AN ENGLISH AFFAIR

RICHARD DAVENPORT-HINES

An English Affair

Sex, Class and Power in the
Age of Profumo

Harper
Press

Harper*Press*
An imprint of HarperCollins*Publishers*
77–85 Fulham Palace Road
London W6 8JB
www.harpercollins.com

First published in Great Britain by Harper*Press* in 2013

1 3 5 7 9 10 8 6 4 2

A catalogue record for this book is available from the British Library

ISBN 978-0-00-743584-5

Set in Minion by Palimpsest Book Production Limited,
Falkirk, Stirlingshire

Printed in Great Britain by Clays Ltd, St Ives plc

*For Jenny, Christopher and Hugo,
and never forgetting Cosmo*

CONTENTS

Though most English men and women cannot 'let themselves go', they love to think and read about people who do throw off inhibitions, either with sex or violence – provided they are punished.

Geoffrey Gorer, 'This is the English', *The People*, 30 September 1951

Snobbery – of all kinds – and prurience are the two most obvious vices of this country.

'Anatomy of Hysteria', *Spectator*, 15 November 1957

One thinks immediately of all the dreary little snobberies, the triviality, the emptiness, the susceptibility to stupid vogues. How drab and provincial we have become! How enslaved to gimmicks! English inventiveness and energy, which used to be an example to the world – have they dried up altogether, or is it simply a bad period we are going through? The two great inventions of the English, their political system and their literature, both seem at the moment rather dwindled and shabby. The parliamentary two-party system has become, whether temporarily or forever, a mere contest between public relation outfits, with professional ad men in the back room.

John Wain, 'The Month', *Twentieth Century*, July 1959

Overture

In May of 1963, when I was nine, Miss Vera Groom, the old spinster who taught me English, asked her class to name a noun beginning with a vowel. There was a new word that I was proud of knowing. I had discovered it from the cook's *Daily Express*. I raised my hand, and in response to a nod from her cried out 'Orgy!' Miss Groom trembled: she gripped the edge of her desk; her face flushed with blood; her skin turned puce. 'You are a foul boy,' she said, and sent me to be caned by the headmaster.

A few days later Mr Wilcox addressed the school. It was the year *Dr No* sold 437,000 copies in paperback. Warner Wilcox was then in his early forties, but seemed old to me. Like many headmasters of his time, he was both overbearing and anxious. Dark-browed, stern, conscientious, he had a jolly wife who could not soothe his pent-up tension. When he rebuked his school, he would spring up and down on his heels, as if he was going to bound forward into the boys and start cuffing them. 'It has come to my attention,' he said in a storm of tense heel-jerks, 'that boys are bringing James Bond novels into school. I will not have them on the premises. They are *sad-is-tic* novels' – he pronounced each syllable of sadistic lingeringly before ending his speech with a savage roar – 'and I will thrash any boy who is found in possession of one.' As soon as I could, I asked a chauffeur what 'sadistic' meant. If he knew, he did not say.

Then in June came prize-giving – ten days after John Profumo's resignation as War Minister, I estimate, and two days before the momentous House of Commons debate on that resignation. The prizes were distributed, and a rousing speech was made by a friend of Wilcox called Renée Soskin. Mrs Soskin was a mother of six. She ran both a farm in Bedfordshire and an import-export business, which she had inherited when her husband died during his morning press-ups a year earlier. Her sister was political editor of the *Observer*, the Sunday newspaper for progressives, and Mrs Soskin, a humane, plucky, helpful woman, was Liberal parliamentary candidate at the 1964 general election for that most high-minded London suburb, Hampstead. She had, indeed, appeared on television promoting Liberal policies for the family, in a party political broadcast for the 1959 general election. A Conservative columnist had called her 'a most intelligent and remarkable lady almost capable of converting me to Liberalism'.[1]

From the prize-giving podium Renée Soskin praised Mr Wilcox, Mr Potts, Mr Lorimer-Thomas (little did she know about Mr Lorimer-Thomas) while I daydreamed. Then she began to praise fee-paying schools, and I was jolted to attention. 'Private schools are more indispensable than ever,' she thundered at the climax of her peroration, 'at this time of Deplorable Breakdown of Public Morals.' The phrase rattled round the hall: 'Deplorable Breakdown of Public Morals'. The adults rustled and glanced at one another. I sensed from the sumptuous indignation in nice Mrs Soskin's voice, and all the silly looks that the adults were exchanging, that 'Public Morals' meant pompous hypocrisy, and that I wanted their breakdown.

I suspect that on that June afternoon it became inevitable that I would write one day about the sexual oppression, guilt and bullying, the whitewashing and blackballing, the lack of irony and absurd confused anger of 'Jack' Profumo's England. The London half-world of Mandy Rice-Davies and Christine Keeler, or rather of their protectors, was the world in which I grew up. My grandparents lived in Bryanston Square, two minutes' walk from Marble Arch. My mother lived in Montagu Mews West, which lay between Bryanston Square and Montagu Square. On the other side of

Bryanston Square lay Bryanston Mews West. It was in a flat there, occupied by the slum landlord Perec Rachman, that the two-way mirror was installed through which steamy voyeurs – perhaps including the osteopath Stephen Ward – watched couples performing on a bed. Ward, the scapegoat of the Profumo Affair, spent the night before his show trial opened at the Old Bailey in a friend's flat in Montagu Square: tabloid newspapers blared that he slept in blue silk pyjamas with a pink curtain in a gilt frame behind the bed. This, indeed, was soft living. Another block to the south-east was Portman Square, where Paul Raymond of Raymond's Revuebar bought the penthouse which he shared with the glamour model Fiona Richmond. Ringo Starr, whom Raymond employed as his interior decorator, rewarded him with a panoply of James Bond gadgets and *parvenu* glitziness.

At the time of her temporary disappearance in March 1963, Christine Keeler lived at Flat 164, Park West, Edgware Road, three minutes' walk from Bryanston Mews West, and a minute further from Montagu Mews West. For a time my father kept a leggy brunette in a flat in Park West. He took me there once in 1963, bounding up to the front door, which he opened with a flourish of his key chain. I asked him why he had a key to the woman's flat. 'I have a key,' he replied with immense satisfaction, 'that opens every door in London.' He meant money. The Edgware Road flat was my induction into sexual deception, duplicitous lives and double standards. I have been standing on tiptoes, trying to peer into secret compartments, ever since.

The irritability of London motoring is a misery that I remember too well. My father bought his first car before driving tests had been devised. His school of motoring was Toad of Toad Hall's. His spiritual home was the fast lane: he never felt more himself than when he was behind a steering wheel with his foot hard on the accelerator. As a Christmas treat for 1959, just after the M1 motorway had opened, he took me for a quick run north from Watford, which I believe may have turned into a dashing 'fun-drive' all the way to Rugby and back. Certainly I recall him saying on the interminable return journey that he would write to the Minister of Transport to complain that trees had been left standing beside the motorway, and might cast dangerous shadows by moonlight. He liked high-velocity travel to lay waste to the landscape.

The speed limit of seventy miles per hour was introduced as a temporary measure in 1965 to cope with enthusiasts like my father. Every few months he would take me to Jack Barclay's car showroom in Berkeley Square. The salesmen were thin men with thin moustaches, sharp suits and sharper eyes. They stood apart from one another, idling by the polished bonnets and winged mascots, but were swift and implacable as they headed for their prey when a customer stepped inside the plate-glass windows: lone sharks, one might say. Sometimes my father drove a Bentley, sometimes a black Alvis. One thing all his cars had in common was no wing-mirrors. Wing-mirrors, my father often told me, spoilt the line of a car. They were effeminate. A good driver, a real man, did not need to look behind him. This creed led to several accidents, many altercations and, for me, one Copernican moment of political revelation.

On a Saturday during the summer after Miss Groom sent me to be beaten, and Mr Wilcox denounced the sadism of James Bond, and Mrs Soskin deplored the breakdown of Public Morals, my father sped me to Park Lane. It was August 1964, and we were in a black Alvis with the hood down. A year earlier workmen had finished converting the sedate old carriage road of Park Lane into a dual carriageway with four lanes on both sides. Old avenues of trees were felled, the eastern meadows of Hyde Park put under macadamised tar, and concrete burrows were excavated so that Mayfair businessmen could park their Jaguars in strip-lit subterranean hideaways. Thinking of Hollywood rather than Paris, Whitehall officials had wanted to foist the name of Park Lane Boulevard as a cosmetic to cover the scars of their vandalism. My father loved the swift new Park Lane as a reminder that England was finished with slowcoaches.

There were other signs of change. Sir Philip Sassoon's great house overlooking the park had lately been torn down, and replaced by a monstrosity that housed the Playboy Club. The developer of the site, Jack Cotton, who lived on Park Lane himself, had, in a show of braggadocio, paid Walter Gropius, the Bauhaus architect, to advise on the redevelopment. Gropius's inspiration, with which London was learning to live, was to assert the un-yielding modernity of the new building by cladding it in concrete rather than the original plan of Portland stone.

We stopped at the Hilton hotel. Its thirty storeys and jutting gimcrack modernity had been opposed at planning stage by 'stick-in-the-muds' whom my father had rejoiced to see quashed. The hotel towered over the rest of Park Lane, and could be seen in its unwieldy disproportions from the far end of Kensington Gardens. It was the first building in London to overlook the gardens of Buckingham Palace, and this objection, too, had been quelled to my father's pleasure. (Thirty years later I was to read the minutes of the Cabinet meeting at which Harold Macmillan's government endorsed this encroachment on the Queen's privacy: the justification given was that American holiday-trippers staying in the Hilton would bring badly needed dollars to revi-talise the ailing English economy.) The site had belonged until 1956 to an old banking family, the Abel-Smiths, who had a mortgage on it. This was a period when debt frightened most people as a weir would scare steady ferrymen, but spurred a bold minority rather as the wide oceans excited fearless pri-vateers. The Abel-Smiths had therefore sold their plot for £550,000 to a property developer called Charles Clore, who bedded both Keeler and Rice-Davies, as it happens. Clore, who borrowed heavily, spent another £5 million turning the site into the Hilton. In the hotel my father and I went to the American coffee shop: he gulped scalding black coffee while I spooned my way through a banana split or knickerbocker glory. I cannot imagine why we were there: perhaps a rival for the brunette was in the offing.

Afterwards, back on wheels, the Hilton behind us, my father stopped his car outside a large, abandoned house of dilapidated stucco on the corner of Hertford Street and Old Park Lane. It was awaiting demolition, he explained. Londonderry House, he added, had belonged to a proud, stupid family who had been friends of Hitler, but the last lord had been a helpless drunk who had died young. Now their day was done, the old house where prime ministers once dawdled on the marble stairs had been sold and was to be torn down. Londonderry House would be smashed for good. It represented a world that impeded progress. My father told me that another hotel for Americans was planned for this site next to the Hilton. It was glorious what competition was going to do. It was marvellous what future prosperity was promised to those who were quick to snatch their chances.

Then my father swung the car round into a full U-turn to head back to Park Lane: no unmanly glances back over the shoulder, no effeminate wing-mirrors to look in, just my father's iron resolve as he pulled out. There followed an almighty screech of brakes, a squeal of tyres, and the sound of a horn held down hard. A black taxi cab behind us had made an emergency halt. As we completed the U-turn and passed the stationary taxi, my father stopped, looked at its driver and gave a harsh, defiant laugh: he was proud of having a chuckle that made people lose their temper or, if they were already angry, re-double their rage. The taxi driver was furious, temporarily powerless, but not, he reminded us, permanently disempowered. As my father drove off chortling, his victim shouted after him the deadly threat: 'Wait until October!'

Everyone knew there was going to be a general election in October. 'A Labour voter,' my father said witheringly. He probably forgot the incident in a trice, but I never did. October came, Sir Alec Douglas-Home was displaced as Prime Minister by Harold Wilson, and I acquired the private incantation: 'Wait until October'. For years, I would repeat the phrase to remind myself that however insecure life already seemed, there was greater instability to come. *Waiting for October* became the title of the self-pitying memoirs that I secretly wrote at the age of fifteen.

This book is not *Waiting for October* in another guise, although it is about insolence, envy and the politics of revenge. Rather, it is a history of the mentalities that made Miss Groom, Mr Wilcox, Mrs Soskin and the Edgware Road brunette. It is a study of *milieux*: the worlds of Harold Macmillan, Jack Profumo, Lord Astor, Stephen Ward. 'How separate we keep ourselves in Britain,' the Labour politician Richard Crossman reflected of the 1960s. 'There is the legal world, the doctors' world, the artistic world, the dramatic world, the political world. We are tremendously separate.'[2] The spheres of politics, medicine, law, journalism, smart society, new money, and espionage – each a discrete segment of British society – all converged into the Profumo Affair of 1963 and detonated a shattering blast. This is a London book, which depicts the capital's good-time girls, property dealers and Fleet Street hacks, and the ways they pointed the rest of the nation. It is about the millionaire with his new Alvis who resented the old order, thought his time had come, and longed to see the demolition ball hit Londonderry House, as well as the taxi driver who hated the millionaire, and thought his time was coming in the October election. It describes the worlds they made, and how none of them got what they wanted.

PART ONE

Cast

ONE

Prime Minister

'I have news today that will bring a gasp from every Tory in Britain,' reported Crossbencher, the political columnist of the *Sunday Express*, on 2 December 1956. 'Mr Harold Macmillan is planning to retire from the Commons.'

What a turnabout this is. Only the other day all the talk was of his rivalry with Mr Richard Austen Butler. He was alight with ambition, his Edwardian moustache bristling for the fray. It is true, of course, that he has lately been dropping a few little hints. In the Commons he talks of looking forward 'to retirement from many of these troubles'. To the Tory 1922 Committee he says he is thinking 'of the viscounty that is my right'. But these are laughed off by most people as typical Macmillan flourishes.

I report that Macmillan means exactly what he says. He intends to go. The reason? Not because of any personal clashes with his colleagues. Not because of any disagreement on policy. But he is sixty-three in February, three years older than [the Prime Minister] Sir Anthony Eden, nine years older than Mr Butler. And suddenly, with absolute clarity, he sees that the nation's highest office is forever beyond his grasp. How sad a moment for a politician who has come so far. The moment when he realises that he is finally out of the race.

The only remaining question: When will Mr Macmillan claim his coronet?

One can imagine the poignant sorrow, the air of noble resolve, affected by Macmillan as he confided in the *Sunday Express* man. A few days later, Brendan Bracken, chairman of the *Financial Times*, reported a similar tale to the *Express* proprietor Lord Beaverbrook, but with a hard-headed gloss. 'Macmillan is telling journalists that he intends to retire from politics and go into the morgue. He declares that he will never serve under Butler. His real intentions are to push his boss out of Number Ten.' A month later, on 10 January 1957, after seductive courting of the parliamentary party, Macmillan became Prime Minister.[1]

Only a consummate politician would brief that he is on the brink of retirement as a device to reach the highest office. Macmillan had foreseen, since November, when he had a privileged talk with Eden's physician, Sir Horace Evans, that failing health would force the Prime Minister's retirement. He knew, too, that many Tories felt, in the backbencher Robert Boothby's words, 'contemptuous disdain' for Rab Butler as a boneless appeaser, and would not have him as Eden's successor at any cost. His ruthless clarity and oblique tactics were outstanding.[2]

Lloyd George was the predecessor whom Macmillan most admired, the arch-spiv among Prime Ministers – shameless, improvising, compassionate, devious, inspired. Macmillan was a politician who mastered both appearances and realities, and understood the differences between the two. He was simultaneously a romantic escapist and sturdy materialist. He studied men's wiles, and knew their weaknesses. He was a world-weary cynic about human vanity yet could be as shocked as a boy scout by the grubbiness of people's motives. Outward calm masked high-strung agitation. He looked like a grandee, had the manners of an Edwardian man-about-town and was one of the last men in England who still put his tongue in his cheek when making a sardonic quip. His self-protective staginess, his toying with appearances, his patrician pose of authoritative nonchalance – all so artfully embedded in the past – were a source of strength and renewal when he was Prime Minister approaching the general election of 1959, but would prove a source of increasing weakness in the years before his resignation in 1963.

Macmillan had been born in 1894 in a tall, thin house in Cadogan Place, where Knightsbridge borders Belgravia. In his parents' home solid comforts were joined with a dread of worldly show and admiration for spartan discipline. Maurice Macmillan, his father, was a partner in the publishing house of Macmillan, an outstanding example of Victorian self-help and constructive idealism, for it had been started by Maurice's father and uncle, themselves the sons of a crofter, a poor tenant farmer, on the Scottish Isle of Arran. Macmillan's mother was a physician's daughter from Indiana, which made him the only Prime Minister (apart from Churchill) to have an American mother. She proved morbidly possessive, withdrawing him from Eton when he was fifteen and sacking his tutor when he was sixteen. His education was further disrupted, for he was an early volunteer in the First World War, which began when he had been only twenty months an undergraduate at Oxford.

Macmillan's war experiences, which proved his courage but shredded his nerves, are of supreme importance in understanding him. Overall he was wounded five times, and bore his scars and disabilities for seventy years. At first, on the Western Front, he was a bomb officer with the Grenadier Guards, training men to throw grenades, and pacifying himself with the novels of Dickens and Scott. In the first battle in which he fought, Loos in 1915, he was shot in the hand and also suffered a head injury. In 1916 he was wounded during a reconnaissance mission to German lines. 'The stench from the dead bodies that lie in heaps around is awful,' he wrote to his mother after the Battle of the Somme. 'We do all the burying that we possibly can.' Once, leading an advance platoon down a moonlit lane near the devastated village of Beaumont-Hamel, he passed a dead German with an outstretched arm rigid in death: his orderly went up and shook it. A few days later, near Delville Wood, he was hit in the knee by shrapnel and in the pelvis by machine-gun bullets. A water bottle in his tunic deflected a bullet from hitting his heart. He rolled into a shell hole in no-man's land, where he lay for twelve hours, feigning death when Germans approached, dosing himself with morphine, and scanning a copy of Aeschylus which he had secreted in his battledress, until a rescue party found him. He nearly died of his wounds, endured several operations and years of gruelling pain. 'The act of death in battle is noble,' he had written to his mother a few days earlier, 'but the physical symptoms and actual appearances of death are, in these terrible circumstances, revolting.' He learnt, as no one should have to learn, to tell how a man had died by the way their body lay. The war left him with sporadic pain, a shuffling gait, a limp handshake and spidery handwriting. It accentuated the apprehensions that had made him such a sad, morbid, unpopular boy at Eton: 'the inside feeling that something awful and unknown was about to happen' which still decoyed him as Prime Minister, and forced him to retreat from the world to spend weekends in bed.[3]

While recuperating from his wounds, Macmillan immersed himself in books to enrich an already well-stocked mind. He had been elected a King's Scholar at Eton in 1906, and was the first K.S. to become Prime Minister since Walpole. He ranked with Asquith as the best-read twentieth-century Prime Minister. He had the longest uninterrupted hold on power of any premier between Asquith and Thatcher. His literary-mindedness intensified when he left the army to become a partner in the family publishing firm. He became responsible for such authors as Kipling, Hardy, Yeats, Hugh Walpole, and Sean O'Casey. Maynard Keynes, who had been the boyhood friend and perhaps lover of Harold's elder brother Daniel, was a Macmillan author with strong influence on his economic ideas. There had not been so literary a Prime Minister since Disraeli, and his love of novels made him the most vivid and alluring of political leaders. He calmed his nerves by happily re-reading Austen, Trollope and Meredith; excited his imagination with Stendhal or Nevil Shute's dystopic tale of radiation sickness after nuclear war; honed himself by reading Anthony Powell ('witty but pointless') as a preliminary training for Proust.[4] His temperament – nervous, subtle and theatrical – was decisive to the colour, texture and shape of the modernisation crisis in British politics and society of 1957–64.

In 1924, Macmillan captured a difficult industrial constituency, Stockton-on-Tees, by unusual methods. He insisted that his local supporters contribute to election expenses, reorganised the local association along democratic lines, declined the help (or handicap) of speakers sent by the central party organisation in London, and left unopened the parcels of official propaganda. His distress at the unemployment and privation of north-east England made him a rebel against economic orthodoxies. In 1927 he and three other young MPs who were styled 'Tory Democrats' issued a milk-and-water Keynesian booklet entitled *Industry and the State.* 'A Tory Democrat,' sneered a socialist professor, 'means you give blankets to the poor if they agree not to ask for eiderdowns.' Nevertheless, Aldous Huxley found much sense in Macmillan's 1931 publication *Reconstruction: A Plea for National Unity*, and told T. S. Eliot: 'I'm glad the young conservatives are waking up.'[5]

Together with Sir Cuthbert Headlam, Macmillan formed the 'Northern Group' of Tory MPs lobbying on behalf of the region. 'He is a curiously self-centred man, and strangely shy and prickly – and yet the more I see of him the more I like him,' Headlam noted after a talk in 1934. Although Headlam advised him to continue pushing progressive ideas, but to stop speaking and voting against the government, Macmillan did not restrain his dissent. He affronted fellow Tories by telling a newspaper interviewer in 1936 that 'a party dominated by second-class brewers and company promoters – a casino capitalism – is not likely to represent anyone but itself'. That year he was the only backbencher to resign the party whip when Baldwin's government lifted sanctions which had been imposed on Mussolini's Italy after the invasion of Abyssinia. Although he rejoined the party after Neville Chamberlain became Prime Minister in 1937, he risked de-selection as a Conservative candidate by continuing opposition to appeasement of dictators. In 1938 he wrote a Keynesian treatise entitled *The Middle Way*, which indicted Conservative economics as callous and complacent, and argued for more consensual, corporatist, expansionist economics. The London Stock Exchange, he suggested, should be replaced by a National Investment Board. This was not the rebellion of a showy, self-seeking mutineer, but the dissent of a man who obstinately, perseveringly, worked out new lines for himself.[6]

In 1940, when Churchill became Prime Minister, he chose Macmillan as Parliamentary Under Secretary at the Ministry of Supply. About a month after this humdrum appointment, Headlam sat beside Macmillan at the long table where members dine together at the Beefsteak Club. 'He is very much the Minister nowadays, but says that he has arrived too late to rise very high,' Headlam noted. 'I can see no reason (except his own personality) for his not getting on – even to the top of the tree – but he is his own worst enemy: he is too self-centred, too obviously cleverer than the rest of us.' Shortly after this Beefsteak evening, Macmillan was motoring in a car with his private secretary, John Wyndham. After desultory conversation, Macmillan fell into brooding silence. Then suddenly, with intense emphasis, but as if talking to himself, he exclaimed: 'I *know* I can do it.'[7]

These glimpses of Macmillan at forty-six – delighted to have reached office, but equivocal about his prospects – are telling. He felt his aptitude for power, but sensed he must disguise his clever ambition. His confidences to Headlam, his exclamation before his most trusted aide Wyndham, prefigure him briefing journalists in 1956 that his political career was over as he poised himself to take supreme control.

At the end of 1942 Churchill offered the post of 'Minister Resident at Allied Forces Headquarters in Algiers' to Macmillan, his second-best candidate, whom he had recently described as 'unstable'. Macmillan accepted without a moment's havering. It proved to be a hard job, unrewarding in outward prestige, but he won praise from those who knew of his behind-the-scenes adroitness. With both the American and Free French representatives he was direct in his approach but insinuating in his ideas. During the closing phase of the war, Macmillan headed the Allied Control Commission in Italy, becoming, said Wyndham, 'Britain's Viceroy of the Mediterranean by stealth'.[8]

By the war's close Macmillan had been married for a quarter of a century. He had met Lady Dorothy Cavendish when he was serving as aide-de-camp to her father, the Duke of Devonshire, who was then Governor-General of Canada. They married – she aged nineteen, he twenty-six – at St Margaret's, Westminster in 1920. The bride's side of the church was filled with hereditary grandees: Devonshires, Salisburys, Lansdownes; the groom's with Macmillan authors, including Thomas Hardy, who signed as one of the witnesses. The young couple took a London house, at 14 Chester Square, on Pimlico's frontier with Belgravia. After 1926 they also shared Birch Grove, a large house newly built in Sussex under the directions of his mother. The marriage deteriorated after 1926, as Dorothy Macmillan chafed under her mother-in-law's meddling intimidation.

One of the Tory Democrats to whom Macmillan was closest in the 1920s was Robert Boothby, a dashing young MP with an unruly mop of black hair and bombastic style of speechifying. Dorothy Macmillan was attracted to him when they met during a shooting and golfing holiday in Scotland in 1928: during a second holiday after Macmillan's defeat in the general election of 1929, she squeezed Boothby's hands meaningfully while they were on the moors. Their affair was consummated during a house party with her Lansdowne cousins at Bowood. Photographs of the pair, taken at Gleneagles, show her as clear-skinned and strong-limbed, with prominent eyebrows and chin, a saucy grin, and the air of an undergraduate. Of the two lovers, Dorothy Macmillan had the dominant temperament.

Boothby was intelligent, but wayward in his habits and ductile in his feelings. 'A fighter with delicate nerves,' Harold Nicolson called him in 1936. Boothby had a look of manly vigour, with a boisterous style, and a reputation as a *coureur des femmes*. Nevertheless, he enjoyed being chased by men during his trips to Weimar Germany, and supposedly enjoyed frottage with fit, ordinary-looking, emotionally straightforward youths. Homosexuality, however, drove public men to suicide or exile in the 1920s, and stalled careers; indeed it was a preoccupation of policemen and blackmailers until partially decriminalised in 1967. 'I detected the danger and sheered away from it,' Boothby later wrote.[9]

Dorothy and Harold Macmillan had one son and three daughters. She fostered the untruth that their youngest daughter Sarah, born in 1930, had been fathered by Boothby, in the hope of provoking her husband to agree to a divorce. Macmillan did not yield to this wish. A solicitor whom he consulted warned that divorce would be an obstacle to receiving ministerial office, and might make Cabinet rank impossible. It might even require him to resign his parliamentary seat (as happened in 1944 when Henry Hunloke MP was in the process of divorce from Dorothy's sister Anne, and seemed likely for a time in 1949 when James Stuart MP, married to another sister, was cited in a divorce). There would have been outcry at Birch Grove, too. His brother Arthur had been ostracised by their mother for marrying a divorcee in 1931, despite consulting the Bishop of London before proceeding with the ceremony.

Until the divorce reforms of 1969, it was necessary for one of the married partners to be judged 'guilty' of adultery or marital cruelty before a divorce could be granted. It was considered deplorable, except in flagrant scandals, for a man to attack his wife's reputation by naming her as the guilty party. Instead, even if the wife had an established lover, the husband was expected to provide evidence of guilt, by such ruses as hiring a woman to accompany him to a Brighton hotel, signing the guestbook ostentatiously, sitting up all night with her playing cards, but having sworn evidence from hotel staff or private detectives that they had spent the night together. Macmillan, who had been neither adulterous nor cruel to his wife, refused to collude in fabricating evidence of marital guilt: still less was he willing to sue her for divorce, and cite Boothby as co-respondent. 'In the break-up of a marriage,' Anthony Powell wrote of the 1930s, 'the world inclines to take the side of the partner with most vitality, rather than the one apparently least to blame'.[10] Sympathy, then, lay with Dorothy Macmillan.

She was too proud and ardent to bother with discretion as an adulteress; her bracing earthiness left no room for subtlety. Her telephone calls to Boothby were made in earshot of her husband and children; she left Boothby's love letters visible about the Birch Grove and Chester Square houses. As he wrote to a parliamentary colleague in 1933, she was 'the most formidable thing in the world – a possessive, single-track woman. She wants me, completely, and she wants my children, and she wants practically nothing else. At every crucial moment she acts instinctively and over-whelmingly.' Over forty years later, in 1977, Boothby gave a similar recapitulation. 'What Dorothy wanted and needed was emotion, on the scale of Isolde. This Harold could not give her, and I did. She was, on the whole, the most selfish and most possessive woman I have ever known.' When he got engaged to an American heiress, she pursued him from Chatsworth, via Paris, to Lisbon. 'We loved each other,' he said, 'and there is really nothing you can do about it, except die.'[11]

Commentators have suggested that Macmillan's distress at his wife's lifelong infidelity (her affair with Boothby lasted until her death in 1966) made him chary of speaking to Profumo directly in 1963, or of confronting the implausibility of the minister's disavowals of an affair with Keeler. This is doubtful, for Downing Street power relaxed Macmillan's inhibitions. 'The PM,' wrote his niece, the young Duchess of Devonshire, in 1958, 'has become much more human all of a sudden and talks about things like Adultery quite nicely.' His prime ministerial diaries show his pleasure in playing the part of a man-of-the-world who knew about kept women, betrayal and divorce. In 1958, after reading the memoirs of the nineteenth-century courtesan Harriette Wilson, he mused that Doris Delavigne, Beaverbrook's Streatham-born mistress (and quondam wife of Beaverbrook's columnist Lord Castlerosse), who took a fatal overdose of barbiturates after being insulted in 1942 in a corridor of the Dorchester hotel by the Duke of Marlborough, was one of the last of the demimondaines. 'This type really depends on the institution of marriage being strict & divorce impossible or rare,' he wrote. 'Now people marry for a year or two & then pass to the next period of what is really licensed concubinage. Since the so-called "upper classes" are as corrupt as they can be, these ladies, like Harriette Wilson, are cut out by "real ladies" – the daughters of our friends. I think the old way was really best.'[12]

It is, however, true that the Profumo Affair snared a specific, secret susceptibility of Macmillan's. The 'foursome', as Harold Wilson slyly called Ward, Profumo, Keeler and the Russian attaché Yevgeny Ivanov, whose convergence was imagined to raise security issues, had met at the Astor house, Cliveden.[13] Thirty years earlier Nancy Astor had made decisive interventions during the Macmillan marital crisis: a visit by Boothby to Cliveden had proved critical to its resolution. Like many people who had been done a good turn, Macmillan did not forgive the Astors for helping him at his nadir. He associated them with memories that he preferred to repress.

Boothby triggered the crisis in September 1932. He told his lover that he could not continue their 'unendurable' half-life together: 'Just an interminable series of agonising "goodbyes" with nothing to go back to. Living always for the next time. Work to hell. Nerves to hell.' Dorothy Macmillan was aghast at Boothby's ultimatum: marriage or a clean break. 'Why did you ever wake me?' she cried at him. 'I never want to see any of my family again. And, without you, life for me is going to be nothing but one big hurt.' She knew that Boothby's political career would be ruined if he eloped with another MP's wife, and that they would have little money to live on. She asked her husband for a divorce, confident that he would agree to collude in providing evidence, and was devastated when in January 1933 he gave an adamant refusal. In desperation she sought sympathy and counsel from Nancy Astor, who gave her the use of a house at Sandwich in Kent as refuge for calm reflection. Lady Astor invited Boothby to Cliveden: there were confabulations in St James's Square with the deserted husband, who also sought his mother-in-law's help. 'Poor Harold had another awful time with me last night, & he talked till 3 in the morning, and is still entirely hard about everything and everybody,' the Duchess of Devonshire wrote to Nancy Astor on 24 January.[14]

Macmillan was exciting himself into a suicidal rage. Around 31 January 1933 he scrawled an agonised pencilled note from 14 Chester Square to his trusted intermediary in his marital negotiations. It is the most emotionally naked document of his that survives, and the fact that it was sent to an Astor may explain his inhibitions, and unforgiving attitude to Bill Astor, when thirty years later a scarring scandal was foisted on Cliveden. 'Dearest Nancy,' he wrote. 'Sorry to bother you. But make it clear to her that I will **never** divorce her' – even if she publicly absconded with Boothby. 'If she does that, I will kill myself. I won't & can't face the children. This is real – not stuff.' Having promised suicide if Dorothy deserted him, he proposed the best way forward. 'If I could feel she was trying to achieve the same ultimate objective as I am, I will do everything to make her life happy. But I must feel that we are working together, as it were. And she must be considerate to my nerves.' If she would try to restore 'normality,' he promised, 'I'll devote anything that [is] left of my life for that – for the children & for her – whom I love more than I can say. Tell her that I am still grateful for the 8 happiest years that mortal man ever had. Nothing can take that away from me.'[15]

A few hours later he sent Nancy Astor a second message: 'You are our angel – and you are really fighting for a soul, as well as for lots of innocent people – e.g. four lovely children.' On 1 February he saw Boothby, and received a letter from Dorothy accepting a compromise. 'It only remains, therefore, for us to help her to build a new life & to heal the wounds,' he told Nancy Astor in a third letter. 'I realise that I can do nothing – except negatively, by leaving her alone.' There was no bridling of his gratitude to Lady Astor for her handling of Boothby. 'Dear, dear Nancy – I know how much I owe to you. When I saw him on Tuesday after he had been at Cliveden, he was in a different mood (I sensed a great change) to any that I had seen at previous interviews. It seemed to me that some of the crust of cynicism had been broken & all the rot with which he had protected himself was rather shattered. Your influence I trace there.' Macmillan believed that their prayers, too, had helped. The continuing strains in the situation were clear in a later confidence of Evie Devonshire's to Lady Astor. Dorothy's temper was stabilised, the duchess wrote, but 'whether she will ever get over her dislike of H is another matter, but she is less hard and angry'.[16]

Macmillan's marital traumas raised a muffled commotion in Society. It was humiliating that parliamentary colleagues knew he was Boothby's cuckold. He donned a mask of indifference, but was instilled with the vengeful ambition and steely endurance that brought him to the premiership in 1957. He described himself to his biographer Alistair Horne as 'this strange, very buttoned-up person'. Strolling in the Birch Grove grounds with Horne, he proffered a hint about himself: 'I think gardens should be divided, so you can't see everything at once.' Pamela Wyndham, wife of his closest confidant as Prime Minister, said he was protean in his shape-shifting: 'one moment you had a salmon in your hand, the next it was a horse'. Significantly, one of his favourite novels was Dumas's *Count of Monte Cristo*, with its hero who returns from the dead in various disguises to wreak revenge on those who had betrayed and humiliated him. An air of cynical mastery was what he aspired to.[17]

Two anecdotes from the day (Thursday 10 January 1957) that Macmillan became Prime Minister show his derogation within his family and his studied nonchalance. In the afternoon he had an audience with the Queen at Buckingham Palace, and accepted her commission to form a government. The news was swiftly broadcast by the BBC. At the Macmillan publishing offices excited staff brought the news to Daniel Macmillan, the eldest brother and chairman of the business. 'Mr Macmillan's been appointed Prime Minister,' they said. 'No,' replied Daniel Macmillan, 'Mr Harold has been appointed Prime Minister.' (A few years later Daniel Macmillan, while lunching at the long table at the Garrick, was bearded by a club bore. 'Is it true,' demanded the bore, 'that President Kennedy speaks to your brother daily on the telephone?' Daniel's reply was deadpan: '*Whyever* would President Kennedy want to do that?') Edward Heath, who was the Tories' highly effective Chief Whip in 1955–59, recalled the evening of the tenth. Macmillan had been Prime Minister for a few hours. 'Where is the Chief Whip? We're off to the Turf to celebrate!' he cried to Downing Street staff. When the two men reached the club in Piccadilly, they found a lone man installed at the bar reading the *Evening Standard* with a front-page headline blazoning Macmillan's appointment. The club man looked up, recognised Macmillan, and asked laconically: 'Any good shooting recently?'

'No,' replied Macmillan.

'What a pity,' said the man. Heath and Macmillan were served their drinks, ordered oysters and steak, and then rose for the dining room. As they left, the man at the bar looked up and said as casually as before, 'Oh, by the way, congratulations.' This was the off-hand behaviour that Macmillan preferred, however ruffled his underlying feelings or agitated his nerves.[18]

Originality could be fatal to men of Macmillan's generation, or indeed to the vast majority of those who had served in the armed forces in either of the world wars. Conformity in clothes, deportment and opinions was the sign of trustworthiness. Conventionality was so strong that when Sir John Widgery was appointed a Judge of the Queen's Bench Division in 1961, there was disgruntlement among lawyers because he would not sacrifice his military-looking moustache, although the English bench was entirely clean-shaven. Indeed, the process by which Macmillan became Prime Minister exemplified conformity in action. After Eden had announced his resignation to the Cabinet on 9 January 1957, the Cabinet members, except Butler and Macmillan, went one by one to Lord Salisbury's room in the Privy Council Office. There they were questioned by Salisbury and the Lord Chancellor, Lord Kilmuir. Their reception by Kilmuir and Salisbury reminded most of them of a visit to the headmaster's study.

Salisbury, who deprecated Rab Butler as a prewar appeaser, did not interview the Cabinet in order of seniority, but began with ministers whom he judged most committed to Macmillan. To each minister Salisbury posed the same question: 'Well, which is it? Wab or Hawold?' He had laid on the table a sheet of notepaper with two columns headed 'Macmillan' and 'Butler' deliberately visible. The names accumulated in the first column, and deterred wobblers from naming Butler; only one minister did so, and he never held ministerial office again. Tory backbenchers, whom Macmillan had been sedulous in cultivating since November, also plumped for him because he seemed more combative than Butler: he had resisted the appeasement policy of which Butler had been a principal exponent. Memories of the war, martial attitudes, and the instilled discipline of 1939–45 were pervasive: twelve years is not a long time, except to children.

'Would you like to join my shooting party?' Macmillan asked men whom he was inviting to join his government. Fifty-two offices changed holders; four ministers left the Cabinet. Forming his administration, as he noted in his diary, 'meant seeing nearly a hundred people and trying to say the right thing to each . . . many considerations had to be born in mind – the right, centre and left of the party; the extreme "Suez" group; the extreme opposition to Suez; the loyal centre – and last, but not least, U and non-U (to use the jargon that Nancy Mitford has popularised) that is, Eton, Winchester, etc. on the one hand; Board school and grammar school on the other.'[19]

To Butler, in October 1957, Macmillan regretted the lack of ruthlessness among his Cabinet colleagues: 'there were no tough guys like Swinton'.[20] The Earl of Swinton, whose dropping from the Cabinet by Eden in 1955 Macmillan had deplored, was a revealing political model for Macmillan to tout: a middle-class professional man, whose marriage had transmuted him into the territorial aristocracy; a first-generation grandee with a moderated swagger; a politician with thirty years of Cabinet experience who had proven his acumen and resilience.

Swinton had once been Philip Lloyd-Greame, a barrister who specialised in mining law. He won the Military Cross on the Somme, and in 1918 was elected for the newly created London suburban constituency of Hendon, a northern equivalent to Bromley, where Macmillan was elected MP in 1945. His Hendon candidature was financially sponsored by Dudley Docker, founding President of the Federation of British Industries, on whose company boards he sat until 1922, when he was appointed President of the Board of Trade at the age of thirty-eight. A die-hard Tory MP called him 'very clever', but not too clever – 'a Sahib'. This MP tried the experiment of inviting the political newcomer to stay for a tennis weekend. 'I like the Lloyd-Greames as a couple not quite entirely,' he decided. 'Across all their actions is written the words "Get On".' When his wife's uncle, the last Lord Masham, died in 1924, she inherited the Swinton estate in Yorkshire, as well as the cash her grandfather had made from inventing the Lister nip comb (which revolutionised Victorian wool-spinning). Lloyd-Greame changed his surname by Royal Licence to Cunliffe-Lister, assumed the responsibilities of a hospitable landed magnate, received his first peerage in 1935, and sat in every Conservative Cabinet until 1938. Churchill appointed him as chairman of the wartime Security Executive in 1940, as Resident Minister in West Africa in 1942 and as Secretary of State for Commonwealth Relations in 1952.[21]

Swinton's elder son was killed in action in 1943, and the younger son, a wartime squadron leader in the RAF, shot himself through the heart in 1956 after years of nervous troubles. Macmillan, who spoke with tears in his eyes to Butler about his only son Maurice's wrestling with alcoholism, felt for the Swintons in their double loss. As Prime Minister he was always pleased to see Philip Swinton, whose judgement he thought peculiarly sound and whose vitality he envied. His visits to Swinton Park – a battlemented, impervious, northern house, which symbolised all that he wished to seem – were a highpoint of his calendar. 'One of the reasons one loves a holiday on the moors is that, in a confused and changing world, the picture in one's mind is not spoilt,' Macmillan wrote to Mollie Swinton after one shooting break. 'If you go to Venice or Florence or Assisi, you might as well be at Victoria Station – masses of tourists, chiefly Germans in shorts. If you go to Yorkshire or Scotland, the hills, the keepers, the farmers, the farmers' sons, the drivers are the same; and (except for the coming of the Land Rover) there is a sense of continuity.'[22]

Macmillan embraced change, although he cherished surface continuities, thought his Foreign Office minister Ian Harvey. The Prime Minister 'understood people, and he cared about them. He knew that politicians who pretended to be ordinary were not respected by the electorate.' He had also learnt before 1940 that his party and the electorate mistrusted showy cleverness, but admired panache, 'even if they did not know the meaning of the word', Harvey judged. 'Above all he understood the make up of the Conservative Party and although he was highly intelligent, he treated stupid people kindly, and there were plenty about in the political field.'[23]

Realising that character is more reliable than brilliance, and that cleverness disrupts political continuities, Macmillan strove to have a balanced government, with members who would never dazzle. As Secretary of State for Air, for example, he appointed (in 1957) George Ward, brother of the Earl of Dudley. 'Poor Geordie! However, he is hard-working & brave, but not quite quick enough for modern life.' As Chancellor of the Exchequer he appointed (in 1958) Derick Heathcoat-Amory, whom he judged 'an awfully nice fellow – rather slow, but very sensible'. To the post of Minister of Power, Macmillan appointed (in 1959) the Earl of Halifax's youngest son, Richard Wood: 'poor Richard (though a charming character) is not very clever'. Wood was undeniably valiant: although a Catholic, he was the solitary minister who voted in favour of decriminalising homosexuality in 1960; his masculinity was irreproachable as both his legs had been amputated after being blasted by a landmine in Tunisia.[24]

Although it proved an electoral mistake in the early 1960s to have a patrician administration full of Scottish earls with such recognisable place names as Selkirk, Dundee and Perth, it was purblind to assume that such men were uninteresting or second-rate. Geordie Selkirk, Macmillan's First Lord of the Admiralty in 1957–59, was shrewd, resilient and adept, although easy to under-rate because he had no taste for self-advertisement. He had read PPE at Oxford, studied at the universities of Paris, Bonn and Vienna, graduated in law from Edinburgh University, practised at the bar and became a QC. At the age of twenty-eight he was commanding officer of the RAF's City of Edinburgh bomber squadron. By his early thirties his expertise in housing and employment problems was recognised by his appointment as Commissioner for Special Areas in Scotland. After war came in 1939, Selkirk was chief intelligence officer to Fighter Command and personal assistant to its commander-in-chief. In 1944, piloting a Wellington bomber above the Bay of Biscay, the aircraft was attacked by five Junker 88 fighters: the windscreen was shot out but Selkirk took deft evasive action – and survived another half century. He was the only member of the staid Athenæum club to marry a captain of the British women's ski team. Promoted to the Cabinet by Eden, his support for Eden's Suez policies was the most anomalous of all the Cabinet, for he was a man (like his fellow Scottish earl, Perth, at the Colonial Office) with staunch independent integrity. Macmillan thought him 'a fine, earnest man', and did right to trust him. Similarly, the Earl of Dundee, whom Macmillan selected as Minister without Portfolio in 1958, and as Minister of State at the Foreign Office in 1961, was no duffer, despite his resemblance to Bulldog Drummond, *pace* a journalist who saw him dealing effectively with Patrice Lumumba during the Congo crisis of 1960: 'a tall handsome presence with a square jaw, a clipped moustache and greying hair'.[25]

There was an assumption that self-made businessmen made more efficient, canny and decisive ministers than the privileged sons of rich men. Some, however, proved as vain, bombastic and calculating as might be expected of men who forsook the boardroom for the public platform. The foremost example was Ernest Marples, who joined Macmillan's first administration as Postmaster General in 1957 and brought automated letter-sorting and subscriber trunk-dialling to British communications. Two years later Marples reached the Cabinet as Minister of Transport. Just as Belisha beacons commemorated a prewar Minister of Transport, so parking meters were the innovative street furniture that symbolised Marples's power. The grandson of the Dukes of Devonshire's head gardener at Chatsworth, and son of an engine fitter, he was educated at a grammar school in Manchester's suburbs. One of his earliest jobs was as gatekeeper at a football ground in Manchester. He made money as a London property developer converting Victorian houses into flats before starting a construction company called Marples Ridgeway, which specialised in docks, power stations and motorways. He married his secretary, and used prostitutes. His self-confidence was boundless. He imagined himself taking large, sure strides towards a great destiny. His appetite for seeing his name in headlines never slaked. A bicycling and fitness fanatic, he died at the age of seventy. John Boyd-Carpenter, the Minister of Pensions, never saw Macmillan laugh more than at a Cabinet meeting when a name was mooted for a public appointment. 'Does anyone know him?' asked the Prime Minister. 'Yes,' volunteered Ernie Marples, 'he once made a proposition to me. I didn't accept. It wasn't quite straight, and anyhow there was nothing in it for me.'[26]

Macmillan, who had been a railway company director before Labour's nationalisation in 1947–48, trusted Marples with the bold scheme of transport rationalisation that was intended to prove the modernity of the Conservatives in the 1960s. The ramshackle railway system was crushed by its accumulated debts and operating deficit. The British Transport Commission, which had a mishmash of responsibilities for running railways, docks, canals and London transport, was ill-managed as well as submissive to the National Union of Railwaymen and Associated Society of Locomotive Engineers and Firemen. Both unions disrupted services with exorbitant pay claims and enforced a regime of restrictive practices: their conservative obstinacy made Bournemouth Tories seem progressive.

Marples convinced Macmillan to appoint a bracing new chairman of the British Transport Commission named Richard Beeching, an accountant who was technical director of ICI (Beeching's annual salary of £24,000 aroused the envious carping in 1961 that then characterised Britain). The choice of Beeching proved calamitous. He was not the infallible cost accountant as pictured by Marples, but botched his analysis of railway costs, and proved cocksure yet unimaginative in his thinking. His recommendations to close one-third of the 18,000-mile railway network were published in March 1963, and endorsed in one of the Cabinet's worst decisions: his proposals were based on false premises, fudged figures and dodgy political expediency; they moreover failed in their purpose of securing the railways on a profitable basis.

'A really remarkable figure,' Macmillan wrote after a two-hour meeting with Marples in April 1963. 'I only wish we had more ministers with his imagination and thoroughness.' However, controversy over the Beeching Axe brought obloquy upon his government, partly because the ministerial presentation was self-advertising, truculent and weak. 'When Mr Marples presented the Beeching Report,' noted a future Labour minister, George Thomson, 'the biggest thing of its kind, we were given to understand, since the Beveridge Report, the operation was intended to show the Conservatives looking forward to the seventies, while the socialists, tied to the railway unions, timorously looked back to the forties. But Mr Marples muffed it monumentally, and suffered a press universally worse than I can remember a minister receiving.' Macmillan, despite his susceptibility to territorial grandees, was hoodwinked by the bouncy self-promotion of rough diamonds, and the myths of infallibility boomed by self-made men.[27]

Derick Heathcoat-Amory's appointment as Chancellor of the Exchequer in 1958 was a better choice by Macmillan than Marples as Minister of Transport in 1959. The assessment of Heathcoat-Amory by Lord Altrincham who, under his later pen name of John Grigg, was one of the canniest political commentators of his generation, had a perfect justness. 'He is often described as "sound", an adjective which in this specialised usage connotes a decently concealed intelligence, more than average efficiency, a willingness to take pains (for instance, in not hurting the feelings of moronic colleagues), a belief in good relations between management and the (not so easily) managed, a fine war record and a squirearchical background. There is, indeed, one feature which might make him suspect – he is opposed to the death penalty – but his friends can plead in mitigation that he has been a zealous huntsman. He is the sort of man who not being first-class pretends to be third-class, and so receives a quite disproportionate amount of credit for being top second-class.'[28]

What of the England and the parliamentary party of which Macmillan took charge in 1957, where men became Prime Minister by pretending to be old-and-done-for and Chancellor of the Exchequer by concealing their intelligence?

In the spring of 1957, Macmillan saw a newspaper story about a seventeen-year-old man, Derek Wiscombe, whose home town of Jarrow-on-Tyne had suffered high unemployment since the 1930s. Wiscombe had applied for a licence to carry furniture and building materials with the intention of passing his driving test and buying a lorry to replace his pony and cart. His application was however rejected after objections from local hauliers, and the state-owned haulage company Pickfords. Macmillan, who never lost his sympathetic interest in the north-east, was vexed by this example of tyrannical regulations protecting vested interests from competition. He prompted William Elliott, the newly elected Tory MP for Newcastle-upon-Tyne North, to organise a fund to pay for Wiscombe's driving lessons and buy him a lorry. With Elliott's help, Wiscombe successfully re-applied for a licence to carry furniture on a lorry bearing L plates. A local businessman was induced to pass Wiscombe some business for starters. Macmillan closed the file with the single word: 'Good'. A few months later, the municipal council at Jarrow found that one of its tenants, Norah Tudor, was supplementing her husband's income by doing embroidery at home. The council ordered her to stop. 'Mrs Tudor is the wife of a worker who earns a good salary,' declared the socialist chairman of the local housing committee. 'It will be no hardship for her to give up her needlework.' As a Tory back-bencher commented, 'this utterance (which Mr Harold Wilson himself could hardly improve on) conveys the politics of envy in a nutshell'. The persecution of Derek Wiscombe and Norah Tudor both occurred in Jarrow, but the mean, restrictive spirit shown by these cases was a national force.[29]

England was a country where the gravy served at main meals made everything taste alike. Dominated by the memory of two world wars, it was more drilled and regimented than at any time in its history, and more strictly regulated. Restaurants and pubs were controlled under onerous rules derived from the Defence of the Realm Act of 1914; audiences stood in respectful silence when the National Anthem was played at the end of every cinema performance; pedestrians still doffed their hats as they passed the Cenotaph memorial to the war dead in Whitehall; family-planning clinics did not dare to give contraceptive advice to the unmarried; every foreigner had to register with their local police station, and report there regularly; businesses needed clearance from the Bank of England for the smallest overseas expenditure; there was a rigid obsession about preserving fixed exchange rates for sterling; the system of Retail Price Maintenance safeguarded shopkeepers from undercutting, and ensured that shoppers could seldom find competitive prices. Though entrepreneur John Bloom was trying to start a consumer revolution with his cut-price 'Rolls Razor' washing machines, the English authorities still frowned on mass consumption, and by imposing taxes that at some levels approached a hundred per cent of income, discouraged it all too effectively. Millions of people were longing to make money, spend money, enjoy the conspicuous spending of money and never apologise for money; but both officials and politicians, whether of the left or the right, wanted to restrict money-making, idealised discomfort as character-building and frugality as manly, scowled at other people's expenditure, thought that the ostentatious enjoyment of wealth was shameful. *It's No Sin to Make a Profit* was the title of Bloom's defiant memoirs.

Macmillan was unperturbed when, two months into his premiership, in March 1957, Lord Salisbury resigned from the Cabinet. Much nonsense was written about Macmillan's relationship with Salisbury (they had both married Cavendish women), and the fracturing of the family circle. In truth Betty Salisbury, who was a nettlesome character, had shown longstanding (and reciprocated) animosity towards Dorothy Macmillan over the Boothby affair. The Conservative Party was not fazed by the rupture with Salisbury. Although constituency associations often had a local nobleman as honorary president, they were run by solicitors, prosperous shopkeepers, men with small businesses and their wives. For these *roturiers*, the Cecils were not a popular bodyguard to have gathered around the seat of power. Two months after the spluttering squib of Salisbury's secession, Macmillan wrote to John Wyndham asking him to join his private office at Downing Street. 'I did not really think my administration could last more than a few weeks; but we now seem to have got over quite a number of jumps in this Grand National course, and having just managed to pull the old mare through the brook and somehow got to the other side, with the same jockey up, and the Cecil colours fallen, I am plucking up my courage.'[30]

The Prime Minister had a salary of £10,000 a year (with £4,000 tax free) but, as there was no permanent domestic staff at Downing Street, Macmillan had to pay five household servants. Wyndham found him calm and considerate with his office staff. Macmillan kept a neat desk, never mislaid papers and had a tremendous power of work. His tastes were frugal. For breakfast he took tea and toast, sometimes with a boiled egg. He might have a gin and tonic or sherry before luncheon, but seldom drank alcohol during the meal. Cold roast beef was his favourite lunchtime dish. Before dinner he would have a glass or two of whisky, and wine at table. When possible on Fridays, before going to Birch Grove or Chequers for the weekend, he enjoyed a schoolroom high tea served at Downing Street in preference to dinner. He liked port, and champagne with agreeable companions. During Lent he forsook alcohol.

The Cabinet Room and secretaries' offices, on the ground floor of 10 Downing Street, were reached by a red-carpeted corridor lined with photographs of defunct Cabinets and busts of bygone premiers. The ambience resembled a Pall Mall club with a historic past, but uneasy finances. Outside the Cabinet Room there was a small lobby with a round table. There, during Cabinet meetings, ministers who were not in the Cabinet would await a summons when the subject under their purview was reached on the agenda. It was, said one of them, 'bleaker than a dentist's waiting room'. When a minister was ushered in, he had to scramble to find an empty chair and hurriedly open his papers; usually he found that the Cabinet had started discussing his subject; indeed, from the glazed eyes as he began his remarks, he realised that somebody else had already said them.[31]

Kenneth Rose likened the Cabinet Room to 'the dining room in a well-to-do boarding house in the neighbourhood of Russell

Square'. Macmillan, though, thought like a clubman, not a boarding-house keeper. 'The RAC or Boodle's?' he asked when, during the Cypriot settlement of 1959, the Cabinet had to decide whether Cyprus should receive full Commonwealth status after independence. 'There was an element of the dining club about his conduct of Cabinets,' Lord Hailsham reminisced. 'There would be quotations from Homer, there would be vague historical analogies; the trade union leaders would be described as medieval barons in the period of the War of the Roses. And some of them would be relevant and some of them would be mildly misleading. But they would all be very amusing and detached.' Ministers learnt 'to watch what he was doing, as well as what he was saying'.[32]

'For him Europe is the super-continent and Great Britain the super-country,' wrote a recent Conservative parliamentary candidate, Lord Altrincham, of Macmillan in 1957. 'In this he resembles Sir Winston Churchill, whom indeed he is clearly much too anxious to resemble. Here, perhaps, is the root cause of his psychological unbalance. He is a pawky Scottish businessman trying to convince himself and others that he is an English aristocrat of the old school.' Although Macmillan was proud of his Scottish crofter ancestry, he projected a patrician English persona. 'Like Sir Winston at the Other Club, Mr Macmillan holds forth in the grand manner at Pratt's – only with this vital difference, that neither the manner nor the setting is his own. As a practical man he is genuine and acceptable; as an imitation grandee he is nauseating.' Yet it was this bogus act – this game of playing the unregenerate grandee – which recommended Macmillan to back-benchers and ministers as they rallied to face the 1959 general election. He may not have been consistently militant during the Suez affair, but he had the air of militancy. Surveying Macmillan's postwar record of Lloyd George-like opportunism, Altrincham predicted that England would soon resemble France, 'where it is accepted that politicians have a code of their own, and most people have an instinctive repugnance to the idea of entering politics'. The appearance of the Prime Minister's wife – the duke's daughter in tweeds and sensible shoes – was part of his deceptive facade, as Altrincham wrote in a profile which uniquely hinted at the Macmillans' domestic irregularities. 'Lady Dorothy is not quite all that she seems in some respects, and a great deal more than she seems in others. To the casual observer she is just a typical English upper-class cup of tea; but on closer inspection he would find that it was laced with liquid of a more stimulating kind.' *Time & Tide*, after interviewing Boothby in 1962, noted a photograph of Lady Dorothy, and a separate one of her husband, in Boothby's Eaton Square drawing room.[33]

The provenance of Tory MPs changed markedly after 1951. Before his promotion to the Lords, Macmillan's Lord Chancellor, Kilmuir, had instigated the Maxwell Fyfe reforms of the Conservative Party organisation (1948–49). These new rules ended the practice of candidates paying their own election expenses or subsidising constituency party funds. Kilmuir intended to discourage men who had made their pile of money in business from deciding that they wanted the status of a MP and collaring a provincial constituency: this malaise resulted in backbenches lined by complacent, inarticulate, politically obtuse money men with the reactionary, inflexible views of late middle age. The new rules also vested the constituency parties with independence in the selection of candidates. Retrospectively, Kilmuir believed that the quality of new MPs elected at the general elections of 1950 and 1951 was high, but thereafter plummeted. Local associations became dismaying in their choice of candidates in seats with handsome majorities. During the 1950s, to Kilmuir's regret, they copied the cardinal error of Labour constituency parties, which had always weakened the efficacy of the parliamentary party by selecting tedious local worthies for safe seats while abler younger candidates were consigned to marginal or unwinnable constituencies. 'Few of the new Members who entered the Commons in 1955 and 1959,' wrote Kilmuir in 1964, 'had achieved a reputation outside Westminster in any field, and far too many of them were obscure local citizens with obscure local interests, incapable – and indeed downright reluctant – to think on a national or international scale. What made this situation particularly annoying was that many excellent candidates, who would have made first-class Members and probably Ministers, were left to fight utterly hopeless seats . . . while the safe seats went to men of far lower calibre.'[34]

The Midlands conurbation, for example, was represented by nonentities with aldermanic paunches which they carried in a stately, self-satisfied way as if they contained dividend coupons: Harold Gurden (elected at Birmingham Selly Oak in 1955), Gordon Matthews (elected at Meriden, 1959), John Hollingworth (Birmingham All Saints, 1959), Leslie Seymour (Birmingham Sparkbrook, 1959), and Leonard Cleaver (Birmingham Yardley, 1959). Clever young William Rees-Mogg was condemned to contest the hopeless seat of Chester-le-Street in 1959 partly because of prejudice in better seats against his Catholicism. According to Rees-Mogg, there were only two Jewish MPs (Harry d'Avigdor-Goldsmid and Keith Joseph) on the Conservative side during the Parliament of 1955–59 and both had the advantage of inherited baronetcies. Margaret Thatcher was selected at Finchley in 1959 solely because a woman seemed less objectionable than her rival, who was Jewish. Julian Critchley, who was one of the 1959 intake, thought it contained 'more than its share of those who could talk nonsense with distinction'.[35]

In January 1957, just before Macmillan replaced Eden, a retired Conservative MP, Christopher Hollis, noted that Eton had ten times as many MPs and ten times as many members of the government than any other school, a disproportion greater than before 1832. He did not think this was inherently undesirable. At the height of the Suez crisis, it was Etonians – the Macmillans' son-in-law Julian Amery and future brother-in-law Victor Hinchingbrooke among the hawks, Jakie Astor, Boothby, Edward Boyle, Anthony Nutting among the doves – who had the courage to refuse blind loyalty to Eden's blunders. Hollis argued 'that in a generally egalitarian society, those who have positions of responsibility will be apt to be too timidly conformist and that a few Old Etonians about the place, bred in a tradition of liberty, ready in their very insolence to value other things above immediate success, are no bad leaven to the general lump'. Hollis had been an intelligent, independent-minded MP who had retired at the 1955 general election because he had not received political advancement, probably because he was suspected of homosexuality. Such was the parliamentary party's fearful recoil from unorthodox opinions or temperament that, as one young backbencher later recalled with shame, 'had I been more mature I might have benefited from his friendship, but as it was I brushed him off as swiftly as I decently could'.[36]

Responding to Hollis, Henry Kerby, a Tory backbencher with links to MI5, stressed the importance in party counsels of men whose families were neither traditional gentry nor hereditary nobility, but had got their wealth, and possibly recent titles, from shareholdings in large businesses. 'The House of Commons is packed with Old Etonians who are no more members of the aristocracy than I am. The Government benches are crowded with Members of Parliament who are Old Etonians only because their fathers could afford to send them to that school.' These MPs were 'representatives of a moneybags plutocracy, however much many of them may try to disguise their origins. The House is crammed with first-generation descendants of hard-faced men who have done very well for themselves in trade of every sort – honourable and otherwise.' (Kerby's point was backed by a survey in 1959 of the country houses in Banbury district, just south of Profumo's constituency of Stratford-on-Avon, which found that of the forty-three houses large enough to be named on the one-inch ordnance survey map, only four had been in the same family for more than two generations.) Constituency selection committees, continued Kerby, were 'dumbstruck' by the sight of prospective candidates sporting the brown ties, with thin blue stripes, that showed the old Etonian. They realised that young men, with that particular fabric round their necks, would quickly reach political patronage and power. 'Money,' Kerby complained, 'lies at the bottom of Old Etonian dominance.'[37]

Angus Maude, a Tory MP who would succeed Profumo at Stratford, explained that once constituency parties were debarred from extracting election expenses and big subscriptions from candidates, they instead demanded that MPs spent more time in constituencies attending to local fusses. Old Etonians, with inherited incomes that exempted them from the need to earn a living, had the free time that constituency associations required. Moreover, the MPs who were most likely to reach office were those who could devote most time to politics. 'OEs', overall, had more free hours than professional and company director MPs. There was a higher proportion of OEs in government posts than on the backbenches because of the low pay of junior ministers: many MPs could not accept office without financial hardship. Macmillan's government, Maude calculated, had seventy ministers, of whom about ten might be called 'self-made'. This scarcely mattered, he argued, because 'a parliamentary party consisting entirely of very clever men would prove the devil to run and might prove extremely dangerous'.[38]

'Those who hope to rule must first learn to obey,' a Harrow housemaster had written thirty years earlier. 'To learn to obey as a fag is part of the routine that is the essence of the English Public School system, and . . . is the wonder of other countries. Who shall say it is not that which has so largely helped to make England the most successful colonising nation, and the just ruler of the backward races of the world?' The instinctive, automatic obedience to their leader felt by most Tory MPs was based on fear of party whips, who reminded them of prefects brandishing canes, or of scragging from other backbenchers. Mark Bonham Carter described his experience after being elected in a Liberal by-election coup in 1958. 'It's just like being back as a new boy at public school – with its rituals and rules, and also its background of convention, which breeds a sense of anxiety and inferiority in people who don't know the rules. Even the smell – the smell of damp stone stairways – is like a school. All you have of your own is a locker – just like a school locker. You don't know where you're allowed to go, and where not – you're always afraid you may be breaking some rule . . . It's just like a public school: and that's why Labour MPs are overawed by it – because they feel that only the Tory MPs know what a public school is like.' Robin Ferrers, who was appointed as a lord-in-waiting by Macmillan in 1962, found front-bench life just like school. 'There are the clever guys. There are the silly clots, too. Like football, you do the best that you can when the ball comes to you in order not to let the side down. At Question Time, if you can make them laugh, it is very satisfying. The schoolboy ethos is never far away – and that is good.'[39]

Sticklers resented any challenge to the prefects' authority. When a decision of the Deputy Speaker's was criticised by Lady Mellor, wife of a Tory MP, at a garden party, Labour MPs complained, and the Commons Privileges Committee censured her. No words that might weaken house *esprit de corps* could be tolerated, especially from anyone as objectionable as a woman with forthright and informed views. During crises, the Conservative parliamentary party resembled a boarding house in which any boy who challenged the housemaster's decisions would be biffed or given a bogging. Even in private sessions, it was bad form to bestir the deferential placidity. When Macmillan, or his successors Douglas-Home and Heath, addressed the 1922 Committee of backbenchers, questions were confined to the closing minutes of the meeting. The questions seldom exceeded the level of those at a constituency ward meeting.[40]

There was a striking homogeneity in the appearance of the Conservative parliamentary party: MPs wore a uniform of stiff white collars or cream silk shirts; dark, well-pressed suits or a black jacket with striped black and grey trousers; sleek Trumper's haircuts and oils. On Fridays, which were called Private Members' Days, when government business was not taken, and the Commons was thinly attended, the Conservative whips wore weekend tweed suits and brogue shoes. Julian Critchley was once standing in the crowded 'No' lobby, waiting to vote, when Sir Jocelyn Lucas, a crusty baronet who bred Sealyhams, accosted him, seized his elbow, hissed 'You're wearin' suede shoes', and stalked off. Lucas never addressed Critchley again. Excessive importance was attached to social standing. 'Some able middle-class Conservatives – like Enoch Powell or Iain Macleod – have gone a long way,' Anthony Wedgwood Benn commented in 1957, 'but one senses that many Tory MPs would prefer to be in the top drawer and out of office than to be out of the drawer and in office.'[41]

Once he became Prime Minister, Macmillan began attending the Derby, cricket matches, and other jollities to settle his image with his party faithful. He excelled in striking poses which projected his personality until it was a palpable force over others. The Tory die-hards had not been fooled by so brilliant a man since Disraeli. His address to Tory peers before the general election of 1959 was 'the best speech I think I have ever heard from a leader addressing his followers', noted blimpish Lord Winterton, who had fifty-five years' parliamentary experience. There were sweeping historical parallels to flatter his auditors' intelligence, and patriotic pride to rouse them. In international affairs, Britain was speeding towards danger 'like a man on a monorail', Macmillan warned the peers, 'but mankind had never known security save perhaps in Antonine age of Ancient [Rome] & Victorian age'. The achievement of full employment with 'one of the highest standards of living in the world' by a nation with few natural resources was possible because Britain was 'rich in brain power as in the time of the first Elizabeth when Europe looked on us as Barbarians who couldn't use a fork'. The Lords – backwoodsmen and activists alike – were rallied by such High Table urbanities.[42]

Critchley recalled a dinner that was arranged for the Prime Minister to meet newly elected backbenchers after the 1959 general election had been won with an improved majority. 'We dined in one room, and then moved to another, where some of us literally sat at his feet. Macmillan was the ideal speaker for the intimate occasion: splendid after dinner, witty, elegant of phrase, skilled at flattering his audience, taking us apparently into his confidence.

He was especially beguiling with the young. He told us, "Revolt by all means; but only on one issue at a time; to do more would be to confuse the whips". Critchley studied Macmillan's mannerisms at close quarters: 'the nervous fingering of his Brigade tie; his curiously hooded eyes which would suddenly open wide, and the famous baring of the teeth. He told us that no one who had not experienced Oxford before the Kaiser's War could know *"la douceur de vivre"*: Humphry Berkeley, a pompous youngster who was among the 1959 intake, admired Macmillan's skill in disguising from his die-hards his intention to grant independence to African colonies as swiftly as possible. He recalled the Prime Minister charming backbenchers after his return from Africa in 1960 with references to the Scottish earl – collateral descendant of a Victorian Viceroy of India – whom he had appointed as Governor-General of the Federation of Rhodesia and Nyasaland: 'It's awfully good of Simon Dalhousie to have taken out to Salisbury the viceregal gold plate which was presented to his ancestor. It's so good for morale.'[43]

'I am always hearing about the Middle Classes,' Macmillan wrote to the Conservative Research Department after a month in office. 'What is it they really want? Can you put it down on a sheet of notepaper, and then I will see whether we can give it to them?'[44] He knew the answer, though, well enough: they wanted a steady onrush of material prosperity, and to recover their margin of advantage over the working class.

The half century between Macmillan's seizing of the premiership in 1957 and the banking collapse of 2008 was exceptional in history as a time of abundance, not scarcity. In all other periods, privation was the common Western experience. Most people were kept on short rations, emotionally and materially; frustration, not satisfaction, provided the keynote of existence. Macmillan offered an end to the stingy circumstances in which women watered down their children's marmalade to make it go further.

Six months into his premiership Macmillan went to Bedford, the county town of the dullest English county. Its population of

60,000 worked in factories making pumps, diesel engines, gas turbines, farm implements, switchgear, tube fittings, transistors, and sweets. There, at the football pitch of the local team on 20 July 1957, Macmillan was guest of honour at a political gala to celebrate the parliamentary career of his Colonial Secretary Alan Lennox-Boyd, the long-serving Conservative MP for Mid-Bedfordshire: a career begun under the aegis of the *ancien régime* Duke of Bedford. No tickets were needed to attend; no 'spin doctors' existed to control the audience; there were no stewards from security firms to evict hecklers, or threaten them under anti-terrorist legislation. It was one of the last open-air political speeches by an English statesman to a genuine mass gathering. Politicians had for generations learnt to pitch their voices to reach thousands, to captivate their audiences and to master the art of impromptu retorts to hecklers. Henceforth they would have to simulate sincerity for television audiences.

The Bedford gala was 'unique in the political annals of the county', reported the local newspaper. 'The Premier received a great welcome from a crowd that had assembled from every part of Bedfordshire.' Macmillan told those who talked of the disintegration of the Empire: 'It is not breaking up; it is growing up.' He warned against complacency at recent advances in prosperity. 'Let's be frank about it: most of our people have never had it so good. Go around the country, go to the industrial towns, go to the farms, and you will see a state of prosperity such as we have never had . . . in the history of this country. What is beginning to worry some of us is "Is it too good to be true?" or perhaps I should say "Is it too good to last?"' The crowd cheered, perhaps because they were polite, perhaps because they were enjoying their afternoon in the sun, but surely not because they liked his warning that there might be bad times ahead. Indeed, the *Bedfordshire Times*, judging perhaps by his manner rather than his words, thought Macmillan had been over-optimistic about the economic future. The paper quoted his remark: 'Most of our people have never had it so good', and commented: 'That is true, but Mr Macmillan said little enough about the slender foundations on which all this prosperity rests.' There was no talk of measures to check inflation. The Prime Minister dismissed 'the fashion for newspapers and political commentators to work up all kinds of stories of troubles and dangers ahead'. The *Bedfordshire Times* thought no 'working-up' was needed: 'the dangers are very real ones, and it is time they are squarely faced'.[45]

At the rally a youngster in a boiler-suit persistently heckled the Prime Minister. One of his interruptions concerned the level of old-age pensions: the Labour Party was calling for the basic rate of old-age pensions to be raised to £3 a week and to be annually adjusted to the cost of living. '*You've* never had it so good,' Macmillan cried back at the heckler, contrasting the youngster's rising wages with the fixed income of a pensioner, rather than targeting everyone in Bedford football ground. According to another account (that of Quentin Skinner, the historian of political thought, then a sixth-former at Bedford school, who was present), the heckler shouted facetiously: 'What about the workers?' Macmillan responded as if a serious objection had been called. It was this phrase that beyond any other became associated with his premiership.[46]

If people's material standards were improving, in Bedford and nationally, there was a perception that, perhaps in consequence, sexual standards were deteriorating. Two years after Macmillan's football-pitch speech, Peter Kennerley of the *Sunday Pictorial* went to Bedford. 'Good-time girls – drunken teenagers – mothers who leave home for the bright lights – and plain unvarnished vice – these are the problems . . . earning the town of Bedford the reputation of "BRITAIN'S SIN TOWN 1959".' Kennerley reported that seven brothels had been raided and closed by Bedford police in the preceding six months. Twenty children from Bedford had been taken into council care in the last four months because their mothers had deserted their homes. A probation officer was quoted as saying that the absconding mothers, like troublesome teenagers, 'go where the money is'. Money in this case meant hundreds of American servicemen from three nearby airbases.[47]

Six weeks after Macmillan's Bedford speech, on 4 September 1957, the Wolfenden Committee on Homosexual Offences and Prostitution in Great Britain published its report. This recommended that homosexual activity between consenting adult men should no longer be criminalised; that penalties for street-soliciting by women should be increased; and that landlords letting premises to prostitutes should be deemed as living off immoral earnings. The recommendations on heterosexual prostitution were adopted in the Street Offences Act, which came into operation in 1959, while the recommendations on homosexuality were resisted.

Although the Profumo Affair would be, exclusively, a tooth-and-claw heterosexual business, reactions to it were part of a continuum of sexual attitudes. The fears, insults and cant surrounding male homosexuality in this period were not restricted in their impact to the communities that were targeted. On the contrary, the obtuseness of intelligent people about sexual motives, the punitive urges, the notion that collective respectability was maintained by newspaper bullying and abasement of vulnerable individuals, the prudish lynch mobs, the deviousness behind the self-righteous wrath of the judiciary – all these defining traits of homophobia erupted nationwide during the summer of 1963, with the Profumo resignation, Ward trial and Denning report.

Writing about Ward's mis-trial, the jurist Louis Blom-Cooper later commented: 'The law does not care for social realities; it bases its action upon highly emotive opinion on what is best for the country's morals.' The truth of this was exemplified by sundry interventions from Lord Hailsham, a barrister who held several Cabinet posts under Macmillan and hoped to succeed him as Prime Minister in 1963. In an epoch when it was unthinkable for Cabinet Ministers to appear in shirtsleeves, Hailsham and Ian Macleod were pioneers among Tory politicians in trying to indicate that they were hustling, businesslike modernisers by tightly buttoning the middle button of their suit jackets. At the time of the Wolfenden committee's appointment, while citing his courtroom expertise, Hailsham had published a scourging essay on homosexual 'corruption'. He was emphatic that male homosexuality was 'a problem of social environment and not of congenital make-up'. For most men, 'the precipitating factor in their abnormality has been initiation by older homosexuals while the personality is still pliable'. Homosexuality was indeed 'a proselytising religion, and initiation by an adept is at once the cause and the occasion of the type of fixation which has led to the increase in homosexual practices'. Hailsham, with his authority as a Queen's Counsel and Bencher of Lincoln's Inn, held that 'homosexual practices are contagious, incurable, and self-perpetuating', that 'homosexuality is, and for fundamentally the same reasons, as much a moral and social issue as heroin addiction'. Homosexuals, he averred, were pederasts by preference. 'No doubt homosexual acts between mature males do take place . . . but the normal attraction of the adult male homosexual is to the young male adolescent or young male adult to the exclusion of others.'

As so often, hostility to same-sex activity splayed into asinine condemnation of heterosexual behaviour. 'Adultery and fornication may be immoral but, on the lowest physical plane, they both involve the use of the complementary physical organs of male and female,' Hailsham explained. However, 'between man and woman the persistent misuse of these organs in any other way is often fraught with grave dangers, emotional, or even physical, to one or both of the participants'. This seems to be a verbose warning that people who enjoyed using either mouths or fingers in their sex lives were in peril of nervous or bodily collapse. Homosexual practices were worse because they used 'non-complementary physical organs', Hailsham continued. 'The psychological consequences of this physical misuse of the bodily organs cannot in the long run be ignored . . . nearly all the homosexuals I have known have been emotionally unbalanced and profoundly unhappy. I do not believe that this is solely or exclusively due to the fear of detection, or of the sense of guilt attaching to practices in fact disapproved of by society. It is inherent in the nature of an activity which seeks a satisfaction for which the bodily organs employed are physically unsuited.'[48]

Hailsham sounded moral alarms monotonously, although the miscreant modernity that he despised was tied to material ease promoted by the government of which he was a member. His inaugural address as Rector of Glasgow University in 1959 flailed 'the emotional, intellectual, moral, political, even the physical litter and chaos of the world today, when truth has almost ceased to be regarded as objective, when kindness is made to depend on political, class or racial affiliations, when only the obvious stands in need of publicity'. He felt revulsion, he declared, 'when I look at popular pin-ups, playboys, millionaires and actresses with the bodies of gods and goddesses and the morals of ferrets lurching from one demoralising emotional crisis to another and never guessing the reason; when I view the leaders of great states, the masters of immense concentrations of power and wealth, gesticulating like monkeys and hurling insults unfit for fishwives; when I reflect on the vapidity of so much that is popular in entertainment, the trite-ness of so much that passes for profundity, the pointlessness and frustration in the popular mood.' In these rounded periods lay the quandary of the Macmillan era, and the trap for Jack Profumo.[49]

Despite the spiritual pride of Hailsham and allies like him, Macmillan won the general election of 1959 because the Tories were more convincing as a party of liberty and progress: Labour, by contrast, seeming conservative and cheeseparing. Profumo's campaign message to the electors of Stratford-on-Avon decried his socialist opponents as regressive killjoys and fretful regulators. 'Most people are suffering from acute political exhaustion. Facts, figures, graphs, slogans, promises, boasts, taunts and threats galore have been chucked about for weeks.' But some things were clear: the Labour government of 1945–51 had failed to meet expectations. 'The Labour leaders were all so keen to establish a Socialist State that they failed to observe what made people tick and what made them kick. They divided us, depressed us, disillusioned us and nearly destroyed us.' By contrast, since 1951, 'we have swept away all the paraphernalia of controls and proved that Conservative freedom does work to the benefit of everyone'. Voters were 'glad to be free of controls; but a Labour Government would clamp them on again . . . This is your life – don't let Labour ruin it.'[50]

Hugh Trevor-Roper, who masterminded Macmillan's election as Chancellor of Oxford University in 1960, thought that the tendency of the times was towards 'a vulgar, jolly, complacent, materialist social democracy'. He found ominous 'the universal absorbent materialism even of spiritual life which has triumphed in America and, unless one fights against it, will gradually triumph here too – has already triumphed in the majority of the population'. A Salford bookmaker's son thought similarly to the Regius Professor of Modern History at Oxford. 'I jumped at the chance,' Albert Finney said in 1961 of his lead in the screen version of Alan Sillitoe's novel *Saturday Night and Sunday Morning*, 'because of what the film had to say about our present-day smash-and-grab society'. Some Tories shuddered at Macmillan's bribery of voters. During elections, declared a discontented backbencher in 1962, each political party entered 'a sort of spiv auction, each one trying to outbid the other with promises of material gain to the masses, in the cynical belief that the electorate is composed of unthinking dupes whose highest aspiration in life is to worship Mammon'.[51]

If Macmillan's England seemed a smash-and-grab society to some, it remained a place of frugal, unimaginative routines for many others. Michael Wharton, the *Daily Telegraph* columnist, lunched every working day in a dingy Fleet Street pub on an identical meal of corned beef sandwiches washed down by brandy and ginger. He ate the same supper each evening at his Battersea flat of lime juice and soda with five fish fingers (never more or less). Yet Wharton felt deep passions, cravings and regrets, as shown by his lament for England in 1961: 'Her empire and influence is almost gone; her patriots are too much ashamed and beaten down with incessant jeers to speak up for her, or if they do, their voices are shrill and ugly with rancour' (a reference to the League of Empire Loyalists, a group of embittered hecklers, opposed to decolonisation, who followed Macmillan about shouting that he was a traitor). As to the countryside, farmers had become 'money-mad mechanics, forever searching for new poisons for the soil which will ensure quick profits at any cost'; fox-hunters chased their quarry around housing estates; Morris dancers cavorted beside atomic power stations; in summer the Lake District was infested by smelly, honking pleasure traffic.

Wharton did not wonder that England, 'the first country to suffer industrialisation and uniquely vulnerable to its final triumph, clings to survivals, landed titles, splendid rituals'. The move towards classlessness was a drift into stereotypes and the culture of grievance. 'Policemen and sociologists, clergymen and psychiatrists are chasing the fashionable hooligans and sex maniacs; housewives yawn in deathly new towns; journalists, television interviewers and experts endlessly discuss the Problems of Today. There is the Problem of Youth, the Problem of Delinquency, the Problem of Coloured Immigration, the Problem of the Eleven Plus, the Problem of Parking.' People thought less in terms of class loyalties, and increasingly as categories of oppressed: 'as teenagers, homosexuals, motorists, misunderstood criminals and so on'. Mammon ruled under Macmillan, Wharton thought. 'Over all this England, with its mingled apathy and desperation, lies a thick fog of money and of the operations of money. The ideal Englishman of the advertisements is no longer an aristocrat; he has become a salesman or a financial speculator. His office skyscrapers shoot up overnight where familiar old buildings have been (and he hires public relations men to tell us how much more beautiful they are than the old buildings and makes us ashamed of ourselves for thinking otherwise); his empires of money grow and combine, grow and combine again, continually devising new needs, new categories of people to feel those needs and buy the goods that will satisfy them, temporarily, until new needs can be devised.'[52]

About the time that Churchill retired as Prime Minister in 1955, the patriotic catchphrases that public men had traditionally parroted abruptly began to seem bogus, weary and redundant. A few months later, after the revelations of the Burgess-Maclean espionage cover-up, the word 'Establishment' was first deployed with the overtone that anything established was suspect. The notion flourished that political, administrative and economic authority was controlled by a secretive sect with strange rites and arcane customs – a mafia comprised of Wykehamists and Etonians. 'There certainly exists in Britain a number of persons, many of them known to each other and sometimes educated together, who exercise considerable power and influence of the kind that is not open to direct public inspection,' wrote the young philosopher Bernard Williams at the time of the general election of 1959. 'Large areas of British life are permeated by mediocrity and the refusal to face genuine issues. Influential figures undoubtedly share, in their own refined complacent way, these characteristics, but they are not the cause of them.' Henry Fairlie, the political journalist who was amongst the most perceptive commentators on Macmillan's premiership, complained in the same year that this demure coinage, 'the Establishment', had been debauched by publicists until it was a harlot of a phrase used promiscuously by dons, novelists, playwrights, artists, actors, critics, scriptwriters and band leaders to denote those in positions of authority whom they disliked. The Establishment's defenders argued that it was rooted in neither class nor sectional interest, and was, therefore, disinterested. Its opponents found this lack of passion or commitment to be depressing, and perhaps reprehensible.[53]

Macmillan's appointment of a Scottish earl, Home, as Foreign Secretary in 1960, and of his wife's nephew, the Duke of Devonshire, to the Commonwealth Relations Office in 1961, provoked the anti-Establishment pundits to fume (although neither man failed at his post). The Tories traditionally believed that the tests of experience and of time were sound guides, but after the 1959 election victory appeals to tradition were no longer winning. Instead, Tory leaders had to place themselves as the people best able to manage change. By 1962, Macmillan was trying to identify his party as the modernisers and Labour as retrogressive: Marples's disastrous transport policies and Britain's ill-fated application to join the Common Market were at the forefront of this strategy.

In July 1962, the *Observer* journalist and former gossip columnist Anthony Sampson published his *Anatomy of Britain* which, on the basis of interviews with political, business and official leaders, presented public life as amateurish, caste-ridden, dithering and cowed. His bestseller operated by the technique of the prewar fellow-travellers who compiled Union of Democratic Control pamphlets: genealogical tables revealing distant, unsuspected cousinhoods; Venn diagrams of overlapping company directorships and schematic representations of power relations all tending to suggest there was a loose conspiracy by undemocratic, debilitated and incompetent fuddy-duddies. Sampson had a priggish belief that people should be spurred hard by overriding moral purposes; in an earlier generation he might have been a disciple of Frank Buchman's Moral Rearmament group. He seemed to idealise men who worked exorbitantly long hours, scorned holidays and judged themselves virtuous for spreading stress in their offices.

Sampson's book chimed with the clashing cymbals of opinion-making in 1962. Jack Plumb, the son of a Leicester shoe factory worker, was a communist in the 1930s, a Bletchley Park code-breaker during the war, a Cambridge history don from 1946 and an avid, frustrated crosspatch with a beady eye for the main chance. 'Your time is coming,' his lifelong confidant C. P. Snow promised him in 1960, 'one can smell it in the air.' Initially Plumb resented tradition: in 1962, for example, he decried the privileged readers of history books as 'those who had nannies, prep-schools, dorms, possess colonels and bishops for cousins, and now take tea once a year on the dead and lonely lawns of the Palace'. In time he proved the very model of an anti-Establishment skirmisher who, once his enemies were routed, annexed their domains of influence and adopted their style and amenities which he had all along irritably envied. Soon he had a rectory in Suffolk and a *moulin* in France, ingratiated himself with philanthropic million-aires and smart noblewomen, looked cocksure in the private apartments of palaces, became a conspicuous member of Brooks's, figured until the last moment among the peers in Harold Wilson's notorious resignation honours list, performed a clumsy political somersault in the hope of prising a coronet from Margaret Thatcher.[54]

Richard Crossman was another opportunistic rhetorician where modernisation and class distinction were concerned. Reviewing Sampson's *Anatomy of Britain* for the *New Statesman*, he pretended that political and economic power was more irresponsibly concen-trated than at any time in living memory. 'Never in our island history have so many been fooled by so few,' he claimed. 'An irreverent attitude to top people is the yeast that makes democracy rise. Without it a free society soon degenerates into a starchy oligarchy, an indigestible complex of collusive interest groups which can only be broken up by subjecting it to constant inves-tigation and public exposure.' Hostile analyses of the Establishment were class-war waged with polysyllables: a device to get one crowd out of power, and another in; to usurp one set of authority figures, and install a different lot. Anti-establishment critics masqueraded as street-fighting egalitarians, but in truth they were jostlers for place in the corridors of power.[55]

Simon Raven was rare among Sampson's reviewers in resisting his thesis. The scolding theme of *Anatomy of Britain* was that 'most educated Englishmen reserve their respect for old-fashioned institutions, such as Eton, Latin, the regimental system and Mr Macmillan, and refuse to recognise the demands of the New Age for such qualities as industrial efficiency and high-pressure sales-manship', wrote Raven. He, however, wanted to be saved from despotic bores who resented people having placid, aimless moments. 'While long-established English institutions tend to be illogical and wasteful, the values which they promote, however limited in their scope, are morally and aesthetically far superior to anything which the new world of admass tastes and applied science can show. If I want to spend my day writing Latin verses or watching cricket, as opposed to selling some beastly machine or rubbishy gimmick over a fat expense account luncheon, who is to say that I am not the better man for it?'[56]

Although Macmillan in 1963 headed a Cabinet with the youngest average age for a century, he was also the Prime Minister who kept his only television set at Birch Grove in the servants' hall. Broadcasting, however, more than newspapers, showed the tendency of the times. 'The formality of BBC official language used to be one of great reassurance; it spoke of order, like guards on trains,' reflected Malcolm Bradbury, lecturer in English Language at Birmingham University, in the spring of 1963. 'Now, in a wave of informality, even the news is changing. The names of contributors to newsreels are frequently mentioned (personal), announcers cough regularly and carefully do not, as they easily can, switch the cough out (informal), the opinions of people in the street are canvassed, though they frequently have none (demo-cratic), and interviewers are aggressive and sometimes even offensive (vernacular). So, personal, informal, democratic and vernacular, becomes the new common speech for all things.'[57]

The challenge for Macmillan, as the protagonists of the Profumo Affair converged towards their crisis, would be to hold onto power in an age of common speech. His attendance at the Derby, the shoots at Swinton, quips about Boodle's which were incomprehensible to ninety-five cent of the electorate, had rallied his parliamentary party after 1957, and brought a thumping elec-toral victory in 1959. But in the new informal, levelling and vernacular age, these poses made his government vulnerable.

TWO

War Minister

When the government minister John Profumo married the film-star Valerie Hobson on New Year's Eve, 1954, a crowd of about fifty bystanders gathered on the pavement in Pont Street, outside St Columba's Church, in Chelsea. Boys on rollerskates, London coppers, and two chimney sweeps made it resemble a scene from *Mary Poppins*. The bride, who was given away by the debonair financier Gerard 'Pop' d'Erlanger, wore a grey suit of vicuna, a new material from Paris, with a high collar and cuffs of sapphire mink. A grey silk bonnet was perched over her red hair. Among the fifteen guests was Leslie Mitchell, the suave-voiced broadcaster who announced the opening of the BBC television service in 1936 and of Independent Television in 1955.

The Profumos flew away on their honeymoon that evening, so spoilt by fortune that the head of Heathrow ordained that free champagne should be provided for them and fellow passengers on their Paris-bound aircraft. Next morning, as their car left the Ritz hotel in Paris, with a motorcycle escort from the US embassy revving its engines, the duty manager hastened out with the MP's pyjamas, which had lain unworn beneath his pillow all night. The Department of Transport gave them the number plate PXH1 ('Profumo Times Hobson equals Number One') and a few years later the Foreign Office issued them with passports numbered 3 and 4. Jack Profumo and Valerie Hobson were a golden couple for press photographers, hotel managers and the image-conscious.

They had met exactly seven years earlier at a fancy dress ball held at the Royal Albert Hall to usher in New Year's Day, 1947. He was dressed as a policeman, she as Madame Récamier (the nineteenth-century Paris hostess commemorated by a type of daybed). She was twenty-nine, with a string of film successes behind her, and stoically married to an inveterate womaniser. He was thirty-one, temporarily out of Parliament, but already with five years' experience as a Conservative MP.

The Profumos were a legal and mercantile family on whom the King of Sardinia bestowed a barony in 1843. The third baron settled in England, became a naturalised British subject and in 1877 founded the Provident Life Association, which made a fortune for his descendants. The Provident enabled lower-middle-class men who could never afford to buy a house outright to take out an endowment assurance policy, pay a small weekly premium and build up a sum which would be held as a deposit when, after five years, they were entitled to borrow several hundred pounds representing the total cost of a house. Their debt would be paid off over twenty-five years.

The grandson and eventual heir to the Provident money and Italian title was born in 1915, and in 1928 started at Harrow School, perched on a hill in Middlesex, ten miles north of London. 'While everybody knows that Englishmen are sent to public schools because that is the only place where they can learn good manners,' Rebecca West wrote in 1953, 'it unfortunately happens that the manners they learn there are recognised as good only by people who have been to the same sort of school, and often appear very bad indeed to everybody else.' There was no school of which this was truer than Harrow. It had its private vocabulary (a boy was called a 'Torpid' until he had turned sixteen or completed two years), arcane rules (boys in their first year had to fasten all three buttons on their jackets, one button in their second year, and thereafter none), special costumes (top hats for all boys on Sundays, a red fez with tassels for football players) and other rigmaroles. 'We lived rather like young Spartans; and were not encouraged to think, imagine, or see anything that we learned in relation to life at large,' John Galsworthy recalled of his years at Harrow. 'In that queer life we had all sorts of unwritten rules of suppression. You must turn up your trousers; must not go out with your umbrella rolled. Your hat must be worn tilted forward; you must not walk more than two abreast until you have reached a certain form . . . you must not talk about yourself or your home people, and for any punishment you must assume complete indifference.' Giles Playfair, who was a pupil shortly before Profumo, emphasised Harrow's ugliness ('the stone floors and staircases, the dark subterranean passages, the dirty blue paint peeling off the walls, the ill-conditioned bed sitting-rooms and the wholly unattractive sanitary accommodation') and philistinism ('"He jaws about poetry", they said, and quite tirelessly and mercilessly, by a process of mental cruelty, they saw to it that I paid the penalty for my indiscretions'). Playfair felt degraded by the fagging system, especially at mealtimes, when he had to assist one irritable butler and two kitchen youths with dirty collars and greasy hair in serving eighty hungry boys.[1]

Harrow School, when Profumo arrived in 1928, was pervaded by militarism, veneration of the dead and sombre pomposity. Memories of the Great War, which had ended ten years earlier, still overshadowed the school. Almost three thousand Harrovians had served, 690 were wounded, and 644 (twenty-two per cent) killed. A huge 'War Memorial Building' was erected amidst a range of old school premises: its 'silent emptiness,' wrote Christopher Tyerman in his superb history, 'appropriate for the hollow anguish and grief caused by the losses'; but its location like 'implanting a dead heart in the school'. There was no forgetting Harrow's Glorious Dead for the school chapel was lined with plaques commemorating hundreds of them. The chaplain appointed in Profumo's time had the Victoria Cross, and joined the Officer Training Corps like other masters. There was army drill, in full khaki, twice a week plus military exercises on Sunday mornings. The soldierliness embedded in the weekly timetables, the rituals of conformity, the zeal of masters in promoting notions of duty and service, exceeded anything that the Edwardians would have desired. The OTC commander was such a martinet in the 1920s that boys protested: despite newspaper coverage of their mutinous discontent, the OTC remained compulsory for Harrovians until 1973.[2]

The headmaster of Harrow School in Profumo's time was Cyril Norwood, who began his career teaching in grammar schools and was nicknamed 'Boots' by Harrovians because his manners seemed common. Masters and pupils thought him abrasive, over-confident and self-publicising. His morality, like that of other weak men masquerading as strong, was stubborn and unimagin-ative. 'His appearance was sallow and plebeian,' recalled Playfair. 'His manner was cold and severe . . . he never welcomed contra-diction or allowed his will to be flouted. He was a bad listener.' When recruiting a new master, in 1929, he sought a good cricketer in holy orders.[3]

Norwood published books with such titles as *The English Tradition of Education*. He saw public schools as a training ground for the hierarchies of adult life. 'It is the business of everybody to obey orders: it is expected that the orders will be reasonable, but they are there not to be criticised but obeyed.' If obedience to orders was the first principle of Norwood's universe, conformity was the basis of his public school code. 'Everyone sees the sense of rules, and the happiness of everyone is found in carrying them out, or conforming to them loyally.' Norwood's Harrow instilled a smooth-mannered duplicity. It taught boys to show outward deference to people for whom they felt little respect. It rewarded them for giving a pleasant smile while conforming to rules that they inwardly scorned. It assured them that compliance to higher authority was the essence of English racial superiority. 'There is an inherited system of morality, which represents the experience of the race, the rules which our ancestors have found to govern the game, and there is a racial character, a setting towards some ideals and not others, towards qualities and types of pursuit which appeal to Frenchmen, and not Englishmen, or to Englishmen, and not Frenchmen.'

A boarding house was a model for the outside world, and its rules – which upheld violence, but punished sex – were applicable there, too. 'It is proper that a House Captain should have the right to cane,' Norwood insisted. 'Caning is not felt by English boys to be a degradation, and it is not so looked upon. It is a quick and effective way of dealing with "uppishness" and insubordination. Nevertheless, if a Housemaster discovered that his captain was making free use of the stick, he would know that his House had gone all wrong.' Norwood's ideal was manliness isolated from sexual fulfilment (a common public-school experience was for a housemaster suddenly to cease thrashing with his cane once he had married and could relax with other outlets). He had no truck with physicians claiming that expulsion was the wrong treatment for schoolboy homosexuality or social masturbation: 'they themselves would never leave a patient with smallpox in a dormitory of healthy people, and it has always seemed astonishing to me that they should think that a schoolmaster should think twice about permitting a detected corrupter to range free inside a school'.[4]

In this Harrow School was a microcosm of English attitudes. 'The English are filled with fear of themselves and their own impulses – and above all of other people', the sociologist Geoffrey Gorer reported in 1951. 'They fear their neighbours; they fear what people would say if they did something a little different from the rest. And this terror of other people's opinions stifles originality and invention, and often prevents the English from enjoying themselves in their own ways.'[5]

The Profumo Affair, one might think, was Norwood-made. Jack Profumo learnt at school how to ape the fearful English version of good behaviour while bent on quietly enjoying himself in his own way. It is hard to imagine that he was ever a shame-faced boy. He discreetly pursued his courses with outward deference but private indifference to the school authorities' moral shams. That morality – still less the empty, fretful orotundity with which it was expressed – bore little resemblance to the imaginations and

49

experiences of any boys or men except the insufferably prim. It provided, though, the antecedent context for the scandals of 1963. Profumo's belief that he could bluff senior ministers with his denial of an affair with Christine Keeler was learnt in the stupid humbug of Norwood's Harrow.

Throughout the mid-twentieth century, schools like Harrow sent to Oxford, as Hugh Trevor-Roper lamented, 'dim paragons of reach-me-down orthodoxy'. In 1933, Profumo, who was dyslexic, went to Brasenose College, Oxford, where he read Agriculture and Political Economy – the least taxing of subjects. Brasenose was not a scholarly college. It was presided over by sozzled dons such as the epicurean Maurice Platnauer, 'a particularly plump, peach-coloured and port-fed rat', together with 'a mountainous old man who drank a bottle of whisky a day' called 'Sonners' Stallybrass, who peered 'through glasses as thick as ginger-beer bottles and was forever veering away from Justinian's views on riparian ownership to Catallus's celebration of oral sex' (the descriptions come from Trevor-Roper and John Mortimer). Jack Profumo had a dashing restless temperament that was well suited to Brasenose, although his carousals were never very boozy. The college luminaries preferred their undergraduates to achieve sporting Blues rather than first-class honours. Profumo, finding the rugby trials too bruising, took up polo, point-to-point riding and pole-vaulting, which earned him three half-Blues. Brasenose's ethos resembled that of the RAF, wrote the college historian: 'athletic, loyal, light-hearted, physically courageous'. Many Brasenose sportsmen, including Profumo, learnt to fly with the Oxford University Air Squadron (Profumo kept his own Gypsy Moth at a Midlands airfield). His son David describes him in early manhood as 'part-daredevil and part-lounge lizard'.[6]

In March 1940, Profumo was elected in a by-election as Conservative MP for Kettering. Aged twenty-five, he was the baby of the House of Commons. When his father died three weeks later, he inherited a fortune, and became fifth baron of the

Kingdom of Sardinia and third baron of the United Kingdom of Italy, but decided that to use his title would hinder his political career. His first vote in the House of Commons, on 8 May, was a momentous occasion. He was one of thirty-three Tory MPs, including Macmillan, who voted with Labour, rather than abstaining as sixty others did, in a vote censuring the Chamberlain government's failure adequately to supply British troops in Norway. The Minister of Health spat on Profumo's shoe. The Tory Chief Whip told him that he was 'an utterly contemptible little shit'.[7]

As pilot officers, flight lieutenants and squadron leaders, Profumo's generation at Brasenose were in the front line during the Battle of Britain – during which many of them perished. Profumo was not an aerial combatant, but served as an air intelligence liaison officer and then a general staff officer until he was posted abroad in 1942. He fought in the battle of Tunis, the invasion of Sicily and the conquest of Italy. He was attached to the staff of Field Marshal Alexander, for whom he liaised with the RAF and United States Army Air Force, and received both American and British decorations.

After losing his parliamentary seat in the Labour general election triumph of 1945, Profumo was promoted brigadier and spent eight months living in the British embassy in Tokyo as second-in-command of the British military mission in the Far East. He was said to have dislodged Enoch Powell from being the youngest brigadier in the British Army. It was at the end of 1946, back in England, and a prospective parliamentary candidate again, that he dressed as a policeman, went to a New Year's Ball and met his future bride.

Valerie Hobson was the daughter of a dud. Her father – Commander Hobson as he liked to be called – devised great schemes, but lacked judgement, perseverance and luck. Once he was offered a chance to invest in a new substance for wrapping bread, called Cellophane, but was sure that housewives would never buy it. He dealt in bric-à-brac, opened a South Kensington bridge club and kept his family in precarious gentility at transitory addresses. One of his few successes was to renounce alcohol after years of unseemly tipsiness. He and his wife shifted about with their two daughters, staying in the spare rooms of patient relations, becoming paying guests in the homes of spinster gentlefolk, moving on within a year before their hosts tired of them. His public face was bluff optimism, but at home there was tetchy despondency.

Valerie Hobson was a plain child with monstrous teeth. But she matured into a beauty, went to RADA, and at the age of sixteen secured her first film part – for which she was paid £20. Three years later, in 1936, while taking part in a Shepperton Studios film called *Eunuch*, she fell in love with a spruce gallant named Anthony Havelock-Allan. Tony Havelock-Allan, too, had a background of feckless, unsettled indigence. At the time of his birth, his father had been managing director of the Northern Counties Spa Water Company, but losing that post in 1907, had tried to keep a wife and three children on an allowance of £200 a year from his elder brother (a Durham baronet). He tried to raise his income by becoming Master of the West Kent Foxhounds with the intention of running the hunt to his personal profit. Instead, after one hunting season, he went bankrupt in 1914. The second son of a bankrupt second son, Tony Havelock-Allan had to skip university, but studied gemmology at Chelsea Polytechnic after getting his first job with the Regent Street jewellers Garrard's. He dallied in Weimar Berlin, met Ravel and Stravinsky during his stint as recording manager of a gramophone company, flogged advertising in Lord Beaverbrook's *Evening Standard* to estate agents, and hired cabaret acts for Ciro's nightclub (where the cocktails 'Sidecar' and 'White Lady' were invented). From Ciro's, Havelock-Allan was recruited by his chum Richard Norton (afterwards Lord Grantley) to be casting director at the English branch of the Hollywood company Paramount Pictures, for whom he became a film producer in 1935.

Havelock-Allan was a practised and calculating philanderer. When he met Valerie Hobson, he was engrossed with Enid

Walker, wife of Count Cosmo de Bosdari. He was pursuing an affair with the actress Kay Kendall, fresh from the flop film musical *London Town*, when ten years later Hobson met Profumo. Having married Havelock-Allan in 1939, Valerie Hobson soon became pregnant and self-induced an abortion by drinking a bottle of gin, hurling herself from a chair and taking a boiling-hot bath. This is one experience that she shared with Christine Keeler, who once tried to induce an abortion with the aid of drugs and knitting-needles. In 1944, Hobson gave birth to a son, Simon, who was diagnosed as having Down's syndrome: a physician offered to give the baby a fatal injection of meningococcal meningitis, but she declined. It is indicative of attitudes in 1944 that the Education Act of that year deemed children with Down's to be 'ineducable' and excluded them from schooling. Simon Havelock-Allan spent most of his boyhood in institutions, and did not speak until he was sixteen. It is not surprising that after such lonely sorrows Valerie Hobson was regarded as prickly and aloof in the film world.

Two of her screen successes were playing aristocrats in films about men escaping from their class. She played a chilly beauty, Edith D'Ascoyne, in *Kind Hearts and Coronets* (1949), the comedy in which a fastidious shop assistant, played by Dennis Price, murdered a succession of his remote cousins in order to escape penury and inherit the dukedom of Chalfont. The murder victims (female as well as male) were all played by Alec Guinness. Edith D'Ascoyne, the widow of the second murder victim (killed in a booby-trapped photographer's darkroom), unknowingly marries her husband's killer (most of the deaths are attributed to accidents). 'A kind of British comedy we hadn't dared to dream about – urbane, satirical, witty, sophisticated,' Cyril Ray greeted it. Hobson played Lady Chell in *The Card* (1952), the film adapted by Eric Ambler from Arnold Bennett's novel. It again starred Alec Guinness, this time as a wide-boy who rises in the world by impertinence and charm. 'Miss Valerie Hobson as Lady Chell performs with great spirit the unladylike tasks set before her,' reported a reviewer. 'Her ride in a runaway mule-cart gives new life to that moribund and fishy tribe – the film aristocrats.'[8]

Valerie Hobson, who was attracted by dashing *coureurs de femmes*, fell for Profumo as swiftly as she had for Havelock-Allan. His vitality was exciting and, as she later wrote, his interests differed from any she had known: 'politics (above all), girls, horses, parties, holidays in the sun, practical jokes, Society gossip, aeroplanes (which he flew himself) and, above all, fun'.[9] She did not want her first foray in adultery to be with him, or to be spoilt by self-conscious guilt, so she first went to bed with another married admirer, probably Whitney Straight, a motor-racing driver and managing director of BOAC (British Overseas Airways Corporation). Shortly after, she and Profumo began their secret affair. The subterfuge of intrigues, he found, intensified the sex.

Hobson became pregnant by Profumo during the summer of 1949. When she told him of the pregnancy as they stood on the battlements of Chenonceaux castle, he reacted lovingly but took it for granted that she would have an abortion. This time, instead of a horrific, self-induced abortion, she underwent the medical procedure known colloquially as a D and C (dilation and curetting) at a nursing-home in Hendon. This second abortion made her suspend the affair. A general election was looming, and her lover could not jeopardise his political prospects by being named in a divorce case involving an actress.

Profumo was elected with a safe majority as Tory MP for the newly created constituency of Stratford-on-Avon in 1950 (his parents' house, Avon Carrow, lay in the constituency, where his unmarried sister still lived). Two years later he succeeded Reginald Maudling as Parliamentary Secretary to the Minister of Civil Aviation, Alan Lennox-Boyd. In the Civil Aviation ministry he enthused about helicopters, and wanted to foist a heliport on Londoners. Subsequently the Civil Aviation and Transport ministries were merged under a single minister, John Boyd-Carpenter – 'spring-heeled Jack' as he was nicknamed. The two parliamentary secretaries of the united department were, Boyd-Carpenter recalled, 'Hugh Molson, cautious, precise, reliable, a little inflexible on the ground transport side, and John Profumo, lively, quick and adroit – the best company in the world.'[10] There are politicians who run on full throttle in their race for power; there are over-wrought firebrands obsessed with principle; and breezy types who scoot along on charm. The latter get people to like them, put them at their ease, recognise their faces, mollify their feelings, nod encouragingly at their remarks, and make apt replies. This was Jack Profumo.

Six months after Profumo's re-election to Parliament, Valerie Hobson went to the opera with Havelock-Allan, let him stay the night and became pregnant. Shortly after her second son was born in April 1951, the couple agreed to divorce – perhaps to facilitate her marriage to a new suitor, the Marquess of Londonderry, a drunkard who swerved between self-pitying submission and ugly aggression. In conformity with the prevalent divorce laws, Havelock-Allan, with his long career of adulteries, had to contrive being caught with a woman in circumstances that seemed to provide proof of adultery, although the woman was a respectable stranger hired for the purpose. After the divorce was accomplished in 1952, Londonderry's attentions became importunate; but Profumo instead bounded back into play. He and the newly freed Valerie Hobson announced their engagement in October 1954. Profumo, saddled with an Italian surname suggestive of women's scents, cannot have helped his flighty reputation among the more wooden-headed MPs by marrying an actress.

Profumo insisted that his bride, who was then starring as the lead in the hit musical *The King and I*, must stop work after she married. She complied reluctantly, though in public she showed a brave front. 'I am giving up all my stage and film work – everything,' she told journalists when she married. 'It is the happiest step I can possibly take, though don't imagine I have not loved my profession. I know lots of men and their wives mix their careers: I want to be a hundred per cent wife.'[11] Similarly, it was unthinkable for Bronwen Pugh, perhaps the highest-paid model in England, to continue her independent working existence after her marriage to Lord Astor in 1960. Both women were obliged by their husbands to uproot a flourishing career; but they were among the luckier women. Choices were far narrower for most others.

Hobson left the stage before the changes in dramatic taste associated with John Whiting's *Marching Song* (1954), John Osborne's *Look Back in Anger* (1956), Shelagh Delaney's *A Taste of Honey* (1958), Arnold Wesker's *The Kitchen* (1959), Harold Pinter's *The Caretaker* (1960) and Keith Waterhouse's *Billy Liar* (1960). In the early fifties, younger playwrights deplored the theatre's dependence on plays written by decorous novelists or verse dramas by Eliot and Fry. 'Well, that marriage broke up,' John Whiting mused in 1961. 'Since then the theatre's been sleeping around with journalism, reportage, propaganda, autobiography and the movies among other things. And the old whore's produced some very odd offspring.'[12] This edgy, ungracious, shop-soiled world was not for Valerie Hobson.

In 1948, Profumo obtained a lease from the Crown Estates of 3 Chester Terrace (telephone: Welbeck 6983), an elegant house designed by Nash overlooking the Regent's Park. Nash's terraces kept a battered look for years after the war; and were only restored in the early 1960s. After the Profumos' marriage their house was revamped with a cool chic that reflected the frosty smartness of their lives. It had a forty-foot drawing room, lit by tall windows, with views of the park beyond. Stéphane Boudin, the Paris interior designer who later advised Jacqueline Kennedy on the redecoration of the White House, imprinted the drawing room with his light version of the Regency style. Side-tables were set on an Aubusson carpet and arrayed with treasures. David Profumo recalled pagodas carved from ivory, an Epstein head, and a bejewelled Fabergé bulldog. It was a special treat for him, when his parents had guests, to hide under the green velvet of one of the side-tables, and nibble rice crackers from a black japanned tin decorated with pink

blossom on its lid. Overall, the boy's upbringing was emotionally chilly.

Smart London did not fully revive after the war until the Season
of 1956. 'For the first time since before the war, the British upper
class has got the bit between its teeth', reported the *New Statesman*
in May of that year. 'Not since the thirties has it consumed so
much bad champagne and dubious caviar, trampled so much
glass underfoot. After years of wartime equality, Crippsian
austerity, servantless mansions, travel allowances, dividend
restraint and triumphant bureaucracy, the Butler Boom is beginning to take effect: Society is scrambling shakily to its feet again
and cocking a tentative snoot at the masses.' It was revealing of
the postwar pusillanimity that rich people enjoying good parties
were thought provocative. Rich people should apologise for their
wealth, the *New Statesman* averred, and should not be seen having
fun. 'The upper-class spending spree – of which the 1956 Season
is the apotheosis – is a form of collective hallucination, a desperate
attempt on the part of Britain's financial and social élite to
persuade itself that nothing has changed. Every all-night party,
every case of champagne, every hamper of *pâté de foie gras* is one
more proof . . . that the Labour Government was just a transitory
nightmare, that equality is . . . receding into the remote distance.'
In the authentic tone of an envious killjoy, the magazine closed
with a whiny question: 'Is it too much to ask, just once, that the
people at the top should set something other than the worst
possible example?'[13]

The *New Statesman* prig disapproved of what he called 'the
leisured class', and was tormented by the thought that somewhere
people might be enjoying themselves. For the prim and pinch-
lipped frowners, who often in these years seemed to constitute
the majority, the only pleasure was in foiling other people's enjoyment. 'The workaday flavour of England today,' wrote James
Morris in 1962, 'is dictated by the middle-aged, born out of the
slough of war and depression, and empty of exuberance. Whose

57

heart has not sunk, to see the elderly, grumpy, sweaty English porter crossly awaiting him at London Airport? Who has not heard the deputy assistant regional manager, with a gleam of his dentures and a hitch of his spectacles, reiterating his unshakeable conviction that it can't be done? Who has not been testily reminded by a frumpish crosspatch in a frilly apron that coffee is only served in the lounge? Who has not felt the deadweight of that worn-out, disillusioned, smug, astigmatic, half-educated generation, weighing lumpishly upon the nation's shoulders?' This was the England against which the Profumos of Chester Terrace were in glamorous rebellion.[14]

In January 1959, Macmillan appointed Profumo as his Minister of State for Foreign Affairs. This promotion was resented by the Tory old guard, who mistrusted the '*Eye-tie*' surname, thought him 'a jumped-up opportunist', and nicknamed him 'the Head Waiter'. One venerable editor judged him an agreeable young man, whose 'advance to ministerial rank had been rapid' for such 'a lightweight'. It is likely that Macmillan, who ranked most men by their attitude to appeasement, favoured Profumo as the youngest and bravest of the thirty-three rebels who had fatally wounded the Chamberlain government in the historic Norway vote of 1940. It is an irony of history that without the fall of Chamberlain, there would have been no Profumo Affair.[15]

As a Foreign Office couple the Profumos began a life of canapés and circuses. They attended official entertainments for foreign ambassadors and envoys at Lancaster House, state dinners and banquets for visiting heads of state at Buckingham Palace, tea with the Queen Mother at Clarence House. Apart from official duties, Valerie Profumo had a busy round of clothes fittings, appointments with hairdressers, and smart lunches. She preferred Italian couture, had an awesome array of stiletto-heeled shoes, and owned a skirt made from python skin. In the reshuffle of July 1960, Macmillan appointed Profumo as Secretary of State for War. The valiant anti-appeaser became one of three service ministers – Peter Carrington (Navy) and Hugh Fraser (RAF) were the others – under the Minister of Defence, Peter Thorneycroft. He proved a vigorous minister, who was a terrier in urging military needs in the interminable contentions over the allocation of expenditure between the three fighting departments.

Valerie Hobson had enjoyed the hectic glamour of Profumo's Foreign Office job. The War Office was equally busy, but less smart, and the incessant official receptions began to become tiresome. Notoriously, the demands of ministerial office, parliamentary attendance and constituency duties made domestic absentees of politicians. 'Goodbye Daddy, we hope you lose,' shouted the three sons of Alan Lennox-Boyd as he left to fight the 1955 election campaign in Mid-Bedfordshire. Some MPs stayed working late at the House. Sir Reginald Manningham-Buller, alone in his Commons room, beavered at legal papers until three in the morning, when other MPs had gone to bed. Profumo, however, may have been among the minority who used late-night sittings to provide alibis for their amorous adventuring. Although quite short in stature and with receding hair, he was an eager flirt who enjoyed the ruses that occurred in the amatory dusk of brief affairs. David Profumo suspects that, while Minister of War, his father had an intrigue with a woman in his own social set, although he was seldom drawn by intelligent, assertive women, preferring 'the painted and, if not exactly the semi-professional, then the obviously fun-loving *amateur*'.[16]

Stanley Baldwin is said to have insisted, in contradistinction to Macmillan's hero Lloyd George, on forming 'a Cabinet of faithful husbands'. He also declared that he wanted his Cabinet to have more old Harrovians than any other administration in history – two aims that were surely incompatible. Other premiers were indifferent to their Cabinet's marital fidelity. There was ready acceptance of extra-matrimonial adventures – so long as the men did not get caught. One way to avoid jeopardising careers was to follow the Duke of Edinburgh's advice: never to have an affair with someone who has less to lose by being found out. Men proved that they were real men by covering for one another. When Eden's health broke after Suez, and he was ordered abroad by Sir Horace Evans, he chose to recuperate at a villa in Jamaica belonging to Ian Fleming. The approach to Fleming was made by Lennox-Boyd who, in order to preserve secrecy, asked if he might borrow the house for a holiday. Fleming concurred, and suggested that their wives should get in touch about the details. 'Oh, you mustn't tell Patsy,' Lennox-Boyd insisted. 'I quite understand, old boy,' replied Fleming, who doubtless never knew that Lennox-Boyd was involved at the time with a male shop assistant at the Army & Navy Stores.[17]

It was divorce that mattered. When Nigel Fisher, MP for Hitchin, was sued for divorce by his wife in 1952, his resignation of the candidature was accepted by his local Conservative Association because Hitchin was a marginal constituency where a candidate who was the 'guilty party' might lose crucial votes. Instead, Fisher was adopted at Surbiton, where the Tories had a safe majority and the anti-divorce vote could be discounted. Eden proved that a divorced man might become Prime Minister; but survivors of the divorce courts were still not nominated as either Aldermen or Lords Mayor of London. Macmillan thought that Eden took 'a risk' in appointing Oliver Poole as chairman of the Conservative Party in 1955 ('like most Conservative leaders nowadays he is a divorcé') although on becoming Prime Minister he replaced Poole with another divorcé, Hailsham. As late as 1957, he felt that Profumo's brother-in-law, Lord Balfour of Inchrye, was precluded from a colonial governorship because he had been divorced.[18]

After six years there was sparring as well as glamour in the Profumo marriage. Valerie Profumo compiled a list of reproaches which suggest how tedious her husband's roaming eye had become. She resented his assumption that all pretty women, or preferably 'girls', were 'fair game' for him. 'You will stretch any manners, at any time, to do this – not quietly and discreetly, but laughing and showing off and behaving like an adolescent,' she complained. 'The way you kiss women you hardly know "goodbye"' was another irritation. So, too, was the tailoring of his trousers ('surely there must be *some* way of concealing your penis'). He seldom stopped scoping the room, she protested, even when they were dancing together.[19]

Despite his flirting at parties and buoyancy at the despatch box, Profumo did not sparkle as a public speaker. The conventionality of his opinions was evident in his respectably prosaic speech at his adoption meeting at the Hippodrome in Stratford before the 1959 general election. Perhaps he judged his constituents aright. The local newspaper allotted more space to reporting that the Marquess of Hertford had served hot-dogs in the grounds of Ragley during a barbecue, at which a hundred accordionists played around a camp fire near the lake, than to reporting the speeches of Lords Mills and Balfour of Inchrye at Profumo's campaign meetings. 'Election? What election?' the *Stratford-upon-Avon Herald* editorialised. 'Hardly a poster seems to raise its head on the hoardings; in villages one or two can be seen, but it seems as if the Indian Summer's soporific spell has bewitched elector and candidate alike, for hardly a voice can be heard raised in anger, let alone politics.' The Conservatives made their headquarters in an Edwardian villa called the Firs. There a band of volunteers worked more quietly than a hive of bees, answering enquiries, addressing envelopes, and despatching posters. The Labour Party's nerve centre in Central Chambers was even quieter, for the candidate and his agent went to solicit votes at factory gates as constituents arrived for work in the early morning, toured villages during the day, and addressed meetings at night. 'Both sides have adopted the "whistle-stop" technique, but their loud-speaker vans seem to have a muted sound, as if they are loth to disturb the householders from "Emergency Ward Ten" or "The Archers". Sundays, by tradition, are rest days (one wonders if they vary much from other days).'[20]

All this typified Profumo's constituency, with its prosperous villages stretching south towards Oxfordshire. Avon Carrow, the Profumo house, lay in the parish of Avon Dassett, near Kineton, midway between the spa town of Leamington and the market town of Banbury. Strong support for Profumo burst from the Banbury hinterland when crisis overwhelmed him in 1963. Banbury was a town which, more than Stratford, reflected the weakening traditions and eroded identity that accompanied provincial England's rising prosperity in the 1950s.

The changes had begun when an aluminium factory started production there in 1933. A corset factory, employing hundreds of women, followed. Soon the cattle, sheep and horse markets, which had been held in the cobbled streets for seven centuries, were resettled across the river under a roof. The marketplace was given a tarmac surface on which cinema-goers could park their cars. A zebra crossing with Belisha beacons was sited by the historic Eleanor Cross, where previously children had played marbles. Long-haul lorries, vans, cars, coaches and motorcycles resembled barbarian warriors as they stormed past the Cross on the north-south road between London and the Midlands conurbation. This road, flanked by stone houses where professional people had once lived in pleasant intimacy, was now a fraught wasteland of de-humanising traffic, where spacious homes were shoddily converted into offices and boarding houses. In the High Street, the Red Lion inn had been demolished for a Woolworths, and the farmers who had done business at its bar had yielded to young mothers with prams. W. H. Smith stood on the site of the Fox, where the fights had once been bloody and blasphemous. A few family concerns survived, but most shops were branches of national chains, and run by managers: Montague Burton the tailor, Dewhurst the butcher, Charles Clore's shoe retailers Freeman, Hardy and Willis were all there.[21]

The aluminium factory at Banbury was, in machinery, techniques, and organisation, unlike anything known in the town before. Previous Banbury industries had been associated with farming products or agricultural tools. Employees were used to small workshops where the 'gaffer' was always visible; but the aluminium managers were, although based locally, often away in Canada, Switzerland, Wales or London. The factory stood 'in green fields beyond the town, surrounded by ten feet of barbed wire, immaculate flower beds, orderly bicycle ranks, and lines of neatly parked cars', reported local sociologist Margaret Stacey. 'The huge white, green-roofed, hangar-like building, with its strange-shaped chimneys and tubes, and its unpredictable noises, seems like something from a different world.' There might be no one visible outside except the guard at the gate, but inside up to 800 men and women toiled. At six in the morning, two in the afternoon, and ten at night, the shift changed, and another 700 to 800 men and women took their places. 'Working life,' wrote Stacey, 'is out of time with home life, with wives' cooking, shopping and sleeping, and with the children's school life, out of time too with the social life of other people.'[22]

The Second World War was a vivid memory in Banbury and Stratford: indeed it created masculine bonds everywhere. 'Possibly it was because neither of us had long been out of the forces, but there was an instant rapport between us,' recalled David Waxman, a physician who met 'Peter' Rachman in 1949. 'In those days, it was still like a brotherhood. You felt akin to anyone who had been in the services.'[23]

The kinship created by war was richly evoked in a film, *The League of Gentlemen*, released in 1960. A group of ex-army officers, shunning the women who have humiliated, scolded, manipulated and bored them, unite in masculine camaraderie and military discipline to rob a million pounds from a City bank. The common fund of memories was drawn on in Granada Television's comedy series *The Army Game*, which gradually became dominated by Bill Fraser playing Sergeant Major Claude Snudge and Alfie Bass playing his stooge, the sly, imbecilic Bootsie. From the autumn of 1960 (running until 1964) Granada screened a spin-off of *The Army Game* called *Bootsie and Snudge*. An average of 17 million people watched its Friday night slot during April and May 1961. Snudge had become the porter of a Pall Mall club with Bootsie as his dogsbody. They carried, wrote a critic, 'the ambivalent, equivocal and sometimes almost flagrantly – though, I suppose, always sublimated – homosexual relationship between these two monsters as far as possible, exploiting all conceivable nuances'.[24]

Wartime affinities were enduring. Attlee and Macmillan were the only Prime Ministers in three centuries to have been seriously wounded in battle. The experience imbued them with compassion and fortitude. Young officers in the trenches, living at close quarters with the men of their platoon, so Macmillan wrote in old age, 'learnt for the first time how to understand, talk with, and feel at home with a whole class of men with whom we could not have come into contact in any other way'. His war record helped him in the Tory leadership, for until the 1960s to have had 'a good war', and especially to have been wounded, rightly commanded respect. Macmillan's limp proved his patriotism. He despised those who (for whatever reason) had avoided active service. 'The trouble with Gaitskell is that he has never seen troops under fire,' he told a dining club of Tory MPs who had been elected in 1959. Three months into Wilson's premiership in 1965 he commented: 'It seems strange that a man who claimed exemption (as a civil servant or the like) at twenty-three and took no part in the six years war, can be PM. We certainly are a forgiving people.'[25]

This was an era when people still saluted as they passed the Cenotaph in Whitehall. 'Rank insubordination' was a phrase that some laughed at, and others recognised had a valuable meaning. A question of precedence arose when Profumo's wartime senior commander Field Marshal Earl Alexander of Tunis dined at Cliveden in 1962. The moment came for the men to leave the dining room to join the ladies. 'By age and distinction,' recorded a fellow guest, 'there was every reason for him to go out first, but he didn't immediately do so, since as an earl his rank was below that of the Marquess of Zetland's. While he hesitated to go, there was a respectful silence, everyone looking towards him with quiet admiration and, by a slight inclination of the head, inviting him to lead the way. A hardly visible expression of pleased assent passed over his face. He went out as it were imperceptibly, as if it just happened that he went out first.' As late as 1978, Lord Denning came within an ace of being disbarred from appointment as Deputy Lieutenant of Hampshire on the grounds that his military service in 1917–19 had been spent in the ranks.[26]

Profumo's son David, who was born in 1955, recalled seeing war-wounded fathers of his school friends – men wearing eyepatches, those who kept an empty sleeve pinned to their jacket, the father whose face was gruesomely disfigured despite all the skill of plastic surgeons. Public men especially needed to show that they had had 'a good war'. Jack Profumo had fought in the battle of Tunis and the invasion of Sicily; as the youngest brigadier in the British Army he had been second-in-command of the British Military Mission in Tokyo. He was still on the military reserve in 1963. The Labour candidate who stood against him at Stratford-on-Avon in 1950–51 had been awarded the Military Cross after the Battle of the Somme in 1916; his Labour opponent in 1955 had served in the Royal Navy; while Joe Stretton, the fifty-year-old Labour candidate for Stratford-on-Avon in the 1959 general election, a Co-op worker and councillor in Rugby, had war service with the Royal Army Ordnance Corps in Italy and Austria.

'Funny how the war was a historical watershed,' mused the Labour MP Wilfred Fienburgh in 1959. 'Every date, every age, had to be translated into terms of how many years before or after the war.' When a man over forty saw a pretty young woman, his calculations were framed by the war: that she was just born when it started, suckling when he paraded for his first rifle drill, toddling and talking when his fighting started, and entering primary school when he was de-mobbed.[27] One wonders if Profumo had comparable thoughts about Christine Keeler, who was a swaddled infant when he was fighting in Italy and not yet at school when he first met his wife.

Profumo's great task as Macmillan's Secretary of State for War was to manage the abolition of National Service, and to return the army to a body of professional volunteers. His political adversary, Colonel George Wigg, jibed that this required him to massage the army's recruitment figures so as to prevent any necessity of reviving conscription. Under the terms of the National Service Act of 1947, all eighteen-year-old men were obliged to serve in the armed forces for eighteen months (raised to two years after the outbreak of the Korean War). More than 2 million youths were called up (6,000 every fortnight): the army took over a million; there were thirty-three soldiers, or twelve airmen, for every sailor. After discharge, conscripts remained on the reserve force for another four years, and liable to recall in the event of an emergency. Although the abolition of National Service was announced in 1957, conscription continued until 1960, and the last conscripts were not released until 1963. Some suspected that the government would be obliged to introduce selective service by ballot, which opponents denounced as tantamount to crimping during the American Civil War. Others regretted the retreat from notions of individual obligations and service to the state.

By 1963 there had never been so many ex-soldiers and ex-sailors in British history. Many people respond well to being drilled: in England, millions of people were respectful of authority, conformist, glad of regular pay and communal amusements. 'Only a fool could resent two years National Service as a waste of time,' wrote the art connoisseur Brian Sewell, who was conscripted in 1952. 'Bullying, brutality, intimidation and fear were among its training tools with raw recruits, victimisation too, but even these had their educative purposes, and were the stimulus of resources of resilience that had not been tapped before.' Many young men, unlike Sewell, seethed at the regimentation and sergeant majors' bullying. With two by-elections pending at Colne Valley and Rotherham in 1963, nearly 700 servicemen tried to escape from the armed services by standing as parliamentary candidates. The government reacted by appointing a panel, chaired by David Karmel QC, to winnow the men. Only twenty-three of the 700 applied to Karmel for interview. A single one was approved: 'Melvyn Ellingham, twenty-four-year-old REME sergeant, yesterday became the first *Army Game* by-election candidate to win his freedom.' He had joined the army aged fifteen, and had two years still to serve as a £14 8s a week electronics technician. 'I'm for the Bomb,' he told the *Daily Express*, but 'against the Common Market. I think a united Europe would only aggravate world tension.'[28]

The psychic air of mid-twentieth-century England was thick with bad memories. Pat Jalland, in her history of English grief in a century of world wars, quotes from the memoir of J. S. Lucas, a private in the Queen's Royal Regiment who, like Profumo, served in the gruelling campaigns in Italy. Before the action at Faenza in 1944, when Lucas was aged twenty-one, he was reunited with his friend Doug, beside whom he had fought in Tunisia. Doug had just asked him for a smoke when a mine exploded. 'My hand was still opening the tin of cigarettes,' wrote Lucas, 'and even as I ran to where he lay, my mind refused to accept the fact of his death. One moment tall, a bit skinny, wickedly satirical, and now – nothing – only a body with a mass of cuts and abrasions and a patch of dirt on his forehead . . . I felt sure that some part of his soul must be hovering about. But he had gone – forever . . . between asking for a fag and getting one.' That night at Faenza, in freezing cold, after heavy losses from shelling, the remnants of Lucas's company took shelter, but he was too hungry and agitated for sleep. 'Before my eyes there passed, in review, a procession of the mates I had lost – faces of chums who had gone in Africa, below Rome and in the battles above Rome. But most clearly I saw those who had died that day. Doug reeling backwards as the concrete mines exploded and Corporal Rich's gentle eyes as he turned away with a goodbye "*ciao*". The whole assembly of these dead comrades stood in a sombre semi-circle around me as if they were waiting and watching until the time should come when I joined their ghostly company.' Next day Lucas was sent to the base psychiatric hospital at Assisi. There the medical officer strove to convince him that, although his grief and battle exhaustion were justified, his shame was not.[29]

A Midlands teenager remembered visiting Portsmouth during the 1950s, and being told that 'Before the War' this bombsite had been a chemist's, or that hole had been a draper's . . . 'Before the War – Before the War' was the sad, weird incantation of the times. All the youth could see were 'stumps of shops, office blocks, houses, streets, piers, just stumps'. The sole undamaged residue of 'Before the War' was swaying wires above the streets, between the rubble and stumps, for trolley-bus power lines survive bombardment and blast. He also visited his mother's family in Cambridgeshire. 'There was the uncle who was half-blown to bits in the First World War, shouting and grunting meaningless sounds as he loaded hay on a truck, and then limping across and shaking my hand and screaming and laughing, and I was very frightened and people said it was a shame, and that he was very intelligent, and couldn't help it, and how it wasn't his fault.'[30]

There were widows and spinsters so lonely that they could fill their teapots with tears. In 1958 the novelist John Braine described eating poached eggs on toast in a London tea shop. The middle-aged woman next to him, 'pale and drab in a skimpy cotton dress clinging to her scraggy body', wore no wedding ring. When she was young, he thought, 'some British general, breathing heavily, would have at last worked out the meaning of attrition and would have issued the order which deposited her future husband screaming on the barbed wire or drowning in the mud, and which left her, forty years later, eating a roll and butter and drinking a glass of orangeade, with dreadful slowness, alone in a London tea shop'. Later he glimpsed the woman again. 'She was walking very slowly, her face a mask of misery, peering from side to side as if looking for help.'[31]

One night in 1963 another novelist, Frederic Raphael, struck up a conversation with two men on the late train from London to Colchester. The more loquacious, at first, was a reporter. He had been a warrant officer in the war, was captured by the Germans, and escaped three times. During one burst from captivity, he said, 'he had killed an Austrian forest ranger whose boots he wanted. After killing him, he discovered the boots were the wrong size.' The second traveller, returning from a dinner at the Society of Chartered Accountants, said little for a time, except to praise the *scampi bonne femme*. 'Finally he broke out: "Have you ever seen a man's face when he knows he's going to die? I have. And if you've seen it once, you don't want to see it again".' He had been a RAF navigator in an aircraft which had a forced landing on an airfield in an area north of Rome held by the Germans. The RAF men knocked out one German who attempted to detain them, and shot the other dead with his own rifle. 'I'll never forget the look on his face; not pretty. When he knew we were going to kill him. You can't describe it. It's just a thing you never forget. Thank God I wasn't the one who had to pull the trigger. I'll never forget the shot. Loudest thing I ever heard in my life.' The German, he added, 'had been a decent chap and shared cigarettes with the man who killed him.' The reporter found Christmas unbearable. The frivolling children made him think of the bombs he had dropped which had incinerated children. Still, he opposed nuclear disarmament, and would drop the H-bomb himself if ordered to. 'Oh yes,' said the accountant, 'so would I.'[32]

These were the ruminative confidences and formative memories that family men shared when unbending on a late night train in 1963. Jack Profumo's England cannot be understood without them.

THREE

Lord

The Astors began at Cliveden with a row. William Waldorf Astor, the New York plutocrat, smarting from the way that he had been traduced by American newspapers during his failed candidatures for the state assembly, settled in England in 1890. Three years later he bought Cliveden, an Italianate pleasure palace perched on a high spacious site above a bend of the Thames, with a magnificent terrace commanding a prospect downstream towards Maidenhead, rather than a short view of the opposite bank.

Immediately he was mired in ill-will. He quarrelled with Cliveden's previous owner, the Duke of Westminster, over so paltry an object as the visitors' book. The Duke denounced the Yankee to the Prince of Wales. Astor gave a sturdy defence to the Prince's Private Secretary, for he was intent on buying his way into the Marlborough House set. In 1895, for example, when he joined the prince's house party at Sandringham, he made a show of paying £1,000 for a pair of bay carriage horses from the royal stud. In appreciation of Astor's outlay, the Prince of Wales, with the Duke of Buccleuch in tow, attended a house party at Cliveden.[1]

Astor's prickliness ensured his unpopularity. Staying with Lord Burton at Rangemore in 1897, the Marquess of Lincolnshire noted of his fellow guest: 'Astor is another instance of the utter inability of American men to get on in England. Here is a man with millions – probably the richest man in the country; and yet he is given to understand that, though he is tolerated on account of his wealth, he is of society and yet not in it.' Astor had represented

70

Ferdinand de Rothschild when Empress Elizabeth of Austria visited London, but her suite 'refused to call him "Thou", though he implored them to do so. Astor assumes a . . . scornful deference to Ladies to whom he is speaking. He evidently resents the way he is treated; but tries not to show it.' Two years later, Lincolnshire met Astor at Lord Lonsdale's racing stud in Rutland. 'He is a social failure. Pompous & proud, with an aggressive air of mock humility . . . The boy (who is Captain of the Boats at Eton) is at present voted a Prig.'[2]

Astor bought a London evening newspaper, the *Pall Mall Gazette*, in order to enhance his social influence, and appointed as its editor a Society swell, Harry Cust. Astor's aunt Caroline, a snob who had imposed the notion of the exclusive 'Four Hundred' on New York City, had inaugurated the custom among New York millionaires of publicising their parties and controlling reputations by issuing tit-bits of news about their guests to the social columns. Astor tried to foist this foolery on London. He gave Cust a list of names, headed by the Duke of Westminster, of people who were never to be mentioned in the *Pall Mall Gazette*, in the mistaken belief that the English nobility cared about being mentioned in newspaper Society paragraphs. At first this was mocked, but in 1900 it brought his social nemesis.

Sir Berkeley Milne, a naval officer in command of the royal yacht (whom the Prince of Wales dubbed Arky-Barky), was taken to a musical evening at Carlton House Terrace by an invited guest who assured him that he would be welcome there. Astor ordered the interloper from his house and inserted a paragraph in the *Pall Mall Gazette* announcing that 'Sir A. B. Milne RN was not invited to Mr Astor's concert.' This upset the *haute monde* more than the Boxer rebellion in China, as Lincolnshire noted at a house party for the Prince of Wales and his mistress Alice Keppel: 'HRH quite open-mouthed with fury: and vows he will never speak to him again.' In retaliation for this royal ostracism, Astor called Mrs Keppel 'a public strumpet', and told people that King Edward VII (as the Prince became after his mother's death in

1901) had been impotent for twenty years. He believed that the government wished to nominate him for a peerage in 1902, but that this was forbidden by the King, 'who hated me'. Thereafter, he said, he never relented in seeking 'to attain what Edward's spite had withheld'.[3]

Cliveden was never a conventional English country house. It was not the centre of a great estate which gave the owner political influence and social prestige in the county. When in 1890 Lord Cadogan, who owned much of Chelsea but no landed estates, spent £175,000 to buy Culford in Suffolk, he acquired a house with 400 acres of parkland and 11,000 acres, and got his eldest son elected as MP for a nearby constituency two years later; and in 1893 the newly created Lord Iveagh, the brewery millionaire, spent £159,000 to buy the 17,000 acre Elveden estate, which made him a power in the district. Although Astor paid a vast sum for Cliveden, he got only 450 acres, comprising woods and riverside pleasure gardens. Cliveden proved a showhouse rather than a powerhouse.

In 1906 Astor gave Cliveden to his elder son, Waldorf, who that year married an American divorcée, Nancy Shaw. The young man, whom Lincolnshire had dismissed as a prig, left Oxford with a social conscience that was rare in an American millionaire. He deplored his father as a selfish reactionary, and wished to make amends by a life of public service. This paragon entered Parliament as MP for Plymouth in 1910, before becoming effectual proprietor of the *Observer*, a Sunday newspaper which his father bought in 1911. He was diagnosed with a weak heart, which made him medically unfit for trench warfare, and spent the early war years monitoring wasteful army organisation. This was an indelible stain on his reputation so far as some Tories and combatants were concerned. His hopes of appointment as the country's first postwar Minister of Health were accordingly frustrated, and his advocacy of public health reforms got him called a 'doctrinaire Socialist' by reactionaries. Nevertheless, by his late thirties, Waldorf Astor was entrenched among the nation's great and good. He was a patient chairman of committees, without a dash of flamboyance, whose attitude to his good causes could be described as reticent enthusiasm (rather as his attitude to his children might be called frigidly tender).[4]

Old man Astor, in the midst of the Kaiser's war, by judicious distribution of £200,000 to King George V's favourite war charities and the fighting funds of both the Conservative and Liberal parties, obtained first a barony and then a viscountcy. When he died in 1919, Waldorf Astor went reluctantly to the House of Lords. His wife was elected for the vacant Plymouth constituency, and became the first woman MP to take her seat in the Commons.

Nancy Astor, when young, was generous, bold and funny, with quick-witted shrewdness and inexhaustible energy; but after turning fifty her sudden amusing parries turned to rash outbursts, and she became a domineering, obstinate and often hurtful spitfire. Her religion put claws on her. She converted to Christian Science in 1914, coaxed her husband into becoming a disciple of Mrs Baker Eddy, and nagged her children along the same lines. Her first marriage had ended because her husband was a dipsomaniac who became sexually importunate when drunk. She and Waldorf were both prudish teetotallers, and her temperance campaigning became notorious for its scolding tone. Before 1914 she kept two infatuated young men, Billy Grenfell and Eddie Winterton, enthralled as her *amis de marie*, though she was the sort of flirt who required only to be the centre of admiring attention: Billy and Eddie were never permitted any pounces.[5]

Nancy Astor had six children: Bobbie Shaw by her first marriage, and four sons and a daughter by her second. The eldest child of her second marriage, William Waldorf Astor (known to his friends as Bill and to his parents as Billie), was born in 1907, and became the last Astor to live at Cliveden. From his mother he received the least affection of all her children, although he strove to win her approval and pretended to believe her Christian Science indoctrination long after he had privately rejected it. She belittled, chastised, and rejected him; and resented the fact that her favourite son, Bobbie, would inherit neither the Astor money nor title. Even in old age she spread discord: as a man in his fifties, Bill would still tense when she bustled into a room; people saw him blanch before her jibes began; and his widow believed that the aortic aneurism that killed him at the age of fifty-eight was partly attributable to the anxiety that his mother had generated. Certainly, her angry obsessions wearied her husband: Waldorf described her in 1951, a year before he died, as ranting against 'Socialism, Roman Catholicism, Psychiatry, the Jews, the Latins and the *Observer*'.[6]

The Astor children suffered from their family's reputation for ostentatious wealth. Bill was held by his ankles out of a school window to see if gold would fall from his pockets. He was victimised by his classics tutor at Eton, Charles Rowlatt – 'rather a nasty bounder at the best of times', he told his mother, 'so I hope you'll ... have his blood'. Rowlatt was an austere bachelor who commanded the Eton Officer Training Corps and heaped Bill's next brother David with work and punishments: 'What annoys me is the way when he loses his temper with me (a daily affair) he always ends up by saying something about all the family talking much too much,' David complained; 'I call it awful cheek but I daren't tell him so.' Nancy Astor was indeed of confounding volubility, and during the 1920s still retained her sense of the ridiculous, though this vanished with the complacent egotism and rudeness of her old age. In Rowlatt's day she amused her children by mimicking the county ladies (and perhaps Eton ushers) deploring 'those vulgar Americans' at Cliveden.[7]

As an undergraduate at New College, Oxford, Bill Astor began to blossom, although Cliveden's proximity to the university made it hard to break his shackles to his parents' home. His outlook as an undergraduate was glossed by his acceptance of conventional proprieties: 'I do like a disciplined life, belonging to a properly organised & ordered society either at the bottom, the middle or the top,' he wrote shortly after the General Strike. Polo, hunting and racing were his chief avocations. He described a flat race in fancy dress at Oxford in 1928. 'We had an oyster and fish and chips lunch and then fared out. I arrayed myself tastefully in a white turban, in which I placed two poppies; a blue sweater, high neck, a red and blue sash and pyjama trousers of broad pink and white stripes. I had a hireling of Mac's, called Nippy, who really went very well. There were all sorts of costumes, Proctors, Scouts, clerics, beards, and so on. It was as muddy as a ditch.'[8]

Bill Astor was thoroughly anglicised for a child of American parents, although he was never convincing as a traditional Englishman. 'There are a lot of Middle West people on board,' he wrote to his mother from the liner *Olympic* as it approached New York. 'The language of course is a difficulty as I understand not everything they say & they hardly understand a thing I say, otherwise we get on splendidly.' He was trained for the responsibilities of public life, and instilled with an international outlook. When in 1929 he was sent to Hanover to live in a family and learn German, provincialism made him shudder. The audience at the local opera house were, he reported, '*repulsive*: in the intervals they go up to a large hall & walk round & round it, very slowly & solemnly: all in ugly ill-fitting dresses & suits'. He recoiled from 'the dirt and perversion and vulgarity that abounds in Berlin', as he reassured his parents. 'The Germans deliberately go out to bring nasty things into their plays. Not funny, just horrible.'[9]

He was also instilled with his father's sense of duty. Both men were meliorists who wished to be competent and kind; but whereas the older man, at a pinch, gave precedence to competence, Bill's preference was for kindness. In 1932 his father secured his appointment as personal secretary to the Earl of Lytton, chairman of the League of Nations' investigation into Japanese aggression in Manchuria. This visit to China (during which he had an affair with a young Russian woman who was a refugee from the Soviet system) triggered his lifelong compassion for war refugees, displaced persons and civilian casualties. Subsequently he attended the League of Nations' discussions in Geneva on the Japanese seizure of Manchuria, deputising for Lytton who was ill. He was adopted as the Conservative parliamentary candidate for East Fulham (no doubt helped by the assurance that Astor money would pay his election expenses and subsidise constituency party funds) and in 1935 joined his mother in the Commons. He subsequently took a tall house in Mayfair at 45 Upper Grosvenor Street. Only a year later he became, through family influence, Parliamentary Private Secretary to Sir Samuel Hoare, who was successively First Lord of the Admiralty and Home Secretary. Bill Astor, who was conscientious and keen to please, visited Czechoslovakia in 1938, and returned with undiminished support for Chamberlain's policy of appeasement.

The phrase 'the Cliveden set' first appeared in a socialist Sunday newspaper of November 1937 in a story about pro-German machinations. The phrase was promoted by the Marxist Claud Cockburn in his newssheet The Week, and popularised by left-wing journalists, who made play with the Astors' (remote) German ancestry. Cliveden, in this smear campaign, became the head-quarters of a conspiracy of manufacturers, bankers, editors, land-lords and diplomatic meddlers, all intent on appeasing Hitler. The Astors at Cliveden, who had been shunned by the Prince of Wales's set at the turn of the century, were to be reviled at the time of the Profumo Affair. But these cycles of denigration were nuga-tory beside the abuse in the late 1930s, when communists and their sympathisers concocted their shabby half-truths about the Cliveden set. Harold Nicolson's trenchant assessment of the Cliveden set was fairer than the communist propaganda. 'The harm which these silly selfish hostesses do is really immense,' he noted in April 1939 of Nancy Astor and a Mayfair counterpart. 'They convey to foreign envoys that policy is decided in their own drawing rooms . . . They wine and dine our younger politicians, and they create an atmosphere of authority and responsibility and grandeur, whereas the whole thing is a mere flatulence of the spirit'.[10]

In 1942, while Bill Astor was serving in the Middle East, his father took two decisions which snubbed him. Lord Astor's friend, Lord Lothian, had instigated in 1938 a change in the law which enabled the National Trust to accept ownership of country houses as well as landscape (he bequeathed his own house, Blickling, to the Trust in 1940), and thus inaugurated a new phase in that charity's protection of rural England. Two years later Lord Astor gave the house at Cliveden, together with 250 acres of gardens and woods, to the National Trust as a way of mitigating death duties. The same year he dismissed the intransigent, elderly editor of the *Observer*, installed a temporary replacement, gave forty-nine per cent of the shares to his second son, David, and indicated that David (then aged thirty) would become postwar editor. Bill, brought up as the heir to Cliveden and expecting to inherit the *Observer*, reeled under this double rebuff.

Bill Astor was thought a superlatively lucky man by those who did not know him well. He lost his Fulham seat in the general election of 1945, failed by a few hundred votes to win High Wycombe in 1950, but was returned to the Commons at the next election in 1951, despite being one of the few Conservative candidates who made clear that (based on his prewar experience as Parliamentary Private Secretary to the Home Secretary) he supported the abolition of capital punishment and opposed birching. His views were influenced by reading Arthur Koestler's death-cell book, *Darkness at Noon*. Unlike many in his party, he believed that 'the de-brutalisation of punishment' resulted in a falling crime rate. His father's death in 1952 sent him to the Lords, and put an end to his ambitions for political office. In the Lords he advocated 'civilised' values: 'arguments based on the emotions of revenge, of righteous indignation and of fear' made bad law, he told peers when speaking against the death penalty in 1956. Homosexuality should not be criminalised, he argued, because 'those of us who are lucky enough to be normal should have nothing but pity for people in that situation'.[11]

With women Bill was fidgety and luckless. In the 1930s he was in love with a married American woman five years his senior who had no wish to wed him. While serving in the war-torn Middle East he had a romance that petered out. Returning to England, he married in June 1945 only a month after the end of fighting in Europe – hastily, as many (including his brother David) did at that time. His bride, Sarah Norton, was recovering from the recent death of a much-loved mother and from a broken engagement to Dorothy Macmillan's nephew, Billy Hartington, who had married someone else and been killed in action in quick succession. (Sarah Norton's father, Lord Grantley, was a monocled clubman who worked in the film business with Valerie Hobson's first husband; Sarah Norton's mother had been Lord Beaverbrook's favourite mistress.)

The newly married Astors suffered the heartbreak of three miscarriages before the birth in 1951 of their only child, William. Sarah Astor subsequently endured serious post-natal depression (a condition not then recognised or understood by physicians). In the thrall of this, during 1952, she left her husband for an Oxford undergraduate who was seven years her junior. There were long, miserable consultations with lawyers and bystanders. One mutual friend spent eight hours with her, urging reconciliation, and then had another long talk with Bill. 'He gave it to her straight from the shoulder, giving home truths about the disastrous effect on a child of a broken home, of the cruelty of her action on me, of the deteriorating effect of this on her own character & her letting the side down generally,' Bill reported that autumn. 'My intention is to sit & do *nothing*; do nothing to create ill-will or make it harder for her to return . . . What hell this all is. But William is *wonderful*, healthy, happy, gregarious, noisy.'[12] The Astors were divorced in 1953, but remained good friends and ensured that their son had an untroubled childhood.

Soon after his first marriage, wishing to provide his wife with her own country house and to plant himself in the Bicester hunting country, Bill Astor had bought Bletchingdon Park, a Palladian house in Oxfordshire, from a penurious bachelor (Lord Valentia) whose heirs were distant and obscure. Bletchingdon was still Bill's legal residence at the time of his divorce in 1953, but was sold immediately after the judicial decree was secured, when he returned to Cliveden. It had lain in desuetude for several years, and he hoped to revive the great days when his mother had drawn smart Society, political lions and literary panthers to the house. While serving in the Middle East he had been nostalgic for the Cliveden parties that were held during Ascot Week: 'tennis and riding in the morning: and all the girls in their best dresses and men in grey top hats fixing on buttonholes and sprays of flowers in the hall at twelve and the cars all lined up and the Royal Procession and Father's colours on the course and polo in the evening and swimming and all the rhododendrons out and for once my parents forgetting politics and giving themselves over to social joy! I hope so much I won't find a new order when I get back: I enjoyed the old order so much.'[13]

The 1950s were an envious decade. Envy was most intense among those who had lately risen in the world, as Geoffrey Gorer noted in 1951. 'Some of the formerly prosperous classes, especially the women, are quite venomous about the advantages the working classes enjoy today, compared with before the war. But they are not as venomous as the working-class and middle-class men who are making good money and getting higher positions. Many of these people are filled with hatred for those they call "the idle rich".' Bill Astor encountered such resentment when he was parliamentary candidate at High Wycombe. If his wife attended a meeting in a fur coat, people seethed: 'Look at her, flaunting her riches!' If she left it at Bletchingdon, they hissed: 'She's dressing down to us! We all know she's got a mink at home!'[14]

Bill Astor's Cliveden regime did not conciliate haters of the idle rich. His belief (broadcast on BBC Radio in 1956) that the management of French stud farms was superior to their English rivals made him further enemies. Yet 'Bill was quite snobbish in an English way', recalled his friend Pamela Cooper. Her son Grey Gowrie thought Bill 'lacked self-belief', despite some remarkable qualities. 'He worried too much about what people thought of him. He was conventional to the degree of not escaping the conventions of upper-class society, but they certainly didn't fit him like a glove.' Some of his guests were the smart end of rag, tag and bobtail. A luncheon guest at Cliveden noted: 'Lord Astor had some anonymous lords and ladies (their personalities and names did not impinge on one).'[15]

This same guest, the writer and connoisseur Maurice Collis, in 1955 watched Astor driving in his Bentley 'accompanied by one of those well-born but colourless chits of girls who are often to be met with at Cliveden'.[16] The girl was twenty-four-year-old Philippa Hunloke, the stage-manager daughter of Dorothy Macmillan's sister Lady Anne Holland-Martin and Harold Macmillan's goddaughter. A fortnight later she married Bill. The couple had a discontented honeymoon in the South of France and at the Astor stud in Ireland, from which they returned estranged, but with the bride pregnant. There was an intimidating collection of guests at the new Lady Astor's first big Cliveden dinner: King Gustav of Sweden, the Dowager Duchess of Rutland, Nancy Astor, the octogenarian pro-consul Lord Hailey, the former head of the Foreign Office Sir Alexander Cadogan, Maurice Collis, an air marshal called Lord Bandon, Isaiah Berlin, and an old courtier called Lady Worsley, all exuding stale, elderly aplomb. Philippa Astor faced her duties as chatelaine of Cliveden with flurried dread.

Moreover, Nancy Astor was captious and undermining to the women in her family circle. She resented her daughters-in-law for supplanting her in her sons' lives, went careening through the family, and grew more destructive with age. Her four Astor sons married a total of eleven times: there is no doubt that her brutal, intrusive rudeness upset her sons' domesticity. Bill's wives, installed in his mother's place at Cliveden, suffered worst of all. 'The most detestable woman in England; boring, rude and guilty of interference in British politics which has brought nothing but disaster,' Isaiah Berlin judged of Nancy in 1954; but said that Bill, who often entertained him at Cliveden, was 'one of the kindest, most public-spirited, human beings'. By the autumn of 1956, Bill Astor's second marriage was so stressful, and soaring his blood pressure to dangerous levels, that he left for New York, and asked Philippa Astor to leave Cliveden before his return (their divorce, however, was not finalised until 1960).[17]

This marital breakdown coincided with the Suez crisis. Bill and his brothers David and Jakie (a Tory backbencher) put themselves at loggerheads with their adopted class by opposing Eden's bungling. They showed themselves as Anglo-Americans, supporters of the Atlantic Alliance, who saw the dangers posed to the English-speaking hegemony by Anglo-French collusion in the Israeli attack without consulting the US government. Bill raised the die-hards' ire by criticising the Suez adventure in the Lords debate on 1 November 1956. The debate had given the impression, he said, 'that it is Colonel Nasser who has mounted a massive invasion into the territory of Israel and whom we are condemning as the aggressor and the invader, rather than the other way around'. It was unclear, he continued, whether Eden's government aimed to displace Nasser from power in Egypt or safeguard shipping through the canal – which, despite dire predictions, had never been disrupted since nationalisation.

Astor did not dare to challenge the official lie that was being asserted, but was brave enough to skewer its inefficacy. 'We may accept – I am sure we all do – what the Government have said, that there is no question of collusion between Israel and ourselves. The trouble is going to be that the Arab states will not believe that.' The Suez crisis had calamitously diverted attention from Eastern Europe, where the communist hegemony was crumbling in Hungary, and 'had the extraordinary effect of bringing America and Russia together against Great Britain'. He reproached, too, the United States for appointing an 'anti-British' ambassador to Cairo, and American managers of oil companies in the Middle East for their gullibility. His intervention offended many people, who cut him in London. A year later he alluded to the unpopularity of Conservative peers with independent views on controversial subjects such as Suez and the death penalty.[18]

On 4 November, David Astor's *Observer* ran its famous Suez editorial: 'We had not realised that our Government was capable of such folly and crookedness . . . Never since 1783 has Great Britain made herself as universally disliked', together with articles demonstrating the political and military fallacies underlying Eden's strategy, and letters from bishops and clerics denouncing the attack on Egypt. Three *Observer* trustees resigned, readers cancelled subscriptions and manufacturers their advertisements. On 5 November, when the Anglo-French force landed at Port Said, and it was reported in the Commons that Egyptian forces were discussing surrender, there was elated uproar among Tory MPs. Jakie Astor alone remained seated: Lennox-Boyd shouted at him, bullyingly, to stand up. On 8 November, Jakie spoke in the Commons against the Suez expedition – one of only eight Tory MPs to do so. A week later David Astor wrote to Iain Macleod urging him to lead younger Tories in repudiation of Eden's leadership. Macleod did not reply to the letter, which he took to Downing Street to show the Cabinet Secretary and Eden's Private Secretary, Freddie Bishop. 'That Astor is using such tactics makes us feel quite sick,' Bishop told Eden.[19]

Although politicians and foreign potentates came to Cliveden, the atmosphere was lighter than in its prewar heyday. Bill Astor kept an open house. Harold Macmillan later quipped that Cliveden was like a hotel, and a regular visitor recalled other guests sitting around 'gossiping in the great hall, as if they were staying in a hotel'.[20] There were no cabals, schemes to reform human nature, unofficial diplomatic initiatives, or grave pronouncements on duty. Instead, Bill Astor strove valiantly to perpetuate the social sheen and resplendent hospitality of the old order. His princely generosity was such that when guests came to Cliveden, their cars would be driven to the garage block, cleaned, polished and filled with petrol for the return journey to

London. Cliveden was so much a millionaire's model estate that if Astor's wife was to be driven across country, one of the two chauffeurs would make a trial run to find the time needed to make the journey at a steady rate: there was no question that any Lady Astor could drive herself.

Bill Astor disliked sitting still. He was always on the move, and seemed to feel lonely without a bevy of people around him. At their best, his guests were diverse, eminent and interesting. The signatures in the visitors' book of Field Marshal Alexander, Alan Lennox-Boyd, John Boyd-Carpenter, Lord Home, Isaiah Berlin, Hugh Trevor-Roper, C. P. Snow, Freya Stark, Mervyn Stockwood, Bill Deakin, and Peter Fleming indicate the diversity and quality of the talk. Astor liked to introduce people to one another, although at the dinner to which he invited the painter Stanley Spencer and cartoonist Osbert Lancaster, the two men eyed one another like dogs, and vied to dominate the conversation. The racing Earl of Derby (who allowed Astor's mares to be serviced by his stallions, and encouraged him to invest in commercial television shares) was bewildered when, after the ladies had withdrawn, he was saddled with Spencer wearing pyjamas under borrowed evening clothes. Astor's munificence also drew parasites and opportunists with smooth manners and envious spirits: those who accepted his food and drink, played his games, had their petrol tanks filled by his chauffeurs, dropped his name, but did not respect him. There were risks in his indiscriminate open-handedness.

After the end of his Commons career and failure of his first marriage, Bill Astor took up charitable work. At a time when the British government imposed onerous, effronting limits on the amounts of sterling that could be taken abroad by travellers, he gave $2 million from his New York funds to support British scholars wishing to study in the United States. The intense suffering that he had seen in Manchuria under Japanese occupation in the 1930s, and in the war-torn Middle East during the 1940s, shaped his benefactions. He supported the Save the

Children Fund, which had been started in 1919 by two English sisters to provide emergency relief for children suffering from malnutrition or other deprivation in the aftermath of the Great War, and was soon responding to famines, earthquakes and floods. Another pet cause was the Ockenden Venture, started in 1951 by three Englishwomen who gave education and vocational training to Latvian and Polish girls from displaced persons camps, and subsequently provided reception centres and resettlement help for refugees. Of the first six girls who joined the Ockenden Venture, one took honours at Nottingham University, two went to Oxford University, one won a scholarship at the Sadler's Wells Ballet School, and another qualified at a technical school.

Astor detested communism and in 1951 proposed launching a global coalition of Protestant Churches to fight atheism, which he felt was softening Western resistance to Soviet penetration.[21] He visited Hong Kong to study the plight of fugitives from Mao's China. It astonished him that English progressives, despite professing their commitment to freedom and humanity, had sided since the 1920s on one issue after another with mass murderers and slave masters as atrocious as any the world had known. Despite all the exposures of communism's brutal inefficiency, written by its victims and repentant dupes, regardless of the thousands who tried every month to escape across communist frontiers, such progressives insisted that this system of servitude represented progress. These delusions were harder than ever to maintain after the Hungarian uprising of November 1956.

With his usual easy munificence, Astor had given a rent-free lease of Parr's Cottage on the Cliveden estate to Zara, Countess of Gowrie, the widow of a former Governor-General of Australia. Lady Gowrie's only son had been killed leading a Commando raid in Tripoli in 1943, and his widow Pamela had subsequently married an army officer named Derek Cooper. In 1956, Astor offered Spring Cottage to the Coopers, but they demurred and the property was taken by Stephen Ward. The Coopers reacted immediately to the agonies of the Hungarian oppressed. They motored to Andau, an Austrian border village, where they helped rescue refugees and shelter them in improvised accommodation. In spare moments they sent descriptive letters to their neighbour Lady Gowrie, which she showed Bill Astor. His niece Jane Willoughby (only daughter of his sister Wissie Ancaster), who had been one of the earliest to start rescue work on the Austro-Hungarian frontier, visited him soliciting a donation. Jane Willoughby's tales, and the fact that he was facing Christmas alone after his wife's departure, spurred him to action.

In December 1956, Astor and his ex-Commando chauffeur drove to Austria in a Land Rover. He installed himself in the comforts of the Hotel Sacher in Vienna, but motored each night into Andau. The refugees, he found, drugged their babies with barbiturates to stop them from betraying their presence to border-guards by crying, trudged across frozen riparian plains covered by rifle fire, tanks and land-mines, crouched at night beside a canal bank until Western volunteers found them and paddled them to safety in a rubber dinghy. Bill Astor's Andau weeks changed the direction of his life: his brother David thought they saved him at the nadir of his confidence, and proved a lifeline, until calamity overwhelmed him with the Profumo Affair.

Subsequently, Astor flew to New York, where he appeared on television talkshows and collected over $100,000 for the refugees. As part of his fund-raising efforts, he compiled a brief Hungarian memoir which he circulated to potential donors:

There were two dramatic moments that stick in my mind. One was on Christmas Eve, a mother and baby arriving quite alone when I was single-handed. The baby doped, with a frost-bitten foot, but it was saved. The other was when a big party of refugees had reached the edge of the canal, and we had got about a dozen of the women and children over. Suddenly a Tommy gun was fired into the air and a security patrol appeared on the other side of the canal, firing shots and Verey flares into the air, and driving the rest of the refugees back. They knelt and wept and prayed, but were driven off at gunpoint when they were only fifty yards from freedom, the security guards firing a few shots at us for good measure. We were left with children separated from their parents, women separated from their husbands, in a state of complete collapse and agony.[22]

There were reminders at Andau of the base stupidity of British journalists. One of the frontier volunteers was John Paterson-Morgan, Lord Cadogan's agent in London and Scotland. 'It was some time before the national newspapers cottoned on to the fact that we were "news", he recalled. Then, one night, a gang of reporters from Fleet Street 'barged' into the emergency surgery where they overwhelmed hard-pressed doctors. Without thought for the refugees and their children, frozen and weary after their ordeal, the reporters chivvied them into standing up and singing the Hungarian national anthem for a crass photo opportunity.[23]

Millions of people in the world had fled from war, oppression or danger, including Chinese, Arabs, Indians, and Pakistanis. Fifteen years after the Second World War there were over 100,000 refugees in Europe, some still living in unofficial camps (at places like Laschenskyhof, near Salzburg) including children who had been born there. To alleviate this suffering, a young Conservative called Timothy Raison suggested a worldwide fundraising effort. World Refugee Year ran from June 1959 to May 1960 with Bill Astor as one of its organisers. In an eloquent speech in the House of Lords he attacked the phrase 'a genuine refugee', which he likened to the nauseating Victorian phrase 'the deserving poor'. It was cruel and stupid, he said, to distinguish between political refugees, in fear of their lives or torture, and economic refugees trying to escape privation. Given the levels of Commonwealth immigration, especially from the Caribbean, it was mean-spirited to exclude East European refugees from communist oppression who, he felt, were more easily assimilated: 'We know perfectly well that with Europeans the Mr Shapiro of one generation becomes the Mr Shepherd of another, and is soon indistinguishable from people in this country.' The previous year's government grant to refugees had been £200,000 out of a budget of £5,254 million, including £44 million on roads: 'If we forwent fifty miles of trunk roads for a year, we could probably solve the European refugee problem.' For every refugee in a camp there were three or four living in garrets, attics, cellars, shanties, or even old buses: he wanted to provide them with houses, furniture, vocational training, and tools of trade.[24]

Astor became chairman of the executive committee of the Standing Conference of British Organisations for Aid to Refugees during this busy time. He made countless speeches and signed thousands of letters. Publicity films were made; promotional books and pamphlets issued; a charity film première, fundraising concerts and a Mansion House dinner were held. He liaised with the Royal Household to win support from the the Royal Family. A pledge of £100,000 was extracted from the government. Harold Macmillan, who spoke at the final rally in the Royal Albert Hall, felt that the campaign 'touched the imagination of the country'.[25] In Britain, over £9 million was raised out of a global total exceeding £35 million. There were few precedents to such fundraising fifty years ago.

Astor's greatest moment of public self-revelation came in a tribute, which was published in *The Times*, to his friend Prince Aly Khan, who had been killed in a car smash while returning from Longchamps races in 1960. It was a cryptic self-portrait, which showed Astor's sense of the discrepancies between public perceptions of heavily publicised individuals and their private characters. 'If only one knew Aly Khan by repute it was easy to preconceive a dislike towards him. When one met him, it was impossible not to be stimulated and attracted by his charm, his perfect manners, his vitality, his gaiety and sense of fun. But if you were fortunate enough to know him really well, and have him as a friend, you acquired a friendship which was incomparable – generous, imaginative, enduring and almost passionately warm.'

Like Astor, Aly Khan had suffered a privileged but lonely child-hood. Just as Astor had been relegated in the inheritance of Cliveden and the *Observer*, Aly Khan had been elided from the succession of the leadership of the Ismaili Muslim community, which his father conferred on Aly Khan's son, Karim. Astor admired Aly Khan as 'the most sportsmanlike of losers', who loyally accepted this adversity. This blow was softened by the Pakistan government naming Aly Khan as its ambassador to the United Nations. This appointment 'produced the most useful, rewarding and happiest days of his life', Astor judged, thinking, too, of his own efforts for refugees. 'Both his staff and the press viewed his arrival at the UN with some doubt. He was a complete success, showing unexpected caution, seriousness and conscientiousness, as well as his usual intelligence and charm.'

Recalling perhaps his loneliness when his marriages failed, Astor affirmed that 'when a friend was going through a bad patch . . . Aly was at his best. He would telephone you from the other side of the world; his houses were at your disposal for as long as you wanted, his sympathy, intuition and imaginative kindness were rocks you could rely on. He was curiously defensive towards the world, and intensely sensitive to real or imagined slights, but if he was sure of your friendship he returned it a hundredfold.' Astor's last sight of his friend 'was an untidy gay figure bustling through London Airport, leaving a trail of laughter by a cheery and courteous word to each person he came into contact with, and each of whom he treated as a human being he was glad to see'. This was how Astor, in 1960, hoped to be remembered.[26]

Bill Astor was one-third playboy, one-third idealist and one-third magnate. Reacting against his finicky upbringing, he was not discriminating in his friendships. He needed to be liked: he was the sort of man who would pay for a friend's honeymoon. 'I always think of Bill as more vulnerable and childish than over-sexed, a man of pillow fights and romping, not some kind of sex maniac,' said Grey Gowrie twenty years after Astor's death.[27] Before the Life Peerages Act of 1958, Astor supported the admission of women to the House of Lords. He was a founder member of the parliamentary committee for British entry into the Common Market, sponsored legislation to introduce lie-detectors into police work, and supported reform of laws covering abortion and divorce. He also had one deadly enemy to whom he had never done a jot of harm. In 1949 his brother David published a profile in the *Observer* of Lord Beaverbrook, describing him as 'a golliwog itching with vitality' and whose editorial policies were 'political baby-talk'. In 1931, the Astors' half-brother, Bobbie Shaw, had been sentenced to five months' imprisonment on a charge of homosexuality. Nancy Astor asked Beaverbrook to use his influence to suppress the story in the *Daily Express* and other newspapers. 'I am deeply grateful to you for the trouble you have taken to keep my name out of the papers,' she later wrote to him. 'Nothing matters very much about me – but I felt I should like to spare the other children.' After the *Observer* profile, Beaverbrook fulminated that the Astors were sanctimonious and ungrateful. His underlings retrieved Bobbie Shaw's dossier, and primed themselves to serve their paymaster's spiteful rage. In 1958, for example, John Gordon, the *Sunday Express* editor, whose virulence about homosexuality was fit for an ayatollah, wrote a vindictive revelation of the Shaw case, which at the last moment was held back. Beaverbrook's staff continued his relentless vendetta against the Astors, which reached its crescendo with the Profumo Affair.[28]

At New Year 1958 in St Moritz, Bill Astor met a twenty-seven-year-old 'model girl' called Bronwen Pugh. She was the Garboesque muse of the couturier Pierre Balmain, standing nearly six feet tall, with piercing blue-green eyes and an all-encompassing instinctive elegance. Her father was a barrister specialising in Welsh coal-mining cases who eventually became a county court judge. Her unusual aura derived, possibly, from a series of mystical experiences which began at the age of seven, when she believed she heard the voice of God speaking to her about the primary importance of love. Bronwen Pugh trained at the Central School of Speech and

Drama before going to teach at a girl's school. Only later did she plunge into modelling. Some thought her too tall for the London catwalks; Cecil Beaton refused to do a photographic portrait because he claimed that her nose was too ugly; but her purposive self-possession proved startling at fashion shows.

In the spring of 1957, Bronwen Pugh went to Paris to model for Balmain. 'Bronwen takes Paris by Scorn', was *Picture Post's* headline. 'Some loathed it. Some were entranced. But everybody remembered that scornful, dirt-beneath-my-feet style of modelling.' Recalling that Pugh has been 'a schoolmistress', *Picture Post* added, 'the glare that quelled the Lower Fourth has become the stare that sweeps the salons at Balmain'. Katharine Whitehorn, who went to see the Paris fashions, reported: 'At Balmain this extraordinary girl somehow acquired a manner of showing dresses which put her instantly on a pedestal. It was half-Bournemouth, half-goddess; scornful, aristocratic, insufferable. It staggered Paris.'[29]

There was confusion among journalists and the public between 'model girls', as Bronwen Pugh and her colleagues were then called, and 'models', as young women were euphemistically docketed when they appeared in newspaper reports of divorce or criminal cases. Anne Cumming-Bell led the way for socially ascendant 'model girls' by marrying the Duke of Rutland in 1946 (newspapers still calling her 'a mannequin' and reporting that she had always insisted on appearing fully-clothed); Norman Hartnell's 'model girl' Jane McNeill married the future Duke of Buccleuch in 1953; Fiona Campbell-Walter married Heini Thyssen-Bornemisza in 1956; Anne Gunning Parker married Sir Anthony Nutting in 1961. Dior's muse Jean Dawnay married a major in the Welsh Guards, Prince George Galitzine, in 1963. These, however, were the rare, publicised exceptions. Many model girls acquired husbands who earned less than themselves. They were unable to save because of the enormous outlay required in shoes, nylons, hats, bags, gloves, cosmetics and hair-dos.

Fiona Campbell-Walter met Heini Thyssen on a St Moritz train rather as Astor and Bronwen Pugh met in the same ski resort. Thyssen wooed her with a Ford Thunderbird, and married her post-haste. 'He had the fastest plane, the best motor car, the most precious paintings,' she is supposed to have said; 'of course he had to have the most beautiful woman.' She was the third of Thyssen's five wives. Talking about her later, with the smugness of a lifelong womaniser, he said: 'She wasn't very intelligent but she would talk endlessly in that wonderful dark brown voice of hers. One day, when we were driving, she asked me a question and I didn't answer. I said: "You've got such a sweet charming voice, you can't expect me to listen to what you're saying as well. Just talk to me".' Thyssen lusted after Campbell-Walter, although he ungallantly said that she looked better dressed than nude. 'When it comes to women,' he philosophised, 'one should not fall madly in love, travel with them, trust or spoil them. One should, however, show jealousy. Women like that.'[30]

Astor was Thyssen's antithesis as a suitor. Between his first luncheon with Bronwen Pugh, and their next, months later, she underwent an unheralded mystical experience which filled her with joy. She read *The Phenomenon of Man*, by the Jesuit Teilhard de Chardin, discovered St Theresa of Avila, and felt transformed. Astor's first words on seeing her again were: 'You've changed, what is it?' Soon he was head over heels. 'I got a shock,' he wrote after watching her on a catwalk, 'as I had always imagined you at work as lovely and gay, and I was knocked off my emotional perch when you looked cold and aloof.' Unlike Thyssen, he appreciated his fiancée's talk. 'The extraordinary thing about you,' he explained, 'is that your mind has survived the chicken chatter of the *cabine* for so long, remaining lively, enquiring, and deep.'[31]

They married at Hampstead register office in October 1960. When news of the impending marriage seeped out the night before, her parents were hounded by journalists. On the wedding day reporters crowded a pub opposite the gates of Cliveden buying rounds in the hope that drinkers would help them to concoct a juicy quote. Dorothy Macmillan, aunt of both Bill's second wife and his first wife's ex-fiancé, had the impertinence to show her disapproval of an ex-model viscountess when she met Bronwen Astor.

The newly married couple were united by humour. He liked boyish practical jokes, while she had a jolly-hockey-sticks sense of fun. She described herself as light-hearted, but not particularly amusing, and Bill as a serious-minded man who liked to be playful. Grey Gowrie, whose grandmother gave the new Lady Astor the nickname of 'The Pencil' because she looked so long and thin, recalled: 'Bill was suddenly bubbly and looked so happy. And she had real energy. "Come on, let's do this, let's have fun," she used to say. She was so much better for him than one of those conventional upper-class wives . . . she gave him back a feeling of being alive.' There were charades, guessing games, songs at the piano as entertainment for guests after dinner. The women sat in groups discussing their children, dogs and horses. Bronwen Astor liked to embroider. There were no erotic carousals.[32]

Many middle-class women, who were expected to abandon their working lives on marriage, were relieved to become the subordinate partners who did not have to take full responsibility for the future. Some found fulfilment playing new roles that were supportive and secondary to their husbands. Bronwen Astor, as the wife of a lordly Croesus, had to accept his settled ways more than most women. Some of her husband's Cliveden guests were condescending towards her because she was not upper class ('the class system was much stronger then', she recalled). Bill Astor, who disliked the way she pronounced 'round', tried to teach her to say 'rauwnd'. She felt socially precarious. Her biographer likened her position to that of a junior partner joining a well-established firm: she had to move discreetly to win acceptance.[33]

Bronwen Astor felt as disempowered by Cliveden's traditions and staff as Maxim de Winter's second wife in Daphne du Maurier's novel *Rebecca*, after moving into his great house Manderley. The household staff in 1960 comprised a chef, assistant cook, butler, valet, housekeeper, laundry maid, sewing maid, three housemaids, two footmen, two secretaries, two stable-hands, two chauffeurs, two carpenters, a night-watchman, a handyman, and eight gardeners. In 1965, shortly before his death, Astor estimated that it cost £40,000 a year to run Cliveden. Everything was already the way that he wanted. His young wife shifted a sofa, replaced some curtains and attempted to make her clothes fill the spacious ward-robes in her dressing room. Her lady's maid, who had come from the Duchess of Roxburghe at Floors Castle, was mortified by how few dresses the new Lady Astor owned. The maid laid out the clothes that she judged should be worn each day by her mistress, who had no choice in the matter; but soon left Cliveden declaring that she could not work for a woman who did not know how to behave. The chef resigned when Bronwen Astor visited the kitchen to discuss the day's menus, and opened the refrigerator to see what was inside; Bill Astor pacified the man's outrage, and she had to apologise.

Nicky Haslam, who had been Bronwen Pugh's walker, recalled visiting the Astors around 1962:

We turned in to the gates of Cliveden [and] . . . circled a vast fountain, its cavorting creatures carved of meat-pink marble, before the last long stretch of drive to the palatial facade. The new Lady Astor, wearing an unusually shapeless mustard-coloured country suit, met us in the vast pseudo-baronial hall. It was strange to see her pouring tea amid tables bearing publications like the *Farmer and Stockbreeder*, and the *Tractor News*, rather than *Jardin des Modes* or *L'Officiel* . . . However rich the Astors, however grand and gilded the Cliveden salons, however *luxe* the food served in them, the upstairs arrangements were curiously Spartan . . . single gentlemen's quarters were narrow bedrooms off school-like corri-dors, not very near a huge communal washroom, and far above the main rooms. The hard mattress in my room did not, however, stop me having a little rest before dinner. I slept through the dressing gong. A footman was sent to wake me, and I hit the dinner table just as an elaborate *soufflé* was being brought into the astonishing blue-and-gold French *boiserie*'d dining room. Bronwen motioned me to my place . . . and I was relieved to find the *soufflé* was the *entrée* rather than the pudding. I hadn't entirely blotted my copybook in this aristocratic, ruling-the-country company.

The next morning Bill Astor took us to meet a friend who had a cottage on the estate. His name was Stephen Ward. Within a few months the scandal of his trial and suicide was to bring irredeemable sorrow into Bronwen and Bill's marriage.[34]

FOUR

Doctor

In the spring of 1960, Randolph Churchill, son of the wartime Prime Minister, ricked his back while lifting a bundle of snowdrops out of his shooting brake. Physicians examined him, radiologists x-rayed him, pharmacists supplied analgesics, but he remained in acute pain. Finally he resorted to an osteopath, who diagnosed his trouble in five minutes and cured it in ten. 'Osteopaths,' Churchill wrote in his *News of the World* column, 'do not make extravagant claims for themselves and do not guarantee cures; but the best of them think that they can be of some help in nearly every ailment and disease save tuberculosis and cancer.' He criticised the General Medical Council which, 'like the Boilermakers Union, is a closed shop, and would like to keep the nation's illness in their own hands whether they can cure it or not'. Churchill's story drew nearly 300 letters from patients praising osteopathy and another ninety enquiring about the practice.[1]

The principles of osteopathic medicine had been founded in the 1870s by a doctor on the American frontier called Andrew Still. All diseases, according to Still, result from abnormalities in or near the joints: the body contains natural antidotes, which can use the nerves and bloodstream to cure physical diseases, but these antidotes are nullified if the skeletal framework is distorted. Still's cures were based on manipulation of what he called 'lesions' in bones, muscles, joints, ligaments caused by injury, infection, physical strain or nervous stress.

England's pre-eminent practitioner of osteopathy, Herbert

Barker, acquired a busy practice in London by calling himself a 'manipulative surgeon' rather than using the old title of bone-setter. He accepted that surgery, anaesthetics and medicines were required to treat many conditions, but succeeded in helping hopeless patients whom orthodox surgery had failed. Although Barker was denounced as a quack by the medical hierarchy, which insisted that the healing arts were the exclusive prerogative of people who had undergone training in teaching hospitals, a grateful nation gave him the accolade of knighthood in 1922. 'He had the gift of healing,' it was written after his death. 'He believed firmly in himself, he exuded confidence, and his personality was striking. He willed his patients back to normal life, and he did not leave them alone until they were cured.'[2]

The British Medical Association resented osteopathy's claim to be a separate science, and defeated the osteopaths' application for statutory recognition in 1935. Hospitals would therefore not appoint osteopaths to their staff, and there was no free osteopathy available under the National Health Service. Instead, a voluntary register of osteopaths was established (with 300 names by 1960). Established practitioners had more fee-paying patients than they could manage. Physicians sent cases of fibrosis, neuritis, sciatica, slipped disc, frozen shoulders, locked ankles, arthritic knees, backache, tennis elbow and flat feet to osteopaths. The patients, after undergoing manipulation and paying their fees, reported good results.

Osteopathy became a modish form of cosseting. Lady Brenda Last in Evelyn Waugh's novel *A Handful of Dust* (1934) went up to London from her husband's gothic seat 'for a day's shopping, hair-cutting or bone-setting (a recreation she particularly enjoyed)', and planned her adultery with a second-rate snob while lying 'luxuriously on the osteopath's table, and her vertebrae, under his strong fingers, snapped like patent fasteners'. Barker felt that many diseases or pains had an element of temperament, nerves, diet or habit in their cause, and therefore urged osteopaths to foster close practitioner-patient relationships: every patient 'must be treated as a personality and not as a "case" – every treatment being different because every patient is different'.[3]

Stephen Ward was attracted by the osteopathic tradition of cultivating personal contacts with patients. He aspired to Sir Herbert Barker's influence, although like Barker's his skills were excluded from the medical mainstream. His position was that of a gifted, ingratiating outsider.

Ward was born in 1912 at Lemsford vicarage in Hertfordshire. The village of Lemsford stands on the edge of the park surrounding Brocket Hall, then the country seat of a Canadian railway millionaire called Lord Mount Stephen. Ward was the middle of three sons of a country clergyman who had married the daughter of an Anglo-Irish landowner. There were coronets in the remoter branches of his family. On his mother's side he was descended from Irish lords called Castlemaine. The traveller Wilfred Thesiger, himself the heir-presumptive of Lord Chelmsford, was his first cousin. Ward attended a public school called Canford, newly opened in 1923 in a sprawling Dorset house which had been the seat of Lord Wimborne. The school's Latin motto 'Nisi dominus frustra' could be irreverently translated as 'Without a Lord everything is in vain', which might have suited Ward in certain moods.

Instead of an English university after Canford, Ward went abroad (like Bill Astor) to improve his foreign languages. He was in Hamburg in 1929–30, where he did translation work for the local office of the Shell Oil Company, and then worked as a Paris tourist guide to fund his French lessons. In 1934 he went to study at the osteopathic training school which had been established forty years earlier at Kirksville, Missouri. This interest in osteopathy may have been spurred by his father's lifelong spinal affliction, which gave him the look of a hunchback. Stephen Ward's qualifications entitled him to practise as a physician in the USA, but were not recognised by the British Medical Association. Henceforth he used the prefix of doctor. (At his trial the prosecution addressed him with wintry scorn as 'Doctor', as if the title were bogus.)

In 1939, Ward enlisted in the Royal Armoured Corps as a private. Later he transferred to the Royal Army Medical Corps, where the refusal of the military authorities to recognise his American medical degree aroused his abiding resentment. He served instead as a stretcher-bearer. After demobilisation he set up an osteopathic practice in Cavendish Square, behind Oxford Street, in 1947. His first important patient, Averell Harriman, was the US ambassador. Harriman's recommendations, and a spreading reputation, brought rich and eminent patients to Ward's consulting rooms: the oil multi-millionaires Paul Getty and Nubar Gulbenkian; Winston Churchill, and his politically inexorable son-in-law Duncan Sandys; other politicos, including Eden, Gaitskell, Rab Butler and Selwyn Lloyd; King Peter of Yugoslavia, Prince Christian of Hanover, the Maharajah of Baroda; film-stars including Elizabeth Taylor, Ava Gardner, Frank Sinatra and Danny Kaye.

Ward was voluble with a rich, resonant voice. He was a sympathetic if inquisitive listener, who combined calculation with impetuosity. At best he seemed charming, kind, plausible, carefree and indiscreet; but he was too sure of his powers of pleasing. One of his patients, an ambassador's wife, Lady Gladwyn, 'disliked his jaunty conceited manner', but acknowledged the efficacy of his techniques. The *Daily Telegraph* editor Sir Colin Coote, whose lumbago was cured by Ward's 'healing hands', found his consultations 'completely normal'. However, as he informed Downing Street confidentially in June 1963, 'Ward chattered incessantly during treatment, so much so that I thought his political views, though childish, might be dangerous.' He consulted David Floyd, the *Telegraph*'s special correspondent on communist affairs, who 'assured me that MI5 knew all about him and, I gathered, actually received reports from him'.[4]

Like all show-offs, Ward loathed being alone. There was nothing self-sufficing about him. His working life and off-duty activities were ruled by a need for company that reflected his fear of solitude. He had an overweening need to win people's esteem. His marriage in 1949 failed after six weeks: his wife, the daughter of a textiles company director, was not typical of his taste in women. Young women with well-educated parents seldom attracted him. Instead he preferred 'girl-spotting' in Oxford Street or coffee bars, and picking up slim-hipped, improvident gamine types, whom he called 'alley cats'.

Vanity, flirting, impudence, fickleness, irresponsibility and indolence were traits that Ward found attractive in women. For some years he lived in a studio flat atop Orme Court near the Notting Hill Gate end of Bayswater Road. It was not, then, a smart address. He let women stay there, without the aim of taking them to bed, because he liked their clutter of underwear, stockings and make-up. Christine Keeler lived with him at Orme Court in a companionate way without sexual activity between them. Their alliance should have been fleeting; but by mischances and indiscretions, their fates became fettered together like those of Lord Alfred Douglas and Oscar Wilde. There was an adolescent tinge to Ward's obsession with sex. Innuendo amused him. With his white Jaguar, his name-dropping and his fantasies of influence, he was a licentious Walter Mitty: Ward might have said, in Gide's words from *The Immoralist*, 'the lowest instinct has always seemed to me the most sincere'.

In 1953–54, Ward acquired a lethal enemy called John Lewis, who had inherited control of a business called Rubber Improvement, and was a hard-driven businessman in a hurry to make millions. Lewis had been elected as a Labour MP in the 1945 general election, later declaring himself a supporter of 'full Socialist planning and control of the world's resources'. His chief parliamentary interventions concerned industrial research and development and controls on scarce materials such as rubber (although as a steward of the Boxing Board of Control, he promoted television sports); but he came to be shunned in the parliamentary party. He achieved fleeting front-page fame by his road-hog behaviour in a Hyde Park traffic jam, which led to a parliamentary investigation in 1951. After losing his seat some months later, Lewis abandoned politics for money-making. He treated his young wife Joy abusively, and was brazen in his pursuit of starlets: 'I've screwed every pretty girl in London,' he crowed. One night, after a drunken row, Joy Lewis fled their flat overlooking the Regent's Park, and took refuge with Stephen Ward. Lewis failed in his attempt to cite Ward in his ferocious divorce, but denounced him to the Inland Revenue, informed the *Daily Express* that he was running a Mayfair call-girl racket, and made anonymous telephone calls to Marylebone police station decrying him as a procurer of women to rich patients. The police found no evidence to support Lewis's unhinged calumnies, but these accusations lay on file, and were a pointer when the police were instructed to investigate if criminal charges could be brought against Ward in 1963.[5]

The osteopath's caprices were invisible to his patients. 'I had no inkling of the shady side of Stephen Ward,' wrote Coote. 'Indeed, if I had been asked whether he had one, I should have guessed that he was not interested in girls.' William Shepherd MP, meeting him for the first time in 1962, similarly assumed that Ward's preference was for youths. Ludovic Kennedy, who watched him on trial in 1963, commented: 'ageing men who look half their years are often fairies; and one wondered whether within this screaming hetero, a homo was not struggling wildly to be let out'. A profile in the *Observer* reported that Ward's girl-chasing was so showy that several acquaintances suspected that his Casanova complex hid 'latent homosexuality or impotence'.[6]

The power and prosperity of Ward's patients defined his status as a practitioner. The fact that his fees were paid by a deposed Balkan monarch, the American oilman who was reported to be the richest man in the world, by Winston Churchill and Hollywood actors, elevated him. He was what his eminent patients made him. His ill-starred destiny proved to be ruled by one practitioner-patient relationship above all others – that with Lord Astor.

In 1949 Bill Astor injured his back in a fall while hunting with the Whaddon Chase. He consulted Ward, who alleviated the pain and persuaded him that he would feel better for an osteopathic massage after every outing in the hunting field. When Ward later cured a bout of neuritis, he was brought into the train of Astor's largesse. Ward was careless about money, and started borrowing from Astor – £1,250 in 1952, for example. It would be harsh to characterise him as a sponger, but fair to call him a presumptuous charmer. Astor introduced Ward to his half-brother Bobbie Shaw, whose joy of life as a young man had been wrecked by guilt, ostracism and imprisonment because of his homosexuality, and who by the 1950s was a miserable drunkard. Shaw's gratitude to Ward took a submissive form. Once, when Ward was tending Shaw for a poisoned arm, David Astor felt that his half-brother needed pharmaceuticals, not osteopathy. Shaw was chary of annoying Ward, who required his patients to trust him without demur, but agreed to consult a physician if Astor telephoned Ward to explain. Ward's reaction was thorny when Astor broke the news: he was always aggrieved when his relations with patients were disrupted by outsiders.

Friendship, Hugh Trevor-Roper noted in 1945, differed between the classes in England. In the lower classes it was expressed by doing helpful kindnesses for each other; in the middle classes it was founded on mutual respect; 'in the world of fashion they simply adore men and women whom one would not dream of trusting round the corner'. Stephen Ward's popularity was a prime case. Like many untrustworthy people, he had the gift of inspiring confidence. As Astor's second marriage unravelled during 1956, he apparently used Ward as an intermediary seeking reconciliation with Philippa Astor. Perhaps in gratitude, Ward was allowed to occupy Spring Cottage, the half-timbered pseudo-Tyrolean hideaway – quaint or ugly depending on one's taste – on the banks of the Thames at Cliveden. Cynthia Gladwyn recalled that on her sole visit, Spring Cottage was 'dusty, untidy and rather sordid', and that she was handed sherry in 'a grubby glass'. Once Ward started using this riverside nook at weekends, he was more than ever in Bill Astor's life. He became the Cliveden jack-in-a-box, always popping up and down from Spring Cottage. He would stroll to the main house, after luncheon at the weekends, massage his landlord's back and give osteopathic manipulation to any guests who wished. Occasionally he was invited to dine. In April 1960, for example, he joined a party including Sir John Wolfenden, the university vice-chancellor who had chaired the official inquiry into prostitution and homosexuality. In reporting this dinner, Maurice Collis, who was another guest, described Ward (who had attended classes at the Slade School of Art) as 'Bill's great friend, and a most charming friendly man who, besides being a Harley Street specialist, is an amateur artist of talent'.[7]

Pamela Cooper, who took a course of treatment with Ward in London, found him amusing and ingratiating. 'However,' she recalled, 'there was something not quite right about Stephen. He could not rest content as a good artist and excellent osteopath, and he presumed on Bill's generosity. Many of Bill's friends did the same – except that Stephen wasn't really a friend.' Her son, Grey Gowrie, enjoyed picnics at Spring Cottage as an Oxford undergraduate. 'They were jolly, not orgiastic. There was a bit of innocent malarkey, swimming in the Thames, but nothing more.' Jack Profumo, who had known Astor since they canvassed together for Conservative votes in Fulham in the 1930s, recalled in old age that after an introduction to Ward by Astor in the early 1950s, he had attended one of Ward's cocktail parties, where he found several starlets. Profumo, who found the osteopath 'charismatic', described Ward's role at Cliveden as 'partly a Court jester, but also a go-getter of girls'.[8]

Ward's preponderant extra-curricular activity was interfering in other people's lives. He acted the part of a wizard casting sexual spells. 'He was full of life, enthusiastic about everything,' Christine Keeler recalled. 'Stephen would always fill an awkward silence with a funny remark, would never put you down for telling a flat joke. He wanted everyone to be as carefree as he was, and was genuinely upset by drooping shoulders.' His thick brown hair, strong jaw and well-toned body were, she thought, attractive: 'when he smiled the whole of his face lit up, and he had the most mesmerising voice that I had ever heard which he used to make you feel important'. She accompanied him when, in June 1961, he moved from Orme Court into a first-floor flat in an unprepossessing little building at 17 Wimpole Mews, Marylebone. Wimpole Mews was a minute's stroll from Ward's consulting rooms at 38 Devonshire Street. It had the further attraction of a public house, where the publican had a special line in attracting pretty young women.[9]

The best summary of Ward was published in David Astor's *Observer* a few days after Ward's criminal trial for living on immoral earnings in 1963. 'He was a compulsive exhibitionist who depended upon audiences to provide him with stimulus and confidence,' the paper averred. 'He was massively indiscreet, and loved showing off right up to the end. He liked to exercise his power over girls, and it may have been this, as much as sexual desire, that impelled him.' Despite his financial and domestic disorderliness, he seemed sure of his professional competence and social influence. He fancied himself as an amateur psychotherapist who understood human foibles and could repair damaged psyches. He prized himself, too, as a subversive, who blurred class distinctions, brought unlikely people together, and introduced poor girls to rich men. Ward was not avaricious: he sought glamour and influence – not money. 'It was this that made much of the prosecution's case seem inherently implausible. To depict him as a straightforward ponce, using his flat as a commercial brothel, seemed out of keeping with Ward's basic ambitions and the peculiar nature of his self-respect.'[10]

A new phase of Ward's career began with a gallery exhibition of his sketches of patients in 1960. He supplied the *Illustrated London News* and then the *Daily Telegraph* with further celebrity sketches. His sitters were as varied as Princess Margaret, the Dukes of Edinburgh and Gloucester, the Cypriot leader Archbishop Makarios, the hire-purchase washing machine tycoon John Bloom, John Betjeman and the comedian Terry-Thomas. Colin Coote commissioned Ward to draw ink sketches for the *Daily Telegraph* of protagonists at Adolf Eichmann's war crimes trial in Jerusalem in 1961. Subsequently Ward complained to Coote that his scheme to sketch the Soviet Politburo had been baffled because he could not get a visa to visit Russia. In the hope of expediting the visa, Coote introduced him at luncheon at the Garrick Club to Yevgeny ('Eugene') Ivanov, the assistant naval attaché at the Russian embassy. David Floyd, the *Telegraph* expert on the Soviet bloc, also attended the lunch. 'Though I only saw Ivanoff once again,' Coote wrote, 'Ward talked a lot about him – so much so that I thought he (Ward) might well be a homosexual. This impression was confirmed at a return lunch to which Ward invited me in a Mayfair restaurant and where Ivanoff was also a guest. As I do not like these gentry, I never went to Ward again for lumbago.'[11]

Ward's hobnobbing at Cliveden was less easy after Astor's re-marriage in October 1960. 'I warned Bill about Stephen,' Bronwen Astor told Peter Stanford. 'From the first time Bill introduced us, I didn't want him at my dinner table.' In fact, he dined there only twice after she became Cliveden's chateleine: for Boxing Day of 1960; and on 30 December 1961. On the first occasion, he was invited to dinner at short notice, because the Astors needed a single man to balance the sexes at the table, and charmed his hostess. Subsequently, at her husband's prompting, she had one Ward treatment: the experience aroused her distaste. 'His conversation was very intrusive,' she thought. 'He asked very personal questions.' She decided not to repeat the experience.[12]

A showdown came in December 1961 when Ward provoked a furious row with Philippa Astor's sister-in-law, Deirdre Grantley, an Oxford-educated young woman. Deirdre Grantley's Hungarian mother Judith Listowel was a staunchly anti-Soviet exile who edited a weekly magazine, *East Europe and Soviet Russia*. Just before Khrushchev's visit to London in 1956, Lady Listowel had launched a press campaign intended to embarrass the Hungarians into releasing her young nephew to travel to freedom, and in November that year, during the Hungarian uprising, she smuggled herself across the border from Austria. More recently, in 1961, the CIA had inspired the Bay of Pigs invasion of Castro's

Cuba. It was therefore rash of Ward to denounce the Hungarian freedom-fighters and the anti-Castro insurgents in scathing terms at the Cliveden dinner. Lady Grantley was angered, and Bill Astor, who had vivid memories of the refugees whom he had helped at Andau, lost his temper and stalked from the room after telling Ward that if those were his views, he should go and live elsewhere. Under Bronwen Astor's calming influence, Bill relented in his threat that Ward must vacate Spring Cottage; but Ward, who feebly protested that he had only meant to indicate that he disliked violence, was not invited to dine at the main house again.

Ward made mischief in upper-class company, and worried about the good opinion of his social inferiors – neither of them traits of a conventional snob. According to Keeler, he seemed proud to be 'a maverick, which I found strange for all the time he also wanted to be part of the in-crowd, especially the high and mighty'. His cliquishness, she added, 'wasn't about money, but the way you wore your hat, who your tailor was'. Ward, so Coote complained, 'would continually drag well-known people into his talk, and refer to them by their Christian names – sometimes the wrong one!' His class-consciousness about his patients matched the mischievous Robin Hood forays in his social life. Ward's outlook differed little from the social self-awareness, the insecurities and compensatory striving, of the medical profession generally, which led to doctors' wives having a reputation as crashing snobs. Medical families had a more precarious social status than legal families, because their standing in communities reflected their patients' standing.[13]

During the 1950s the medical profession became less respected and more openly criticised than at any time in previous history. It was partly that professional authority had been weakened by the formation of the National Health Service in 1948. Physicians found that after being 'nationalised', they were answerable to 'a vast, impersonal, remarkably uninformed machine with a predilection for having its million and one queries answered in triplicate', as was lamented in 1954. The taxpayers who funded the service felt they could make new demands of their physicians. 'Since everyone was forced to pay a whacking great weekly premium for medical insurance, nearly everybody, not unexpectedly, thought they might as well get something out of it . . . so the stream of importunate demanding free chits to the dentist, free wigs, postal votes, corsets, milk, orange juice, vitamin tablets, pensions, invalid chairs, beds, water cushions, taxi rides to hospital, crutches, bandages, artificial limbs . . . dogged us wherever we went.' Patients, especially less sick ones, were disrespectful to physicians, whom they treated as functionaries trying to cheat them out of their rightful entitlements. General practitioners were paid according to the number of patients listed in their NHS practices, and found that if they did not prescribe, or overprescribe, what their patients wished, their patients would transfer to other doctors' lists. This was a particular problem with housewives seeking amphetamines or barbiturates.[14]

The medical profession was hit by the creeping iconoclasm of the 1950s. 'The mood today is to criticise everything,' Harold Macmillan wrote in 1957. 'It may pass, but I have never known the press and the public so sensitive or so hypercritical. I think it is because they are all so terribly well off. English people never seem to show their best except when they are in great trouble.' Sir Arthur Porritt, President of the Royal College of Surgeons, felt the injustice of physicians being less esteemed than in earlier generations. The trouble, he complained in 1962, was that few physicians could any longer master all aspects of medicine, which weakened medical authority so far as some patients were concerned. Physicians, Porritt emphasised, faced duties that nobody else carried. 'A doctor's stock-in-trade is life and death. People tend to forget that he has a heavier responsibility than any millionaire, property dealer or business tycoon.'[15]

One of the contentious issues facing the Macmillan administration on its formation in 1957 was doctors' pay. Discontent on this issue festered into the 1960s. In their protests about remuneration, physicians were subliminally asking to be restored as objects of respect before the NHS masses. The *News of the World* headline 'THESE DOCTORS MAKE ME ANGRY' was an example of the denigration. It headed complaints in 1960 about the difficulty of winning compensation for blunders when the medical world acted as a self-protecting Establishment and closed ranks at the first whiff of an action for medical negligence. 'By all means let us salute the devotion of thousands of those who treat us in our infirmities. But isn't it time they realised that they are increasingly the paid privileged servants of the citizen, not the fellow conspirators of a secret vocation. A new professionalism, a new outlook on responsibility to a tax-paying, better-educated public, is stirring all around us. It's time it reached the doctors.'[16]

The British Medical Association reacted to the changed public mood by upholding a severe, restrictive morality in its official dealings. Throughout the BMA's memorandum to the Wolfenden committee on homosexuality and prostitution, when referring to sexual activity, the word 'indulgence' was used instead of 'pleasure'. 'The proper use of sex, the primary purpose of which is creative, is related to the individual's responsibility to himself and the nation,' the BMA asserted, meaning that sex without the possibility of pregnancy was improper, and probably shameful. 'At the present time doctors observe their patients in an environment favourable to sexual indulgence, and surrounded by irresponsibility, selfishness and a preoccupation with immediate materialistic satisfaction. There is also no lack of stimulation to sexual appetite. Suggestive advertisements abound on the street hoardings and in the Underground; provocative articles and illustrations appear in the daily and, especially, the Sunday newspapers; magazines and cheap novels with lurid covers frequently provide suggestive reading matter; and the erotic nature of many films and stage shows is but thinly veiled.'

The BMA offered far-fetched explanations for the perceived epidemic of homosexuality: 'Many men see in homosexual practices a way of satisfying their sexual desires without running the risks of the *sequelae* of heterosexual intercourse. They believe, for example, that there is no danger of contracting venereal disease in homosexual activity. Other men adopt homosexual practices as a substitute for extra-marital heterosexual intercourse because there is no fear of causing pregnancy or emotional complications as in the life of a woman.' Male homosexuality aroused, perhaps even deserved, public hostility, the BMA testified, because of the propensity of its practitioners in 'positions of authority to give preferential treatment to homosexuals or to require homosexual subjection as an expedient for promotion. The existence of practising homosexuals in the Church, Parliament, Civil Service, Armed Forces, Press, radio, stage and other institutions constitutes a special problem.' Sexual acts between men were 'repulsive', in the diagnosis of the BMA. 'Homosexuals congregating blatantly in public houses, streets, and restaurants are an outrage to public decency. Effeminate men wearing make-up and using scent are objectionable to everybody.' The physicians concluded that if 'degenerate sodomists' persist in their debauchery despite repeated imprisonment, 'it would be in the public interest to deal with them in the same way as mentally deranged offenders'.[17]

This was the morality of the BMA at the time when Ward was 'girl-spotting' in Oxford Street, enjoying women's stockings hanging over chairs in his flat, and revelling in the lazy caprices of the girls he befriended. Although he aspired to the prestige of the royal physician Lord Evans, and the influence of Macmillan's medical adviser Sir John Richardson, his destiny lay with the blaring headlines associated with the murderous physicians, Crippen, Bodkin Adams and Shipman. During 1963 he was victimised by politicians, framed by policemen, deserted by patients, betrayed by girlfriends, reviled by lawyers, and smeared by Lord Denning. For a while, osteopathy fell in reputation to the level of quackery which claimed to cure warts by rubbing them with toads. It was three years only since Randolph Churchill had ricked his back lifting a bundle of snowdrops, but it seemed another age.

FIVE

Good-Time Girls

'A procession of downtrodden wives, bullied mothers, cast-off mistresses; the jilted, the enticed, the abandoned; harlots, door-mats, birds in gilded cages.' This was how women were pictured by a dress-shop saleswoman in Elizabeth Taylor's 1951 novel, *A Game of Hide-and-Seek*. Richard Crossman, who in 1954 married his third wife, a young Oxford graduate in Politics, Philosophy and Economics, used to say complacently to visitors in front of her: 'If you're going to marry, you want to marry either an alpha girl or a doormat: *I* married a doormat.'[1]

Although young women had few direct, open routes to inde-pendence, some managed to find oblique, discreet ways of asserting themselves well before the social and sexual convulsions of 1967–68. Women at the time of the Profumo Affair had been subjugated by domestic constraints, sexual assumptions and judicial oppres-sion which they resisted with stealthy opinions, defiant conduct and wayward impulses. For every overbearing masculine voice trying to punish female independence, or devalue women's opin-ions, there were less audible voices insisting with obstinate integrity that they would not do as the men said. It was from the social *milieu* of the 1950s that Christine Keeler and Mandy Rice-Davies emerged: two 'good-time girls' who refused to be doormats.

The spirit of these times was represented by the Sexual Offences Act of 1956. This far-reaching legislation was prepared in committee, and passed unanimously without a word of debate in either the Commons or the Lords. It covered eventualities

109

that were hard to imagine (Section 1 specified that a man committed rape if he induced a married woman to have sexual intercourse with him by impersonating her husband), and showed the hidden stresses of the period by criminalising activities that many people thought inoffensive. Section 23 (which was invoked after the arrest of Stephen Ward in 1963) created the criminal offence of procuration of a girl under twenty-one. This provision meant that if someone introduced a male to a woman who was over the age of consent (sixteen), but under the age of twenty-one, and the pair subsequently had a sexual romp, then the introducer had committed a criminal offence. Introducing a man to such a girl at a party or in a pub, or joining in his bantering chat-up, could be the prelude to a criminal offence if they later had sex together (anywhere in the world). By the early 1960s most university undergraduates, and much of the population under twenty-five, were criminals if the law was interpreted as it was in the charges levelled against Ward. As this law remained in force until 1994/95, many readers of this book will have committed the crime of procuration.

This provision of the criminal law – silently enacted so far as the public or press were concerned – was a Maginot Line in defence of what was called young women's 'virtue'. It was the work of legislators who were middle-aged or elderly, and overwhelmingly male: indeed women were excluded from membership of the House of Lords until 1958. It remained an exorbitant challenge for English women to have self-reliant lives. They were subordinated to men, and expected to feign gratitude for their subjugation. Valerie Hobson and Bronwen Pugh, for example, were required by their husbands, Jack Profumo and Bill Astor, to abandon shining careers after their marriages, and thereafter to chirp prettily like songbirds in gilded cages. Women were promised influence and masculine protection, though not the comprehensive respect of men, if they accepted roles that were secondary, insincere, compliant and manipulative. At times it seemed that the alternatives posed for women were to settle for a patronising bore as a husband, or to be venturesome and risk being hurt by the sort of predatory lechers who exploited Christine Keeler.

An article headlined 'HOW TO GET A HUSBAND' from the *Sunday Pictorial* of 1962 reveals the prevalent attitudes:

Let's suppose . . . that you have been dating a single man for some time. Gradually, and in an irresistible, gentlemanly manner, he is taking the initiative. Even if you would like the experience yourself, you probably feel deep down inside that intercourse out of wedlock would be wrong.

So the questions that dash through your mind are:

IS this really necessary to win him?

WILL he respect me more afterwards – or less?

DOES he really intend to marry me, or is he stringing me along?

Many a man does not want to marry a woman with whom he has had a pre-marital relationship. If he was taught in his early life that 'nice girls' don't surrender before marriage, he might find himself losing respect for the woman who gives in – in which case his reaction might be one of disgust. Worse still, he might feel that he would never be able to trust such a woman. Yet this same man will exert all manner of persuasion to engage the woman in going all the way. So it's up to her to set the pace and offer resistance, if she has her limits.

But if you are not going to yield to his entreaties to join him in bed, don't just sit there and sulk. Give him a real lecture on your monumental respect for the act as a marital rite. Convince him, if you can, that you have stored up ardour and fire that will create a holocaust once you have a marriage certificate in your hot little hand . . .

Here is a programme that will help you in your struggle.

ONE: If, at the end of a date, your escort insists on a long session of kissing, engage his aid in the preparation of a little snack. Avoid being blunt. Men don't like to be told firmly.

TWO: Plan your dates around people – card parties, cocktail parties, barbecues, stage plays, films, dancing, club activities, or just getting together with a group.

THREE: Try to achieve a real sense of affection and intimacy through conversation.

FOUR: No matter how badly you want to, don't go on a trip with him, except possibly a weekend jaunt with a group.

Don't yield cheaply, if yielding is what you are going to do. Don't be grudging. Cry a little, but also bite his ear. Tell him that he has made you feel like a real woman for the first time. Tell him that this is what you were created for, and that you have found the ultimate happiness. He may have just wanted to sample the merchandise on a trial-run basis. But if you are smart, you can create such an emotional climate that he will be begging you to become his wife.[2]

The notions that copulation represented conquest for a man and surrender for a woman, that sex was a compounded sequence of discomforts for women, that they were weak, vulnerable creatures who were justified in using their 'sexual favours' to manipulate and take passive-aggressive control of men, were all implicit in 'How to Get a Husband'. The article upheld codes of sexual decorum – differently nuanced between the classes – which acted as bulwarks against masculine sexual rapacity.

Women were demeaned, if not incriminated, when they showed lust. During the Profumo Affair and Ward trial, the following words were used synonymously: girlfriend, model, nightclub hostess, dancer, artiste, good-time girl, Society belle, party girl, gold-digger, short-term mistress, enthusiastic amateur, masseuse, call-girl, scrubber, adolescent drab, common tart, prostitute, whore. 'Nymphomaniac' – the epithet used by men to devalue women with a higher notch-rate than they had managed – became prevalent at this time (it had been popularised by reviewers' descriptions of Justine, the voluptuous protagonist of Lawrence Durrell's *Alexandria Quartet* published in 1957–60). The notion

Harold Macmillan with his Lord Chancellor, Kilmuir, leaving St Paul's Cathedral in glossy silk hats in 1958. Discretion, conformity and restraint were valued in Establishment England. (Getty Images)

The Prime Minister in more vernacular mood at Earls Court motor show in 1957. Cheap little cars were a symbol of the jolly, complacent materialism and gimcrack modernity of 1957–64. (Getty Images)

Jack Profumo looking vital, eager and sleek at his Ministry of Aviation desk in 1953. (Popperfoto/Getty Images)

Valerie and Jack Profumo after their son David's baptism in the Crypt Chapel of the House of Commons in 1956. (Mary Evans/Interfoto Agentur)

Cliveden, the Italianate
show-place overlooking the
Thames, where Bill Astor
dispensed princely hospitality.
(Getty Images)

Bronwen and Bill Astor in
the grounds at Cliveden after
their marriage in 1960. Their
happiness was quenched and
their lives were sullied by
the events of 1963.
(Popperfoto/Getty Images)

Bill Astor's Cliveden jester, Stephen Ward – carefree, kindly, meddling and sensual. 'He was massively indiscreet, and loved showing off right up to the end.'
(Popperfoto/Getty Images)

Spring Cottage, Stephen Ward's Cliveden hide-out, around the time that it was burgled and searched by journalists. His parties there were 'innocent malarkey, swimming in the Thames, but nothing more'.
(Getty Images)

The pudgy refugee and slum landlord Peter Rachman at his cluttered desk in his chaotic basement office in Bayswater. (Popperfoto/Getty Images)

The house in Bryanston Mews West where Rachman kept Mandy Rice-Davies. Stephen Ward took over the tenancy after Rachman's death. (Mirrorpix)

Sub-editors toiling in a newsroom in 1953 to rake up scandals, publicise slurs and pillory the vulnerable. (Getty Images)

Hugh Cudlipp ensured that his newspapers were provocative in every issue and supremely confident of their own importance. They defied conventions, broke taboos, punctured pomposity and jeered at tradition. (Getty Images)

Eugene Ivanov, the Russian naval attaché. Journalists and Labour Party leaders pretended to believe the dubious tale that he had an affair with Christine Keeler.
(Popperfoto/Getty Images)

The Minister of War, Jack Profumo, with the boys and a new Saladin tank in 1960.
(Mary Evans/Interfoto Agentur)

The swimming pool at Cliveden where Jack met Christine and Eugene in July 1961.

that men were 'naturally' overpoweringly and excusably raunchier than women was pervasive. 'Nothing can stop a bloke once he gets into that state,' said a Hertfordshire man: 'be a hell of a job to do that.' 'The biological urge to have her overcame everything,' explained a barrister in extenuation of his client Harvey Holford who had married a woman fifteen years his junior, beaten and shot her dead. Dual standards abounded in 1963. When a night-watchman at John Bloom's washing machine company found an 'office girl' attending to a salesman with his trousers down, the man was reprimanded but the woman was sacked.[3]

During the Macmillan years these attitudes covered the surface of society like a stifling blanket. A small boy was taken by his nanny, around 1961, for a meal at a Wimpy Bar – a chain of proto-Macdonald's serving hamburgers in buns with onion rings and chips, in which his favourite treat was squeezing slurpy, sweetened ketchup from an over-sized, luridly red plastic tomato. On the wall there was a puzzling notice proclaiming that no 'unaccompanied woman', or pairs of women, would be served after 9.30 or 10 at night. He quizzed his nanny about this. 'Oh, they might be up to no good, you see,' she replied cryptically. It seemed a fixed public notion of the 1960s that any woman, or pairs of women, out at night in public spaces, without a man, were offering sex and contaminating their surroundings.

To challenge what many inwardly knew to be nonsense was simply not respectable. For all the talk of 'Swinging London', little changed in the sixties. 'Women still can't go alone where they want to without arousing adverse comments – it's even socially difficult when two women, without male escorts, go somewhere together,' Colin MacInnes reported in 1968. There were glares if a solitary woman went to a bar or restaurant: it was assumed that she was on the game. 'The Ritz hotel is the only place in London where the chic and the style are such that a lone woman is not frowned at in bar or dining room.'[4]

A splendid young journalist and features editor of *Vogue*, Siriol Hugh-Jones, browsed through the *Oxford Dictionary of Quotations* in 1961 to discover what male writers thought of her gender: 'women wail for demon lovers; wake to love; are weak and feeble; like dewdrops, fountains and troublesome cattle; a dish for the gods; the last thing civilised by Man; small-souled; and have no characters at all. Byron hates them dumpy, and Meredith deeply regrets that their sense is with their senses all mixed in.' Hugh-Jones recalled that when she was confirmed by a bishop, his address hinged on the memorable words: 'My dear little daughters, don't take yourselves too seriously.' She resented an advertising campaign by the *Observer* in 1961, which praised the newspaper's newly recruited film critic, Penelope Gilliatt, while insulting her gender: 'She is also that unusual thing, a woman who is a wit.' It made Gilliatt sound, thought Hugh-Jones, as outlandish as a woman with a green nose.[5]

The patronising mistrust of women was evident in a BBC television interview with Nancy Astor intended to celebrate her eightieth birthday in 1959. 'Do you think, looking back, that women are as suited mentally to public life as men?' she was asked. 'I think they are more suited,' she replied, 'because they're not so easily flattered as men are. I can guarantee any woman can get any man if she's got enough flattery.' The interviewer persisted in his belittling. 'A lot of men say that women are emotionally unstable, and that their judgement is therefore a bit subjective?' he asked again. Nancy Astor erupted at this vainglorious masculinity: 'I guarantee you can get any man, and I'll tell you how . . . [Bitterly] "Tell me about yourself," and off they go!' It was because of Nancy Astor that, when the introduction of life peerages was debated in 1953, Lord Llewellin wished to exclude women from the bill – not because they were ignorant, but because they were considered mouthy. 'Political women,' he declared, rummaging through his experiences with Nancy Astor in the Commons, 'are inclined to be "bossy"', with 'a tremendous number of bees in their bonnets'.[6]

If women in the Macmillan years were not gentle daughters or dewdrops, then they were Wimpy Bar sluts or bossy-boots. During the debate on life peerages in 1957, Lord Rea suggested that the title of future life peeresses should be 'Matron' rather than Baroness. The innovation of women MPs had not been 'a roaring success', claimed twenty-eight-year-old Lord Ferrers, who was rare in saying publicly what untold men muttered among themselves. If one looked at women MPs, they were not 'an exciting example of the attractiveness of the opposite sex', he complained. 'I hate the idea of your Lordships' House becoming a repository for over-exuberant politicians . . . Frankly, I find women in politics highly distasteful. In general, they are organising, they are pushing . . . Some of them do not even know where loyalty to their country lies.' Ferrers believed that nature and custom had decreed that men were suited to some duties rather than women. 'It is generally accepted that the man should bear the major responsibility in life . . . a man's judgment is generally more logical and less tempestuous than a woman's. Why should we then encourage women to eat their way, like acid into metal, into positions of trust and responsibility which previously men have held?' If women were permitted to legislate in Parliament's upper chamber, their emancipation might reach unthinkable extremes. 'Shall we follow the rather vulgar example set by Americans of having female ambassadors? Will the judges, for whom we have so rich and well-deserved respect, be drawn from the serried ranks of the ladies?' It would be a pollution to feminise the Lords: 'We like women; we admire them; sometimes we even grow fond of them; but we do not want them here.'[7]

Not only were women excluded from the upper house of Parliament until 1958; married women's signatures were seldom accepted without their husband's endorsement so that they were unable to raise loans or make contracts independently. When, in 1961, the Cambridge graduate Jessica Mann underwent a Caesarean birth, it was her husband who was required by the hospital to give permission by signing the consent form. The social conservatism of this period, as entrenched in the Labour Party as in the Conservatives, created pent-up rebellion. Its archetypal heroine was the near-angelic housewife, always unselfish and patient, spreading harmony, and making decent men out of horny brutes and dutiful children from filthy brats. The delightful radio programme *Listen with Mother*, which provided happy hours of intimacy for children and their mothers, represented an ideal that was worth striving for. The distinctions between uplifting ideals and delusive fantasy are, however, easily blurred.[8]

In Wilfred Fienburgh's autobiographical novel of 1959 about the Parliamentary Labour Party, an MP takes his young girlfriend on a Thames pleasureboat from Westminster to Greenwich. They sit together in the prow watching the Shell-Mex building and Somerset House slide past. He asks what ambitions she has had. 'All the usual ones,' she replies, 'to be a netball captain, a film-star, the lot, all at once. It's much simpler now. I want a home, a few round, bronzed, tow-haired children, a car in the garage and a sprinkler making music on the lawn.' As the solicitor Michael Rubenstein lamented in 1963, 'for young people today there is a tremendous build-up to the idea that marriage is bliss'. The make-believe that everyone should expect marital compatibility made disillusionment inevitable, Rubenstein thought. He deplored the sham whereby couples pretended that mutual indifference, lit by occasional sparks of reciprocated impatience, represented mature content. 'All over the country there are young and not so young couples, each partner bewildered, bored, miserable and lonely, but for the sake of the children, for the sake of public "face", for fear of the soul-rotting alternative – pretending.'[9]

Increasing numbers of people recognised the imperfections of their marriages: women were less resigned to lifelong discontent. Divorce reform was recognised as a way of equalising the position of women; and the soaring of postwar marital unrest led to the appointment of the Royal Commission on Marriage and Divorce, with the judge Lord Morton of Henryton as chairman. After five years of deliberations, in the same year as the new Sexual Offences Act of 1956, Morton's commissioners produced a vast tome, packed with inferences and laments, which was described at the time as 'official humbug'. The lawyers who predominated as Morton's colleagues were trained in precedent and the interpretation of statutes, and adept at musty, sententious altercation. They had no experience, though, in assembling or analysing social data. From fathomless depths of subjective ignorance they pronounced that the rising incidence of divorce arose from 'a tendency to take the duties and responsibilities of marriage less seriously than formerly'. They upheld a view of marriage not as a contract between the two individuals who married, but as the two spouses' contract with the state. Marriage was seen as a social institution rather than an emotional partnership. It served the greater good of society rather than individual happiness.[10]

Morton's commissioners were unanimous that matrimonial fault – the legal fictions of guilt and innocence – rather than a breakdown of trust and sympathy, should be retained as the basis for divorce. If marriage was a contract between two people and the state, adultery was a breach of that contract, and therefore one party must be punished as guilty and the other rewarded as innocent. Morton's commissioners had the mulishness of people fighting in the last ditch against insurgency. They even discussed abolishing divorce altogether as a way of curbing the renegades. Ultimately, they recommended that the abolition of divorce should be reconsidered if the divorce rate continued to rise. Just as the Sexual Offences Act of 1956 had to be amended in 1967, so the Commission's mindset was overthrown by the Divorce Reform Act of 1969.

Marital disillusion and infidelities were the stock of English cinema. Tony Havelock-Allan, Valerie Hobson's first husband, produced that classic film (scripted by Noël Coward) *Brief Encounter* in 1945. This tale of unconsummated adulterous passion between a physician and an unfulfilled housewife was first previewed in a cinema near Chatham dockyards. The reaction from the naval audience was so derisive that the director thought of burning the negative, but the themes of stilted cravings and emotional paralysis struck responsive chords among the

117

married middle classes. Hobson herself had a succession of film roles in which she played a wife in a failed or disappointing marriage. Her characters were coddled economically, but left with meagre emotional rations. In *The Interrupted Journey* (1949) she had the part of a middle-class suburban wife whose husband is eloping with another woman when he is caught in a train smash. In *Voice of Merrill* (1952), Hobson played Alycia Roche, trapped in a loveless marriage with an overbearing husband whom (with her lover) she schemes to poison. In *Background* (1953) she played Barbie Lomax, who agrees with her husband that their marriage is dead, and would be better buried by a divorce. Though their decision is rationalised to their three children, the latter are so grieved by the prospect of parents living in different houses that the adults' hopes of divorce are relinquished. In *Knave of Hearts* (1954) Hobson played the wife of a philanderer. In each of these films, the promise of conjugal trust and happiness was a trap, or source of frustration. Marriage in these celluloid versions connoted at best sterile security and botched compromises: at worst, humiliation.

Many adults knew this disillusion, from Downing Street to the housing estates. When Dorothy Macmillan accepted in 1933 that her husband would not divorce her, she wrote that she was 'reconciled to going on as we are. Of course that can't be forever but it is no good looking too far ahead.' In the event, the Macmillans remained together for another thirty-three years, albeit, as Dorothy said, having 'got rid of all illusions & shams'. She described to Nancy Astor how she had been summoned to Chatsworth for rebuke by her mother, the Duchess of Devonshire: 'She'll have to get out of her head that my soul is like a bottle being swept along by a raging river & that she & the family have got to fish it out, & that my body is a suitcase to be picked up & put down & sent off & watched! I am in point of fact 32½ & a human being & I'm not going to be packed about like a suitcase any more.' Dorothy Macmillan was desperate to escape the surveillance of her husband, mother-in-law and mother; refused to be either downtrodden wife or bullied daughter; determined to be neither doormat nor bird in gilded cage. Her liberty mattered as much as her lover. 'I've not gone off to Bob because of the children & I am perfectly willing to make a façade up to a point with Harold. As a matter of fact he agrees, or says he agrees with what I say, but he is so weak that if Mother tells him something is bad for my soul, he'll completely change his mind and persuade himself that it's his Duty to save the same soul.' She had told him that he could visit Birch Grove whenever he wished: 'it's his house, his children, but all I want is to feel that I haven't always *got* to be there with him & that I can go away if & when I want to, without incessant badgerings. If I'm hemmed in by the family & virtually imprisoned I can always go off, not to Bob, but alone.'[11]

More than once Dorothy Macmillan likened herself to a suitcase that was filled, emptied, humped and knocked about. Other women, too, felt they were being treated like bags. Wayland Kennet's study of Paddington prostitutes, published in 1959, quoted one who faked orgasms if paid enough. 'There's some of them lies still as stones, they think it's more ladylike or something; but I say they don't know which side their bread's buttered. Listen; if you lie still the bloke may spend half the night sweating away. But if you bash it about a bit he'll come all the quicker and get out and away and leave you in peace.' Indeed she knew tricks 'so that with a bit of luck they come before they even get into me. When they do I look ever so loving and say: "Traitor". Well, I'm not paid to be just a bag, am I?'[12]

Lena Jeger, a postman's daughter whose physician husband was Labour MP for St Pancras, worked with a family planning clinic in Somers Town until she went to the Commons in 1953 after a by-election caused by her husband's death. She reported that until the early 1950s, working-class women were loath to use pessaries, rubber caps, diaphragms or sponges. Women, for example, who inserted a cervical cap in expectation of sex with their husbands later in the evening, were thought to be taking the sexual initiative in a wanton way, which sullied them. A middle-aged mother of five, who 'fell again on the change', had explained why she had not resorted to the clinic: 'My husband says to leave all that to him, and that if I interfere with myself he won't have anything to do with me.' By 1962, Jeger reported, such attitudes had receded. 'Small families have become almost a convention, a status symbol, and those with four or more children often hasten to explain that this was by deliberate decision because they like a lot of children.' The changes in attitude and practice were partly attributable to the improved types of condoms – latex, and above all pre-lubricated – that became available in the mid-1950s. Generally, young working-class wives had come to despise those who failed to protect themselves. This overthrow of old prejudices seemed encouraging to Jeger because it had all but eliminated 'the exhausted, impoverished and prematurely aged, who used to come to my husband's East End surgery with their tormented little calendars of fear, believing it was "their lot" to have, as one woman put it, "one at the breast or one in the belly".'[13]

When Joyce Robinson married in 1949 she had no apprehension of loneliness and left her secretarial job to devote herself to marriage. 'My husband was then a hairdresser and we had a four-roomed flat which I could clean out in a couple of hours. Then I just sat around being married. Sometimes I visited friends for tea. After six weeks I couldn't stand it any longer, just sitting around like a plum pudding.' To reduce her drooping isolation, she took part-time work, which she relinquished when pregnant with her first child in 1952. Young children kept her busy – 'I thought it wrong to be away for work in their early years' – but 'if you spend all your time with young children you almost forget how to talk to adults. And the fewer people you see, the less you can think of what to say to them.' Joyce Robinson restored sanity by working two mornings a week as a builder's secretary: 'I advise all my women friends not to work at home. Go out. See people outside your home even if it's only at the bus stop.' Her husband, meanwhile, started working nightshifts in the telephone exchange at Slough. Joyce Robinson felt ashamed that she spent less time on housework than other wives. 'I'm always apologising about it and I shouldn't. I say to visitors in case the house isn't tidy enough, "Well, you must excuse us, we live in a perpetual weekend".' She felt that women who said they put their home and family first preferred housework to humanity. 'They put objects before people. The polishing must be done on Mondays or they feel terrible. I don't.'[14]

Many authority figures wanted to make the Joyce Robinsons feel guilty. Journalists wrote approvingly: 'Mum was a stay-at-home housewife'. Although the number of juvenile delinquents was infinitesimal compared with the number of mothers in full or part-time work, authorities, on scant evidence, insisted that working mothers caused crime. 'Nearly everyone would now accept that lack of mother-love is an important cause of crime,' declared Peter Scott, a physician at the Maudsley Hospital, psychiatrist at Brixton prison and Home Office consultant in 1954. Under the guise of condemning women for working, Scott indicted them for escaping domestic servitude. 'If mother works it may mean that she must do so, but quite as often we find that she scarcely gains anything financially; it is very common to find that what the mother gains in wages she loses in paying a baby-minder, in fares, in the canteen of the factory, and in a reduction of father's house-keeping allowance . . . what she really gains is a feeling of independence, and an escape from what her home has to come mean for her.'[15]

This was a time when physicians could be found to blame everything from autism to homosexuality on bad mothering. John Bowlby of the Tavistock Clinic wrote a shameful book, *Childcare and the Growth of Love* (1953), based on his study of atypical children who had undergone the extreme disturbance of being bombed out of their homes and housed in wartime institutions, to argue that small children experienced separation anxiety if they did not have constant access to their mothers. It was a key text in the emergence of a new craft called 'parenting' – a middle-class secular faith, with bogus scientific paraphernalia like Christian

Science – which justified competitive egotism by parents and reiterative fault-finding by parenting experts. 'When a child steals sugar,' the psychoanalyst Donald Winnicott propounded, 'he is looking for the good mother, his own, from whom he has a right to take what sweetness is there.' The salvos against wilful women, and their weak men, never relented. 'The boy,' wrote a psychiatrist about teenagers who stole cars for joyrides, 'usually comes from the rather better-class home, but he may have an over-possessive, dominating mother and, perhaps, an ineffectual father.'[16]

As some women began to assert themselves, working to improve their independence, status and satisfactions, expanding their experiences and choices – all of these advances made with crablike stealth – there were people intent on subduing or rebuking them. 'If I had my way,' Lord Ailwyn told Parliament in 1961, 'I would introduce a law forbidding mothers with young children to leave them all day and go out to work. Surely a woman with a husband at work should remain at home and look after her children.' Ailwyn wished to make family allowances paid by the state to mothers, 'these bonuses, or bounties, or whatever they call them', eight shillings weekly for the second child rising to ten shillings for succeeding children, 'conditional on the mother remaining at home and bringing up her children in the way she should'.[17]

The reprimands of Scott and Ailwyn were the protests of men who feared that the women of the Macmillan years could not be stopped from their insubordinate courses. 'The mothers of today,' wrote Cecil King of Mirror Group Newspapers, 'are so anxious to have a job or go out to bingo that they neglect their functions as mothers.' The respect traditionally shown to women was bound to be forfeited if they preferred jobs to 'self-sacrifice'. As late as 1979, the Secretary of State for Health and Social Services in the Cabinet of the first woman Prime Minister promised a radio audience, 'as the need for women's paid work outside the family evaporates . . . we may expect a gradual return to the education of women for domestic labour'.[18]

Increasingly during the 1950s, some young women rejected

semi-official, masculine notions of womanhood and shuddered at the idea of being a selfless *Listen with Mother* housewife. Significantly, women's broadcasters began the discreet, almost inaudible radio discussion of judicial regulation of sexual preference. *Woman's Hour*, in 1955, was the first BBC programme to utter the word 'homosexual': the innovation would have been too threatening during any programme to which men listened in numbers. Marjorie Proops of the *Daily Mirror* claimed to find in 1964 'a new don't-care-what-men-think attitude among females'. The fact was that 'women, after years of struggling to please, allure, delight and generally grovel to men, suddenly got tired of the whole thing'.[19]

Pamela Green – the first woman to appear all-but-naked in a British feature film, *Peeping Tom*, in 1960 – did not feel devalued by sexualised work because she made good money out of it, and made sure to control her own images. She was born in 1929, and enrolled at the St Martin's School of Art when she was eighteen. She paid her London rent by working as an artist's model, but found that she could earn better money by posing for photographers who produced the decorous nude studies, often lit to resemble classical statuary, used in such magazines as *Lilliput* and *Men Only*. Green, who was lithe with long blonde hair, did hundreds of topless or naked shots used to adorn barrack-room lockers and garage workshops. In 1951 she pranced in the chorus of *Paris to Piccadilly*, a Folies Bergère comedy spectacle starring Norman Wisdom, and staged by Bernard Delfont and Val Parnell at the Prince of Wales Theatre.

After a brief marriage to a stagehand, Green fell in with George Harrison Marks, a clapped-out comedian with a beatnik beard and drink problem. She taught him to pose shots of nude women, and to retouch prints. They sold discreetly wrapped postcards of nude photographs of her through Soho newsagents and some of the seedier bookshops. With the profits from these postcards she and Marks launched a magazine called *Kamera* in 1957. Green designed the costumes and backdrops, and posed in tempting disguises such as the sultry, flame-haired 'Rita Landré'. For other photoshoots she applied 'Pancake Negro' (Max Factor, boot polish and baby oil) to become an exotic princess. *Kamera*'s kitsch eroticism resulted in reported weekly sales of 150,000 copies.

When the director Michael Powell was casting the role of a model in his film *Peeping Tom*, he visited Green and Marks's studio in Gerrard Street, Soho asking for 'Rita Landré', whom he had seen in *Kamera*. After explaining her multiple identities, Green posed for him in a setting, which she had painted herself, of a cobbled Paris street with an arched alley. Powell not only cast Green in his film, but used her backdrop design in *Peeping Tom*. When Green reached the Pinewood film studio, she found it thronged with lookers-on, including the ogling cast of *Carry On Constable*, which was being shot nearby. In Powell's film, Green stripped down to a G-string to play a model who is murdered by a duffel-coated photographer who impales young women on the leg of his camera tripod.

'What *are* we coming to, what sort of people are we in this country, to make, or see, or seem to want (so that it gets made) a film like this?' asked the critic Isabel Quigly. It was 'the sickest and filthiest film' that she had seen. There had been sleek horrors before, 'but never such insinuating, under-the-skin horrors, and never quite such a bland effort to make it look as if this isn't for nuts but for normal homely filmgoers like you and me.' The voyeur-murderer had, as a child, been subjected to psychological testing whereby his reactions to cruel, terrifying and erotic experiences were filmed and analysed. These experiments stimulate a compulsion to ram tripods into young women's throats so that he can record their last agonies: he provides a mirror so that they watch themselves die. As accompaniment to his own death by self-spiking, he plays tapes of his screams as a tormented child. 'Children's terror used as entertainment, atrocious cruelty put on the screen for fun,' deplored Quigly. 'The madman murderer is played all through as hero – handsome, tormented, lovable, a glamorous contrast to the heroine's alternative youths – and dies in the sort of well-it-was-worth-it huddle with his girl that Cocteau used at the end of *L'éternel retour*.[20]

English sleaze merchants of the 1950s shot eight-millimetre black-and-white films, lasting two or three minutes, in which women disrobed, but stayed tantalisingly short of full nudity. These films could be bought in Soho or by mail order from firms that advertised in magazines like *Photo Studio*, and watched by men on home projectors. Pamela Green graced some of these. She also starred in *Naked as Nature Intended*, the first 'sexploitation' film, directed by Marks, who avoided censorship by persuading the authorities that five girls, scampering naked in a gravel pit at Gerrard's Cross, lobbing a beachball that during the shoot was constantly blown off by gusts of wind, made a sincere, even idealistic, film about naturism. 'Hello, do you come here often?' was the film's single line of dialogue. In 1964, Green featured in an obscenity trial after a Clackmannanshire schoolboy went to a showing of her nude film *The Window Dresser*, and afterwards confessed to his father: 'I cannot tell a lie. I am a ruined boy forever.' In time, she retired to the Isle of Wight, where she became a stalwart of the Women's Institute.[21]

This was the Mammary Age, in which the public became obsessed, wrote a commentator in 1957, with 'the Cult of the Big Top'. Diana Dors was Queen of the Blonde Bombshells. Born in 1931, with the original surname of Fluck, she was the daughter of a Swindon railway clerk. She attended the Rank Charm School but, after appearing in several flop films, Rank let her contract lapse. In 1951 she married Dennis Hamilton, a spiv whose father managed a Luton pub. Hamilton, who hit her and bullied her into abortions, exploited her platinum blonde hair, full lips and curvy figure to promote her as a 'sex symbol' – a term coined in the 1950s. 'Beneath her robust and open-hearted physical allure,' wrote Kenneth Tynan in 1952, 'Miss Dors conceals the soul of an ugly duckling, a boisterous and jolly child, eager to be liked. She is an unabashed parodist of desire.' When Marilyn Monroe became well-known in England in 1953, after her appearance in the films *Gentlemen Prefer Blondes* and *How to Marry a Millionaire*, Hamilton projected Dors as the English Marilyn. Publicity stunts were arranged for press photographers: once, for example, he sent Dors afloat in a Venice gondola wearing a diamond-studded mink bikini. Her appearance as a condemned murderer in the film *Yield to the Night* (1956), inspired by the trial and execution of Ruth Ellis, showed dramatic talent; but Hamilton ensured that her acting was sacrificed to her 'celebrity' status.[22]

The 1950s were the pioneering decade of the sex party in England: the epoch when an insulated lust, which had hitherto been associated with Continental brothels in wartime, began to be indulged behind the curtained windows of private homes. English sex parties fell short of orgies. There were no group antics or polymorphous exchanges. The male performers were anxious not to touch one another, and to keep their bodies – still more their fluids – apart. Hamilton held sex parties at the London flat where he lived with Dors. The comedian Bob Monkhouse recalled going to one at which 'stag films' were shown on a noisy home projector. There were wafts of amyl nitrite (a chemical that intensified men's orgasms) in the room. At intervals, male guests with starlets were ushered by Hamilton to a meagre bedroom with a mirrored ceiling. Monkhouse had fifteen minutes; Hamilton whispered: 'Make the most of it'.

In 1956, Dors and Hamilton bought a sprawling house called Woodhurst on the Thames at Maidenhead, where a bedroom – so the *Sunday Express* primly described – featured a 'draped canopy hanging over the bed with an inset circular mirror reflecting the eiderdown'. One of the spare bedrooms at Woodhurst had a two-way mirror through which voyeurs could watch couples performing on the bed. This mirror was later bought by Hamilton's friend Peter Rachman, installed in Rachman's love-nest in Bryanston Mews West, smashed there by his girlfriend Mandy Rice-Davies, and was later misleadingly invoked by lawyers, including Lord Denning, intent on blackguarding Stephen Ward. John Bloom, who invested in the El Toro Club in Finchley Road in 1958, recalled Hamilton as 'the king of this whirlwind world' of nightclubs: 'a big tough man with an apparently insatiable desire for girls and parties'. Bloom was abashed by the nude swimmers in the Woodhurst pool, and indeed by the parties: 'the whole concept of them – a hundred per cent sex'. Hamilton died in 1959 (depleted by wild living, thought Bloom), while Dors was seeking to divorce him.[23]

Later that year Stafford Somerfield, newly appointed as editor of the circulation-declining *News of the World*, determined to have smashing impact. He paid Dors, who had by then married an American comedian, £36,000 for her confessional memoirs which he ran under the title 'Swinging Dors' during January and February 1960. The memoirs supposedly boosted *News of the World* circulation by 100,000 copies. They were celebratory, but with guilty, punitive touches. 'At sixteen I learned to play a card game called "Strip Jack Naked",' Dors wrote. 'Those who draw Court cards become strippers. The others sit back and watch. If you draw a Jack you let yourself be stripped.' In adulthood she progressed to naughtier revelry. 'There were no half measures at my parties. Like flags being struck after a battle, off came the sweaters, bras and panties. In fact, it was a case of off with everything – except the lights . . . Every night was party night.'[24]

Out with the bad – in with the good – was the theme of Dors's confessions. 'As I look round the new home in Virginia Water in Surrey I now share with my husband Dickie Dawson – with its lovely indoor swimming pool and superb nursery – and savour my new-found domesticity, I shudder to remember what went on in my Chelsea home with Dennis. My cheeks burn to recall the succession of stage-struck girls who were betrayed under my roof – some willingly, others carried away by the unaccustomed attention of "top film people" and the drinks.' Voyeurism had a special appeal to *News of the World* readers, of course. 'It was all done by mirrors. But the mirror Dennis used was a very special one.'[25] Dors's memoirs were decried by the Archbishop of

Canterbury and the Press Council. She grew plumper, her film work receded and in 1967 she was declared bankrupt.

If Dors was the *ersatz* Monroe, then the glamour model 'Sabrina' (real name Norma Sykes) was the *ersatz* Dors. Sykes was born at Stockport in 1936, daughter of a factory mechanic and a seamstress who later opened a small hotel at Blackpool. She contracted polio in girlhood, and endured years under medical orders. At the age of sixteen she went to London, where she worked as a waitress and posed nude to decorate the backs of playing cards. She tried to get modelling work from Harrison Marks, but was rejected – perhaps because at that time her waist size matched that of her bust. In 1955 the comedian Arthur Askey noticed her picture in a magazine. He invited her to his office, where he found that she could not sing, dance or act. Her Lancashire accent, too, jarred. But because her measurements were now 41–19–36, Askey put her on his television programme *Before Your Very Eyes* as a 'dumb blonde'. Viewers were so enthusiastic about her bust that she was moved centre stage for the next episode. Her stage name 'Sabrina' was coined.

Soon she was hired to attend shop openings and publicity stunts. In 1957, for example, she graced the launch of the Vauxhall Victor motor car (a four-door saloon with chrome trimming and a touch of Chevrolet swank), and spent a night at Thoresby Hall in Nottinghamshire (newly opened for sightseers in order to pay death duties levied after the recent death of its owner, Lord Manvers). When booked to star in the revue *Plaisirs de Paris*, Sabrina was paid to do nothing but stand with her chest held firm. In Askey's boisterous comedy-western *Ramsbottom Rides Again* (1956), she appeared alongside Sid James and Frankie Vaughan, but hardly uttered a word. In the film *Blue Murder at St Trinian's* (1957) she was given star billing after Alastair Sim, above Terry-Thomas, Joyce Grenfell and Terry Scott, but played a swot who stayed in bed with a book, and never spoke. She bobbed in the background behind Dickie Henderson in a 1957 revue at the Prince of Wales Theatre. Every week she signed thousands of pin-up photographs. A young schoolmaster at St Custard's prep school, in the classic Nigel Molesworth school novel, had one such picture, and daydreamed about her.[26]

Sabrina's agent, Joe Matthews, was profiled in the *Spectator* of 1957 as representative of a new generation of self-made men. A cockney with a sharp weather-beaten face, he had discovered his flair for publicity when working as a stage manager. Then he opened a shop (flanked by an undertaker's and a supplier of jellied eels) selling photographs of American stars at 148E Lambeth Walk. During 1955–58 he operated as Sabrina's Svengali, managing her celebrity appearances and publicising her charms. Among his stunts, Matthews insured Sabrina's breasts for £100,000: she was promised compensation of £2,500 for every inch her bust measurement shrank below forty inches. Another device to curry publicity was to spend £2,700 buying a yellow and white Chevrolet for Sabrina, together with the registration number S41 (her bust measurement). Matthews drummed-up press interest in her romance with an American film-star, Steve Cochran: speculation about whether she would meet him on arrival at Heathrow airport relegated mine disasters from front pages. Dancing with Cochran at the Pigalle restaurant in 1957 she let her shoulder strap slip, and paparazzi snapped her in an expression of rapture.

After Sabrina scored a hit speaking at the Variety Club lunch, Matthews boasted: 'It was splendid corn – I wrote it.' The Variety Club was an exuberantly masculine showbiz charity with which he enjoyed cooperating. His reaction was different when Antonella Kerr, the Marchioness of Lothian, invited Sabrina to speak at the Women of the Year luncheon at the Savoy hotel. 'Tony' Lothian was a broadcaster who had spent her adolescence in Nazi Germany, voted Labour after the war and was married to one of the Catholic representatives on the Wolfenden committee. Her idea of an annual luncheon for women high-achievers – enabling women to meet one another and develop networks of shared affinities and plans, honouring women for outstanding work that was not headline-grabbing – was initially derided, especially by men who thought that the weaker sex could achieve little without male protection, and should either look like Sabrina or stay at home. Eventually Lady Lothian enlisted the support of Odette Churchill Hallowes, a survivor of polio and a year's blindness in childhood, who had been parachuted by the Special Operations Executive into Nazi-occupied France, served with the resistance, survived Ravensbrück concentration camp, and was the first woman to receive the George Cross. Lothian, Hallowes and Lady Georgina Coleridge finally launched these enjoyable, estimable luncheons, which also raised funds for blind charities, in 1955.

Matthews, however, liked his women weak and helpless, and revelled in the growing cult of ill-manners and brazen disrespect. When approached by Lady Lothian, he decided the uppity women needed to be toyed with and snubbed. There would be 'better publicity', he reckoned, if Sabrina disrupted the luncheon with his gimmicks. 'When a countess or something asked her to speak at this Savoy lunch I made all sorts of impossible demands like them hiring a special plane to bring her down from Blackpool. Finally they dropped the idea of her speaking. Anyway, she went to the lunch, and after the coffee walked out.' To the journalists who had been primed by Matthews to follow Sabrina, she claimed to be hurt that she had not been asked to speak, and read some wisecracks that were widely if not respectfully reported.

It was, as Matthews intended, an insult to all the good, strong women who organised and attended the luncheon (Sabrina's walk-out occurred during a speech by a Pakistani woman who had represented her country at the United Nations – just the sort to threaten Matthews' sense of male supremacy). With the rodomontade of one man speaking to another about a woman under his control, Matthews 'wouldn't like to say whether I think the kid's got talent ... Let's put it this way, I think the bust attracts 'em and then they realise that she has a beautiful face.' Matthews said Sabrina was 'not intellectually inclined. I've only known her to write one letter, and that was to me ... I've got her invitations to parties at which they've been dukes and earls, but it wasn't a success. She would talk to them for a bit, but they never seemed to get real friendly. They didn't seem to have much in common.'[27]

Sabrina was not so simple and downtrodden that she did not resent this denigration by her agent. In 1958 she took herself, with her earning-power, out of Matthew's ambit towards Hollywood. One journalist recalled seeing her at three o'clock in the morning, sitting forlornly at the white baby grand piano in her barely furnished apartment near Sunset Boulevard, picking out the tune 'I've Got the World on a String' with one bejewelled finger. 'You know,' she said, 'when I finally do go back to London I'm going back big. You know? I'll make those people who laughed at me laugh on the other sides of their faces. For a long time I didn't know what it was I wanted. Now I know . . . Just a little respect. It goes a long way. Respect.'

Sabrina went first to Australia, where she was swindled by a druggy impresario, toured Venezuela, and had a part in an American film, *Satan in High Heels*, about a burlesque dancer, her junkie husband and a lesbian club owner, which was refused a certificate by the British film censors in 1963. That year she returned to London, aged twenty-six, with English derision of her still rankling, to open beside Arthur Askey at the Saturday night Palladium show on 23 March. One interviewer found her in a Mayfair hotel, wearing shocking-pink tights and a body-hugging sweater. 'I've got eight minks,' she told him happily. 'They cost me three years' work. Not one gift among the lot.'[28]

Sabrina's Palladium run coincided with the public breaking of the Profumo Affair: she was knocked out of the photoshoots by Christine Keeler. It coincided, too, with the climax of the murder trial of a nightclub owner who had shot his wife, a case that provided some background noise to the Profumo Affair, and similar judicial bias as the Ward trial. This sad, squalid story was eloquent of young women's muddled aspirations, marital incompatibility, the legitimisation of male violence to discipline unruly wives, and men's angry fright at suggestions of sexual inadequacy.

In 1960, Christine Hughes, the petite, semi-literate or dyslexic nineteen-year-old daughter of a Saltdean confectioner, eloped with a man in his late thirties, Harvey Holford, owner of the Whisky-A-Go-Go coffee bar and the Blue Gardenia nightclub in Brighton. Journalists raised a hue and cry, which tracked them to Scotland. Her parents took legal action to prevent her marriage, but relented when she became pregnant. The Holfords' daughter, Karen, was born in 1961. Holford looked impressive, motoring through Brighton in a scarlet Pontiac Parisienne, but his bride's pleasure in married life soon waned. Marriage for her, as for Dorothy Macmillan, meant restrictions, demands and routines. In 1962 she and a hairdresser friend, Valerie Hatcher, left on a summer holiday together.

Without his wife in the kitchen, Holford, as he piteously told the all-male jury at his trial, was forced to subsist on Shredded Wheat and fishcakes. The lustrous summer heat made her voluptuous. In Paris she slept with a Swiss barman, in San Remo with a German drummer. After being ejected from her hotel for taking two boys, whom she had met on the beach, back for the night, she shifted to Juan-les-Pins. There she met Richard Reader Harris, a Conservative MP, who took her for a spin in his Bentley convertible.

In addition to being negotiating secretary of the National Union of Fire Officers, Harris was a director of John Bloom's company, Rolls Razor. Bloom was a boom tycoon who had been making a fortune in washing machines and had introduced competition to the retail of household durables. Washing machines offered emancipation to women from drudgery (one of the Hotpoint models was called 'the Liberator'). The lower-middle-class housewife Mavis Parkinson, in Angela Thirkell's novel of domesticity *Close Quarters* (1958), wept with relief when she won a washing machine in a raffle. The novelist Elizabeth Taylor in 1961 described a television advertisement in which a packet of soap powder, capering on tiny legs, sang a ditty before diving into a washing machine, after which a head of jostling bubbles appeared, singing too: images that were both patronising and promised salvation. Until Bloom, manufacturers did not compete on price, but spent large advertising budgets claiming high performance or technical innovations to justify the cost of their products. Some washing machines during the 1950s cost an average of six weeks' wages. Bloom supplied cut-price washing machines on hire purchase terms, and undermined Retail Price Maintenance: around seventeen per cent of households owned a washing machine in 1955; twenty-nine per cent in 1958; and sixty per cent in 1966.[29]

Christine Holford, Hatcher, Harris, Bloom and another couple went together to the casino at Cannes, then to Harris's rented summer home at Cap Ferrat. This was subsequently depicted as a luxurious villa, but was in fact a scruffy, sparsely furnished peasant cottage. According to widely publicised accounts, Bloom took Christine Holford upstairs to the only bedroom, while Harris slept downstairs on a sofa. Bloom's version is more plausible. According to him, six people sat up talking, drinking and dozing together until dawn. Christine Holford regaled them with stories of her bad marriage. She took no one to bed, but made breakfast for all six of them. Weeks later, Bloom continued, he met Holford for the second and last time – for tea in Harris's house in Montagu Mews (just east of Bryanston Mews where a gun was fired at Christine Keeler soon afterwards). They were shocked by her appearance: her hair had been shorn, her face was puffed like a football, and dark glasses failed to hide black eyes. Her husband, she said, had found her summer diary, dragged her to the edge of a cliff, threatened to hurl her off, and then beat her. 'There was little either of us could do to comfort her,' Bloom recalled. 'Her marriage was a disaster, and that was that. I never saw her again.' She was murdered a few weeks later.[30]

Holford's testimony at his trial was intended to devalue the woman he had killed, and secure a verdict of manslaughter rather than murder. By his account, his wife, after returning to England in August 1962, was obsessed by Bloom's wealth. 'She told me he had made £4 million in four years. She said he was so rich that in one day when his shares were up threepence, he made £75,000. She said: "Think what he would have made if they had gone up 1/6d". Bloom would install her in a Monte Carlo apartment or Mayfair house, she added. Holford referred to the recent suicides of Marilyn Monroe and the actress Patricia Marlowe. 'I said: "There are two women who had everything in the world that money could give them, but they did not have their happiness . . . You would be like a diseased animal waiting in the room for him to use you."' Holford and his barrister made a virtue of the fact that in cuckolded anguish, on 14 August, he had battered his wife with his fists – inflicting extensive cuts and bruises, a nosebleed and black eyes – before cropping her hair, later explaining it was 'the standard treatment in Germany for a loose woman'. After this brutality he attempted reconciliation, giving her a primrose-coloured Ford Anglia costing £440 for her twenty-first birthday in September, and taking her for a slap-up evening to hear Frankie Vaughan sing at the Talk of the Town cabaret restaurant.[31]

In an appeal to the jurymen's chauvinism, Holford testified that his wife boasted that 'foreigners were marvellous lovers especially Germans'. When he asked her confidante Valerie Hatcher why she thought his wife had slept with Bloom, she quoted Christine's remark: 'Such a big one for such a little man.' This 'shattered' him, he said. Holford, who worried about his potency, had been prescribed by his physician a desensitising ointment Nupocain, which was supposed to curb premature ejaculation, although it could hardly reduce the anxiety that triggered his poor performance. His wife's manner when they discussed sex was 'scornful and yet somehow triumphant', he testified. 'I felt like something that had crawled from under a rock.' One night 'she undressed and lay down first and said: "Come and show me how good you are".' But when he thought of her lying ready for Bloom, 'I just could not feel anything . . . I did not feel like a man.' On a later evening, when he spoke of his civil action against Bloom for enticement of his wife's affections, he claimed: 'She said,

"Don't be ridiculous you can't fight a millionaire and an MP." She said, "You are getting out of your class, little man . . . he could buy and sell you a million times over". After he called her 'a slut', she retorted that now her shorn hair had grown back, she was going to Bloom: 'He has got a bigger one than you, little boy . . . You can stop crying about Karen [their daughter] because she is not yours.'[32] Holford snatched a gun from a cupboard and shot her six times through the jaw, right temple, left ear and genitals.

While awaiting trial for murder Holford sued Bloom for alienating his wife's affections: the diversionary antics of this civil action softened the public mood before his criminal trial. 'Holford's wife was accosted in the South of France by a man known as Reader Harris [and] was taken to a villa where the enticement took place,' his counsel told the Court of Appeal. But when counsel added that 'Bloom devoted himself exclusively to Christine Holford, telling how rich he was,' Lord Justice Sellers interrupted. 'What has that got to do with a jury any more than a judge?'[33] The police, assuring Bloom that his name was being introduced to raise tactical confusion, declined to call him as a witness in the murder trial. They preferred a simple case to go to court because it made a conviction likelier; the defence repeatedly smeared the dead woman and Bloom, and the prosecution was complicit in this. These were familiar tactics: the prosecution in the Vassall espionage trial of 1962 accepted statements from the defendant which simplified the case, but were surely untrue; Lord Astor, Charles Clore and Emil Savundra – men with whom Keeler or Rice-Davies claimed to have gone to bed (in Astor's case, wrongly) – were not called to testify in Ward's trial in 1963 because their evidence might have made the accusations and denials too complex for a jury.

Holford described his wife as 'a marvellous girl and mother until she met that bastard Bloom', prosecuting counsel told Lewes Assizes. The star prosecution witness was Valerie Hatcher. 'Washing-machine tycoon John Bloom dazzled twenty-one-year-old Christine

Holford by the way he made love to her and by never-ending talks about his immense wealth,' she testified (pace the Daily Express report). 'In a whisper, Valerie dramatically told the jury at Lewes Assizes: "After her night with Bloom at a Cannes villa, Christine compared Bloom's performance with her husband's and said some pretty nasty things about her husband in the sexual sense."'[34] (As a reminder of the pressure for every man to be a super-stud, the Express's serialisation of Ian Fleming's On Her Majesty's Secret Service ran on the page following the murder trial reports.) Christine Holford's last letter to Valerie Hatcher was read out in court: 'Harvey said that I would be nothing but a high-class P and I would never be able to live with myself. It is very difficult because my feelings for Harvey are nil, gone, finished, kaput.' Also quoted was another letter to Holford: 'We can never be happy together and I would only end up being another Momma, cleaning and working seventeen hours a day.'[35] Bloom was probably not her lover; but certainly to her he was the saviour of overburdened housewives.

The trial's climax came when the wife-killer took the stand. 'Yesterday, weeping club-owner Harvey Holford told the jury trying him for capital murder how he shot his twenty-one-year-old wife Christine – his "Princess",' reported the Daily Express. He testified that she repeatedly complained (the emotive word used in court was 'taunted') about his sexual technique. 'Asked about love-making, Holford said in a low voice: "She seemed to become cold, frigid. She told me she did not think I satisfied her any more."'[36]

The judge, Sir Geoffrey Streatfeild, was sympathetic to the defendant when summing up to the all-male jury. The dead woman, considered as a wife, was 'an insincere, spoilt young child with but few tender sparks for him', Streatfeild said. 'Do you think you can really cast any stones at him for cutting off her hair?' he asked the jurymen. 'Who in the world in his right senses,' he also asked, 'would criticise Harvey Holford for bringing an enticement action against John Bloom?' (It should be reiterated that Bloom had been discouraged by police from testifying: his denial of an affair would have convinced many auditors.) Streatfeild stressed Christine Holford's comparison of the sexual prowess of 'this millionaire washing-machine manufacturer' with her husband's swerves between premature ejaculation and impotence. He alluded to her jibe that Holford was underendowed compared with Bloom, an accusation, said the judge, 'which for reasons of decency, I suppose, has not been printed in the newspapers and which preceded her death'. (This was no doubt Holford's justificatory gloss for firing his gun at his dying wife's genitalia.) 'Can you imagine any words more calculated . . . to sear deeply into a man's soul?' Streatfeild continued: 'Think of the contempt of the last words "little boy".' This belittling of the defendant as physically meagre, and pathetic in performance, was intolerable provocation, the judge instructed. 'How would any man react when the wife goes out of the way first of all to mock his sexual capability, and then, true or not, tells him the child is not his?'[37]

The jurymen acquitted Holford of murder, but convicted him of manslaughter on grounds of both provocation and diminished responsibility. He was sentenced to three years, and paroled in 1964.

The questions of male sexual ineptitude and ignorance aired at Holford's trial had seldom been publicly broached before the publication in 1948 of Alfred Kinsey's *Sexual Behavior in the Human Male*. The Home Office in 1953 was indignant at the 'disgraceful furore' raised by 'the gutter press' at the publication of Kinsey's sequel, *Sexual Behavior in the Human Female*, which hinted that 'the more a young girl allows herself to be lasciviously mauled, the better her chances of a happy marriage': such passages might 'encourage some youngsters to excess'. The chapter on masturbation was 'hardly edifying', but the most objectionable passage to the official mind was a section that might encourage 'pre-marital coitus' by stating that antibiotics provided 'simple and rapid cures for the two principal venereal diseases'. Misinformation seemed preferable to the Home Office's man: 'Fear of disease is perhaps the most potent factor in restraining many young men from promiscuous immorality . . . and to remove that deterrent gratuitously (even if, which I doubt, the assumption is valid) seems to me to be monstrously irresponsible.' The official concluded that parents would object to adolescents reading Kinsey's reports, but that the government need not prosecute a treatise that was 'long, technical and dull, and . . . expensive'.[38]

Ten years after these tense, repressive, joyless ebullitions from the Home Office, so clearly intended to spread guilt and misery, Marjorie Proops was being jubilantly uninhibited in publications that were neither dull nor expensive. As the agony aunt employed by *Mirror* newspapers, she assumed that newly married women would already be sexually experienced, that they could discuss their sex lives, and state their needs – although in the early 1960s sex in bed was still reserved for the married. 'He started kissing me,' a young woman said in 1962. 'He asked if I would like to go to bed with him and I said: "Only married people do that." When he asked if I wanted intercourse I told him only engaged couples did it.'[39]

Easter brides of 1963 were regaled with Marje Proops's advice. 'Most girls have had some kind of sex experience before marriage,' she wrote, but in the back seats of cars, dark doorways or 'swiftly, in the parlour, when THEY'VE gone to bed, with ears fearfully strained in case one of them comes down. The quick fumblings in a not-very-private corner at a crowded party, or the rapid assaults on each other in the back of a Mini Minor, do not add up to the kind of sex you will share after the wedding, when you will be alone and in bed together for the first time.' Once a couple had a marital bed, Proops hoped they would discover that 'sex is an art and not a fumble'. Because 'sex before the wedding is almost always shadowed by fear of pregnancy, guilt, terror of being found out', it was often anxious, inhibited and flat. 'Sex after the wedding is very different as you Easter Brides are about to discover. Lucky you!' She urged brides to 'tell him what you need and ask him about his needs . . . you'll discover the art of sex by experiment, learning as you go. And if you are a bit slow on the uptake – or he is – buy a book.' Proops insisted that sex was not a dangerous instinct to be repressed but a pleasure to be mastered. 'Take the myth, so often propounded by those who have very little of it, that sex isn't everything,' she wrote in 1963, midway between the Profumo resignation and the Ward trial. Prudes who asserted that sex was unimportant 'can't possibly have heard of Freud, who maintained it was the impulse behind everything we do, say, think, feel, dream. Without it (or without the best of it) life is arid, boring, wearying, unenticing, uneventful, uninspiring. With it (or the best of it) life is rewarding, exciting, moving, amusing, exhilarating and splendid.'[40]

Proops's cheery outlook was not in evidence when, in November 1962, the Italian proprietors of the Milan, a basement café in St Anne's Court, Soho, with a secluded corner nicknamed 'the Grotto', were prosecuted for permitting disorderly conduct. The police evidence had the tut-tutting prurience that the *News of the World* relished. Police Constable Thomas Jones testified that in one corner 'two couples were kissing and embracing. In each case the girl was sitting on the man's lap. One man said something to his girl who replied: "Well, you're not getting it here".' Jones had watched a beatnik girl dancing with a man near the jukebox. 'The girl was wearing a low-cut blouse and the man put his fingers under her bra at the back and pulled it . . . Then there was a couple known as David and Ann. As they danced David stroked the girl's neck and nibbled her ear.' Sexy backchat, teasing play with bra straps, nibbled ears – all this constituted disorderly conduct, or what the Marylebone magistrate John Phipps denounced as 'revolting behaviour'.[41]

Where should Christine Keeler and Mandy Rice-Davies be located in this terrain? Somewhere in the hinterland between Pamela Green, Diana Dors and Sabrina, whose 'sex appeal' brought fame and fugitive prosperity, and those young women from the industrial provinces who felt they had nothing to offer but sexual relief for the men who found them in the London streets. If Mandy Rice-Davies resembled one of Proops's modern women, who found that life without sex was arid, Christine Keeler resembled Christine Holford: chaotic, lurching from one escapade to another, sexy-looking but not always enjoying sex; improvising moves, and ill-starred.

Christine Keeler was born in 1942. Her father, Colin, was adopted and took the surname of Keeler from his adoptive family. He married a seventeen-year-old girl from West Ham, Julia Payne, in 1941, but soon deserted his home, and changed surnames again. After a divorce in 1949, he worked as a photographer at Butlin's holiday camp at Clacton. Keeler acquired a quasi-stepfather, Edward Huish, whom she was told to call 'Dad', although her mother did not marry him until 1976. The trio went to live in two converted railway carriages a few yards from the Thames riverbank at Hythe End Road, Wraysbury, a dingy backwater between Staines and Windsor where people lived in bungalows, shacks and caravans surrounded by gravel pits and grime. The carriages had neither running hot water nor electricity until the mid-1950s. There was no privacy: the child soon learnt the sounds and sights of her mother's sex life. At the age of nine she was sent to a holiday home at Littlehampton after the school health inspector judged her to be malnourished. She was bicycle-mad, tinkered with cars, built a go-cart, climbed trees, threw the javelin. Aged twelve she started a paper-round (earning fourteen shillings a week). This dim, larval phase of her life ended with puberty. As a baby-sitting teenager the fathers would try to catch her alone, to kiss, fondle or rub against her, which she loathed. After an overture from her stepfather, she kept a small knife under her pillow at night. He was jealous and aggressive when she acquired boyfriends.

At the age of fifteen, in 1957, Keeler got a job stock-taking in a London gown showroom. She tried modelling there, but the manager kept cornering her for a sexual tussle, so she left. Next she worked as a waitress in a Greek restaurant. She had some modelling pictures taken by a photographer in his studio: 'I was quite frightened of him because he was queer and I had never met one before.'[42] A photograph of her was printed in *Tit-bits* magazine in 1958. In addition to Wraysbury youths, she was involved with a Ghanian cleaner at the gown showroom, and a black American airman from an encampment at Staines. At the age of seventeen, after gruesome attempts to induce an abortion, she gave premature birth, in April 1959, to a son, Peter, who died six days later in a Windsor hospital. The episode must have been fearsome, lonely and numbing. She left the Wraysbury gravel-pit carriages shortly afterwards.

Newspapers and magazines became obsessed with modelling during the 1950s. 'If a scandal or divorce is reported, more often than not a model seems to be involved,' Dior's muse Jean Dawnay observed in 1956. 'Most of the girls mentioned just call themselves models for want of a better name. The fact that they have done one photograph at some time makes them a model in their own eyes.' Keeler lacked the discipline and perseverance for haute couture modelling: she was too quickly bored. 'There comes a day,' Dawnay wrote of the genuine model, 'usually after about five years, when she is sick to death of everything connected with fashion and would like to go round in a pudding cloth. She is fed up with the continual round of posing with vacuous expressions or artificial smiles, the endless making-up and hair-doing, the tiring fittings, the tedious showing to a continual sea of anonymous faces, the empty, empty words about new lines, cuts, colours.' It would have taken three days, not five years, for this life to pall for Keeler. 'In an age when time is all-important,' Dawnay thought, 'everyone seems to be looking for shortcuts in life and getting something for nothing with the least effort involved.' Keeler and Rice-Davies became quintessential short-cut, low-effort girls.[43]

At school Keeler acquired the nickname 'Sabrina' once her breasts developed: she aspired, perhaps, to be a Sabrina who did not have to work. Like other 'models', she found a job in a night-club, where her haziness suited the amorphous clientele who hoped to smudge their nights and blot out memories of their days. Anthony Powell wrote in 1957 of 'that anonymous, indistinct race of nightclub frequenters, as undifferentiated and lacking in individuality as the congregation at a funeral'.[44]

Nightclubs were also high roads into big money for their owners. As a boy of sixteen, Geoffrey Quinn sold wartime scarcities such as shoelaces, hair nets, perfume and nail varnish from market stalls in the Lancashire mill towns of Rochdale and Oldham. Conscripted into a colliery on Lord Manvers's land in Yorkshire, he absconded in 1943 to Soho, where he became a 'pavement pusher' or 'kerb boy' dealing in petrol and clothing coupons. He grew the pencil moustache that was the identifying mark of a spiv. After the war, he worked as a variety artiste specialising in mind-reading and psychic healing. In 1952, after changing his name, he started the Paul Raymond Variety Agency, based in attics above a coffee bar in Charing Cross Road. He staged such shows as *Folies Parisienne*, advertised as including 'The Banned Reefer Dance, performed by the Dangerous Girl with the Low Neckline'. The programme for his Burlesque of 1955 boasted that glamorous nudes would stand in poses imitated from 'stars of sex-appeal' including Sabrina's 'nationally publicised Nude Photograph pose'. Printed at the bottom of the programme, for those punters who were queasy, was a hygienic assurance: 'In the interest of Public Health, this Theatre is disinfected throughout with Jeyes Fluid.'[45]

Strippers had to remain as static as Dresden china shepherd-esses, not moving a muscle, to conform to the Lord Chamberlain's regulations on theatrical censorship (the official from the Lord Chamberlain's department charged with monitoring stripshows was called Sir George Titman). A striptease show in King's Lynn had to be shortened in 1957 because of freezing cold weather. 'If we shiver and move any part of our body during a pose, we would lose our licence,' explained a young woman whose act was to stand naked and unflinching while her brother threw axes at her. Her name, reported the *Sunday Pictorial*, was Margaret Shufflebottom.[46]

Raymond's Revuebar, which opened in 1958, engorged him with money (he bought the club's freehold for £14,000 in 1960 with a suitcase of damp, musty banknotes). It was a negligible setback in 1961 when he was fined £5,000 at London Sessions, where the chairman told him: 'Your establishment and others have been vying with each other to see what degrees of disgustingness they can introduce to attract members of all classes who are only too ready, out of curiosity or lust, to see the filth portrayed in this establishment.'[47] Secure in the Big Time, Paul Raymond bought a yacht, which he named *Veste Demite*, a Latinist nun's translation of 'Get 'Em Orf'. Raymond was the King Spiv: his Revuebar was the frontline of the new Soho. Keeler, however, got her break at an older-established outfit, Murray's Club, where there was no need for Jeyes Fluid.

Murray's was prosperous but fading under its elderly proprietor, Oswald Murray, called Percy by men friends, but 'Pops' by his girls. Sometimes he was said to be a wounded major from the Kaiser's war. In the 1920s he had kept a café at La Zoute in Belgium, until his wife (a local soubrette) abandoned him and their children. He ran a nightclub in Brussels before opening Murray's Club in Beak Street, Soho during the 1930s. To avoid the strict licensing laws, which prohibited the drinking of alcohol after eleven at night, Murray's was run on the 'bottle party' system. Customers pretended to be there by prior invitation and drank alcohol which they had supposedly ordered earlier. During Hitler's war it was an 'officers only' establishment from which other ranks were barred. Murray's Club looked tawdry by daylight, but ritzy enough by night. Murray's son David, who had served with the Special Operations Executive during the war, installed a revolving stage and a spotlight system which – skimping and improvisation providing keynotes for the 1950s – he cobbled together from car headlamp bulbs and tin cans.[48]

As dancers cavorted at the front of Murray's cabaret, the real draw stood in the background: beautiful, bare-breasted, motionless showgirls. The girls were beckoned during the intervals between shows to join customers at their tables, where they earned commission on drinks orders. Murray expected them to sip fruit-cup while they coaxed the customers to order over-priced champagne: the tally of drinks they got ordered were called 'scalps'. He made a show of insisting that his low-paid girls did not meet customers outside the club after shows, but this was unenforceable, and just a ploy to enforce discretion. Some of Murray's girls sold sex for money: others gave men a 'good time', and received presents in return. Probably a few were set up in flats in Marylebone or Maida Vale.

Keeler was one of the near-naked girls who stood immovably in the background during Murray's cabaret. Twenty years later, the journalists Philip Knightley and Caroline Kennedy interviewed people who knew her when she worked there: 'She spoke quietly and with effort, as if always trying to remember lessons. She moved very sensuously, and let men know that she was aware of the effect that this had on them.' The key to her attraction, Knightley and Kennedy suggested, was that she resembled 'a sexually aware twelve-year-old girl who has dressed up in her mother's clothes, put on her mother's make-up and is prepared to play at being a woman'. Their depiction suggests a teenager whose manner was both compliant and evasive, like a bullied child.[49]

It was at Murray's that Keeler met Ward. She went to live in his Bayswater Road flat, but did not become his mistress. He took her to parties: she had affairs, casual sex, and was set on course to be enticed and abandoned. A young law student called Noel Howard-Jones met her in Ward's flat in 1960. 'I was a randy twenty-year-old and here was this pretty girl who seemed available,' he recalled two decades later. 'I couldn't take her to my room, so we'd go to bed in Stephen's flat when he was at his consulting rooms. Sometimes I'd pick her up on a Saturday, and we'd buy a couple of bottles of wine and some food and I'd take her down to Stephen's cottage on the back of my motor scooter.' After a few months, the affair 'fizzled out', Howard-Jones said. 'I didn't drop her. She didn't drop me. We just dropped each other. She was disappointingly dull in bed, and after a while it was a struggle to make conversation with her. Once you got beyond clothes and gossip there was nothing left.'[50]

Jack Profumo seems to have been better satisfied by the sex: perhaps he did not notice if women were dull in bed; perhaps Keeler found him more exciting than Howard-Jones. Still, he too was dismissive of her conversation. 'All she knew was about make-up and her hair, and about gramophone records and a little about nightclubs,' he said later. These disobliging views come from sexual partners who picked her up and dropped her. Another man, who met her relaxing with women friends such as Paula Hamilton-Marshall and knew her only socially, found her quick, witty and good fun.[51]

'She is a very, very pretty girl,' Sybille Bedford wrote of Keeler in 1963. 'All the curves and lines are as good as they can be, the head has charm and grace, and there is a faint oriental touch about the face: the pure smoothness, the hint of high cheekbone, the slant of eyes, oh yes, no doubt that she could be devastatingly sexually attractive. But there are other things, and they are frightening. Not only the mean little voice is a giveaway, the look on the face is avid, stubborn, closed.' Bedford watched her testifying at Stephen Ward's trial. 'For all the sleekness, the sexiness, there is a lack of life, as if the sex were pre-fabricated sex, deep-freeze sex, displayed like the dish of fruit in a colour photograph.' She sensed 'a blank absence of spirit, a fundamental inpenetrability of the kind one associates only with the hardest kind of poverty'.[52]

Life was always less hard and battering for Marilyn ('Mandy') Rice-Davies. Born in 1944, she was the daughter an ex-policeman who worked for the Dunlop tyre company. At home in a three-up-two-down semi in Blenheim Road, Shirley, Solihull, she experienced what Penelope Fitzgerald called 'the inexhaustible fund of tranquil pessimism peculiar to the English Midlands'. Frustration was the ruling emotion of her childhood. She saw life as a tedious ordeal: 'If it was sausages and mash for tea, it had to be Monday.' She was an intractable, wilful girl, who seemed more knowing than her parents, and got what she wanted – including a pony called Laddie. The routines at Sherman's Cross Secondary Modern School were burdensome: she was racked with yearning for showy freedom and eager for the confidences of her classmates who had plunged into sexual affairs by the age of fifteen. She felt superior to them, though, when on evening visits to Laddie, she saw them dolled up in 'baggy mohair sweaters, dirndl skirts over multi-coloured nylon net petticoats and white ankle socks all set up for an evening's chatting up on street corners or hanging around the juke-box in the over-lit coffee bar'.[53]

When she was sixteen, working in the china department of Marshall & Snelgrove's Birmingham store, the shop staged a fashion show to coincide with the Birmingham première of a topical comedy film about the crime wave, *Make Mine Mink*. Mandy Rice-Davies was picked as a Marshall & Snelgrove catwalk star. Wearing a dress from the model gown department, with mink coat from the fur room and festooned in jewellery, her hair lacquered into a bouffant extravaganza, she posed for photographs with the film's stars, Terry-Thomas and Hattie Jacques. Primed by this success, she went to London to appear as 'Miss Austin' at the Motor Show of 1960. Soon she passed an audition at Murray's cabaret club. There she met Christine Keeler, who taught her about cosmetics and false eyelashes. After two months, she and Keeler left Murray's, took a flat together in Comeragh Road, Barons Court, and called themselves models. They starved all day, because they had no money for food and knew little about kitchens, waiting for men whom they knew from Murray's to ring with invitations to supper.

One distinction between them was their taste in men. Ever since her pubescent involvement with airbase Americans, Keeler had been susceptible to black men. Public opinion was so ignorant and backward in the 1960s that inter-racial sexual activity was anathematised: in the 1980s Lord Denning still worried about the risks of mixed-race juries. Keeler's involvement with black men was thought shocking and shameful. In June 1963, at the height of the Profumo Affair, J. Edgar Hoover of the FBI, who hankered for the imposition of sexual apartheid between blacks and whites, became fixated on Keeler's attraction to 'coloured men', and this solidified his conviction that British sexual and security looseness was a menace to the United States. His agents scoured London before corralling three US airmen, who were repatriated to an air base in Washington DC, where they were interrogated for days and subjected to lie-detector tests. 'The three Negroes had met Keeler in low-class nightclubs, generally frequented by non-Caucasian elements in London,' an FBI dossier noted. 'The investigation is designed to determine whether Keeler had attempted to pump them for intelligence data which they might have in connection with their Air Force assignments.'[54]

By contrast, Rice-Davies was drawn to Jewish men. She was squired by, among others, the property developer Walter Flack. Eventually she married an Israeli, opened clubs in Tel Aviv and converted to Judaism. One evening she and Keeler were invited to the Savoy restaurant by two Americans. There Keeler gave a shriek of recognition directed at a plump bald man with diamond cufflinks and handstitched crocodile shoes. His name was Perec Rachman. She had first met him when she and Ward were flat-hunting together, and inspected a flat in Bryanston Mews West which, it transpired, belonged to Rachman (whom neither of them had previously met). Subsequently Keeler had left Ward's protection and been kept, briefly, by Rachman. The Americans now discovered that the two girls' mix of artful backchat and trilling laughter could swiftly curdle. They were ditched after supper by their dates, who returned to Comeragh Road, where Rachman joined them. He arrived in the clutches of a possessive blonde who tried to boss the girls, and strafed the room with verbal crossfire.

Rachman eventually left after fixing a date with Rice-Davies for the following evening. He arrived in his Rolls, took her for supper and to bed, and when she had passed his probationary period, established her in his Bryanston Mews West flat. She loved its rose-pink carpet, green and gold upholstery and gilded Welsh harp in the corner. He forbade her to bring German-made products into the house. She said he tried to teach her French and Hebrew. He was so fond of vocabulary, she suggested, that he would be pleased that he was responsible for a new word in the *Oxford English Dictionary*: Rachmanism, defined as the extortion or exploitation by a landlord of tenants of dilapidated or slum property.

Rice-Davies was sharp and wary: she always wanted the gilded cage. Keeler, whose later fortunes were bleaker and whose divagations seemed unhappier, launched a tirade against her ex-ally in 2001. 'Mandy Rice-Davies was a true tart,' she wrote. 'There was always shock on her face whenever she thought she might have to do more than lie on her back to make a living.' She resented the way her ex-friend had exploited the Profumo Affair: 'Mandy handed out quotes as readily as her sexual services. I hope the sex was better value.' She mocked Rice-Davies's single-mindedness: 'Everything about her said "I Want to Marry a Millionaire"; she might as well have carried a placard.'[55] Rice-Davies, at least, lived by the *Sunday Pictorial* precepts of 'How to Get a Husband'.

SIX

Landlords

'Long ago in 1945 all the nice people in London were poor, allowing for exceptions. The streets of the cities were lined with buildings in bad repair or in no repair at all, bombsites piled with stony rubble, houses like giant teeth in which decay had been drilled out, leaving only the cavity. Some bomb-ripped buildings looked like the ruins of ancient castles until, at a closer view, the wallpapers of various quite normal rooms would be visible, room above room, exposed, as on a stage, with one wall missing; sometimes a lavatory chain would dangle over nothing from a fourth- or fifth-floor ceiling; most of all the staircases survived, like a new art form, leading up and up to an unspecified destination that made unusual demands on the mind's eye. All the nice people were poor; at least, that was a general axiom, the best of the rich being poor in spirit.'[1] Muriel Spark's evocation of the damage, dejection and deadly drabness of London could have been applied to the capital for a dozen years after 1945. It was a period when to pinch and scrape suggested respectability. Only head waiters and car dealers fawned on the nouveau riche. But when Spark recalled those years – she wrote in 1963 – the war ruins and shabbiness seemed historic. So, too, did the accompanying beliefs that discomfort was virtuous, mortifications were character-building and that millionaires ought to be quietly ashamed.

After 1957, Londoners had made a dash for modernity. Property developers like Charles Clore and Jack Cotton trans-formed the centre of the capital with a brutal phallic modernity that provided both the aesthetic and the ecology of the Profumo Affair. Cotton lived on the new arterial dual carriageway, Park Lane, with its onrush of traffic like lancers riding pell-mell into battle. Clore had a house in the parallel Park Street, a narrow one-way thoroughfare in which cars idled and edged forward, like infantrymen fidgety in their trenches, then advanced in tense rushes when the traffic lights at the corner with Oxford Street turned green, as if hurtling across no-man's land while being raked by machine-gun fire.

Mayfair, Marylebone, Soho and Notting Hill provided the terrain of the Profumo Affair. Its protagonists were Londoners. Lord Astor lived in Upper Grosvenor Street, two minutes' walk from Clore and three from Cotton; Stephen Ward and Perec Rachman lived a few minutes apart in nearby Marylebone mews; Jack Profumo lived by the Regent's Park; Christine Keeler shifted between Notting Hill and Marble Arch. Both Keeler and Rice-Davies had come to London to find money, excitement and the main chance, and to discard poverty, monotony and futility. The nebulous sexual market in which they were players had its counterparts in the London property market, and the rough new world of contested takeovers. 'The lasting damage to British society,' recalled a beatnik who became a hippy, 'was not committed by the hairy evangelists of permissiveness, but was the work of the property developers.'[2]

Isabel Quigly saw the film *The Seventh Veil* twice – once in London, and then a hundred miles away in the country. In one sequence the heroine was urged by a dissolute painter to elope with him to Italy. 'Do you mean to get married?' she asked. 'Oh,' replied the artist, 'I never thought of that!' The London audience heard this dialogue without a snigger, Quigly recalled, but in the country it provoked 'a long gasp, followed by such a cackle of outrage, mixed with a sort of whistling admiration at the sheer metropolitan coolness of it, as drowned the dialogue for the next five minutes'. England, overall, had a morbid fear of London. The dominance of London in national anxiety about morality intensified during the Festival of Britain in 1951 and the

Coronation year of 1953. Purity campaigners insisted that land-mark London required special protection from unruly or dangerous sexualities, namely street prostitution and male homosexuality. Sunday newspapers warned that 'immorality' in the capital incited misbehaviour across the country. London's supposedly expansive, invasive turpitude dominated successive moral panics and press stunts about vice. The report in 1957 of the Wolfenden committee devised the basis of nationwide legisla-tion on prostitution solely from the experience of central London streets and backstreets.[3]

During 1943–44, Patrick Abercrombie, Professor of Town Planning at London University, devised detailed plans for the systematic redevelopment of the capital to repair the effects of wartime bombing, to obliterate mouldering slums and to deter the jumbled sprawl associated with speculative profiteering. These comprehensive plans expressed both progressive hopes and social anxiety: planners wanted to regulate, control and repress the burgeoning, undisciplined development of London and keep it on clean lines; they believed that rebuilt, sanitised townscapes, with tight planning regulations, would create paragons of clean living. Spurred by Abercrombie, Westminster City Council proposed in 1946 to demolish 130 acres of Soho, rebuild and rezone it to meet the needs of impatient motorists, disperse its denizens, and concentrate the remnants of its population in salu-brious, purpose-built blocks of flats. This plan envisaged the demolition of the Royal Opera House in contaminated Covent Garden, and its relocation in the hygienic purlieus of Belgravia.[4]

Planning was enshrined in statute by the Town and Country Planning Act of 1947. This was the brainchild of Lewis Silkin, the first Minister of Town and Country Planning to hold Cabinet rank. He had been born in Poplar, a few months after Jack the Ripper's murders in nearby Whitechapel, the son of a Lithuanian-born shopkeeper who taught Hebrew. Though he won a mathematical scholarship to Worcester College, Oxford, his headmaster decided that the son of East End Jews was unsuitable for university

151

education, and kiboshed his chance. Instead, Silkin went to work in the East India Docks before mustering the funds for a year at London University. Music and country rambles were his abiding loves in youth: he used to stride through the countryside singing aloud with joy of life. He became a solicitor's clerk, and then a solicitor. As chairman of the London County Council's housing committee in the inter-war years, propelling schemes for the rebuilding of slums, he loathed the way that individuals made money out of property development. His aim was to remove the profit motive, and to bestow the ownership of development rights on local communities, rather than landowners or companies.

Few MPs understood what they voted through in Silkin's Town and Country Planning Act, which stripped development rights from landlords, and vested new powers in local planning authorities. During the 1950s the Labour Party propounded that housing was 'no longer a proper field for the profit motive, and must be regarded as a social service'. Local authorities, Labour proposed, should be empowered to acquire properties for 'structural rehabilitation'.[5] The act contained an item called the 'Third Schedule', which allowed owners of existing buildings to make minor improvements without paying the charge levied on all other building work to discourage promiscuous development and prevent the waste of scant resources.

Macmillan, who was appointed Minister of Housing by Churchill in 1951, rejected Silkin's creed of idealistic dirigisme as cumbersome and restrictive. His Housing, Repairs and Rents Act of 1954 abolished the development charge, but left the Third Schedule, which permitted buildings to be extended by up to ten per cent of their cubic capacity. This had few implications when developers were busy rebuilding bombsites. After 1957, however, they began demolishing older office blocks and erecting replacements with low ceilings, fewer corridors and stairwells, and open-plan offices. The developers not only exploited Schedule Three to achieve ten per cent greater cubic capacity, but arranged their amenities so that the working interiors far exceeded this percentage.

'Plot ratios' – devised in the 1940s with the intention of setting limits on the density of workers in given areas – were another factor. A plot ratio was the relationship between the area of the site and the gross floor area of the building. A developer could have a ratio of 1:1 by covering the entire site by a one-storey building. Alternatively the development could be set back from the road, so that not all the site was covered, but with more storeys rising skyward – an objectionable prospect to Silkin, who disliked the dehumanising scale of tower blocks. Developers cared only to cram as much onto sites as was permissible under plot ratio rules. The London County Council planning department, staffed by guileless milk-and-water idealists focussed on improving the housing stock, was startled by this red-blooded grasping. Entrepreneurs who resented any authority over them, and behaved to officials like quick, clever schoolboys making fools of fretful, unimaginative schoolmasters, enjoyed foiling the regulations and baffling the planners' intentions. Plot ratio was described by one player as 'a commercial joke and a commercial jackpot'.[6]

The lifting of building restrictions in 1954 by Macmillan ignited a London property boom which thundered on until 1964, when the incoming Labour government reimposed strict controls. Twenty-four million square feet of new office space was built in central London in the decade from 1954. Jack Cotton estimated in 1961 that the best office sites in Manhattan commanded just over £2 per square foot, while the best sites in the City of London were worth £3. Hence the spires and pinnacles, in cheap, flimsy materials, that soared in the age of I'm All Right Jack. The boom brought princely wealth to Cotton, Clore, Max Rayne, Max Joseph, Felix Fenston, Harry Hyams and others. It needed men who were traditionally disempowered but bursting with retaliatory initiative to see the possibilities, put together the deals, change England's urban environment forever, and act as forcing agents of change in the Macmillan era. The property developers were an assault echelon on the status quo as well as the literal demolishers of old England. The governmental throttling of supply and demand, which Silkin had enacted, created conditions in which these men became as rich as Greek shipowners or Texan oilmen. They aroused intense resentment. 'If you're making pots of money, you're exploiting somebody,' said a Tyneside miner and union official in 1963. 'You can disguise it any way you like, it's exploitation.'[7]

Local authorities ladled out planning consents for office blocks, shop developments and town centre schemes. Tenants were eager for space. Money was loaned on easy terms for the borrower: long-term rates were five or six per cent at a time when inflation was running at three or four per cent. Borrowers did not have to part with any equity. The return on cost of new properties was seldom less than ten per cent. The value of a completed building was not based on its building cost, but on a calculation involving the annual rental income from the tenant of the completed building, the length of the lease, and rent review provisions. These calculations could double the value of the property over its building cost. Private companies owning new buildings could be floated on the Stock Exchange with immense profit to their promoters. There was a bull market in the City which ran from 1958 until 29 May 1962 – the Flash Crash, when the plunge on Wall Street was the worst on any day since 1929. During those easy years investors could sell shares half an hour after buying them, and keep all profits tax free. There were some fifty property companies listed on the London Stock Exchange in 1958 (often family-owned urban estates); two years later there were about two hundred, most of which scarred the country with coarse architecture.

The developers hired architects with proven ability to obtain – swiftly – the planners' agreement to schemes with maximum possible density. About ten architectural practices were adept at the necessary negotiations and exploitation of loopholes. Foremost among these was Richard Seifert's firm. The property boom of the Macmillan era can be measured by the fact that he had twelve employees in 1955 and about two hundred in 1966. His buildings had the disposable modernity of sputniks and moon rockets, as their names showed: fourteen-storey Planet House in Chiltern

Street, near Baker Street station, completed in 1960; eleven-storey Orbit House in Blackfriars Road, completed in 1962; the oval Space House in Kingsway, completed in 1963 for Hyams, but left vacant for years; Telstar House in Eastbourne Terrace, Paddington, completed in 1963, but vacant for years. The office complex at Euston Station, which necessitated the demolition of Euston Arch; the Royal Garden Hotel ruining the approaches to Kensington Palace; Centre Point, creating motor-traffic canyons and killing pavement life on the corner of Charing Cross Road and Oxford Street; the Park Towers Hotel in Knightsbridge wrecking the scale of Lowndes Square. These were Seifert buildings which exploited the plot ratio formula in order to soar high.

Sir Mortimer Warren of the Church Commissioners admitted that most of the office blocks with which he was involved with Max Rayne, including Telstar House, looked as if they had been designed by accountants. On one occasion when Felix Fenston approved a development, his architect noticed that in studying the plans he had been holding them upside down. When Clore was asked of which development he was proudest, he named an ugly block in Southwark Bridge Road because it was 'one of the largest office developments in London' which had been 'built in record time', for Ernest Marples's Ministry of Transport. He scoffed at 'architectural triumphs which end in bankruptcy'.[8]

Seifert's activities showed that vital forces – individuals little interested in community discipline or collective virtue – were pitted against the orderly plans of men like Abercrombie and Silkin. The defeat of the pure-minded planners was like a parable of London sexual life, with the purity campaigners fighting a failing battle with the libertines. 'Kiss Goodnight, Sweetheart!' was the way that a jovial cockney called Joe Levy, one of the great estate agents turned property developer, used to show that he was calling a deal off. In 1939, when the leading prewar developer Jack Phillips, a desperate gambler, was going broke, Levy and his brother took over his estate agency. He also adopted Phillips's business credo: 'If you can't make a damned good living within three square miles of Piccadilly Circus, don't try in this profession. And never go into a back street.'[9] This advice for estate agents worked as well for sex workers.

A new generation of agents and property developers dominated the London scene from the late 1940s. Although most had prewar experience of the property market, they retained the eager pliancy of young men. Few of the agents who diversified into property development had sat the examinations of the Royal Institute of Chartered Surveyors. Indeed, the established chartered surveyors of the period, accustomed to prewar conditions of static or falling values, kept their minds fixed on present stability, and were poor judges of future possibilities. Traditionally they lived by their fees, and did not sully themselves with the profits of property development.

The first developments by Levy and his brother (in 1937) were three depots for the Dunlop Rubber Company in Mile End, Brixton and Greenwich; £50,000 for this project was loaned to them by Robert Clark, a Paisley-born mogul of the film industry. The Levy brothers both served in the fire service during the war, working three days at a stretch, with two days off. On their free days they did plenty of buying and selling as the bombs fell. After the war they resumed dealings with Robert Clark, and together formed a development company called Stock Conversion, which undertook a vast scheme on Euston Square which had been rejected by Clore – with whom they did many early deals. 'You never know,' Levy joked of his alliance with Clark, 'what can happen when a Scotsman and a Jewish boy get together. Why does it work so well? Because they would go blind watching one another if they weren't together.'[10] There were no grudges among Levy's business collaborators: he made fortunes for them. His last years were devoted to the charitable foundation that he established with his profits.

One of Levy's lucrative connections was with the Italian-born Charles Forte. Forte opened his first milk bar in Regent Street in 1935, and began serving a novelty called milkshakes. Further milk bars followed in Charing Cross Road, Oxford Street and Leicester Square. During the depths of postwar austerity, Forte began collaborating with Levy, who taught him the technique of buying and leasebacks of property. At Levy's prompting, he bought the Lyons tearoom at Rainbow Corner on Shaftesbury Avenue, near Piccadilly Circus, with a £35,000 loan from Prudential Assurance. By leasing part of the site to himself at rent of £4,000 a year, and leasing the rest to other tenants at £8,000, he achieved an annual income of £12,000. Thereafter he enlarged his fortune by property deals as well as catering, and became known as a property financier as much as a restaurateur. In 1950 he leased the Criterion building on the south side of Piccadilly Circus at an annual rent of £12,000, used its Marble Hall as a cafeteria, serving Chicken Maryland, ice gateaux and the like, and leased back other parts of the building. In 1953 – again advised by Levy – Forte bought the Café Monico site at Piccadilly Circus. A year later he bought the Café Royal building in Regent Street. Journalists nicknamed him 'Mr Piccadilly'. In 1958, Forte bought his first hotel, the Waldorf, for £600,000, which he raised by selling his lease of the Monico site to Jack Cotton for £500,000. He then arranged a sale and leaseback deal with Prudential Assurance on the Waldorf.

By 1960, Forte was a top table guest at Cotton's famous annual luncheon at the Dorchester hotel. He did several property deals with Isaac Wolfson, from whom he bought a store at Oxford Circus in 1961. Anthony Sampson noted the retreat of industrialisation under Macmillan and the ascendancy of the property men: 'The era of Nuffield and de Havilland is being succeeded by the era of Charles Forte and Jack Cotton.' Forte was 'one of the most respected businessmen in England', reported the *Daily Express* in 1963 when he bought 1,200 acres at West Horsley in Surrey from the Bowater paper-making family. 'Now he has joined the landed squirearchy.'[11]

The leading London developers were driven by 'a profound psychological and social need for acceptance', according to

Charles Gordon, who was a journalist on the *Investors' Chronicle* before becoming a consultant to the Clore-Cotton conglomerate. Their decisions were often the result of a defiant impulse that hid anxiety or lack of social confidence: they wanted to impress or annoy authority figures, ex-partners, competitors, unappreciative parents and resented siblings; big money for them was protective. Clore once asked his friend George Weidenfeld during a dinner, 'What do you really think of all these people I've got here? What do they think of me in the West End?' When Weidenfeld replied that some admired him but others could not quell their prejudices, Clore raised his voice defiantly: 'To hell with them! Who needs them? They're all bastards and bitches!'[12]

Developers hid their insecurities in schemes that were big enough to justify them doing whatever they wanted. The London property man was an 'insecure animal whose main drive is vanity and whose main passion is a worship of prestige', Gordon judged. 'His headlong quests for creating wealth, implementing deals, mergers, takeovers, is really a quest for approbation, not for money and possessions *per se*, not for power *per se*, but for approbation from people mostly as insecure as himself.' This was also the view of the psychiatrist Bernard Camber, who treated one or two developers and used to give them books by Alfred Adler, inventor of the 'inferiority complex'.[13]

The social exclusion of Jewish East Enders, exemplified by the sabotage of Silkin's Oxford scholarship, and Judaism's prized sense of difference, contributed to these feelings. The murderous savagery of the Holocaust mattered more. Many developers were lavish benefactors of the state of Israel. For them the days of submission and propitiation were over. They neither made apologies nor offered truces. They had the intractable anger that was voiced by the author Frederic Raphael in 1963: 'We tried being patriotic, we tried being philanthropic, we tried being everything, and it didn't do us a damned bit of good. If they want to kill us, they'll kill us. What does it matter what we do?

We'll do what we want to do and be damned to the lot of them.'[14]

The Macmillan years were characterised by an unprecedented consumer boom and retailing convulsion. England ceased to be a nation of shopkeepers, and became a nation of multiple retailers. Grocery shops provided self-service counters, supermarkets proliferated and retail chains came to dominate high streets. Some developers, such as Wolfson and Clore, were retailers too. They were aggressive modernisers overturning the habits and values of traditional business.

Margaret Stacey noted that, during the 1950s, in the Profumos' nearest market town, Banbury, traditionally minded shopkeepers did not open branches in the town's outlying districts, where there were only 'corner shops' or Co-op branches. Banbury's drapers, ironmongers and grocers had capital for expansion, but not the urge. They were sure of their social position and neighbours' approval. They felt no compulsion to make a show. Their reputation in Banbury as 'nice people', in Muriel Spark's phrase, mattered more than making as much money as possible. In delegating to branch managers they would forfeit personal contacts, which they prized, between 'gaffer' and employee, and between shopkeeper and customer. If the expansion failed, the shopkeeper's business would succumb, and he would lose his standing in the town. If he prospered, he would outclass his peers, and be cast adrift socially: his acceptance in richer strata would be slow. It was men with these gently self-limiting values whom Wolfson and Clore, mercenary rebels or freebooters, were putting out of business.[15]

Anthony Sampson in 1962 named five men as the foremost corporate raiders whose takeovers had made them 'the heads of colossal empires' within the previous ten years: Isaac Wolfson, Charles Clore, Hugh Fraser, Cecil King and Roy Thomson. Of these, Wolfson, though he was at Cliveden during the weekend when Profumo met Keeler, had no part in the Affair. Cecil King, however, figured in it. Clore was the 'Charles' who featured in Stephen Ward's trial. Although Keeler later denied that she had sex with him, a different tale was told in order to convict Ward. Rice-Davies, too, claimed Clore as a sexual partner. Walter Flack, Clore's co-director at City Centre Properties, was also numbered among her protectors. Perec Rachman, who kept both Keeler and Rice-Davies, is the third property dealer who featured in the Profumo Affair – most infamously of all, as it proved.

Charles Clore's parents had shifted to London to escape the anti-Semitism and russification of their native Latvia. He was born in 1904 in Mile End. He nearly drowned as a small boy, and thereafter was scared of getting out of his depth: literally, for the swimming pool at his country house was only chest deep and he always donned waterwings in it. Figuratively, too, he kept on land that was under his control. He stood apart as a child, always neat and unruffled, never joining the boisterous street games of his East End boyhood. When young he worked in his father's textile business and lived with his family at 18 Elm Park Avenue, Tottenham. In 1928 he became licensee of the Electric Palace Cinema in Cricklewood, and two years later of the Super Cinema in Walthamstow.

Next he became licensee of the Prince of Wales Theatre, which had a prime site between Piccadilly Circus and Leicester Square. In 1934 he was nominally responsible for staging a revue there, *Sourire de Paris*, a licentious slapstick in which plumbers interrupted a honeymooning couple, and men shoved a pretty girl behind a curtain and emerged flourishing her corset and knickers. The reactionary prudes of the Lord Chamberlain's Department insisted as conditions of the revue being staged on the non-suggestive pronunciation of the surname Winterbottom, and the deletion of a scene in which a man blew a raspberry at his wife, together with all mention of the Marquis de Sade. After the play had opened, the official censor George Titman attended a performance. 'It was a tawdry and vulgar entertainment and quite unworthy of a West End Theatre,' he reported; a comedian produced 'a very decided "raspberry", made with his hand and mouth . . . I consider it gross impertinence to include this filthy noise'. At the Lord Chamberlain's instigation, Clore was convicted on 21 February 1934 and fined £16 with nine guineas costs, for breaching the censorship regulations. 'The average Englishman finds vulgarity and filth repugnant,' fumed the magistrate who fined Clore after warning that the reputation of all London theatres was injured by this 'disgusting stuff'. Although Titman privately wrote that 'during these proceedings, Mr Clore has behaved in an exemplary manner, and I believe his concern at being in conflict with the Lord Chamberlain to be genuine', the affair of the blown raspberry was preserved in Metropolitan Police files, where it was treated as if Clore had been convicted of obscenity. A few months later, Scotland Yard received an anonymous letter denouncing Clore for 'attempting to procure chorus girls . . . for immoral purposes', but detectives found no evidence to support this allegation.[16]

Clore in 1939 led a syndicate that paid £250,000 to buy the London Casino, a cabaret restaurant with a revolving circular dance floor, in Old Compton Street, Soho (now the Prince Edward Theatre). Reporting this deal, *The Times* described Clore as 'a well-known dealer in property'. In official papers he called himself, on the basis of owning the Token Construction Company, a government building contractor. His purchase for £120,000 of the Dowager Countess of Seafield's 50,000-acre Balmacaan estate in Inverness-shire led to parliamentary questions in 1943, and a request by the Secretary of State for Scotland for a confidential Scotland Yard investigation of this 'land speculator'. The request was handled by Sir Norman Kendal, Assistant Commissioner of Metropolitan Police, who shortly before the German invasion of Poland in 1939 had cancelled an official visit to the Nazis which would have included a lecture on policing methods by SS-Gruppenführer Reinhard Heydrich and a tour of the Dachau facilities. ('I am more sorry than I can tell you to miss seeing you and all my other friends,' Kendal wrote to Heydrich's deputy, 'but we must hope for better luck some other time.') Little surprise, then, that Kendal characterised Clore to the Chief Constable of Edinburgh, for the Secretary of State's information, as 'an unscrupulous Jew upon whose word no reliance whatever can be placed', and reported a hotchpotch of hearsay, before concluding, 'anyone having any dealings with him must keep both eyes wide open'.[17]

After D-Day in 1944, Clore began buying commercial sites. His company directorships proliferated. He was targeted in further anonymous letters to Scotland Yard and the Director of Public Prosecutions ('Clore is a Jew of the worst type who flagrantly flouts the laws and traffics generally in black market business,' began one denunciation, eighteen months after the enormity of the Holocaust was known); but police enquiries found no grounds to prosecute him.[18]

It was Clore in 1953, rather than, as has been claimed, Siegmund Warburg in 1958, who masterminded the first-ever hostile takeover, in which a controlling shareholding in a public company was bought on the open market with the intention of ousting the company's management and board. Clore's target was J. Sears' Tru-Form Boot Company, which owned 950 footwear shops, and several factories. Stealthily, he bought Sears shares, through nominees, and accumulated a secret 'warehoused' holding. Then, without prior consultation with the Sears directors, at a time when their company's shares were valued at about fourteen shillings, and yielded an income of about fourpence a share, he offered forty shillings in cash for each share, combined with an alternative offer whereby the shareholders could retain twenty per cent of their equity interest. Shareholders who took this option did well. There was a furious battle, with much retaliatory newspaper comment, all of which Clore relished. The Sears directors tried to rally their shareholders' support with the assurance that over £6 million could be raised by selling properties. As the properties were valued in Sears's books at £2.3 million, irritated shareholders voted for Clore, who got control of seventy per cent of the equity. He sold the freeholds of the shoe shops to insurance companies at a large capital profit, but continued to sell shoes from them. After the Sears deal, Brendan Bracken traduced Clore as one of 'the invading Israelites'.[19]

Contested takeovers suited the brutality of Clore's character. 'The phrase "takeover bid"', said the Labour politician Anthony Crosland in 1954, 'conjures a picture, half-glamorous and half-repellent, of tough, astute and immensely rich financiers coolly gambling on the Stock Exchange for stakes that are measured in millions of pounds.' It was a moot question, thought Crosland, whether to call such men the 'apotheosis of the spiv' or the 'best type of merchant adventurer'. Either way, they repudiated traditional notions of respectability and trampled accepted codes of behaviour. Their bounds seemed illimitable. In 1963, in a satirical song about parvenus, Michael Flanders and Donald Swann sang: 'Hell has just been taken over by a friend of Charlie Clore.'[20]

The developers were proud of being danger men. They were not public school boys trained by rules about the number of buttons that might be fastened on a blazer, or to venerate spurious traditions. They scorned, and in turn were despised by, the old guard. 'For a long time there has been no fundamental change in the board,' Sir John Hanbury-Williams, chairman of Courtaulds, mused in 1952. 'There has been a Gentlemen's Club atmosphere in the Board Room, and it is true to say that over the years this has spread to all Departments of our business. It is, in fact, part of the goodwill of the Company, which we must safeguard.' Similarly, the financial coordinator of Shell who emphasised that profit was the prime end of business was told to 'tone it down a bit'. One of ICI's divisional chairmen said proudly: 'We think of ourselves as being a university with a purpose.' Another senior ICI man had an alternate corporate ideal: 'We are very similar to the Administrative Class of the Civil Service.' The military baronet who was Director General of the Institute of Directors described his organisation with satisfaction in 1962 as 'a gigantic Old Boy network'. Men who thought like this were as much Clore's prey as the Banbury shopkeepers.[21]

Clore acquired other shoe retailers, such as Dolcis (250 shops bought for £5.8 million in 1956), combining these into the British Shoe Corporation, which in the 1960s controlled almost one-quarter of the British retail shoe trade. His other acquisitions included the Mappin and Webb jewellery group in 1957 and Lewis's Investment Trust (controlling Selfridges) in 1965. His property company, City and Central Investments, spent years acquiring land near Park Lane and obtaining planning permissions to build a skyscraper hotel, for which in 1960 Clore signed a contract with the American hotelier Conrad Hilton. One passer-by, who blanched at the hotel's execrable design, commented in 1963: 'I resent belonging to a society which gets, for instance, such things as London's new Hilton hotel.'[22]

Early in Queen Elizabeth II's reign, Clore and his wife were launched in London Society by Loelia, Duchess of Westminster, who oversaw the guest list of their first ball and coaxed the smart and worldly to accept Clore's invitations. 'They liked "Charlie boy" for his malapropisms and social gaffes, and they liked him even more when his French wife . . . left him to stand on his own unsteady social feet,' wrote his friend George Weidenfeld, who 'watched the interplay between the newly risen tycoon and his socially unassailable mentors with fascination and amusement. I loved Charlie Clore for himself and because he provided priceless anthropological source material.' Soon, according to Beaverbrook, Clore ranked with Niarchos and Onassis, the Greek shipowners, as the social leaders on the French Riviera – besought at parties from Monte Carlo to Cannes. When approached in 1962 by the Society magazine *Queen* for a profile, he allowed them to photograph the prize cow of his Berkshire farm, but refused to be quoted: 'I haven't got a bad eye at ping-pong,' was almost his only on-the-record remark. He had an imperious presence. 'All his life,' wrote Charles Gordon, 'he had the feeling of divine right, that he was superior.' His privileges had to be indisputable: he was resolved never to make amends. If he suspected that his staff served him less than the best, they were given a drubbing. It was unforgivable to serve him with pears for dessert: pears were 'provincial – his most pejorative word'; for him only the choicest, out-of-season grapes would satisfy. 'He worshipped at only one altar: money,' Gordon continued. 'His grasping for it was a form of gluttony, an appetite that was never satisfied.'[23]

Clore declared that he was always unhappy and had never known anyone who could truthfully say they were happy. His sexual pride and possessiveness were outraged when his wife left him in 1956. Thereafter he embarked on a libidinous rampage that lasted almost until his death. 'His virility and his appetite for women unnerved many of his social and business acquaintances, leading them to accept a subordinate status in their personal relationships and therefore inferior terms in their business transactions with him,' Gordon said. 'He would always win. He would always get what he wanted. Not only all the money in the world, but all the girls in the world. Girls were for his pleasure, the taller and younger the better, and every night if possible, right into his seventies until his final illness. In his prime it was any girl of any social level. All that mattered was availability.' Some businessmen, who wanted to make deals with him, procured girls for him. 'His sexual will was indomitable. Some women were attracted by it; others fought it and succumbed; others were repelled by it.' Dinner parties were ruined by his relentless groping of women sitting beside him, whom he had first met only an hour earlier. 'He couldn't wait; he had to have it now. He hadn't the slightest concern for the sexual niceties.'[24]

Henry Fairlie egged Macmillan to recommend Clore for a life peerage in 1961: 'I would not be the only one who would attend the House of Lords if it was known that Lord Clore was to take part in the annual debate on the Budget.' But when Simon Raven in 1962 decried the 'money-grubbing' modernisers and 'hatchet-faced middlemen guzzling smoked salmon in Quaglino's', who wished to replace 'complacency, nepotism, charm, the amateur spirit' with barbarisms like 'technical efficiency, professionalism, smart sales talk', he showed the forces arrayed against Clore.[25]

Clore liked to move among the gentile aristocracy. Lord Fermoy, whose granddaughter became Diana, Princess of Wales, was his first ornamental 'guinea-pig' director – of a company underwriting capital issues formed in 1937. He regarded the Fermoy class, as he did most people, with contempt. When he went to Deauville for the August races he could be seen scrutinising the banquettes in the bar of his hotel to find someone who wanted to be seen having a drink with Charlie Clore. There was always someone who would buy Clore's drinks, consult his views, nod keenly at his gruff, disobliging remarks, and (if his stooge were accompanied by a young second wife) tolerate her being undressed by Clore's sharp, cold eyes or groped by his small manicured hands. He said that he would never marry his long-term companion, the Marchioness of Milford Haven, because what he liked best about her was her title. He cherished his East End accent, and liked to disrupt smart dinners with the remark: 'I'm just a little Jewish boy who has learned one or two things in life.'[26]

Clore was the embodiment of the modernisation crisis in Macmillan's England. That he was a breaker as well as a builder was shown by the scuppering of two men, Jack Cotton and Walter Flack, after Clore agreed in 1960 to merge his City and Central Investments property portfolio with their City Centre Properties.

Jack Cotton was born at Edgbaston in 1903. His father was an import-export merchant trading in silver plate cutlery, and treasurer of Birmingham's chief synagogue. When he passed the examinations of the Auctioneers' Institute, his mother lent him £50 with which, on his twenty-first birthday, he opened his own estate agency in Birmingham. Cotton acted as a middleman between farmers and speculative builders interested in suburban ribbon development around Birmingham in the early 1930s. His first great development was peculiarly satisfying: the demolition of King Edward VI Grammar School in Birmingham, where as a pupil he had been victimised, and its replacement by an office block. Cotton had completed his education at Corinth House, a special boarding house for Jewish boys at Cheltenham College. The housemaster, Daniel Lipson, was elected in a famous by-election of 1937 as the Independent Conservative MP for Cheltenham after members of the constituency party refused to endorse the candidature of a Jew; he was accepted as a Conservative by the Prime Minister, Chamberlain, but Cheltenham Conservative Association continued to refuse him membership.

During the war Cotton served in the Home Guard and was employed by the government in factory building. He was a British delegate of the World Jewish Congress in 1945, and visited the USA to promote emigration to Palestine. In the early months of peace, he was expelled from the Auctioneers' Institute after a dodgy deal. He left Birmingham, separating from his wife around the same time, and moved into suite 120 at the Dorchester hotel on Park Lane. Cecil Beaton described the Dorchester's habitués around this time as 'Cabinet Ministers and their self-consciously respectable wives; hatchet-jawed, iron grey brigadiers; calf-like airmen off duty; tarts on duty; actresses (also); *déclassé* Society people; cheap musicians; and motor-car agents.' So, too, did Elizabeth Bowen's lover, Charles Ritchie: 'In the Dorchester the sweepings of the Riviera have been washed up – pot-bellied, sallow, sleek-haired nervous gentlemen with loose mouths and wobbly chins, wearing suede shoes and checked suits, and thin painted women with fox capes, long silk legs and small artificial curls.' It was a rendezvous of new-money millionaires, and old. Associated with the Dorchester, too, were the 'Hyde Park Rangers', as Park Lane street-walkers were known. They warmed themselves on cold nights by an air vent known as 'the hotplate' at the hotel's rear.[27]

Cotton could stroll along any street in central London, or provincial high street, and value each site. He took fast decisions which investors trusted. He imbued confidence in nervous money men. When his schemes grew too big for his company City Centre Properties to finance alone, he entered development partnerships with Legal and General Assurance and Pearl Insurance – collaborations that were widely copied. Cotton was the first developer to realise that pension funds were better partners than insurance companies because their investment managers could take a longer view. The pension funds of ICI, Imperial Tobacco, and Unilever had all financed his developments by the early 1960s.

When Cotton's daughter married a stockbroker in 1957, he rented a special train to carry guests from the ceremony in Birmingham to the reception in London. Newspaper headlines about 'The Mink and Champagne Express' stood above tales of his ostentatious hospitality. Cotton relished the attention, which felt like a tribute to him. Thenceforth he was always available to journalists, and thrived as a capitalist for the headlines. In 1958 he had an attack of mumps which left distressing after-effects. To compensate for his diminished potency, Cotton became 'over-assertive and hyper-active', said Gordon, who saw him often. 'His constant search for new partners, his striving for new associations, new friends, new projects, his accelerating all-consuming obsession with publicity were part of his attempt . . . to find a substitute for his loss of virility.' Cotton was racked by Clore's sexual arrogance. His envy of other men's potency gnawed at him. He became obsessed with size. As he admitted in 1962, 'I feel I'm growing smaller as I grow older.'[28]

Buildings erected by City Centre Properties had to be big and obvious. His most enduring monuments were phallic eyesores like the Big Top shop complex in Birmingham or the misnamed Campden Hill Towers at Notting Hill Gate. There was monotony, Cotton felt, in districts where buildings were the same height. He thought his developments brought thrills to the skyline. 'Have you been through Notting Hill lately?' he asked an interviewer. 'Well, go and look. There you get an example of broken skyline with a very tall block of flats and lower units near it, and your eyes travel up.' A man who lived in the shadow of this development recorded how his house shuddered as for months the mechanical pile-drivers slammed down every few seconds. Cracks appeared in several rooms: it was like being under German aerial bombardment.[29]

Cotton lived with the ex-nanny of his children. He treasured a small, ginger teddy bear in a striped blazer inscribed: 'I may look busy. I am the boss.' He collected miniature bottles, and laughed uproariously at the Crazy Gang. Paintings by Renoir and Fantin-Latour hung on the walls of his Dorchester suite. An Osbert Lancaster cartoon in the *Daily Express* of 1962 featured a caricature of a Jewish plutocrat, clutching a cigar and sitting beneath a picture of an ugly skyscraper resembling the Hilton hotel: 'Withdraw that offer for Berkeley Square and buy a Renoir – quick!' he barks into his telephone. The Dorchester suite became a haunt from which Cotton's truer friends were expelled by sly sycophants, who plied him with booze in the hope of tempting him to market tips. Solitude was intolerable to him. His armada of vehicles was headed by a monarchical Rolls-Royce, with the number plate JC1, and descended to a shooting brake, JC9. He trademarked his spruce, gleaming appearance by sporting a bow tie which matched the folded handkerchief in his breast pocket; there was usually a red carnation in his buttonhole from the greenhouses at his Marlow-on-Thames home. His exuberant showmanship reminded one interviewer of an impresario. Another journalist, who found Cotton's accent 'hard to place', likened him to a leading actor: 'pink face, sensitive nose and mouth, and dark hair that tends to curl'.[30]

City Centre Properties retained its name after its merger in 1960 with Clore's City and Central Investments (the new company had an inflated stock market valuation of £65 million). Cotton remained chairman. Hitherto his staff had comprised a few accountants, clerks, and typists. He kept the details of his business in his head, or in a few files which were heaped on a spare bed in his Dorchester lair. The suite was littered with maps of London, newspaper cuttings and surveyors' reports. It had a private tele-phone switchboard, a pretty telephonist and vivacious secretaries. These methods proved too haphazard for an expanded dominion in which Clore was the other potentate. After hammering by Clore and sniping from institutional shareholders, Cotton relinquished City Centre's chairmanship in July 1963.[31] His shares in the company (held by family trusts) were sold in November for £8.5 million to a consortium headed by Wolfson. A month after leaving City Centre's board in 1964, Cotton died of a heart attack in the Bahamas. He had outlived by a year his own victim, Walter Flack.

There was nothing stifled or cloistered about Flack. He had been born in 1915 to parents who wished him to become a solicitor. Having failed to matriculate at secondary school, he talked his way into a Mayfair estate agency which trained several eminent developers, including Harry Hyams and Maxwell Joseph. He was inordinately proud of reaching the rank of sergeant during the Second World War. After demobilisation, he returned to his old firm, but was sacked after a row with its senior partner, who objected to the smoke from his long, curly pipe. Flack set up as a property developer on his own account, and in 1958 paid £11,000 for a shell company, Murrayfield, which acted as the vehicle for his schemes. He recruited as its non-executive chairman his wartime commander, Field Marshal Sir Claude Auchinleck, whom he revered. He was so proud of his association with 'the Auk' that he commissioned a bronze bust of the Field Marshal which was put on a pedestal in the bow-fronted, ground-floor window of Murrayfield's offices in St James's Street. The bow window and bust were the reasons for his eccentricity in locating his offices in the middle of clubland.

Murrayfield specialised in provincial shopping centres. Its schemes required long preliminary negotiations with councillors and council officials. As most of the councils which launched major redevelopments of their town centres in this period were Labour-controlled, Flack cultivated Sir Frank Price, the influential Labour leader in Birmingham, whose contacts proved invaluable to Murrayfield. The company's first major development was a shopping centre in Basildon New Town, Essex. The Basildon worthies liked Flack's scheme, but asked if he had the financial clout to put it through. Flack rose from his chair, paced back and forth across the council chamber in frowning thought before exclaiming to the committee: 'I've got the answer: I'll give you my personal guarantee!' The worthies were charmed by this performance, and settled terms with Flack.[32]

A City editor's profile in 1963 catches the man. 'Walter Flack loved to be known as Sergeant Flack, a rank he gained with the Eighth Army. He told me once: "It is a very respectable rank, cock." He formed the Sergeants' Club – a drinking and dining get-together of sergeants who made a big postwar success. Sergeant Flack was its chairman.' He also gave an annual 'Knees Up, Mother Brown' party for old-age pensioners at a Westminster pub, where he sometimes served behind the bar for fun. His wife Louise, an intense and vivid woman, 'had married him long before he reached the big time. It was she who kept him "ticking", for he had the moody up-and-down temperament that often goes with brilliance.'[33]

Flack brandished his confidence, and tried to keep his insecurity hidden in a lead-lined box. He had the mannerisms of a cheeky errand boy. His smile was wide, but his gaiety was disarming. He was both direct and sly. He told stories with the timing of a musical-hall comedian. 'He was sometimes so winning it was dangerous to be in his company, safer to write a letter or to negotiate with him on the telephone,' Gordon recalled. 'Even that provided no immunity from his powerful wheedling charm.' Flack loved cricket, and was a voracious, self-improving reader, who took up new interests with ephemeral zest. Heraldry became one of his fleeting enthusiasms: in 1961 he obtained a grant of armorial bearings from the College of Arms featuring a heraldic version of bricks and mortar with the motto 'Bien Bâtir' ('Good to Build'). His steam-yacht Isambard Brunel was named after one of his heroes. People either liked his gusto, or mistrusted him as too bouncy. He had a streak of malice, and could be cruel. This side of his temperament did not fit with the rest of him; he wore it,

171

said Gordon, like somebody else's overcoat. Flack drank alcohol too deeply (the whisky sometimes started at ten in the morning), and became envenomed when drunk.[34]

Flack liked lording it in pubs, but hunted people with titles. In 1961 he invited Gordon for what he called a *'tayte-a-tayte'* in Murrayfield's offices, with the bronze statue of Auchinleck confronting passers-by. Flack was beaming with pride as he introduced Gordon to the other men collected in his shiny mock-Regency room: Dickon Lumley, young heir of Lord Scarbrough, the Lord Chamberlain; Anthony Berry, a Tory parliamentary candidate and son of Lord Kemsley; a stockbroker, Rupert Loewenstein – 'Prince Loewenstein, he underscored'; and then Flack swelled, his waistcoat with its gold watch-chain bulging round his plump girth, his voice resembling a music-hall compère announcing his star act, as he introduced Archduke Otto von Habsburg, son of the last Emperor of Austria. 'You know the Prince, of course,' he said to Gordon.[35]

In 1959, in order to alleviate Murrayfield's high leverage, Flack agreed a deal with Cotton involving an exchange of shares between Murrayfield and City Centre Properties. Two years later Murrayfield was completely absorbed into City Centre, by then Britain's largest property company. Flack, who joined its board, was not disposed to defer to Cotton or Clore: the latter in particular found him too much of a buck.

Mandy Rice-Davies's claim that she had an affair with Flack surfaced once he was dead and unable to issue denials, but certainly, during 1962, he separated from his wife, with whom he was well-matched in vivacity and louche charm. In January 1963, he crumpled under the buffeting of his clashes with Cotton, and resigned from City Centre Properties. On 22 March (aged forty-seven), he had the death that Clore peculiarly dreaded – by drowning. He was found by his chauffeur immersed in a bath in his flat in Whitehall Court: he had taken barbiturates with alcohol. The coroner's verdict accepted that he had accidentally fallen asleep while washing. Even if he did not intend to kill himself, there was a despondent rashness about his last weeks. His widow, who inherited his estate (valued at £840,801 in 1963), settled on Cap Ferrat, with a yacht at Villefranche. She felt a rueful tenderness for his memory, and bitterness towards Cotton and Clore for hounding him to perdition.

Flack was a tangle of a man: bumptious, vulnerable and self-destructive. There were anomalies, too, about that great hate-figure of 1963, the slum landlord Rachman, at once a brute and victimised refugee, whose surname inspired a hostile epithet, Rachmanism, but whose villainy came with redeeming traits and extenuating experiences.

Perec Rachman was a Polish Jew born at Lvov in 1919. As a dentist's son, he had a middle-class upbringing. 'The Polish attitude to the Jews was one of disgust, like someone who has bitten into a piece of bad fish, and can neither swallow nor spit it out,' recalled a contemporary who fled to Palestine. 'The fear in every Jewish home, the fear we never talked about, but which we were unintentionally injected with, was the chilling fear that perhaps we really were not clean enough, that we really were too noisy and pushy, too clever and money-grubbing.' It was instilled in these children that they must remain polite when insulted by drunkards, that they must never haggle, that their manners should be submissive and smiling. 'We must always speak to them in good, correct Polish, so they couldn't say that we were defiling their language, but that we mustn't speak in Polish that was too high, so they couldn't say we had ambitions over our station.' There was an obsession, too, with hygiene: 'even a single child with dirty hair who spread lice could damage the reputation of the entire Jewish people'. This was the mentality in which Rachman spent his boyhood; and against which his adulthood was a furious, wounded, panicky reaction.[36]

In 1940, after the German invasion of Poland, Rachman aged twenty-one was forced into a chain-gang building an autobahn towards Russia. His parents vanished into the oblivion of the concentration camps; years later, in England, when asked what had happened to them, he would shrug silently. After escaping from German captivity, he fled towards the Soviet Union, where he nearly starved to death. He used to say that he survived by stealing a barrel of caviar, which he had to eat long after its richness had sickened him: thereafter the sight of the black fishy eggs made him retch. Another story was that hunger drove him to eat human turds, but he liked to add savagely: 'I never ate German shit. At least no one can say I ever ate *that*.'[37] Even if one discounts the factual accuracy of these tales, they expressed a psychological truth for Rachman. The caviar and the shit showed what life felt like for him.

After capture by Soviet forces, Rachman was sent to a labour camp in the Arctic Circle. When Hitler sent troops to invade Russia and rid the world of the Jewish-Bolshevik menace, Rachman was drafted into a Polish army corps organised by the Russians, which joined the invasion of Italy in 1943. Rachman worked in the corps' supply depot, where he proved indispensable in procuring and dispensing soap, cigarettes, chocolate and coffee which could be exchanged by soldiers for the sexual services of Italian women. He learnt passable German, Russian and Italian by 1945, when he began teaching himself English. A Polish second-lieutenant who met him at this time remembered him as a stereotype, 'always trying to get something out of you – always looking for an opening to do a deal'.[38]

Rachman remained with the occupying troops in Italy until December 1946, when he sailed for Britain. He was kept in Polish corps resettlement camps in Scotland during a notoriously harsh winter. In 1947 he was moved to a resettlement camp in Oxfordshire, where he amused his dormitory companions by kissing goodnight at bedtime Rita Hayworth's face on a wall poster. In 1948 he took his first English job, in Cohen's veneer factory, earning £4 10s a week. He rented a squalid room in Stepney, and got evening work as a washer-up at Bloom's, the famous Jewish restaurant in Whitechapel. After about eight months he went to work in a tailor's workshop in Soho, and got better digs at Golders Green. He was eager for social acceptance, but as a middle-class Polish Jew whose upbringing had instilled the notion that he was primarily a Pole and secondarily a Jew, his avidity made him inadmissible in every set. Polish exiles in London certainly rejected him. 'He spoke the average Polish,' said Karol Zbyszewski, editor of *Dziennik Polski*, London's daily Polish-language newspaper, 'not like most Jews making a hundred mistakes in every sentence.' After Rachman's death, Zbyszewski complained that he had been quoted as saying that Rachman had made him feel ashamed at being Polish. 'I never said such a thing,' Zbyszewski insisted. 'I said I was ashamed Rachman *claimed* to be a Pole – because he was not a Pole. He was a Jew, and that's a very different thing.'[39]

Around 1950, Rachman left Golders Green for a Paddington bedsit. He was selling cheap suitcases, uncured sheepskin, and contraband Swiss watches. 'The best time to catch me in my office is between 4 p.m. and 5 p.m.,' he would tell men with whom he was trying to fix a deal. He gave them the number of a red telephone kiosk on a Paddington street, and ensconced himself inside for an hour each afternoon heedless of angry thumps on the door. In every way he prowled like a fox at the edge of a poultry farm. He was surrounded in Paddington, as before in Soho, by prostitutes whom he used when he could afford them. 'Women,' he said, 'are like food. You are fond of chicken? OK. But eat it every day and you'll soon be bored. Now try a little duck, and the chicken will taste much better.'[40]

A brunette called Gloria, whose pimp was a black jazz musician, suggested to him that he should start a flat-letting agency. The idea was that he would rent flats in his own name, and sub-let them to individual prostitutes (two women working together counted as a brothel, but a lone female in a flat was beyond legal reach). Rachman opened a letting agency at the corner of Westbourne Grove with Monmouth Road: his stygian office, beneath pavement level, was reached by descending the narrow stone stairs into a basement. A rent of £5 a week was entered in prostitutes' rent books, but Rachman took an additional £10 a week in cash. Other landlords in the vicinity used him as letting agent and rent collector; he also emptied pennies from gas meters into a bucket which he carried with him.

In 1954 Rachman formed his first companies, Six Norfolk Square Ltd and Eight Norfolk Square Ltd, in collaboration with the property dealer Cyril Foux, and the latter's solicitor brother. Cyril Foux was a sharp, natty man, quick-moving but oblique, with a near-spiv moustache and a sardonic attitude to those he thought fools. He had been born in Hackney in 1920, married a girl with rich parents, Leila Leigh, at Hendon in 1951, and acquired smart offices in Maddox Street, Mayfair. Norfolk Square, a short walk from Paddington station, was lined by small hotels of the sort described by Anthony Powell in 1955 as pervaded by 'an air of secret, melancholy guilt'.[41]

A nearby area of similar dinginess was the Charecroft Estate, terraces of tall mid-Victorian houses abutting Shepherds Bush Green, with leases reverting in the late 1950s and early 1960s (the freeholds were owned by a charity called the Campden Trustees). The premises were packed by tenants paying statutorily controlled low rents, and had a high turnover of landlords who wished to avoid repair bills. A property dealer called Lieutenant Colonel George Sinclair bought a batch of end-of-lease properties on the Charecroft Estate, and sold thirty of them to Rachman. Sinclair had a quaint address: 'The House Beyond', The Avenue, Farnham Common, not far from his registered offices in Slough; and a quaint hobby, too, driving carriage and horses.

Victorian speculative builders had erected terraces of houses throughout Bloomsbury, Islington, Kensington, and Pimlico, on sites leased from aristocratic families which still owned swathes of the capital's land. As with the Charecroft Estate, the lessees granted ninety-nine-year leases to the tenants, which meant that many central London leases were due to expire between 1950 and 1975. The Victorians had envisaged that when their heirs repossessed their freeholds, the properties would have risen in status and increased in value. Instead, as the size of families shrank and servants became scarcer, families moved from big terraced houses to smaller suburban properties. Those people who owned their leases, and stayed behind, sub-let floors to cover running costs. Soon the floors were sub-divided, and surreptitiously sub-sub-let, room by room, turning desirable houses into squalid, even disreputable rooming houses. Freeholders stopped enforcing the terms of leases or resisting sub-letting. Moreover, few landlords could afford proper upkeep of such buildings during the long postwar period of statutory rent control, when the rents of sitting tenants in unfurnished flats and rooms were frozen at 1939 levels. Even if landlords managed to dislodge the sitting tenants, and let furnished rooms at uncontrolled rents, they did not smarten the exteriors of their properties for fear of attracting the interest of tax collectors or other snoopers.[42]

One of the Victorian speculative developments, which had been forsaken by the middle classes, was the Colville Estate, comprising five-storey stucco houses with porticos and balustrades built in too northern a district of Kensington to be fashionable. The accommodation, twenty-seven per cent of which had been vacant before the war, was monstrously overpopulated by 1945. 'There wasn't a cupboard that didn't have somebody in it,' recalled Mark Strutt, who together with a Norfolk baronet had inherited control of the estate. 'The houses had been sub-let and sub-sub-let without our consent, and they were filled with prostitutes, burglars, murderers and negroes,' he complained. He and the baronet decided that Colville was 'not an estate that our sort of families should be associated with', and could not face the outcry that would be aroused if they evicted existing tenants so that the muddle of rented rooms could be converted into proper flats.[43]

In 1950 they sold the Colville Estate to a speculator named Benson Greenall, who had been born at Ashton-under-Lyne in 1890, enlisted in the Cheshire Regiment in August 1914, was appointed as a Housing and Town Planning Inspector under the

Ministry of Health in 1925, but had become a developer by 1929 when he bought historic Lansdowne House, off Piccadilly, after the death of the old marquess – Dorothy Macmillan's uncle. He subsequently erected a block containing ninety-five luxury flats, offices, the Austin car showroom, a cinema and restaurant in Lansdowne House's gardens which dominated the south side of Berkeley Square. He floated Lansdowne House (Berkeley Square) Limited with gratifying profit in 1936. At a time when British taxpayers were being mulcted by their government, it was Greenall who in 1948 pioneered the development of Grand Cayman Island as an offshore tax haven. Noticing that the island, twenty miles by six in area, rising from a gin-coloured stretch of the Caribbean waters, was exempt from taxation, he brought the first bank to Georgetown, established an airfield, built a hotel and launched that most lucrative light industry: tax evasion. His second wife, Melisande Dalrymple, whom he married in 1946, was related to Oscar Wilde.

Greenall bought the Colville Estate for £250,000, which he paid by negotiating a hundred per cent mortgage. As the Labour government had imposed a lending limit of £50,000, he split the estate between five companies, each of which borrowed £50,000 from a clearing bank. Greenall sold his Colville properties in parcels during the next few years: his profits partly funded his pioneering developments on Grand Cayman Island during the 1950s. Years of poor maintenance meant that most Colville lessees were in default of their leases. The new freeholders scared them with Notices of Dilapidations, whereby the law would oblige them to spend thousands of pounds repairing the houses to comply with their leases; then bought back the leases themselves, and thus got control of their properties. Lacking the qualms of the Strutts, Greenall issued notices to quit to unprotected tenants, and sold a hundred Colville houses to George Sinclair, with whom Rachman had dealt over the Charecroft Estate.

Sinclair introduced Rachman to Abraham Kramer, a method-ical, quietly spoken solicitor with a practice in Portland Place specialising in property. Kramer controlled money held in trust, which he used to loan to clients to fund their purchases of property from Sinclair. In 1955, at Sinclair's instigation, Kramer formed a shell (non-trading) company called Rimmywood Investments of which his wife Dorothy was the nominal director. Rimmywood became the vehicle for Rachman's activities. A mortgage of £9,600 was advanced to Rimmywood by Unilever's Union Pension Trust, which dealt with Sinclair and Kramer, but never directly with Rachman. He thus acquired four houses in St Stephen's Gardens, and six in Powis Terrace ('our driver was shocked by the squalor of Powis Terrace', Christopher Isherwood wrote after visiting David Hockney there: 'peeling houses, trashcans spilling over sidewalks, seedy shops run by thin pop-eyed Pakistanis'). Next year, in 1956, Rimmywood acquired four more Powis Terrace houses, and one in Colville Terrace. Also in 1956 Sinclair and Kramer obtained a mortgage of £6,700 from Union Pension Trust for a shell company called Flynbrook Securities, which acquired three houses in Colville Road, and four in Powis Gardens. Some months later Rachman became sole shareholder in Flynbrook.[44]

Next, he took over the shares in Rillianwood Investments, a company holding twenty tail-end leases in Wymering Mansions, a run-down Edwardian mansion block on the Paddington side of Maida Vale (it was to be from there, in 1966, that Harry Roberts set out to steal a get-away car for a robbery, and ended up shooting dead three policemen at Shepherds Bush). Other Rachman companies bought further houses in Colville Terrace, Powis Terrace and Powis Square. By the end of 1956, Rachman controlled thirty houses near Shepherds Bush Green, twenty flats in Wymering Mansions, and thirty houses in Notting Hill.

Rent control and security of tenure only applied to 'stats' – statutorily controlled sitting tenants of unfurnished lettings. Tenants of furnished flats and rooms (with their narrow beds, chipped washstands, cupboards with wobbly legs standing on worn linoleum floors) had no protection, and could be given a month's notice to quit. In consequence, Rachman let his flats and rooms furnished whenever possible. Rents became decontrolled once 'stats' vacated their homes: rents far above 1939 values could then be levied on new tenants. Rachman's preferred technique for dislodging 'stats' was what he called 'putting in the *schwartzers*'.[45] He hired black thugs to intimidate white tenants, or occasionally deployed white hooligans against black tenants, and obtained vacant possession by coercion. Bullies with Alsatians would wrench the doors of communal lavatories off their hinges, sever gas, water, and electricity supplies, break into flats, smash furniture, rip up floorboards, remove roof tiles, and conduct interminable, filthy building work. Deafening music would be played to stop tenants from getting a night's sleep. Once properties were vacated, Rachman would 'sweat' them, either by overcrowding them with Caribbean immigrants, or by leasing them at high rents to brothel keepers or shebeens. His profiteering from racial tensions, and that of many other unscrupulous landlords, contributed to the Notting Hill race riots of 1958.

Rachman was able to collect £10,000 a year in rent for a house which cost him £1,500. By 1959 he controlled about eighty houses. The muddle of interlocking companies fronted by nominee directors made it impossible to identify the beneficial owner of a property, which frustrated the serving of sanitary notices or certificates of disrepair. Companies were wound up, and properties reassigned to other companies, in order to keep a defective drain festering and drive out the statutory tenants. The Metropolitan Police, Ministry of Housing, council officials, public health authorities, and rent tribunals all tried to catch him in legal nets, but their meshes were too wide.

Before the Race Relations Act of 1965 outlawed discrimination on the basis of skin colour and ethnicity, immigrants faced cards in rooming-house front windows specifying 'No Coloureds'. They were expected to apologise for causing embarrassment. 'I find it most strange,' wrote a refugee from South African apartheid in 1962, 'that I am expected, on the telephone, to say that *I* am sorry that a landlady is sorry that she does not take Coloureds.' Those landladies who said, as if bestowing a royal favour, 'I don't mind Coloureds', nevertheless imposed humiliating rules on their tenants, such as a maximum of two visitors at a time.[46]

Rachman was exceptional in letting rooms to black people who could not otherwise find accommodation. He charged £6 a week for a flat for which a statutorily controlled tenant paid only £1. Sometimes he was patient with black tenants who fell into rent arrears; perhaps he felt affinities with them. Like Rachman, they belonged to a minority which was apprehended as anti-social by the majority. In reaction, like him, some chose to be seen and heard flouting the manners of the host community and to sail as close-hauled as possible to the law. 'To the West Indian he was a saviour, and people still have a lot of respect for him,' Rachman's biographer was told by a Caribbean social worker whom she interviewed in the 1970s. 'He was a swinging guy,' said a Jamaican. 'He liked us, and we liked him.' He would offer 'a tenner' to West Indian men loitering on the Notting Hill streets if they would clear a house of 'stat' tenants for him. 'He had his strong-arm men like everybody else,' said one of his enforcers, 'but basically he was a good bloke. While he was alive, I never heard anything against him, and when he died I was sad.'[47]

Rachman was short, chubby-faced, plump and balding. He wore tinted spectacles, which gave him a sinister look. A gold bracelet, which was locked to his wrist, was supposedly inscribed with serial numbers of his Swiss bank accounts and safe combinations. He always had a roll of banknotes in his pocket and sported Churchillian cigars. Despite his silk shirts, cashmere suits, and crocodile shoes, he looked sloppy. In his early years in England, when he was poor, he impressed several acquaintances with his thoughtful kindness. Later, although he was moody, people often found him polite, reasonably intelligent and mildly amusing. In prosperity his fleet of motor cars included a red Rolls-Royce saloon, and a blue Rolls-Royce convertible, in which he liked to drive about London showing off flashy blondes.

The Kenco coffee house in Queensway, rather than his basement office, was where Rachman spent his mornings seeing contacts and making cash deals. He would lunch in an expense account Mayfair restaurant, such as the Coq d'Or or Les Ambassadeurs, with a blonde. During his afternoons he played chess at a Polish restaurant, Daquise, near South Kensington station, or sat in the Kardomah coffee house in the King's Road, ogling the passing Chelsea girls. He diversified into club management, first with a basement gambling club at the New Court Hotel in Inverness Terrace, Paddington; then with the El Condor nightclub (later renamed La Discotheque) in Wardour Street, Soho; and finally the 150 Club, a decorous gambling den in Earls Court Road. In the evenings he would make a round from the New Court, via El Condor, to the 150.

Contamination was Rachman's obsessive fear. The world seemed to him a mire of dirt and effluent. People, too, were filthy in their secretions. Memories of the lice that infested him during the war, disgust at the cockroaches, ants, fleas and worms with which the planet teemed, drove him to take three baths a day, with a bottle of the disinfectant Dettol poured into the steaming water each time. Unless he scrubbed, the creepy-crawlies would take over. He drenched himself in eau de cologne, and wore silk underwear to counteract memories of the coarse soiled rags of the Soviet labour camp. He never drank alcohol, would request mineral water when he ate out, refused to drink from glasses in case they were dirty and swilled his water straight from the bottle. He accused a waiter who touched the rim of a bottle of mineral water while opening it of trying to poison him. Before eating in a restaurant he would inspect its kitchen, and yell reproaches if he thought that the cutlery was unclean. The Spanish au pair at his Hampstead Garden Suburb house had to sterilise cutlery after each meal. Rachman would rinse and re-rinse plates himself before he would let meals be served to his guests; plates reached the table dripping wet. To the end of his life, as security against starvation, he hoarded snacks under his bed and stockpiled his homes with food.

Servility combined with aggression in Rachman's character. He was both affectionate and mistrustful. He oscillated between raucous generosity to his intimates and pre-emptive inhumanity against strangers. He liked the company of handsome wrestlers as much as he did decorative blondes, for he longed for rough and tumble. He said: 'If you have one true friend you are lucky. If you have two you are very lucky. If you tell me you have three you must be a liar.'[48] Serge Paplinski, who had been dragooned into the Polish partisans at the age of thirteen and had a murderous wartime history, was spotted by Rachman on a London street sometime after his expulsion from St Martin's College of Art in Soho. Rachman counted Paplinski as one of his two true friends. Paplinski was debonair, affectionate but scatterbrained: Rachman's decision to employ him to keep his business records and manage the Monmouth Road office ensured that both records and office were chaotic.

Denis Hamilton, Diana Dors's husband, was Rachman's boon companion. Hamilton's sexual dissipation so delighted him that – in addition to his London base, flat 609 in Clive Court, a Maida Vale block of mansion flats which was five minutes' drive from his office – he occupied an annexe in Hamilton's house, Woodhurst, near Maidenhead. Shaken by Hamilton's death in 1959, Rachman left Woodhurst, and replaced the Clive Court flat with Bishopstone, a sham-Georgian house in Hampstead Garden Suburb's opulent Winnington Road – two minutes' walk (although it is doubtful if he ever walked) from the Malibu-style house that Cyril and Leila Foux built in the grounds of her parents, the Kennedy Leighs. Rachman furnished Bishopstone with gilt furniture, including a piano which he prized in the belief that it has been owned by the Polish wife of Louis XV. He took boyish delight in the gadget that opened his garage doors electronically, and in his refrigerator where he kept his tennis balls cool. He also took over a small, modern, ugly house in Marylebone – 1 Bryanston Mews West – from Cyril Foux in 1959. The two-way mirror from Woodhurst, through which voyeurs enjoyed the action in Hamilton's spare bedroom, was moved there. Mandy Rice-Davies later smashed it; but it was repeatedly mentioned by the prosecution at Stephen Ward's trial as if Ward had installed it.

In 1959 three West Indian tenants, including Michael de Freitas (the future black activist and murderer, Michael X), had their rents reduced by the West London Rent Tribunal: de Freitas from £8 to £4; the others from £6 to £3, and £3 to £2. Thereafter, there was an outpouring of applications to rent tribunals from tenants of Rachman and other landlords. He neither appeared nor was legally represented at any of the hearings. The complaints of Donald Chesworth, Labour member for North Kensington on London County Council, about Rachman's housing rackets were handled gingerly by the Metropolitan Police: Detective Super-intendent George Taylor noted that Chesworth 'was of "Left Wing" tendencies and a "Fellow Traveller".'[49]

Ten cases of intimidation were submitted to the Directorate of Public Prosecutions, which judged that there was insufficient evidence to prosecute. The DPP seemed reluctant to support tenants against landlords, reckoned that the threats were 'quite trivial', and was contemptuous of the testimony of sex workers. Serge Paplinkski's threats against May McCash (alias Mary Scott, who had convictions for brothel-keeping and soliciting) were judged 'not very severe, merely telling her that they would cut off the electricity and strip the house of wallpaper'. Rachman's warning to June Hilton, alias Bury, 'that he could be "naughty",' was not taken seriously given that she had forty-three convictions for prostitution. As to Chesworth's motives in organising the tenants, the DPP dismissed these as 'political'.[50] The police inves-tigated whether Rachman was committing the criminal offence of living off immoral earnings: an officer disguised as a coster trundling a barrow kept watch on suspect houses; but no charges were brought.

None of this rattled Rachman, but he felt insecure as a 'state-less person', and was distraught when in April 1959 his application to become a British subject was rejected by the Home Office. As he desired the security of a British passport he transferred the Monmouth Street letting agency to young Etonians, Julian March Phillips de Lisle and Anthony Sykes, who were to be pilloried by the *Daily Mirror* in the summer of 1963. He sold most of his tenement houses: two of the exceptions, 23 Nevern Square and 5 West Cromwell Road, were both mortgaged through Cyril Foux, whom he joined in several property syndicates. Rachman bought and sold the Streatham Hill Theatre, and moved on to the Golders Green Hippodrome. 'He was carving his niche,' said an estate agent who often saw him. 'Lots of top-drawer people ate well at his expense. Everyone says that if he'd lived, he'd have ended up being knighted.'[51]

The jeweller Kutchinsky supplied Rachman with a cache of 22-carat gold watches. Spotting a pretty woman in a club or restaurant, he would beckon her over, and slip a watch onto her wrist. He liked to be 'blown' in offices, for this avoided the intimacy of bedrooms: oral sex, he believed, reduced the risk of venereal infections. Like Clore, he preferred sex to be perfunctory, yet performed in such a way that tribute was paid to his wealth. In 1959, after acquiring his Bryanston Mews hideaway from Cyril Foux, he decided to keep a mistress there, as a status symbol as much as to relieve his satyriasis. That summer he installed seventeen-year-old Christine Keeler, gave her a sports car, and treated her as if she was a mechanical dummy. After lunch, he would tug Keeler into the bedroom, and, without preliminaries, make her sit astride him with her back towards him so that she never saw his face. 'Sex to Peter Rachman was like cleaning his teeth, and I was the toothpaste,' she memorably said.[52]

Rachman was invited to Stephen Ward's cottage on the Cliveden estate once. Keeler claimed that during the weekend, he accompanied her and Ward to see the big house. She said that he stood on Cliveden's famous terrace, raised his arms above his head and with clenched fists cried: 'This is what I want! *This* is what I want!' Ward, she said, turned to her and sneered: 'This is something he can never buy – not for all his money.'[53] Histrionic tales like this say more about the taste for lurid racial stereotypes than the reality of Rachman. In contrast with Keeler, Rice-Davies, whom he kept during 1961–62 in Bryanston Mews, spoke well of him.

Rachman died in November 1962, and in July 1963 became a national hate-figure, vilified above all by Labour MPs and the Labour-supporting *Mirror* newspapers. Flack survived him by five months; Cotton died early in 1964. In the spring of that year, a columnist on the *Financial Times*, who was a Labour supporter, noted one unifying opinion shared by every party member from Konni Zilliacus on the left to Douglas Jay on the right, which he summarised as: 'Moneymaking is an unpleasant business. At best it is distasteful, more usually it is morally repugnant, and at worse it is close on criminal.' Rachman's activities intensified Labour's hostility to both money-making and regulatory de-control. 'Slick talk about Conservative freedom,' wrote Marjorie Proops of the *Daily Mirror* during the 1964 general election, 'means freedom for the Rachmans of this noble land.'[54]

Clore, Cotton and Flack, as much as Rachman, were the targets when, in the summer of 1964, shortly before the general election, a trade unionist caught a national mood by decrying the land deals of 'super spiv tycoons'. 'Curbing the racketeer,' Harold Wilson promised, three weeks before he became Prime Minister, was a Labour priority: 'the squalid property deals which merely produce vast profits and ultimately send up the prices of people's home have no place in a New Britain.' None of the Labour leaders, though, admitted that socialist regulation had inadvertently created the chance for this massive money-making. Rules, whether they govern sexual morality or financial probity, regardless of whether they are justifiable or undesirable, always provoke bold recalcitrants to devise clever, defiant ways to breach them.[55]

SEVEN

Hacks

The Profumo Affair was made in Fleet Street more than in Wimpole Mews or Cliveden. It was incited, publicised and exploited by journalists. It erupted during a phase of newspaper history when editors reacted to falling circulation with aggressive pursuit of stories and scapegoats; and it was seized as a godsent chance by some newspaper proprietors to skewer targets of their own. Whereas Lord Beaverbrook's staff at Express Newspapers paid and manipulated Christine Keeler and other Profumo Affair protagonists as a means of envenoming the old man's feud with the Astors, the men at Mirror Group Newspapers played a bigger game. Their involvement began with a deal to buy Keeler's story, which they hoped to run as a scandalous circulation stunt. It escalated into a campaign, with ruthlessly plotted tactics, to inflict mortal injuries not merely on the Macmillan government and the Establishment, but on ways of life which the Mirror chiefs, Cecil King and Hugh Cudlipp, both envied and resented, even as they brashly emulated them. The Profumo Affair aroused a Fleet Street frenzy of ferocity. It managed to glorify what was shabby, and had an enduring influence on investigative journalism.

Already, for more than half a century, journalists had been creating a headline blizzard of sensational crimes, lewd scandals and quirky escapades. They relished dramatising the confrontations between deviance and control that were manifested in manhunts, criminal trials and judicial punishments. The burglar

Alfie Hinds, who escaped three times from high security prisons during the late 1950s but was always recaptured, became the darling of the tabloids because he epitomised the breaking of bounds and the reassertion of control: his wife, and later he himself, sold their memories for lucrative serialisation. The gutter press, with its entertaining scrapes and vicarious punishment, provided a histrionic morality for its readers and frontier markers for society. Its contents were a map of moral landscaping, showing the contours of normality, the roads to right and wrong, the boundaries that must not be crossed.[1]

Popular journalism was modelled on the pillory. It was intended to make money for newspaper proprietors, to cover them in glory and to buy them influence. Sensationalism defined the product. Snobbery – increasingly it was inverted snobbery – was mixed with puritanism. The formula for Sunday newspapers was supremely punitive: they were meant to hurt. An editor, who was a self-described puritan, declared his credo to the Royal Commission on Divorce in 1910. 'The simple faith of our fore-fathers in the All-Seeing Eye of God has departed from the Man in the Street. Our only modern substitute for Him is the Press. Gag the Press under whatever pretexts of prudish propriety you please, and you destroy the last remaining pillory by which it is possible to impose some restraint on the lawless lust of Man.'[2]

Until late in the twentieth century the overwhelming majority of the English hid what they felt, did, and thought: from child-hood they were taught to conceal their desires, appetites, physical necessities; adults maintained a tacit conspiracy to keep them hidden. But the game for journalists was to trample discretion, catch people out, and pelt them with retributive publicity. Hugh Cudlipp, former editor of the *Sunday Pictorial*, wrote in 1953 of its rival the *News of the World*: 'This is no hole-in-the-corner, nasty-minded little news-sheet. The *News of the World* is a national institution. It is a newspaper which goes into two-thirds of our homes, and to which great judges and statesmen have been happy to contribute.' He quoted the retort of its proprietor, Lord Riddell, to someone who complained that it recorded crime: 'No,' said Riddell, 'it records punishment.'[3]

Victorian England abominated Sunday newspapers as radical, infidel and disreputable. When, in 1899, Lord Burnham's *Daily Telegraph* began to publish seven days a week, and was copied by Lord Northcliffe's *Daily Mail*, Baptists, Presbyterians and Congregationalists censured both men, who abandoned their Sunday editions. The demand for weekend news of the Western Front in 1914–18, however, made popular Sunday newspapers irresistible. Although national press readership rose during that war, the combined circulation of nationals did not exceed the figures for local newspapers until 1923. During the next fifteen years, the habit of reading national newspapers spread from the lower-middle class to the working class. The Sunday press boomed: by 1939 almost the entire population saw a Sunday newspaper, while two-thirds saw a national daily. For millions the conscientious pleasure of Sundays was sharing the morbid indignation of its mass-market newspapers.

Circulation, which rose during the Second World War, peaked in 1950–51, when Sunday newspapers sold over 30 million copies a week, and national dailies 16.6 million a day. Thereafter, television, especially the commercial channel ITV inaugurated in 1955, drove sales downwards. In 1959 the ten national Sunday newspapers sold 27 million copies, and the eight national dailies under 16 million. Almost every household still took at least one Sunday newspaper – many households took two or three – but the *News of the World*, which sold 8 million copies weekly in 1950, dispersed only 6,665,000 weekly by 1958. Some optimists hoped that this meant that working-class sexual taboos and salacity were receding. At the end of 1961, the *News of the World* led circulation figures with 6.6 million followed by three Mirror Group Newspapers: *The People* (5.5 million); *Sunday Pictorial* (5.3 million); *Daily Mirror* (4.6 million). Lord Beaverbrook's *Sunday Express* and *Daily Express* followed with 4.5 million and 4.3 million respectively. *The Times*, of which Bill Astor's uncle Lord Astor of Hever had been chief proprietor since 1922, had a circulation of about a quarter of a million, while the Astor-edited *Observer* was approaching three-quarters of a million.

Chequebook journalism began when the *News of the World* paid the defence costs of John Haigh, 'the Acid Bath Murderer', in return for his exclusive memoir in 1949. Editors had long known that sex stories sold their papers. After 1955, faced with competition from ITV, they told their staff to produce sizzling stories with lots of pictures to vie with screen images. Rising newspaper production costs, keen competition for advertising revenue and the battle in the middle and lower ends of the market meant that print journalism by the late 1950s aimed to titillate more than ever – while keeping its patina of prudish rectitude. Cyril Connolly in 1963 could not imagine England without sexual inhibitions, lavatory jokes, lust murders, 'its virgins and sadists of all ages and sexes, its squeamishness and evasions'.[4]

The National Union of Journalists insisted that tyro journalists must serve an apprenticeship on provincial newspapers – just as a left-wing cabal in Equity tried to insist that actors must serve in provincial repertory before they could be allowed into London theatres. English reporters, wrote an American journalist in 1965, were toughies 'with provincial accents and newspaper tea-boy educations; many of them held the old spit-and-polish, school-of-hard-knocks, learn-the-hard-way-on-the-stone, and other equally soporific philosophies for journalistic success. Public schools were never mentioned.' Newsrooms were pugnacious and chauvinistic. Women were a tiny minority among Fleet Street journalists, excluded from the Press Clubs in London and Manchester, ritually humiliated in the rowdy Fleet Street bars, and estranged by the long hours, hard-drinking, and oafishness. Racist mentalities were also commonplace in newsrooms until late in the twentieth century, even on newspapers which campaigned against landlords' 'colour bars'. 'Come in, Tom,' beckoned Reg Payne, editor of the *Sunday Pictorial*, to Tom Mangold, a young recruit from the *Croydon Advertiser*, 'the *Pic* wants to do a serious sociological' – Payne garbled the six-syllabled word – 'experiment. Go up and dress yourself as a fuckin' nigger.'[5]

For five years Peter Wildeblood worked for the *Daily Mail*. He was successively general reporter, gossip columnist, assistant drama critic, and diplomatic correspondent. He covered King Farouk of Egypt's honeymoon, Don Carlos de Beistegui's masked costume ball in Venice, the Craig and Bentley shooting at Croydon, and the Queen's Coronation. He delved into the Acid Bath Murderer's boyhood in the Plymouth Brethren, hunted for Burgess and Maclean on the French Riviera, and waded through the East Coast floods. 'Fleet Street is a hard-working, nervous community with shabby suits and nicotine-stained fingers, living on beer and sandwiches and catching the last train home to the suburbs,' he wrote. 'Its contacts with the great, wide, lurid world about which it writes are usually brief, disenchanting and fraught with suspicion on both sides. At one moment a reporter may be trying to gatecrash an earl's wedding in a hired morning coat; an hour later he is in Stepney, persuading a group of stevedores that, at heart, he is one of them.'

Reporters' nerves were always jumpy lest (unknown to them) a good story was happening round the corner. They faced hostility everywhere. They were controlled by pawky managers who 'peddled tragedy, sensation and heartbreak as casually as though they were cartloads of cabbage', and exploited a 'false, over-coloured and sentimental view of life'. It was hard for Wildeblood to imagine work in which his homosexuality was more of 'a handicap' than journalism, for Fleet Street had the morality of the saloon bar: 'every sexual excess was talked about and tolerated, provided it was "normal"'. When Nancy Spain was recruited as a *Daily Express* book reviewer in 1952, its editor described her to his proprietor Beaverbrook as 'a raging Lesbian', whose manliness made her a 'circus freak'. *Express* journalists feared their paper might become a 'laughing-stock' by employing her.[6]

Peter Earle was the *News of the World* journalist who did much to publicise the Profumo Affair. He had been investigating call-girl rings for some time, and was scampering ahead of the pack in 1963. Earle was a tall, gangly man who cultivated clandestine contacts with policemen and criminals. They would telephone him with tips, using codenames such as 'Grey Wolf' or 'Fiery Horseman'. He was unfailingly ceremonious with 'ladies', though he called his wife Dumbo. Office colleagues were addressed as 'old cock' or 'my old china'. Earle's speech was peppered with phrases like 'Gadzooks!' or 'By Jove!' When he agreed with someone, he exclaimed: 'Great Scot, you're right!' To quell office disputes he would say: 'Let there be no murmuring.'

Earle was the archetype of the seedy Fleet Street drunk. He scarcely ate, but survived on oceans of whisky, which he called 'the amber liquid'. He held court in the upstairs bar of the *News of the World* pub, the Tipperary in Bouverie Street, or at weekends in the Printer's Pie in Fleet Street. 'Hostelry' and 'watering-hole' were his words for pubs. 'Barman, replenishment for my friends,' he would call when ordering a round. Earle had a prodigious memory for the details of old stories, talked like Samuel Johnson, and was an avid gawper at bosoms. Dressed in his Gannex rain-coat, he left on investigative forays clutching a briefcase which was empty except for a whisky bottle. His doorstep technique was based on devastating effrontery; his questioning was indignant; and if rebuffed he mustered a baleful glare of wounded dignity. Either because he could not write intelligible English or because he was always drunk, his copy was unusable. He jumbled his facts and muddled their sequence. Subs had to read his incoherent copy, patiently talk him through it, and prise out a story that was fit to be printed.

Fleet Street in Earle's heyday was quickened by the commercial strategies and journalistic innovations of a formidable duo, Cecil King and Hugh Cudlipp, who controlled Mirror Group News-papers. Beginning in 1958, King pursued an aggressive merger and takeover strategy in newspaper and magazine publishing: the great combine that he created was in 1963 renamed International Publishing Corporation (IPC). King and Cudlipp proved to be the proprietors who exploited the Profumo Affair most effectively for their own purposes, which were to divert the currents of political power, to install a Labour Prime Minister in Downing Street, to entrench the privileges of their allies and to command domineering influence in a new social regime which was supposedly to be characterised by salubrious modernity and merciless egalitarianism.

The *Daily Mirror* had been founded by Northcliffe in 1903 as a snobby publication for office girls who aspired to become gentle-women. Taken over by Northcliffe's brother Lord Rothermere, it remained until 1935 an ailing, torpid newspaper losing readers under fusty management. Thereafter, with Rothermere's nephew King as its grey eminence and Cudlipp as its features editor, the *Daily Mirror* chased young working-class readers with politics that were left-leaning and insubordinate. In 1937, King appointed Cudlipp as editor of the *Daily Mirror*'s sister paper, the *Sunday Pictorial*. Together the two men deftly repositioned both news-papers. They became market leaders of 'the cheap press', as it was described in 1937, 'that strange, crooked mirror which distorts the world for our entertainment'.[7]

A representative issue of the *Sunday Pictorial* of March 1939 had an editorial headlined 'The New MAN!' It lauded its male readers with a rhetoric that was to be revived and loudened during the Macmillan years. 'There is no smug complacency about the New Man of the New Britain. He's awake, virile, courageous, eager to defend his hard-won freedom, resolved at all costs to remain supreme. The mind of the New Man is no longer clogged with worn-out doctrines and moral shams.' In the same issue of 1939 there was an equally characteristic feature depicting Mayfair in terms that dived from inverted snobbery to salacity. 'Shiny limousines glide through the quiet streets. Disdainful duchesses take pompous Pekinese on shopping expeditions. Ducal mansions look down their noses at £10,000 cottages. Butlers buttle; head-waiters pocket £5 tips; and smart page boys scurry across the roads laden with the merchandise of Hartnell and Molyneux.'

However, the backstreets behind 'skyscraper hotels and blocks of luxury flats' were 'honeycombed with flatlets kept by ladies of easy virtue'.[8]

In 1945, King's newspapers helped Labour to win a swingeing victory in the general election. 'You must remember,' Churchill's daughter warned of the impending Conservative defeat, 'the *Daily Mirror* is *widely* read by all Ranks and especially the Other Ranks.' Its tone was youthful, demotic and irreverent. King and Cudlipp subjected the secrets of sex and power to the same levelling demystification. They identified sexual candour with modernity, cheeriness and populism. Their democratic openness hit the circulation of the *News of the World*, with its sickly hypocrisies and furtive guiltiness.[9]

Of all English newspapers, the *Sunday Pictorial* gave most coverage to the publication in 1948 of Kinsey's American research, *Sexual Behavior in the Human Male*. The paper then resolved to finance complementary research into English sexual attitudes by Tom Harrisson's Mass Observation network: 2,052 members of the public were interviewed, while 450 members of Mass Observation's voluntary panel gave information. The results were published by the *Sunday Pictorial* in a five-part serial during 1949. This was a rare example of the Sunday press not displaying repressive, derogatory malice about sexual secrets, and typified the Cudlipp-King approach to explaining the riddles of political and erotic power. One-third of respondents approved of sex outside marriage, particularly among engaged couples. Two-thirds favoured birth control. A quarter of husbands and a fifth of wives admitted adultery. Forty-nine per cent of bachelors and thirty-eight per cent of spinsters claimed experience of intercourse. A quarter of men had used prostitutes; twelve per cent had experienced 'homosexual relations'; another eight per cent admitted milder same-sex contacts. Ninety-five per cent of men and sixty-six per cent of women said they had masturbated. A Labour MP who was chairman of the *Birmingham Town Crier* denounced the articles: 'I have a girl who is still at school, and she takes the

Pictorial. The recent *Sunday Pictorial* articles are real "stinkers". Who went to bed with whom and how many times, is no sort of Sunday morning breakfast reading for young girls and boys.'[10]

Coverage of John Christie's necrophilia in the Rillington Place murder trial of June 1953, more than the weekly Sunday circulation stunts, aroused revulsion. The General Council of the Press was launched during that summer – funded by newspaper owners and with council membership restricted to newspaper editors – to evade the threat of statutory regulation of press conduct. The Council met quarterly, and issued colourless, starchy reports of its deliberations. The second of these, in October 1953, deplored 'the unwholesome exploitation of sex by certain newspapers', which was 'calculated to injure public morals, especially as newspapers and periodicals are seen and read by young persons'. However, editors of populist newspapers showed a studied insolence towards the General Council, especially during its inaugural phase under the chairmanship of Lord Astor of Hever, the remote, high-minded proprietor of *The Times*. The General Council remained an organisation of lofty self-esteem but neutered powers even after its restructuring as the Press Council in 1962.[11]

'Newspapers and periodicals, by their unwholesome exploitation of sex, are corrupting the moral sense of the nation,' Geoffrey Fisher, the Archbishop of Canterbury, declared in November 1953. 'The papers in question have owners and editors, sub-editors and reporters, men with wives and families and domestic virtues. They cannot really enjoy the passage through their own minds of what they put into the minds of others. Will they not bravely face a reformation of heart, of moral judgment, of public duty, and of journalistic practice?' The Archbishop called also for a revival of old notions of privacy, 'which would abolish the smart, impudent and offensive ways of referring to individuals and their private concerns, which spoil so much of modern journalism'. Sir Victor Gollancz, despite publishing a mordant pen portrait of Fisher, nevertheless agreed with him about yellow journalism. 'With the vilest of motives, to increase profit,' Gollancz wrote in

1953, 'the million-circulation newspapers have gone all out to titillate those sadistic and lascivious instincts that lie dormant in almost everyone; for this is the way, they think rightly or wrongly, to get more readers and down their rivals.' C. S. Lewis similarly denounced proprietors and editors who profited from spreading 'envy, hatred, suspicion and confusion'. The trouble was that no one hesitated to drink, joke or shake hands with journalists, any less than to read their stories. They enjoyed 'all the sense of secret power and all the sweets of a perpetually gratified inferiority complex while at the same time having the *entrée* to honest society'.[12]

In November 1953, Cudlipp responded to this outcry with his three-part series: 'Sex, Crime, and the Press'. 'The *Daily Mirror* is not a pompous newspaper,' he declared. 'We are flippant about flippant matters, serious about serious ones – but we try not to be a bore about anything.' His newspapers never truckled to puritanism. 'The whole nation laughed at the silly attempt made to agitate Shropshire Women's Institutes into demanding a ban on pictures of girls wearing bikinis . . . What's disgusting about a pretty girl – if you aren't faded and jealous?' His newspapers were righteous campaigners. 'When we learn of evils it's our job to expose them. We detest hypocrisy. We give plain meanings in plain words . . . Fogies object to us because we're lively. WE think it a crime against life to be tiresome. We're a cheeky, daring, gay newspaper. But we're blowed if we are a dirty newspaper.' Cudlipp's phrases were more plausible than those of King, who argued that reports of violence in his newspapers diverted people from committing murder. 'Crime vicariously enjoyed in print is a substitute for violent crime itself,' he argued in 1963. 'If some people can read about murder, their murderous instincts will be sufficiently satisfied to remove the temptation to commit an actual murder themselves.'[13]

A paradox of the 1950s was that as the English increasingly claimed sexual acts as the private business of consenting adults, beyond the purview of clergy, magistrates and police, there was simultaneously a growing desire for the intimate details of people's lives to be exposed to the dazzling searchlights of newspaper prurience. The collection of 'human interest' stories or the photographs that illustrated them was unscrupulous. It was to remedy a deteriorating situation that Lord Mancroft in 1961 introduced in the House of Lords his Right of Privacy Bill, which was intended to protect privacy and give rights of redress. It would have enabled the suing of journalists who published, without the plaintiffs' consent, information about their personal affairs which was calculated to distress or embarrass.

To show the need of such legislation, Mancroft cited the invasion by newsmen and photographers of the Munich hospital where the Manchester United manager Matt Busby and surviving players in his soccer team lay after their air crash of 1958, and similar intrusion when Aneurin Bevan lay mortally ill in hospital in 1960. He cited the bullying of Sir John Huggins at the time of his divorce and re-marriage in 1958; the callous, humiliating publicity given to the emigration plans of the parents of a convicted murderer; and the harrying of Colonel Christopher Hunter. At a quarter past one on the morning after his lovelorn daughter had committed suicide, Hunter's front doorbell was rung. A voice called: 'It's the police.' Colonel Hunter and his wife came down from bed, unhappy and confused, in their dressing gowns, to be caught on their front doorstep by a flashlight photographer, who then sped off in a car.[14]

Reporters and photographers, wearing pork-pie hats and scruffy raincoats, had no qualms about invading their quarry's house: clambering over a wall into the garden; entering by an open window in summertime; ringing the doorbell, shoving past whoever answered the door, and firing a fusillade of questions once they had marched inside. If their quarry left home by car, one or two of them would swerve their vehicles in front, and drive slowly on the crown of the road to prevent overtaking, while the rest followed in a phalanx behind. Reporters and photographers were proud of their deceptions: inveigling their way into houses pretending to be meter readers; equipping themselves with flowers or grapes and invading hospital rooms masquerading as relatives; waylaying children on their way home from school; threatening incessant persecution ('I'm going to be here all day, and we'll go on asking until you talk to us') or harassment of loved ones ('If you won't tell us, we know who to ask'); breaking confidences; bribing and suborning; inventing unattributed quotes. Sir Richard Glyn had constituents whose baby had been murdered by a maniac: 'The mother,' Glyn complained in 1963, 'almost unconscious from shock, was receiving medical attention when the house was invaded by a journalist and a photographer. The latter forced his way into her bedroom in order to obtain "an exclusive picture" and had to be ejected by other members of the family.'[15]

The Duke of Atholl and his fellow press peers resisted Mancroft's Bill as an unjustifiable restriction on journalists' duty to report fearlessly; but it was the Lord Chancellor, Kilmuir, who squashed the bill on behalf of the government. His disingenuous speech implied that Lord Porter's committee on defamation had, after conscientious thought, reported in 1948 that it was impractical to legislate to ensure privacy. In truth, Porter's committee had reported that privacy was outside the terms of their remit. Kilmuir also objected that such cases would have to be tried before juries, who were unreliable in the amounts they awarded in damages. He did not explain why, if libel and slander actions were tried before juries, privacy cases should not be. Kilmuir denied that protection for privacy in England failed the standards set by the Universal Declaration of Human Rights (1948) and the European Convention for the Protection of Human Rights (1950) which, he falsely insisted, applied only to interference by governments in individual privacy. Kilmuir refused to refer privacy for consideration by the Law Reform Committee.[16]

Although the government was scared of confronting press abuses, Macmillan as Prime Minister was increasingly exasperated by what he saw as Fleet Street's vulgar stupidity. 'The only exception to the deterioration of all the Press into treating politics, economics, finance, literature with a sort of "servants' hall gossip" technique is *The Times*, he wrote in 1961. 'It is sometimes very silly; often intellectually patronising; but it is *not* corrupt.'[17] His dislike of press stunts was to lead him to confront Fleet Street exaggerations at the time of the Vassall spy case in 1962 – a confrontation that proved decisive to the development of the Profumo Affair. Moreover, despite Macmillan's qualified praise, *The Times* did not fulfil all that its buyers wanted from their newspapers: forty-four per cent of its readers also read the *Daily Express* in 1958, and thirty-two per cent read the *Daily Mirror*.

Beaverbrook's *Express* newspapers were seedbeds of ancient rancour. They pursued vendettas, smeared people and magnified spiteful gossip. A friend of the old man recounted in 1962 that when he mentioned that he would like to contribute an article, Beaverbrook purred softly, 'Whom do you wish to attack?' Beaverbrook typically used his power to persecute a reclusive baronet, Sir John Ellerman, from envy that he had inherited £20 million at the age of twenty-two. For a quarter of a century his newspapers inserted disobliging paragraphs about the Duke of Hamilton, partly because he was a duke, but chiefly because Hamilton as a young parliamentary candidate had rejected an offer of Beaverbrook's support during a by-election. Other rebuffs were revenged. In 1949, hearing of Isaiah Berlin's scintillating diplomatic reports on American politics and society, Beaverbrook summoned the Oxford don and asked him to write for *Express* newspapers. He was incredulous when the young man did not immediately submit to his overtures. He could arrange luxurious living, he told Berlin: 'there could be – and it was an offer, he declared, that was not made to many – there could be a discreet flat where Berlin could entertain – a lady; indeed ladies, if need be, could even materialise'. Berlin resisted these blandishments, and shortly afterwards a BBC radio talk by him was decried in a leading article in the *Evening Standard* which Beaverbrook had perhaps dictated to one of his minions. Slurs and innuendos abounded in Beaverbrook's newspapers. Macmillan noted in his diary in 1957 that they had sunk to the level of *Confidential* (an American scandal sheet), by entrapment of the Foreign Secretary, Selwyn Lloyd. While holidaying in Spain, Lloyd was tracked by a *Daily Express* cameraman, who snapped him walking with a friend and the friend's wife. The husband, however, was excised from a doctored photograph of Lloyd with the woman published under the caption 'Who is the *Señorita*?' 'Beaverbrook,' thought Macmillan, 'could stoop no lower.'[18]

J. B. Priestley had Beaverbrook in mind when he wrote in 1962 that he did not resent the power of newspapers to criticise everything and everybody. What he disliked was 'their conviction that they are among the sacred objects and persons above all criticism, and that any public man bold enough to challenge this conviction may become the subject of a vendetta, disguised as honest newsgathering, that may last for years'.[19] Few newsmen felt more sacrosanct from criticism than the Mirror Group's Cecil Harmsworth King.

King was born in 1901. His mother, whom he hated, was a sister of Northcliffe and Rothermere. She held that monotony was improving for children. King's eldest brother died at the battle of Ypres; his cousins Vere and Vyvyan Harmsworth – the Rothermere heirs – were killed in the First World War too; another cousin, Alfred Harmsworth, was castrated by wounds sustained at the Somme. Worse still was the calamity of King's school holidays in the last year of the war. He and his surviving brother were pupils at Winchester College. After visiting their parents in Dublin in 1918, their mother sent them back to Winchester on separate Irish Sea steamers. At the last moment, King asked to travel on the earlier ship: his brother, who took his place on the *Leinster*, drowned when it was torpedoed by a German submarine. King's cold, twisted sorrow, like his conviction that he was predestined for supreme power, was intensified by this tragedy. He wrote in his memoirs that he had hated himself until old age, and always hankered for suicide. For most of his adulthood he suffered from psoriasis – raw bleeding skin and scales – which deepened his woebegone moods. His self-loathing, though, had a self-congratulatory tinge.

The *Daily Mail* managing director who was ordered to give King his first job threatened but failed to break him. King became a director of his uncle Rothermere's *Daily Mirror* in 1929. He led the new regime that was installed there in the 1930s. Its keynotes became more assertive after the abdication crisis of 1936, during which the *Daily Mirror* was less deferential than other newspapers. Thereafter it was always class-conscious, with jibes at aristocratic adultery. King selected Hugh Cudlipp, an abrasive young Welshman, as the *Daily Mirror*'s features editor in 1935. When King was appointed as editorial director of the *Sunday Pictorial* in 1937, Cudlipp, aged just twenty-four, was his choice as editor.

Cudlipp had been born in Cardiff in 1913, son of a commercial traveller in eggs and bacon, and grandson of a docks policeman. He was relieved to finish with schooling at the age of fourteen. His journalistic apprenticeship was served on a weekly newspaper serving a dormitory seaside suburb of Cardiff. At the age of fifteen he left Wales to work for Lord Kemsley's *Manchester Evening Chronicle*. He thrived as a district reporter covering Blackpool: watching the English working classes holidaying was, he believed, an invaluable training for populist journalism. In 1932 he transferred to one of Kemsley's Fleet Street titles, the *Sunday Chronicle*, where he was appointed features editor at the age of twenty. Three years later he joined the *Daily Mirror*.

Cudlipp enlisted in 1940, and fought on active service before launching the British forces' newspaper, *Union Jack*. His military experiences honed his understanding of his readers' aspirations as much as his training in Blackpool. They raised him in the world's view, too: this bagman's son was demobilised in 1946 with the rank of lieutenant colonel. In 1951, King made him editorial director of both the *Daily Mirror* and *Sunday Pictorial*. For the next seventeen years the two men collaborated in a formidable partnership. By the early 1960s the Mirror Group owned the *Sunday Pictorial*, *The People* (together commanding over forty per cent of Sunday sales), the *Daily Herald* and *Daily Mirror*, together with the six leading women's magazines published in Britain, and held one-quarter of the shares in Associated Television.

Cudlipp never read a book if he could avoid it. He found it unbearable to sit still in a theatre for more than one act. It was as if plays were newspaper columns: it should be enough to read the first paragraph to get the story. His books *Publish and Be Damned!* (1953) and *At Your Peril* (1962) were ghosted for him. In them, Cudlipp resembled a celebrity cook praising his own recipes. His journalism was 'rumbustious', *At Your Peril* boasted. 'Defying the conventions. Hastening the inevitable in social change. Cocking a snook at the hoary traditions and pomposities of our times. Fighting the taboos.' Cudlipp's working credo ran: 'Say it first, get away with it first, and others will follow. At all events, say it first.' For a newspaper to boom in popularity, 'it must be alarmingly provocative in every issue and abundantly confident of its own importance'.[20]

A survey of English journalism extolled the Cudlipp-King regime in 1957: 'the *Daily Mirror* has kicked, jeered, argued, fought, joked and shouted its way up. It has insulted powerful men. Its editors have been brought to court. It has been threatened with suppression. It has been called subversive, irresponsible, pornographic. Always it has kept on the side of the "ordinary" people.' More than any other newspaper the *Daily Mirror* had identified itself with 'the century of the common man'. With its 'spluttering outrage', and clamorous, denunciatory headlines, it was primarily 'a paper of opposition'. What readers noticed most, though, were 'the strip cartoons, the teasing cuties, the babies, the sob-stuff, the bottoms and busts'.[21]

Harold Macmillan lunched with King and Cudlipp in 1955. 'I don't think I've ever seen a more unpleasant type than Mr King. Mr Cudlipp (I wd say) though quite reckless, was not without a certain bias towards the interests of his country, always supposing that his personal interests were not involved.' Meeting them again for luncheon a year later he judged them 'as good a pair of ruffians as you cd find anywhere'. In 1957 the Macmillans gave a Downing Street luncheon for Cudlipp: 'He is able, & not unreasonable – altho' naturally, like all such journalists, without any scruples about truth, morality, good faith & the like.'[22]

King stood six feet four inches tall. His rumpled clothes showed his indifference to convention. Humankind, he believed, would live in brutal chaos unless discipline was imposed on the morass of fools by a strong leader. He dealt with letters by returning them with brusque responses written in biro in his even, sprawling script. Sometimes he sealed envelopes with a strip of sellotape. He loathed late nights, and stalked out of public dinners before ten regardless of the eminence of the speakers or his neighbours at table. For thirty years, despite his newspapers' denunciations of the Tories' grouse-moor image, he owned a shooting estate in Aberdeenshire, where the bags were mainly grouse.

Every year King made stately business tours of the Commonwealth: his newspapers in Nigeria, Ghana and Sierra Leone were as valued by him as those in London. He selected office lackeys to accompany him, put them under his surveillance and delivered trenchant assessments: 'That goose will never be a swan'; 'Not ruthless enough'; 'No fire in his belly'. The lackeys returned with tales of their own: how he 'fought his way through a mob of four hundred excited gibbering Indians to buy a ticket for a native cinema in Bombay', as they told Cudlipp; 'the loud guffaw that astonished a group of nude African villagers when King discovered that the total equipment of their mud hat consisted of a sleeping mat, an eating bowl – and a selection of Hollywood pin-ups stuck on the wall'. In advance of his aircraft landing, his favourite meals were ordered: groundnut stew and palm oil chop. A fog of imperial condescension enveloped King's tours. 'He has pow-wows with the African editors and the commercial staffs, listening with patience to their problems and aspirations:

203

with affection they call him "the father of the family", Cudlipp described. 'When the pow-wows are over, and he has listened to the politicians in their fine new buildings in the city, King wanders off on safari in the villages in his ill-fitting linen suit and floppy straw hat, talking with the chiefs in their mud huts or palaces, and giving lumps of sugar to the hordes of delighted, gurgling children who follow him around with smiles as long and broad as sliced melon.'[23]

Carnal possession was King's only means of mitigating his emotional isolation. 'Sex to me is suffering,' he copied into his commonplace book. 'This is what it means, has meant since my first pubertal longings, the fire in my head and loins, sometimes such that any woman, my mother or any other, would have helped; and what it has meant through two marriages and now into my sixties. I mean suffering identical with the pangs of Tantalus, a mental and physical hunger, a desperate longing for that which I can see, which is all around, but which I cannot touch at will – and touch, physical contact, is essential for any easement of my condition – but . . . which, even when perhaps briefly I can satiate or at least blunt its ferocity, returns next moment more urgent than ever.' King was dismissive of moral panics about changes in sexual conduct, and credited his news-papers' frankness for inducing these changes: 'a great deal of the tut-tutting is due to the fact that working-class morals have invaded the middle classes'. Whereas men paid for illicit affairs in money, venereal infection, wifely reproaches or scandal, he admonished women that their 'promiscuity had to be paid for' in other ways. It was not a question of hell-fire, 'but a woman tends to leave a bit of herself behind with each lover and at the end is so dispersed that she can never reassemble herself and become a complete woman. Perhaps this was the origin of the phrase "a ruined woman".'[24]

Presumably King prided himself on leaving each of the many women with whom he had affairs reduced by their final parting. He warned his first wife before their marriage that he had no intention of fidelity, but she was too naive to understand what he meant. 'Love-making,' he told her, 'is the only form of athletics that interests me in the least. It is the only handcraft too! In one form or another it is the only pleasure in life worth talking about.' His target was to have a dozen women a year. He propositioned his wife's twin sister, and her friends, as well as taking mistresses from his office. In the 1950s, when he invited his young daughter-in-law to holiday with him without her husband, she concluded that he had designs. He subjected his wife to invasive interrogation about her thoughts, beliefs and emotions, and criticised her replies relentlessly; but when he explained his hopes and vulnerability with unremitting emphasis, he required her responses to be wholly uncritical. King's wife lurched into depression with occasional bouts of paranoid aggression. Following electric shock treatment, she spiralled by the mid-1950s into horrifying delusions, furies and self-loathing.[25]

In 1955, King began an affair with Ruth Railton, a choral conductor who a few years earlier had founded the National Youth Orchestra, which the *Daily Mirror* sponsored. Telling his adult daughter that he was going to live with another woman, he said that he could not yet give her name: 'Let us call her Marilyn Monroe'. Railton, explains King's biographer, 'pictured herself occupying a bower of metaphorical fluffy clouds and pink roses from which she exuded love, kindness, sensitivity, spirituality and truth', but in truth was 'jealous, merciless, fiercely manipulative and an inveterate liar'. She claimed to have fought with the Dutch wartime resistance and therefore to be the object of postwar Nazi death threats; to have trained in sexual technique in a Paris brothel; to have been an Olympic rider, Dior model, ballerina and psychic consulted by police in murder cases. She convinced King that she possessed paranormal powers, and claimed that she could make herself invisible. He finally married her in October 1962, three days after his divorce was finalised. Several of his colleagues at Mirror Group applied the word 'evil' to her. One called her 'a maniac'.[26]

*

Hugh Cudlipp was twenty-two when he married a fellow journalist, Bunny Parnell, an upholsterer's daughter. During their miserable, wet honeymoon in the Channel Islands she announced that Tom Darlow, editor of *John Bull*, was her lover. This affair continued unabated through her marriage. When she became pregnant by Darlow, she tried to hide the paternity of the child by telling Cudlipp that she wanted his baby and inveigling him into unprotected sex. It was only when she died, in 1938, following a Caesarean birth in which the baby also died, that Cudlipp realised her ruse. A few hours after his wife's death, Cudlipp went to the *Sunday Pictorial* office to check the late edition. An assistant suggested substituting a new front-page lead, proffering a freshly received report with the words, 'this is a better human interest story than that one'. Cudlipp replied: 'Don't talk to me about human interest tonight.'[27]

Cudlipp liked flirting with pretty women, taking them on dates, and seducing them. 'They are tired of thinking, they are tired of working, they are tired of planning; they simply want to be loved, and they simply want babies,' he told *Sunday Pictorial* readers in an article of 1939 about women:

> *The young woman of to-day still talks a certain amount of drivel about her career, but she'd sooner forget all about it if a man worth marrying proposed to her* . . . The truth is just this: That if the New Man of the New Britain is virile and courageous, the New Woman wants to be nothing more than the sort of mate he deserves.
>
> *Back to the home. That is where the modern woman wants to go.* She will deny it until she is blue in the gills, but she wants to go back there just the same. With her cooking, and her sewing, and her man, and her baby. Does she want to serve groceries over the counter, dish up cosmetics and lotions in a beauty parlour, weave materials for other women's dresses in a mill, or tap the keys of a typewriter in a dreary, dusty office? Not on your life![28]

For several years Cudlipp had an affair with a *Mirror* journalist, Eileen Ascroft, and in 1945, after her divorce, the couple married. She was a ruthless operator surrounded by dazed human sacrifices to her ambition. During the 1950s the Cudlipps were the most successful couple in Fleet Street. There was adultery on both sides in the marriage. Ascroft supposedly had an affair with one of their chauffeurs (the Cudlipps had a battery of secretaries, housekeepers and drivers to support their high-pressure lives). She had a long tangle with a married man whom she had met during the war. One has a sense of desperate flings masquerading as *soigné* diversions. An obvious affair with one of her husband's closest colleagues was tolerated by Cudlipp, who was involved with her friend Jodi Hyland, editor of *Woman's Mirror* (whose devotion he however had to share with a pug with a weak bladder). A revealing aspect of Cudlipp's adulteries in this period was that the great democrat enjoyed exercising *droit de seigneur* by having sex with the wives of men who worked for him. It added to his feeling of sexual power. He liked to tarnish what he could not permanently possess.

Cudlipp was profiled by the *Observer* in 1961 as 'one of those earnest, clever, bold, rhetorical men who seem to have been given a hard push at an early age, after which they have never been able to remain still. At the age of forty-seven Cudlipp cultivates tycoonery: telephones interrupt, the gin is freely offered, the cigars look like truncheons, the jokes to subordinates are tinged with meaning, and Cudlipp's charm alternates rapidly with Cudlipp's brusqueness.' The paper found in him that cardinal virtue of the 1960s: edginess. 'He is better at toppling the mighty, at seeing the catch in things, than he is at taking his own beliefs seriously; this is a highly contemporary talent . . . there's no doubt that Cudlipp is about the most successful journalist in Britain when it comes to pleasing the public.'[29]

Eileen Cudlipp died in 1962 of an overdose of Carbrital, a hypnotic sleeping-draught. In the preceding week Cudlipp's book, *At Your Peril*, had been launched with a round of parties. On the evening before her death the Cudlipps attended a party at

Sonning-on-Thames, where they had a new house, but she motored back from the party to their London house, also on the Thames, at Strand-on-the-Green, near Hammersmith. This was ostensibly because the curtains were not yet hung in their Sonning bedroom. 'Sorry to desert you,' she wrote in a note to her husband, 'but I had to try & get some sleep. As you know I haven't slept for nights – probably the excitement of the book. After Dr Thomas' excellent pills & a good night's rest I'll be down feeling fine.' Although the inquest recorded a verdict of accidental death, a few of the dead woman's friends and her many enemies believed she had killed herself. A year later Cudlipp married Jodi Hyland.[30]

Until the early 1960s, Cecil King drank copiously. During long expense-account lunches he would order an aperitif, wine with the meal, and brandy afterwards. When he reached home in the evenings, he would down a treble gin and tonic before killing a bottle of wine. At parties he drank heavily to loosen his tongue. He liked martinis. He would leave his glass at a small distance, affect not to notice when it was filled by a waiter, and swallow the refreshed glass in a gulp. In restaurants he ordered wine by the magnum. (He also ate in a hurry, swallowing each of his breakfast fried eggs in one gulp.) King renounced alcohol on physician's orders at the age of sixty, outlived two hard-drinking sons, and in sobriety was more frustrated than ever.

Until the early 1960s, visitors to Cudlipp's office before eleven in the morning would be offered a beer, except on days of celebration, when there would be a champagne conference at 10.30. After eleven he used to open a bottle of white wine. Like King, Cudlipp had power lunches accompanied by aperitifs, wine, and digestifs. He had blazing rows when drunk. His behaviour and judgement became so unreliable that King, having sobered himself up, insisted that his colleague must stop drinking. Cudlipp agreed to renounce spirits, except brandy, which he counted as wine.

The egalitarianism of King and Cudlipp was undetectable in Mirror Group's brash, self-conscious skyscraper offices, built on the site of a bombed drapery at Holborn Circus at a cost of £9.5 million, and opened in 1961. There had seldom been an office so status conscious in its interior arrangements. Every employee's place in the hierarchy was assessed with inexorable logic and fixed by fine gradations. King had a private lift to his ninth-floor suite, which as symbol of his paramountcy contained an open-grate fireplace – the first one ever installed in a centrally heated, air-conditioned office in a smokeless zone. King also had his own dining room, bedroom, kitchen, bathroom and luxurious carpeting. Cudlipp, by contrast, had only a refrigerator, bedroom, private lavatory and shower; but his bedroom was designated as his 'studio' to show that he was the creative ace rather than financial brains of the business.

Other directors had built-in cocktail cabinets and televisions, but to signal the importance of advertising revenue, only the advertising director had his own refrigerator. Whereas directors had rubber underlay to their carpets, editors had felt. Journalists were reduced to rubber-tiled floors, with no carpets. Only directors could lock their office doors from inside. Deputy editors had venetian blinds and metal desks rather than the curtains and wooden desks of editors. Men with double-pedestal desks knew their superiority to single-pedestal men. Top men's offices had brick walls, the next level of prestige had walls of frosted glass from floor to ceiling; the middle-rankers had frosted glass only halfway; and the subordinates worked behind plain glass. The office telephone directory printed some extension numbers in blue, to indicate that only internal numbers could be dialled from that instrument. Numbers printed in green indicated that the instrument could be used to dial external local numbers. Red numbers denoted a telephone which could connect to operators to make trunk and overseas calls. Racing tipsters (red telephones on double-pedestal desks) outranked news reporters (green telephones on single-pedestal desks). Chief sub-editors excelled sub-editors because they could eat in the executives' restaurant, instead of the staff cafeteria, although never, of course, in the directors' dining room.[31]

King specialised in destructive criticism, and had a jealous, levelling spirit. His resentments and Cudlipp's envy ensured that their papers pilloried nepotism and the Old School Tie, although King was the Wykehamist nephew of Northcliffe and Rothermere. Moreover, despite his newspapers' diatribes against Eton, King sent two of his sons to the school, and his other boy to Winchester. Eventually the *Daily Mirror* denounced Eton so viciously that one governor proposed Michael King's expulsion. Other pupils became so hostile that the youth insisted on leaving Eton, to the sorrow of his masters, and went to work in a Glasgow shipyard. King and Cudlipp taunted privilege and decried luxury; but while their columnist Cassandra inveighed against those who dined in expensive restaurants during food rationing, they ate in the costliest places. Cudlipp said in 1962 that his newspapers were fighting notions 'that all life begins on the playing fields of Eton. That it gets its second breath in a college in Oxford or Cambridge. Its third breath as a major in the officers' mess of the Household Cavalry. Its fourth breath in an exclusive West End club. And its last breath as an obscure and impoverished parson in a quaint English village.' He ranged his newspapers against 'a restricted ruling clique, an upper crust of polite and discreet intellectuals, belonging to the same class and clubs, marrying the same sort of women and producing the same sort of children'.[32]

These editorial tactics gelled with the thinking of Labour politicians like Wilfred Fienburgh, who believed that many Labour supporters were only jerked into voting at elections if they had something to vote *against*. When Labour won its great election victory in 1945, and one newly elected MP shouted in the Commons 'We are the Masters now!', the parliamentary party assumed that because it was the working-class party, and the working class far outnumbered the rest of the electorate, they were guaranteed to remain the permanent government. Labour MPs were puzzled, if not affronted, when it proved that they had no automatic majority. Fienburgh deduced that Labour voters in 1945, 1950 and 1951 feared that the Tories would return to mass unemployment, and filed into the polling booths to vote *against*. But there was no industrial depression or mass unemployment under the governments of Churchill, Eden and Macmillan; nothing for Labour supporters to fear or vote against at the general elections of 1955 and 1959. The decision of ten per cent of these voters not to vote contributed to the party's defeat, Fienburgh judged. 'The pot-bellied cartoon capitalist has ground very few faces. Indeed, he has provided a few million television screens to which working-class faces have been glued. There were in consequence no bogey men to vote against in 1955.'[33]

Cudlipp urged Labour to revive its vote by using Macmillan's toffs as bogeymen. 'As you're bound to lose next time, let's lose on a fine anti-privilege campaign,' he urged Richard Crossman in 1958. Macmillan's triumph in the general election of 1959, whereby the Conservatives increased their majority from sixty to one hundred, dismayed him. He blamed himself for misinterpreting his readers' temper, and declared a holiday from politics. Crossman disappeared as a *Daily Mirror* columnist; the 1945 slogan 'Forward with the People' was discarded overnight, and the newspaper proclaimed that its new emphasis would be on 'YOUTH'. The newspaper signalled this change by substituting the 'Life Story of Tommy Steele', the Bermondsey boy who became England's first rock'n'roll teen idol, for its usual editorial. Other newspapers made money by starting moral panics about the young, belabouring them with insults, and criticising those like the Mirror Group who pandered to them. 'It is natural,' King retorted magisterially in 1963, 'when we are worried about juvenile delinquency or sexual promiscuity to seek scapegoats. The root causes, the decay of religion, the abdication of parental authority, earlier puberty, greater mobility and life in large cities, are too unmanageable, and it is easier to blame the newspapers.'[34]

Cudlipp's truce with privilege was short-lived. Mirror journalists soon devised new angles to stab at tradition, civility and amateurism while promoting clichés about innovation and expertise. The imagery of their *Wake Up, Britain!* campaign, for example, contrasted Mr Yesterday, a gent with furled umbrella, briefcase, bowler hat, and breastpocket white handkerchief, with Mr Today, equipped with space helmet and futuristic protective uniform fit for an experimental laboratory. The *Daily Mirror* was not, Cudlipp boasted in 1962, one of those newspapers 'treating the usually vain pronouncements of Archbishops as if they were the word of God; imagining that the demise of an unknown peer in a midnight crash between expensive limousines was of any greater moment than the unhappy end of a railway wheel-tapper crushed between buffers in the sidings at Crewe on a wet Sunday morning; extolling the aplomb of wealthy, titled drones gambling at Deauville and ignoring the harassed joys of the plebeian customers at the Margate whelk stall where the vinegar, though watered, is free'.[35]

Most popular newspapers raised as much dirt and noise as they could during the Profumo Affair – but by unthinking reflex. They wanted to raise circulation by sensational stories and shameless stunts. Beaverbrook's *Express* papers had a side agenda of hurting the Astors. The King-Cudlipp newspapers, by contrast, had premeditated, coherent tactics to accomplish their strategic aim of damaging the reputation and confidence of Macmillan's government. Their newspapers were the ones that seized on the Keeler-Profumo affair not as a weapon for a general thumping of the Conservative Party, but as a poisoned stiletto which, if carefully inserted, would kill off a political class. They made the Profumo Affair into the ignition point of Britain's modernisation crisis, which had been seething since 1958. Their strategy was facilitated by the changes in public mood that had occurred during the seven years of Macmillan affluence.

'Ours is an acquisitive society, interested mainly in its physical wellbeing and the possession and enjoyment of luxuries,' King summarised. 'The cohesion of the family itself, aided by the fireside television set and the family car, is stronger than for generations.' The fireside television proved a more powerfully levelling device even than Mirror Group Newspapers. In 1951 there were 764,000 combined television and radio licences. Stimulated by the Coronation in 1953, this figure had risen to over 4 million by 1955 – the year when ITV was inaugurated. There were 10 million television sets in 1960 (by which year seventy-two per cent of people had access to both channels) and 13 million by 1964. Each set commanded the room in which it was installed. 'There it sits,' wrote a television critic, 'shouting slogans and snatches of song, and wasting your time, and grabbing your attention.'[36]

For years broadcasters were forbidden from discussing on air any subject that was to be debated in Parliament within the next fortnight. In 1955, for example, panellists on BBC's *In the News* could not animadvert on the hydrogen bomb because it was soon to be discussed in the Commons. When challenged on this suppression Churchill, as Prime Minister, insisted that it would be 'shocking' for debates to be forestalled 'by persons who had not the status or responsibility of Members of Parliament'. The rule became insupportable during the Suez crisis, was suspended experimentally, and abolished in July 1957.[37]

The BBC continued to uphold exacting standards, hierarchical authority and seemliness. It was, wrote a former programme assistant, Penelope Fitzgerald, 'a cross between a civil service, a powerful moral force and an amateur theatrical company which wasn't too sure where the next week's money was coming from'. Apart from vaudeville entertainment, it produced bland, deferential programmes. Henry Fairlie in 1959 pictured the scene when a minister or trade unionist arrived for interview. As the eminent visitor is ushered into the 'hospitality' room, a BBC mandarin, whose eye has been fixed on the door, 'bolts the last corner of his sandwich and advances, hand outstretched, an obsequious smile laid across a face which is sallow from days spent in fruitless committees; he breathes the ritual BBC welcome to eminent persons, "How good of you to come", and, overcome, relapses into a bold offer of a glass of sherry; if this is the kind of programme in which the eminent person is to be questioned by a number of journalists, the next fifteen minutes are spent in introducing him to his inquisitors, with the smiling, ritual reassurance, "I don't think you have anything to fear from Mr – "; nor does he, for Mr – has already pointed out to him that the point of the programme is, not to put the eminent person on the spot, but to "reveal his personality". If a moment arose during the broadcast when a sharp question seemed likely to pin the interviewee finally to one unambiguous statement, the chairman would save him with an interruption of amiable fatuity: 'I think we have had enough of that question. May I ask, Sir, if it is true that your hobby is fishing?'[38]

ITV, by contrast, emerged after loud controversy. Its birth was marked with fanfares and fireworks. It set out to make money. Programmes grabbed attention by challenging settled notions. There was less of the balming equanimity of BBC output. Associated Television's scriptwriter Wilfred Greatorex felt that the commercial channels brought bracing change to broadcasting. 'As a monopoly public service, the BBC spoke with an Establishment voice and gave many of its programmes an official hand-out flavour: it was stuffy, academic, able to make cultured noises and to indulge a sickening capacity for genuflection in the presence of the mighty. There were all those safe question-masters with unquestionable degrees and calm, neutral voices. There were all those standard-English accents.' Greatorex judged that commercial television was developing by the mid-1960s towards 'classlessness, not surprisingly for it has grown out of the meritocracy'.[39]

Admittedly, the BBC's satirical programme *That Was The Week That Was*, broadcast from November 1962 until December 1963, jeered at the men in power – sometimes for good, well-researched reasons – as it launched its stars on their route towards Mayfair flats, columns in *The Times*, ducal fathers-in-law, knighthoods and multi-millions. The satirists' tone of voice, wrote Malcolm Bradbury in 1963, was 'quizzical, demanding, informal, vernacular, often faintly offensive and doctrinaire'. More temperately, the BBC police series *Z-Cars*, launched in 1962, taught viewers that while it was necessary to respect authority, the people who held authority were neither better nor worse than anyone else. It seems, though, that anti-Establishment organisations and individuals were protected from irreverence. Although Tony Hancock's television comedy scriptwriters, Alan Simpson and Ray Galton, were not Campaign for Nuclear Disarmament supporters, they dropped the idea of hanging a CND banner on the wall of Hancock's bedsit lest it bring CND into ridicule. Even progressive intellectuals recognised this bias against unfashionable authority and towards obstructive defiance. 'Maybe,' mused Michael Frayn in 1961, 'we should be trying to inculcate a sense of duty, instead of exploiting the bolshie streak which runs through the otherwise orderly geology of the British character, engender a respect for authority, instead of drilling down to that layer of pure nihilism which makes people open to the suggestion that the Commanding Officer is an ass just because he is the Commanding Officer.' It might be beneficial to remind commanding officers of the fragility of their authority, and to remind their underlings of their power, but unlimited derision of authority seemed facile, unfair and destructive to Frayn.[40]

'Television,' wrote Cyril Connolly in 1963, 'is the greatest single factor for change in people's lives and probably has done much to undermine English puritanism'. The goggle-box, as it was called, started to show criminals, prostitutes, and the sexually or socially marginalised being interviewed full-face without murky lighting to disguise their identities. It was abolishing shame. There were no full-frontal glimpses when Dan Farson visited a nudist camp, but several backward shots: 'Thank goodness,' wrote an affronted mother, speaking for the *News of the World*'s England rather than the *Sunday Mirror*'s, 'that my son, aged twenty-four, was out playing table-tennis and thus spared the shame of watching'.[41]

EIGHT

Spies

Harold Macmillan seldom lost his temper publicly. He did so, however, at an Oxford dinner of 1981 held in honour of Hugh Trevor-Roper. Sir Michael Howard, one of the official historians of wartime intelligence, had just made a jocular speech referring to the double agent codenamed Garbo. The ex-Prime Minister rose to declare that he had never heard such a shocking speech in his life: national security was no joking matter; indeed, it should seldom be mentioned. This represented the uniform view of intelligence held in Whitehall. 'In Britain the activities of the intelligence and security services have always been regarded in much the same light as marital sex,' as Howard explained four years later. 'Everyone knows that it goes on and is quite content that it should, but to speak, write or ask questions about it is regarded as exceedingly bad form. So far as official government policy is concerned, the British security and intelligence services, MI5 and MI6, do not exist. Intelligence is brought by the storks, and enemy agents are found under gooseberry bushes. Government records bearing on intelligence activities are either industriously "weeded" or kept indefinitely closed. Members of Parliament who ask questions are heard in icy silence and choked off with the most abrupt and inexplicit of replies.' The history of espionage, Howard lamented, was the preserve of 'inquisitive journalists, disgruntled professionals and imaginative fiction writers – categories that confusingly overlap'.[1]

Perhaps it is not surprising that Macmillan's humour failed him in 1981, for espionage cases repeatedly disrupted his exercise of power. It fell to him as Foreign Secretary in 1955 to give a tricky Commons statement on the defection of the diplomats Guy Burgess and Donald Maclean to Moscow. (He decided against recalling his own discussion thirty years earlier with a senior Foreign Office man about applying for a diplomatic post. 'You will be asked lots of questions,' he was told, 'but there are only two that matter: What is the name of your father; Who is your boot-maker?') The first great reverse of his premiership was the failure of the Paris summit of 1960, which Khrushchev sabotaged on the pretext of indignation over the American U-2 spy plane. The collapse of confidence in his political prescience was started by the Vassall spy case of 1962, and intensified by the stunts about national security staged by his enemies during the Profumo Affair.[2]

Sex, class and official secrecy were connected taboos. The uproar after the disappearance of Burgess and Maclean aroused class tensions. They were public school men, Cambridge graduates, alcoholics: Burgess an outright member of the 'Homintern', and Maclean bisexual. They had been recruited into government service by social contacts; they had been shielded by friends; and they had proved traitors. Journalists from less privileged backgrounds, who felt socially excluded from the civil service, decried the system that had nurtured both men. Insiders lost their sacrosanct aura; outsiders felt free to express their animosity.

Two cases involving Englishmen who worked in the Moscow embassy and spied for the Russians – those of William Marshall and John Vassall – show the continuing importance of class resentment in the public presentation of espionage trials. In both cases, the explanation of motives and narrative agreement shared by prosecutors and defenders were of dubious accuracy. As the murder trial of Harvey Holford showed in 1963, there were stories that it suited the defence to advance, and the prosecution not to challenge, in order to simplify the course of trials and appease public feeling. The Vassall case was the essential prelude to the Profumo Affair. The Profumo Affair was the Vassall case prolonged by other means. Marshall's trial, with its attendant publicity, foreshadowed them both.

William Marshall was born in December 1927. His father was a bus driver (who was disabled from work after his vehicle was hit by a wartime bomb blast) and his mother worked in a newsagents. 'His home,' Rebecca West reported, 'was in a street of little brick houses down in Wandsworth, the kind of street from which ability keeps pushing up, and occasionally misses its way, if it reads the wrong books and misunderstands what it reads.' He trained at the British School of Telegraphy, in Stockwell, before attesting for military service in 1945. He served in Palestine during 1947, and then in Egypt. When he was released from the army in 1948, his commanding officer wrote a testimonial that he was 'of clean and sober habits', conscientious and trustworthy. Marshall joined the Diplomatic Wireless Service, which posted him to the MI6 wireless station at the strategic Suez Canal port of Ismailia. He made persistent efforts to reach the Moscow embassy, where he spent a fraught year of service from December 1950. 'Marshall was the perfect example of the type who should not be sent here,' noted an embassy official. 'He was an introvert, anti-social to a degree I have never seen before. At staff cocktail parties he would be found in a corner behind a screen, if he turned up at all . . . He was most difficult to draw into conversation, and he had a meanness which it would be difficult to surpass. If asked to give a cigarette to a colleague, he would ask for the cigarette back the following day.' By the autumn of 1951 there were fears that Marshall would suffer a breakdown if he remained in Moscow. He was moved to the SIS communications department at Hanslope in Buckinghamshire. He lived in a hostel at Bletchley, but often visited his parents Ethel and Bill at 36 Elborough Road, Southfields.[3]

In London, the security services kept under surveillance Pavel Kuznetsov, the stocky, impassive Second Secretary at the Soviet embassy, who lived in Holland Villas Road, Kensington – 'a fading but handsome part of West London'.[4] His contacts with journalists and Labour MPs were monitored. On 25 April 1952, Kuznetsov's shadowers saw him meet a young man, who proved to be Marshall, at the Century Elite Cinema in Kingston-upon-Thames. The pair lunched together in the Normandy restaurant of the nearby Bentall's department store. Two other tables in the restaurant were occupied by burly secret policemen: Special Branch officers kept watch from one, as Kuznetsov must have spotted; Soviet agents from the other. Oddly for the location of a clandestine rendezvous, the restaurant had wide plate-glass windows at pavement level, so that the three tables of agents were as visible to the bus stop queues as tropical fish in a brightly lit aquarium. The surprising openness of the assignation continued: after lunching, Kuznetsov took his dupe to a riverside park where in open view Marshall showed papers and drew maps for him. It could not have been easier for Special Branch to monitor their targets. This was espionage as charade.

Instead of designating dismal public houses and obscure haunts as their meeting places, Kuznetsov took his stooge – who was a physical oddity, preternaturally tall, thin and narrow-chested, with a swan's neck and pitted lumps bulging from pallid cheeks – to assignations where his cheap tailoring would be conspicuous. Marshall's appointments diary, which Special Branch seized, showed that he had met Kuznetsov on 2 January 1952 for lunch at the Berkeley Hotel, Piccadilly; on 5 January for dinner at the Pigalle restaurant, Piccadilly; on 14 January for lunch at the Criterion restaurant at Piccadilly Circus; on 7 March for dinner at Chez Auguste in Frith Street, Soho; on 17 March for lunch at the Royal Court Hotel in Sloane Square. The Soviets, it seemed, wanted either to unsettle the English authorities with a spy trial, or to divert them from a more important agent. Marshall's secrets from Hanslope Park were low grade.

On 13 June, Kuznetsov met Marshall in Wandsworth's King George's Park, which was then bisected by a colony of prefabricated houses inhabited by bombed-out Londoners. On one side of the prefabs there was a café, swimming pool, playground and other discreet nooks. But it was to the other side – a wide playing field with three exposed benches and a cinder track – that the Russian guided the youth. Kuznetsov sat on one bench, and cannot have missed the Special Branch party settling on another. Yet he continued in ostentatious confabulation even after the Special Branch men upped from the furthermost bench, and occupied the one nearest to Kuznetsov. Eventually they made their arrests.

Marshall's line to his interrogators was saturated in self-pity and inverted snobbery. 'I flew to Moscow arriving there on 31 December 1950, and started work at the British Embassy,' he stated. 'I was a misfit at the Embassy from the start. The people there were not in my class of people, and I led a very solitary life. I kept to myself, spoke to as few people as possible, did my work as well as I could, and just waited for the time to go home. I was disgusted with the pettiness of life at the Embassy.' He soon became 'impressed by the efforts of the Russian people and by their ideals'. After several days of interrogation, Special Branch summarised Marshall as 'a morose self-contained individual with few friends . . . hesitant and indecisive'. Dick White, Director General of MI5, was summoned to Chartwell to report on the case to the Prime Minister. Churchill received him in bed, heard him attentively, offered him a cigar and sent him away for a drink.[5]

After Marshall's conviction at the Old Bailey on 10 July 1952, newspapers gave sentimental extenuations of his conduct. The *Daily Mirror* reported his case under the headline 'Downfall of a dupe!' and described him as a 'young misfit'. His parents, who owned a clock that chimed with the Harry Lime theme music from Orson Welles's film *The Third Man*, gave an interview to the Labour Party's Sunday newspaper, *Reynolds News*, in which parental distress mingled with prim disapproval of cocktail parties. 'Three weeks ago one of the most terrible blows which can fall on a working-class family descended on us. The police snatched a son away.' Ethel and Bill insisted that he was a dupe. 'Such a lad never deliberately gave away the secrets of England, the country he loved, to a foreign power.' They were being shunned in Southfields. 'Some people will not speak to us now. And when we go out everyone stares. "Fancy bringing up a son like that," they say.' When he was sentenced his mother called out, 'Keep your chin up', and now the Marshalls were trying to do the same.[6]

Six months after Marshall's conviction, Jim Skardon of MI5 interrogated him at Wormwood Scrubs prison. Marshall protested that he had been 'absolutely alone at the Old Bailey, and no stronger than a trawler in a contest against the dreadnought of the law. He always felt that he had no chance.' Once Skardon had got Marshall talking, he was 'unable to stop a flow of muddled abuse of the capitalist world, as Marshall sees it through the jaundiced eyes of an embittered young Communist. All the ideas to which he gave expression are heard from the lips of Communists at Spouter's Corner, and it seemed that he had collected together in a photographic sort of way a mass of information tending to show that the common people are oppressed by the middle and upper classes. The ideas simply tumbled from his lips in no sort of order.' Speaking of his father's disabling injuries from the wartime bomb, Marshall demanded: 'What did they care when he was blown out of his bus? All they wanted to know was where he left the bus.' Towards the Moscow embassy staff he remained bitter. 'Call themselves gentlemen – beer is not good enough for them, all they want is whisky. And what about the girl who had to be sent home pregnant after one month? Bah! The Russians laugh at 'em! It was the same with our officers in the Middle East – the natives used to smirk at their behaviour.'[7]

The staff at the British embassy in Moscow in Marshall's time numbered about a hundred. There were technicians, typists, cipher clerks, radio operators, and other clerical employees: their busy lives were evoked in the published diaries of the embassy's chirpy night-watchman, Harold Elvin's *A Cockney in Moscow*. The diplomats – the Ambassador, First Secretary, and attachés – were in a minority. Yet Marshall's statement after his arrest

221

gave a different impression: he was estranged by the luxurious pride of upper-class snobs, whose attention to him was fitful and derisory until, in lonely humiliation, he agreed to spy. It is more likely that he had been solicited by the Russians in Ismailia, that they flattered him into believing that his low-grade leaks were valued, but always envisaged his discovery by the British authorities. Nevertheless, journalists and their readers were eager to swallow Marshall's tale that he felt a social reject, stranded out of his class among attachés who were as haughty as archdukes and as icy as alpine glaciers. This explanation, which exculpated the working-class youth but incriminated the high-ups, made Marshall rare among traitors in receiving sympathy. The jury found him guilty, but asked for mercy in the sentencing. The judge condemned him to five years' imprisonment, instead of the maximum possible of fourteen, which meant that with remission he was freed after three years.[8]

One of Marshall's Moscow colleagues, during interview by the security services, said that although Marshall owned sexology books, he doubted if he was 'a practising pervert of any kind'.[9] Worries about the link between homosexuality, diplomacy and espionage after the Burgess and Maclean defections partly explained the illegal methods with which police collected evidence and the vehement tenacity with which the Director of Public Prosecutions pursued the Montagu of Beaulieu case of 1954 (an unpleasant legal stunt in which three young upper-class Englishmen were convicted of sexual activity with two RAF men), for one of the defendants, Peter Wildeblood, was diplomatic correspondent of the *Daily Mail*. As more revelations about Burgess and Maclean emerged during 1955, this aspect was hysterically stressed. The front page of the special 'EVIL MEN' issue of the *Sunday Pictorial* (25 September 1955) blared that the 'sordid secret of homosexuality' provided a key to the betrayal. Cecil King felt fearful loathing of homosexuality. He severed contact in early middle age with his two closest Oxford friends after belatedly realising their preferences. Thereafter, in private conversation, he often accused influential men of secret inversion. Probably he felt so betrayed and sullied by his Oxford friendships that he incited the 'Evil Men' issue of 1955.

'The wretched, squalid truth about Burgess and Maclean is that they were sex perverts,' shouted the *Sunday Pictorial*. 'There has for years existed inside the Foreign Office service a chain or clique of perverted men.' By their machinations Burgess and Maclean were 'protected' and public morality suffered 'hoodwinking'. Under the headline 'Danger to Britain', the story continued: 'Homosexuals – men who indulge in "unnatural" love for one another – are known to be bad security risks. They are easily won over as traitors. Foreign agents seek them out as spies.' As an addendum, seven years later, Cudlipp wrote of the 'Evil Men' articles: 'doctors, social workers and the wretched homosexuals themselves recognised this as a sincere attempt to get at the root of a spreading fungus.' He regretted, though, 'that nothing practical was done to solve the worst aspect of the problem – the protection of children from the perverts'.[10]

At a by-election in 1954 there had been elected to Parliament a Tory MP called Captain Henry Kerby. He spoke Russian, and translated for Khrushchev and Bulganin during their 1956 visit to England. 'Sinister' was how Peter Rawlinson, Macmillan's Solicitor-General, described Kerby, 'a hugely unlikeable man, trusted by few'. He was suspected of leaking the parliamentary party's soul-searching at the height of the Suez crisis to the lobby correspondent of the *Daily Express*; he was MI5's plant in the Commons, and reported parliamentary gossip to the security services. When an all-party Civil Liberties group was inaugurated by MPs in 1962–63, Kerby insinuated himself into the post of vice-chairman, and, doubtless, acted as MI5's mole. After being dropped by MI5 in 1966, he became a Labour Party informant of confidential Tory discussions. Kerby, with this background, gave a front-page interview which the *Sunday Pictorial* headlined: 'Who is hiding the man who tipped off these sex perverts?' Kerby decried 'the "brotherhood" of perverted men' responsible for the

continuing cover-up of 'flagrant homosexuality' among diploma-
tists: 'there are still many people of this ilk today in the Foreign
Service'. Popular indignation should not be frustrated. 'The
British people are still denied the names of those Foreign Office
officials who shielded both traitors during their service.' He
wanted a witch-hunt: 'The archaic tradition of Ministers manfully
shouldering and shielding Civil Servants at the Foreign Office is
ABSURD and DANGEROUS.' The 'positive vetting' that followed
Burgess and Maclean, intended to placate agitators like Kerby,
was neither rational nor productive. Alistair Horne, who was an
intelligence analyst of Soviet satellite activities in the Balkans,
noted that 'the two most brilliant intelligence operators under
whom I worked were both homosexual'. The campaign to identify
and exclude such men, he reckoned, 'caused a loss of talent to
the secret services comparable to Louis XIV's ill-conceived expulsion of the Huguenots from France'.[11]

The Labour frontbencher George Brown joined in the *Sunday
Pictorial* onslaught. 'This is the jet age. The era of moving damn
fast.' Yet diplomats, he said, were 'cynical, long-haired young
gentlemen toddling from one cocktail party to another, never
meeting ordinary people, and proclaiming a belief in nothing at
all.' It is odd that he thought cynicism and scepticism were undesirable traits in diplomacy: did he prefer naïveté and credulity?
Interesting, too, that Brown held the Marshall family's view of
cocktails as sinful. Brown was indignant that when he had visited
Buenos Aires in 1954, he had been forced to sit through an 'Alice-
in-Wonderland dinner' with embassy staff. 'Every attempt I made
to discuss Argentina and British prospects there was met with
levity . . . The final curtain was pretty fine disorder, as I lost my
temper and displayed how unsuitable I would be for the appointment to the cynical, ineffectual, prattling body we call our diplomatic service.' This was from a man who was notorious for
drunken aggression. Macmillan noted, after giving a confidential
briefing to Labour Privy Councillors on Lord Radcliffe's inquiry
into the George Blake spy case in 1962: 'George Brown was so

rude that I could have kicked him out of the room. But it is not malice. He is just common & so ill-bred as not to be conscious of his boorish behaviour. He is one of those few men who is more disagreeable sober than drunk.'[12]

Bill Astor initiated a Lords debate on the Burgess-Maclean disappearances on 22 November 1955. The government's attempts at suppression had been misguided, he said: 'It is far better to get the truth out and finished with than to try to save prestige by hiding it.' He did not say outright that the government's White Paper on the subject had been a whitewash, but invoking a comic song of Stanley Holloway's, likened it to 'the magistrate in the sad affair of young Albert and the lion, who came to the conclusion "No one was really to blame"'. Some of his remarks made wry retrospective reading once his toleration of the louche Stephen Ward had brought him low. 'I was one of the few people who never knew Guy Burgess, and apparently I missed a lot,' Astor said. 'By all accounts, he was one of the most amusing and clever conversationalists there was, who charmed a great many people. But he was drunken, dirty and a sexual pervert. He had been ever since his school days. He made no pretence about it.' Astor felt that MPs and officials 'should have a higher standard of personal conduct, whether they are in their office or not, than those who engage in commercial and private pursuits'. Profumo was not listening.[13]

After becoming Prime Minister in 1957, Macmillan put his greatest efforts into international diplomacy intended to avert nuclear war between the Soviet Union and the United States. He hoped to revive the era of personal diplomacy during which Churchill, Roosevelt and Stalin settled the world at Tehran and Yalta, although his first encounter with the Soviet leader at a diplomatic conference in Paris had startled him. 'Khrushchev is an obscene figure; very fat, with a great paunch; eats and drinks greedily; interrupts boisterously,' he noted. In 1959, when Macmillan flew to Moscow on a diplomatic initiative, he was first publicly humiliated by the Soviet leaders. 'I fucked the Prime Minister with a telephone pole,' said Khrushchev. Then he was granted concessions, which turned his visit into a public relations triumph with his own electorate, although his common ground with the communists remained negligible. Malcolm Muggeridge attended a speech of Macmillan's in Kiev during this visit. 'He was dressed in a tweed ensemble suitable for rural occasions, worn, I should suppose, at many a Conservative garden fête. His speech, delivered with old style elegance, referred to how, in the eleventh century, a Ukrainian princess had married into the English royal house. Might not this union, he went on, be regarded as a happy augury for future relations between two countries whose history and traditions had so much in common?' Muggeridge studied the officials and plain-clothes policemen as Macmillan's oratory washed over them. 'In just one or two of their faces I thought I detected a faint trace of wonderment; a tiny flicker of an eyelid, a minute fold of incredulity round the mouth. The others remained inscrutable, their pleasure in their former princess's London nuptials, if any, well under control.'[14]

The next stage of Macmillan's diplomatic strategy – the Four Power Summit in Paris in 1960 – was wrecked when a US spy plane was shot down over Russia, its pilot captured and Eisenhower's White House caught in puerile lies. The Russians had known of the spy flights for years, but the incident provided Khrushchev with the sledgehammer with which to smash the Paris summit. 'In his crude arrogance, and acting like a Court buffoon, this wily Russian peasant got far more out of his blatant sabotage act than he could have achieved by hours of diplomacy,' wrote the diplomatic correspondent Honor Balfour. He issued an intolerably provocative ultimatum to Eisenhower, which included a ludicrous moment when, denying Soviet espionage, he raised his hands towards heaven crying, 'As God is my witness, my hands are clean and my soul is pure.' After ranting that the American people must grovel, he went to bellow at 3,000 journalists in the Palais de Chaillot. 'It was a revolting and frightening performance,' noted Balfour. 'The fat fleshy face swelled to a ruddy pulp. The little piggy eyes shrank to darts of wily evil. The voice roared and the fist stabbed in alarming resemblance to Hitler in the Nuremburg stadium.' The sequel in which this raging brute reverted to 'a roly-poly of jollity served only to aggravate the horror of the scene'.[15]

The collapse of the Paris summit was Macmillan's gravest reverse since becoming Prime Minister. 'This was the moment,' said one of his aides, when 'he suddenly realised that Britain counted for nothing; he couldn't move Ike to make a gesture towards Khrushchev, and de Gaulle was simply not interested. I think this represented a real watershed in his life.' Macmillan felt sick at heart, as he recorded in his diary back in England. 'The summit – on which I had set high hopes and for which I worked for over two years – has blown up, like a volcano! It is ignominious; it is tragic; it is almost incredible.' It was a chill, drizzly day, he added in his diary. He rested in bed, read *Dombey and Son*, and dozed.[16]

'Russia,' wrote a commentator in 1961 after the spy plane revelations, 'has suddenly brought into public view all those activities which are traditionally carried on in a decent obscurity, not because they are wrong, but because they involve prestige – the passions, the conceit, the self-regarding complacency of the peoples of the world and their leaders. As a result, the public which, particularly in England, has been cosily snuggling into 1910, is being bumped and banged into the icy air and blows and counterblows of the 1960s.'[17] A few days later the arrest of five Soviet agents who comprised the Portland spy ring, operating in the Admiralty Underwater Weapons Establishment, made the bumping feel rougher.

In September 1962, in the month of *Dr No*'s film première, Toby Mathew, the Director of Public Prosecutions, marched into the office of Peter Rawlinson, the Solicitor-General. 'Sit down, Solicitor,' said Mathew looking pleased with himself. 'You will need to. We have arrested a spy who is a bugger, and a minister is involved.' A few years earlier the two men had been in court together: Mathew had gone in triumph to watch the sentencing of Lord Montagu of Beaulieu and Peter Wildeblood in the homosexuality show trial of 1954. Rawlinson had defended Wildeblood, and felt ardent sympathy for him. When, in response to the excesses of this case, the Wolfenden inquiry had been appointed, Mathew had testified that 'young men should be taught that these habits are dirty, degrading and harmful, and the negation of decent manhood'.[18]

The spy was John Vassall, an Admiralty official who had been a cipher clerk in the British embassy in Moscow. Born in 1924, Vassall was the son of a luckless, precarious Anglican clergyman. His memoirs gave a wistful, snobbish account of the public schools that his parents considered for him and the reasons for their rejection: Trinity College, Glenalmond – but fares to Scotland were too expensive; Marlborough – but boys were forbidden to wear overcoats in winter; Charterhouse – but Mrs Vassall disliked Lady Fletcher, the headmaster's wife, a vivacious, cultivated woman not unlike herself. Mentioning these imposing schools somehow hid the obscurity of the final choice, Monmouth, on the Welsh borders, so exiguously funded that it suffered demotion soon after Vassall left and became a grammar school. 'Reading about Vassall,' wrote the cultural historian Marcus Cunliffe in 1963, 'I pounce with cruel enlightenment upon the disclosure that this debonair creature went to Monmouth Grammar School, and left at sixteen. What an apprenticeship . . . he must have served in concealing that stigma before he moved on to wider evasions.' Vassall prompted Cunliffe to muse on snobbery, that 'non-violent, second-rate and above all hermetic vice'. Its effects were 'cosy, indirect, inhibiting, malicious. The art is to put oneself at ease by making someone else uneasy.'[19]

Money shortages forced Vassall to leave school early: he felt the loss keenly, saying that it deprived him of his chance to go to Oxford after the war. He perforce took jobs in a branch of the Midland Bank and as a temporary clerk in the Admiralty. In 1943 he was conscripted into the Royal Air Force, where he became an expert photographer, handling Leica cameras, developing pictures and making prints. After his demobilisation in 1947, he became a clerical officer in the Admiralty.

At Monmouth, Vassall enjoyed sex with handsome, masterly, older boys. 'I lived in a secret world,' he recalled. 'My whole being was stimulated by my sense of their virility.' London in wartime, with the black-out and servicemen on leave, offered boundless opportunities. He became an experienced mover in the capital's semi-clandestine sexuality. Rebecca West depicted him as a doe-eyed, soft-voiced dandy who was sincere in his kindliness. He was suspected of legacy-hunting, because he liked the company of old ladies; but although some of them were rich, he was equally attentive to old ladies who were poor. He played bridge well, was a model railways enthusiast, musical and churchy. Supremely, though, he was a much-courted 'queen', whose admirers included rich, clever and moderately important men. 'They made his life in London amusing, and when he went abroad, even so far as Egypt and Mexico, he was passed from host to host. He was very successful in this sphere, which meant that he was not merely playful and girlish, but could hold his own in an outlaw world where tact, toughness and vigilance had to be constantly on the draw.'[20]

In 1954, Vassall applied for a post as a clerk on the naval attaché's staff at the British embassy in Moscow. He depicted his application as a chance impulse, dictated by his desire to see the world; but this is improbable. At the time of his detention in 1962, during the tribunal of investigation of 1963 and in his memoirs published in 1975, he gave a consistent account, which is worth recapitulating to show its implausibility. Like Marshall before him, Vassall suggested that he would not have been tempted to espionage if the English had not been snobbish. After reaching Moscow, he was invited for luncheon by the ambassador and his wife, Sir William and Lady Hayter. He found their manners starchy; his note of thanks afterwards to Lady

Hayter was thought effusive; his angling to join her bridge parties was snubbed. The naval attaché for whom he worked, says Vassall, rebuked him for infiltrating circles above his 'station'. His retrospective complaints that the Hayters were aloof, that the embassy hierarchy was rigid, and that protocol was relentless, were uncannily like Marshall's. It was, one must assume, part of the Soviet training that English spies, if caught, had to parrot tales of class stigma and subjugation.[21]

His loneliness, by his account, drew him to an embassy interpreter named Sigmund Mikhailsky. While dining with Mikhailsky, he was decoyed, he said, by a young man who 'looked at me with fire in his eyes and showed me with his smile how passionate he felt'. The decoy began to meet him for sexual bouts. They went together to dinner at a smart hotel. There, Vassall hinted, his wine was doped, for he became extra-suggestible, was guided to a divan, told to strip naked and to brandish his underpants above his head. Three men joined him, and he was photographed under harsh lights. 'When I cried out to someone that what was going on was painful I was told that it would not last much longer, but it felt endless to me,' he recalled. 'When they had finished . . . I asked if I might go to a bathroom to tidy myself up . . . On my return I was dressed properly, and we all behaved as if nothing had happened. It was like a painful dream.' Months later, Vassall continued, he met a soldier, 'a tall, slim man, upright and fair of face', 'gentle but firm', with whom he was then surprised in bed by policemen, who brandished the earlier photographs, and threatened Vassall with arrest. He claimed that he did not confide his quandary to embassy officials because of their class-exclusiveness. Instead, he agreed to spy after being threatened with Lubyanka prison: 'I was terrified of being sexually and psychologically assaulted by specially trained experts, and I had fearful dreams of hooks, spikes and instruments being placed on my body and private parts.'[22]

The story of his entrapment was told by Vassall as a long rigmarole, with an uneven splattering of details and vagueness.

Would he have lost his head in this way? Only a weak, helpless fool would have submitted to KGB threats of exposure, and Vassall was hardy, smart and resourceful. If he was so timid and submissive when blackmailed for sexual indiscretions, he would not have had the nerves for years of high-level espionage. No one who met him thought he was easily ruffled, or inexperienced in the world's ways. 'His friends had a special liability to be blackmailed, as skiers have a special liability to break their legs,' so Rebecca West observed. 'If Vassall really had been blackmailed . . . he would have gone to the right member of the Embassy to make his report, and made it in terms likely to bleach the embarrassment out of the blushing occasion, he would have made the journey home with just the right camping humour, he would have dined out on the story at home, telling the story in two different ways to please the two different sorts of people, and if he had found the atmosphere chilly in Whitehall he would have found some shelter in an art gallery or interior decorator's shop where the air was balmier.'[23]

Vassall began taking documents from the naval attaché's office, giving them to Soviet agents for photographing, and then returning them. On returning to the Naval Intelligence Department in London in 1956, he regularly photographed secret documents. After a year he was appointed as assistant secretary in the private office of the Civil Lord of the Admiralty – a Scottish MP, Thomas Galbraith, who proved courteous and friendly. Tam Galbraith was a typical figure in the Conservative Party of the 1950s in that he seemed to journalists to be a patrician Oxonian, with pleasant manners but no force of character, whereas he came from a hardheaded family which had made its recent fortune as accountants and pub owners in Glasgow. There were no secret dossiers to be filched or photographed in Galbraith's office. On a few occasions Vassall acted as a courier taking papers from Whitehall to Galbraith's Scottish home, Barskimming. He never stayed for more than a scratch lunch. In 1959, when Galbraith was appointed Parliamentary Under Secretary for Scotland, Vassall was posted to the Fleet section, where he had access to secret documents. He suspended spying when the Portland Spy scandal broke, but resumed in December 1961. Information received in April 1962 from the Soviet defector Anatoliy Golitsyn led to his detection. Harold Macmillan, when Thorneycroft, the Minister of Defence, and Carrington, First Lord of the Admiralty, told him on 28 September of Vassall's arrest, predicted: 'There will be another big row, worked up by the Press, over this.'[24]

After an Old Bailey trial held partly held *in camera*, Vassall was sentenced to eighteen years of imprisonment on 22 October – the first day of the Cuban missile crisis, which brought the world to the brink of nuclear war. The prosecution accepted his story of the compromising photographs as the reason that from 1954 until 1962 he supplied his Soviet controllers with documents. The judge endorsed this tale in his summing-up. The House of Commons debate after the trial invigorated this improbable mish-mash, which was popular with the press – always keen on tales of voyeurism, and avid to magnify sexual turpitude. Lord Radcliffe's tribunal of investigation did not challenge the legend. It enforced the view that Vassall was flighty, malleable and timid, which seemed less threatening than the reality that he was a resilient, subtle man whose treachery gave the Russians a rich fund of secrets.

The notion that Vassall had a protector in Whitehall, who probably secretly shared the same criminal sexual tastes, appealed to those journalists who made their money by seeking people for pillorying. They started to hunt down the powerful queer who had inveigled the little pansy-boy into the Admiralty, protected him and promoted him. Brendan Mulholland of the *Daily Mail*, for example, visited Galbraith, without appointment, at Barskimming on 11 October. He claimed to have interviewed Galbraith for up to an hour: Galbraith said they might have spoken tersely for as little as five minutes. Yet, on the day after Vassall's conviction, Mulholland published a fanciful account of the spy's visits to Scotland. 'In his eighteenth-century mansion Mr Galbraith and his assistants waited for Vassall – their trusted

SPIES

courier a paid servant of Moscow.' After arrival, Vassall 'mingled with the other weekend visitors. He would listen so attentively that he made a good impression on his superiors . . . Over the weekend Vassall had plenty of time to develop his friendships. There were often as many as thirty people staying at Barskimming.' Lest readers had forgotten Vassall's sexuality, Mulholland provided some reminders: 'his love of music was a basis for many an opening . . . and he always had the correct clothes for the occasion'.[25] Mulholland later claimed that his fantasy was based on informants in the district, but the figure of thirty guests was demonstrably false; the seams and patches of his Vassall reports were easily unpicked, and found to be fictional in details and gist. So, too, were the *Daily Mail*'s claims on the same day, 23 October, that Vassall owned a hundred ties, nineteen suits, three dozen shirts and twelve pair of shoes.

Seven years earlier, in 1955, Arthur Christiansen, editor of the *Daily Express*, had told Beaverbrook that he had identified a 'notorious homosexual' on the Foreign Office Selection Board.[26] Now an adapted version of this fantasy emerged for the Admiralty. The *Sunday Express* on 28 October – the Sunday when Kennedy won the Cuban missile crisis – insinuated that Vassall had been too close to the luckless Galbraith. Galbraith had sent a few brief, banal notes to Vassall, some discussing office carpets and crockery. 'My dear Vassall,' Galbraith had written in one message, 'Goodness knows what you will think of me for having taken so long to write. We were both delighted to receive your charming card of congratulation and I would have thanked you ages ago except for the fact that the Scottish Office, when Parliament is sitting, keeps me more busy than the Admiralty.' To some drab minds the words 'charming' and 'My dear Vassall' suggested sodomy. A further attraction of Galbraith as a target for pillorying was that he was heir to a peerage: it was a recent title, but sounded sonorous – Strathclyde.

In order to pay for his defence, Vassall sold his memoirs to the *Sunday Pictorial* for £7,000. The first instalment appeared on the first Sunday after his conviction, 28 October. The Mirror Group required arch sexiness, salacious guilt and inverted snobbery for its money. One passage described Vassall's consolations when he went to board at Monmouth School away from his mother: 'I experienced a terrible loneliness without her. My need of companionship was obvious to some of the other boys. An older boy from the rugby fifteen made approaches to me while I was playing the piano. And one night, after lights out in the dormitory, a boy crept into my bed to comfort me in my loneliness. I never forgave myself for these incidents. To help me forget I buried myself in work.' The *Sunday Pictorial* highlighted Vassall's bracing lack of snobbery in Moscow, and the stifling class discrimination of others: 'Soon I was on first-name terms with senior diplomats from many European countries and America. "John," they used to tell me, "you are so much less reserved than the average Englishman we meet." I suppose I was. My mother had always encouraged me to mix freely with barons and barrow-boys alike. But it was being whispered at the British Embassy that I was living way above my social standing. They branded me as a social climber. I ignored their gossip. My foreign friends reassured me that I was the perfect Englishman. I was proud of that.' The second instalment on 4 November – headlined 'HOW THE RUSSIAN SPY MASTERS BROKE ME DOWN' – was illustrated by a photo of Vassall reclining on his back wearing nothing but a tight white bathing costume and sporting an impressive bulge.[27]

Under the front-page headline 'SPY CATCHERS NAME "SEX RISK" MEN', Norman Lucas had the lead story in the issue of the *Sunday Pictorial* carrying the first instalment of Vassall's memoirs. 'Civil servants with homosexual tendencies were especially vulnerable as security risks,' Lucas explained. 'Several groups of these men have been traced and broken up in Whitehall,' he added mendaciously. 'A secret list prepared by detectives names homosexuals who hold top Government posts.' A week later, under the front-page headline 'THE LETTERS IN VASSALL'S FLAT', the *Pictorial* of 4 November reported that 'before Vassall was sentenced for spying he talked of the urgent need for an inquiry into sex blackmail of people who work in Government departments . . . he warned that such an inquiry – to weed out homosexuals and bi-sexuals in high office – would be unlikely to succeed: "Many of the types who would be vetted in such an investigation are respectable married men holding senior posts. No one would suspect them of abnormal sexual practices," he said.'

The *News of the World* had to vie with the *Sunday Pictorial*'s exclusive serialisation as best it could. On 28 October it ran a story about Norman Rickard, a thirty-eight-year-old Admiralty victualling supply clerk, who had been strangled in his basement bedsit flat in Elgin Avenue, Maida Vale, on 19 February 1962. There is no reason to trust any assertion in the story, which showed the ugly temper of the times. 'When he left his office in the evening he threw off his dull suit and dressed himself in a black leather jacket, tight blue jeans, a check shirt, high-heeled cowboy boots with silver buckles and thin blue leather gloves. He was a more obviously squalid character than Vassall, as wearing this fancy dress he wandered around the Marble Arch trying to make friends with other men. Nine months ago he met the wrong man. He was found naked, strangled and trussed in a cupboard in his flat.' After this lubricious description, the *News of the World* moved into its customary mode of scare-mongering and sermonising – garnished with the mad suggestion that Guy Burgess was the spymaster who had recruited and run Vassall. 'There are many of these low-salaried twilight people working in places where they can betray their country to indulge their perverted pleasures . . . There must be no more Rickards, no more Vassalls, in this kind of employment. FOR BURGESS SITS IN MOSCOW LIKE A PATIENT TOAD AWAITING HIS NEXT WILLING VICTIM.'[28]

A fortnight later the Mirror Group's *People* took up the Rickard story. Its reporter Roy East alleged that Rickard had been recruited three months before his death by the Admiralty Security Department to inform on homosexuals. East suggested that

Rickard had been investigating Vassall before his death – oblivious of the fact that this was two months before the authorities' earliest inklings that there was an Admiralty spy. East scouted gay bars looking for informants who, he claimed, had seen Rickard drinking with Vassall. He stressed, though, to Lord Radcliffe's tribunal, that he was not homosexual, but happily married with three children.

This was not the only mischief being made. William Shepherd, the Tory MP for Cheadle, who was to play a part in the Profumo Affair, had links with MI5. His loud, denunciatory voice had been clamourous during the parliamentary debates on Wolfenden. Homosexuality was acquired, not 'congenital', he insisted; 'inverts' indulged in such acts so as to seem 'fashionable'; 'incest is a much more natural act than homosexuality'. The male homosexual, he explained, was pitted against society. 'His mind becomes twisted and distorted because he feels he is not as other men are . . . He is always beset by fears of discovery. The more sensitive ones wear a hunted look . . . homosexuality sets up a society within a society, and this is indeed sinister.' Shepherd wrote in early November to Macmillan, complaining about certain ministers who, he said, were risking exposure. Macmillan replied sceptically, but asked him to consult the Chief Whip, Brigadier Martin Redmayne. At his meeting with Redmayne, Shepherd took a similar line to the *Sunday Pictorial* about 'buggers in high places'. 'I told Martin that he ought to know what I knew about these men,' Shepherd recalled, 'including one very high minister who was involved with young boys. I said he ought to have access to what they knew across the road, which was then Scotland Yard.'[29]

George Brown, who had penned a scurrilous attack on British diplomats when the *Sunday Pictorial* was running its campaign against 'Foreign Office perverts' in 1955, returned to the fray in 1962. 'We cannot leave the Vassall case as it is,' he thundered in a Commons debate on 5 November. 'There are other letters in existence, copies of which I and, no doubt, others have seen, the originals of which are in the hands of what are called the "authorities", which indicate a degree of Ministerial responsibility, which goes far beyond the ordinary business of a Minister in charge.' This palaver was a description of Galbraith's genial, innocuous letters – though no one ever called Brown amiable or harmless. Galbraith had done no more than show patient civility to a pleasant but perhaps socially pressing clerk. Brown, who was detested for his brutality by civil servants who had to work with him in the 1960s, showed harsh inverted snobbery in suggesting that Galbraith's politeness exceeded the acceptable. Several of his front-bench colleagues felt 'sensitive' at his innuendos about Galbraith and Vassall: Anthony Crosland had seduced Roy Jenkins when they were Oxford undergraduates; Richard Crossman and others had had youthful episodes ('Dick has known unnatural joys,' wrote Maurice Bowra); Hugh Gaitskell had gallantly sided with Lord Montagu of Beaulieu when he was being insulted by brutish diners in a restaurant following his release from prison. Such men knew what sordid nonsense Brown was talking.[30]

A day or so after Brown's aspersions, Redmayne, William Deedes (the Cabinet minister charged with press relations) and two of Macmillan's private secretaries consulted together before attending a late night discussion with the Prime Minister, who had been exhausted by the Cuban missile crisis. While they wished to avoid panic reactions, they were fraught about male friendships. Reviewing Galbraith's notes to Vassall – it is misrepresentation to call them letters – Deedes said they were 'narcissistic', which was a codeword for homosexual, with the implication that Galbraith was 'almost certainly improperly involved' with Vassall. Deedes was perennially muddleheaded about such matters: when the bill that partially decriminalised homosexuality was debated four years later, he tabled an unsuccessful amendment 'exempting university staff and schoolmasters from any relaxation in the restrictions on buggery'.[31]

Most people at the Deedes-Redmayne meeting were retrospectively so ashamed of their part in it that they either lied or misremembered their conduct. Although Macmillan recognised

Galbraith's missives as innocuous, he was so weary and rattled that he sent Redmayne to extract Galbraith's resignation. On 8 November, a few hours after the full texts of Galbraith's notes were published in the morning papers, it was announced that he had resigned from the government (the announcement was accompanied by public declarations of regret from Macmillan which constituted shameless hypocrisy given that he had forced the resignation).

With the publication of Galbraith's missives, the sensible view was that 'Mr George Brown and the *Daily Express* [came to] look a little foolish'. But Beaverbrook's newspaper had already changed tack. On 8 November, Percy Hoskins, its crime reporter, effectively accused Lord Carrington of treason by suggesting that as First Lord of the Admiralty, he had known for eighteen months before Vassall's arrest that there was a spy in his department but concealed this from Macmillan. This falsehood was followed next day by another emanating from Douglas Clark, political correspondent of the *Daily Express*, a companionable man but unscrupulous operator, who 'revelled in the drama, intrigue and interplay of personalities at Westminster and was the complete Beaverbrook man', according to Macmillan's press secretary, Harold Evans. Clark's story pretended that after Hoskins's revelation, Carrington had received an abrupt summons to see the Prime Minister, who was minded to sack him. A photograph of the First Lord having a drink at an official dinner was published under the headline, 'Doesn't Lord Carrington Care?' The Labour Party began by crying for his dismissal.[32]

Macmillan was incensed: he longed for the purveyors of lies to be punished and delivered in the Commons a speech of striking pugnacity. He announced the appointment of a tribunal inquiry into the Vassall case under the chairmanship of Lord Radcliffe. He inveighed, too, against the wild inaccuracies of the witch-hunting press and the innuendoes of some members of the Parliamentary Labour Party. 'The time has come,' he declared, 'for men of propriety and decency not to tolerate the growth of what I can only call the spirit of Titus Oates and Senator McCarthy.' For once he had the support of Nigel Birch, who spoke of 'venomous libels' and filthy slurs. Humphry Berkeley decried Brown's 'squalid attempt at character assassination'. There were speeches from Labour MPs who were to be at the forefront of the Profumo Affair: George Wigg, Richard Crossman. The socialist Michael Foot seethed with synthetic indignation: 'The Prime Minister, with matchless insolence, talked of McCarthy, but he is the man who is asking the House to institute the McCarthy procedure. He is the most brazen McCarthy of the lot.' This was a nadir in opposition politics. As Macmillan spoke, reported a lobby correspondent, 'he seemed completely at his ease and looked as if he had just come from a stroll in his part of the country. With a resonant voice, and in a dark suit of clothes that would be a credit to the best tailor in Britain, he gave the impression that the whole affair. . . required a calm atmosphere, and not the realm of melodrama.' The lobby correspondent added that 'this unfortunate scandal is one in which the whole nation can feel nothing but a sense of shame', but it is unclear if he included his fellow journalists in the obliquity.[33]

'I have made a lot of enemies in the Press today,' Macmillan told Evans on 11 November, 'but I am an old man and I don't really care.' He thought the newspaper distortions had reached intolerable levels of cheapness. 'How did you recognise a homosexual?' he asked Evans. 'It was said that women could do so more easily than men.' He doubted if acceptance of the Wolfenden recommendations would make blackmail more difficult: 'it was not the avowed and complete homosexual who was vulnerable, but the man who did not go quite that far, who in part had a normal sexual life and felt ashamed of his aberrations.' Macmillan recorded in his diary on 15 November that in a week of Cabinet meetings, conferences with the Japanese Prime Minister, and ongoing tensions over Cuba and Yemen, 'we have wasted *all* the rest of the time on the Vassall spy case. On this there has been a continual running crisis – involving (rightly or wrongly) Mr

Galbraith's resignation (he having written some foolish if innocuous letters to Vassall when both were in the Admiralty), and a
sort of mass hysteria worked up by the Press & the less reputable
members of the Opposition like Brown & Crossman & Gordon-
Walker.' This had 'culminated in an accusation of treachery
against both Galbraith & Ld Carrington (First Lord) and against
the Board of the Admiralty'. His necessary response was the
appointment of the Radcliffe tribunal, a manoeuvre which had
caused him 'infinite trouble to prepare. But the speech was, I
think, the most impressive & successful which I have ever delivered in Parliament. Many congratulations poured in during
today.'[34]

Radcliffe's report, published in April 1963, disparaged Vassall
as an effeminate weakling ('a bit of a miss') who 'had been addicted
to homosexual practices from youth', but concluded that nothing
in his conduct or talk had indicated homosexuality even to astute
observers. This conclusion led the *Sunday Mirror*, as King and
Cudlipp had recently renamed the *Sunday Pictorial*, to publish
an exposé by their former Hollywood correspondent, Lionel
Crane, entitled 'How to Spot a Potential Homo'. The search for
tell-tale signs became so silly that an MI5 officer had an unheralded visit from Special Branch, and was interrogated about his
sexual habits, because Duncan Sandys, the hard-man of the
Macmillan Cabinet, had reported that the officer 'smoked his
cigarettes like a woman' and was therefore a security risk.[35]

On 4 February 1963, the Fleet Street journalists Brendan
Mulholland and Reg Foster were sentenced to six months and
three months' imprisonment respectively for contempt after
refusing to reveal to the Radcliffe tribunal their sources for stories
describing Vassall buying women's clothes in West End stores
and attending sex parties. They went to prison masquerading as
martyrs in the sacred cause of press freedom; but the truth is that
they did not want to admit that they were liars who had invented
their stories. Everyone knew it. But Fleet Street turned them into
figures of heroic probity, extolling their moral courage in

defending high principles, and went gunning for Macmillan's government in revenge attacks.

Journalists were 'seething with anger' at the jailing of Mulholland and Foster, wrote Paul Johnson in his truculent *New Statesman* column of 22 March. 'They blame the judges but, above all, they blame Harold Macmillan, who made it quite plain, in outlining the Vassall tribunal's terms of reference to the Commons, that he was out to get the press. I wonder if Mr Macmillan has quite understood what he has let himself in for. He is about to fight an election in which he will need every friend he has got. At the moment, he has none whatsoever in Fleet Street.' Everyone there, although Johnson did not say so in print, knew the rumours tying Jack Profumo to a call-girl. The last flying punch in his article was thrown at a target that was obvious despite being unnamed: 'any Tory minister or MP (or, for that matter, judge or barrister) who gets involved in a scandal during the next year or so, must expect – I regret to say – the full treatment'.[36]

PART TWO

Drama

NINE

Acting Up

Living at Cliveden was like inhabiting the stage of an opera house. The landscape resembled a scenic backdrop. People made dramatic entrances. They had different routes from offstage to front stage. There was an incentive to perform. Understudies itched for prominent parts. Non-players scavenged for visitors' passes to go backstage and catch the actors déshabillé in their dressing rooms. The Profumo Affair was a drama in which the protagonists converged from varied directions. The theme of the opera was the damage done by unintended consequences.

The fatal convergences began in 1960, when Yevgeny Ivanov arrived as assistant naval attaché at the Russian embassy in London. He was less coarse than most communist diplomats, although a rumbustious drinker. In pursuance of his duty to manipulate 'agents of influence', he visited the offices of the *Daily Telegraph*, where he met the editor Sir Colin Coote, who was a patient of Stephen Ward's. Coote, who knew that Ward was keen to visit the Soviet Union, invited him to meet Ivanov over luncheon at the Garrick Club. Ivanov began meeting Ward socially. Like Kuznetsov in the Marshall case, he was under surveillance. He assumed from the outset that Ward, as a conspicuous contact of his, would be approached by MI5.

On 8 June 1961, a MI5 officer named Keith Wagstaffe, who used the alias of Woods, lunched with Ward in a Marylebone restaurant to discuss his friendship with Ivanov. Wagstaffe reported that 'Ward, who has an attractive personality and who talks well', was of doubtful reliability. He added that when he took tea with Ward at 17 Wimpole Mews, he was introduced 'to a young girl, whose name I did not catch, who was obviously sharing the house with him. She was heavily painted and considerably overdressed, and I wonder whether this is corroborating evidence that he has been involved in the call-girl racket.' Probably Ward agreed at this time to cooperate with MI5 in reporting significant comments from Ivanov, although probably not in a scheme to suborn or entrap him. Whether Ivanov provided misinformation, or sound material that the Soviets wished MI5 to have, Ward was the conduit for it.[1]

A month later, on the weekend of 8–9 July 1961, Ward organised a party at Spring Cottage. His Saturday guests included the law student Noel Howard-Jones, Keeler, and a pretty young hitch-hiker picked up near Slough. The group resembled a microcosm of King's Road swingers (a scene that had been flourishing since 1958) until on Sunday morning they were joined by Ivanov.[2]

A more formal party was held at the big house. Its hostess, Bronwen Astor, was five months pregnant. The President of Pakistan, Field Marshal Ayub Khan, on his way to Washington to confer with the Kennedy administration, was guest of honour. Profumo, as Secretary of State for War, was invited for the whole weekend with his wife for their first Cliveden visit. For Saturday luncheon the Astors had Lord Mountbatten, his daughter and son-in-law Pamela and David Hicks; both Dalkeiths (Jane McNeill had been a fellow model of Bronwen Pugh's before she married the Duke of Buccleuch's son); Bill Astor's aunt Pauline Spender-Clay; Sophie Moss (the former Polish Countess Zofia Tarnowska, who had been an SOE camp-follower in Cairo during the war and was afterwards involved in refugee work); and two creative bachelors, the interior decorator Derek Patmore, and Felix Kelly, who designed nostalgic stage sets and painted portraits of domestic architecture and romantic country-house interiors. Some luncheon guests were replaced by fresh dinner guests on Saturday's hot summer evening: Sir Osbert Lancaster, the architectural writer and creator of the immortal Maudie Littlehampton in his front-page *Daily Express* cartoons, and Sir Roy Harrod, Macmillan's economic adviser from Oxford, together with their wives. Billa and Roy Harrod were regular visitors to Cliveden where they enjoyed the luxurious hospitality while thinking that the opulence had a comic element.

Bill and Bronwen Astor took their guests for a stroll after dinner on Saturday to admire a newly installed statue of their son riding a dolphin. Near the house there was a walled garden containing a tennis court abutting a stone-flagged swimming pool with cupola-domed changing cubicles at one end: the expanse was more spacious and elegant than the electric blue plastic pools that in Macmillan's England were becoming a suburban status symbol. Astor and Profumo sauntered ahead of the others, opened the gate in the high wall, and found Ward and three Spring Cottage visitors frolicking. One of them was Keeler, who had just lost her swimsuit or the bra part of her bikini in a prank, and had swathed herself in a towel. Forty years later, and not reliably, Profumo recalled that Astor slapped her backside playfully and said, 'Jack, this is Christine Keeler.'[3]

With the exception of Roy Harrod, who stayed sitting in the main house, the guests ambled to the poolside closely behind Bill Astor. A few of them found costumes in the pool house, and swam. *News of the World* journalists later paid Keeler to say that Astor and Profumo chased her naked round the pool. Other money-making inventions had Bronwen Astor arriving at the pool in a tiara, and Ward turning on the floodlights so that everyone could watch Keeler emerging naked from the water. Keeler's vivid tale that she and another woman had clambered onto the shoulders of Astor and Ayub Khan in the pool later aroused Anglo-Pakistani diplomatic ructions. Afterwards, Ward's group was invited to the main house for drinks. Lady Harrod had brisk intelligence, unflagging energy and unquenchable zest: her meeting with the farouche Keeler must have been enjoyable for connoisseurs of human comedy. There seemed to the Harrods nothing exceptional about this Cliveden visit – Keeler and the other young woman from Spring Cottage seemed part of a beautiful background – and it was nearly two years later before they realised that they had been present at a historic conjunction.[4]

Profumo had been introduced to Ward by Astor about ten years earlier, but had not met him for years. Earlier that Saturday, Astor asked Profumo if he remembered Ward, whom he brought to the Profumos' bedroom, where the osteopath gave Valerie Profumo a neck massage. She found him 'creepy', she said later, and evaded his efforts to give her a second massage on the Sunday. Many accounts of this weekend and its sequel – even from responsible sources – are inaccurate. Richard Lamb, whose history *The Macmillan Years* is of first-class reliability, drops his standards in the welter of confusing stories about the scandal. The Profumos were never 'on very friendly terms with Ward', as Lamb states; they did not 'discreetly but rigorously cut' him after August 1961; Keeler was not 'the mistress of Stephen Ward'; 'Keeler's known liaison with Ivanov' probably never happened.[5]

On Sunday morning, 9 July, while Astor took Ayub Khan to inspect the Cliveden stud, some of his guests mingled with Ward's group at the swimming pool. Ivanov had a swimming race with Profumo. When Profumo asked Keeler for her telephone number, she directed him to Ward. The osteopath, who seemed pleased by the approach, said his number was in the telephone directory. Later that morning two multi-millionaires, Nubar Gulbenkian and Sir Isaac Wolfson, arrived with their wives at the main house as luncheon guests to replace the Harrods and Lancasters.

During Sunday afternoon, Ivanov began a drunken binge which continued after he had driven Keeler back to Ward's flat in Wimpole Mews. This evening became crucial eighteen months later, in January 1963, when Keeler was being paid for her sexual reminiscences about Profumo. Encouraged by journalists who were offering £1,000 for a sensational story, she then began to say that she and Ivanov had gone to bed together that night at

Wimpole Mews. It is striking that, although sexual discretion was not her métier, no one could recall her mentioning her night with Ivanov before January 1963, when journalists first saw their chance to run stories pretending that official secrets had been jeopardised by her multiple affairs. The value of her account of coupling with Ivanov, as it was finally published in the *News of the World* on 16 June 1963, after all legal inhibitions had been broken by Profumo's resignation, can be easily judged:

> Here was my perfect specimen of a man. And he wanted me. He couldn't have stopped now anyway. We crashed across the room. A little table went flying. He pinioned me in a corner by the door. I relaxed. Because he was just kissing me with all the power of a man in a frenzy of passion.
>
> I made a last attempt to get away. But he caught hold of me. Our very impetus carried us through the door, and we half fell into my bedroom. There was my little bed, with its blue coverlet, and the little pink dressing-table. From that second I too threw all reserve to the winds. But . . . I was afraid he would hate me afterwards . . . But he was like a god . . . Clumsy perhaps, but only because he wanted me . . .
>
> But later came the grim shadows, when he was lying beside me. I could sense his sadness; the deep black gloom that I am told all Russians feel after they have done something they feel they shouldn't have done . . . What had happened between us was something as old as time . . .
>
> I never dreamed I might be the girl who rocked the Government. I know nothing of high affairs . . . All I know is that when I allowed Eugene to love me I was young and free.[6]

There is every reason to discount Keeler's memory, which profited newspapers by enabling them to run scare stories that the Secretary of State for War and a Russian spy had both been lovers, around the same time, of the same 'good-time girl'. The *News of the World* story also reinforced its view that aroused men could not be expected to stop themselves; that men despised women who yielded to them; and that sexual clumsiness in men was an admirable sign of passion rather than evidence of their selfish incompetence.

Reverting to a chronological account of the sequel to the Cliveden weekend, on Monday 10 July, Ward telephoned his MI5 handler Wagstaffe ('Woods') to arrange a meeting. Two days later he reported that Ivanov and Profumo had met at Cliveden; that Ivanov and Keeler had been binge-drinking together; and that Ivanov had asked him to elicit when the United States was going to arm West Germany with nuclear weapons. Astor, on that same Monday, according to his secretary, telephoned to rebuke Ward for bringing the girls and Ivanov to the pool, on the Sunday morning, when he had a house party including the President of Pakistan and the Secretary of War. 'You damned fool,' he is supposed to have said. This tale is doubtful. Young women from Spring Cottage were often found at the Cliveden swimming pool when the Astors had house parties, as shown by the draft of the evidence that Profumo later submitted to Lord Denning: 'All the girls were very young, and very pretty, and very common, and I remember that subsequently my sister, Lady Balfour of Inchrye, who was there with her husband a week or so before, had said that she and her husband were absolutely scandalised that Bill should allow this man Ward to go up to the pool with all these common tarts.'[7]

Profumo rang young, pretty Christine Keeler – 'common' though she was – to arrange an assignation on the weekend after their first meeting, while his wife was visiting his Warwickshire constituency. Profumo's subsequent line was that they met for sex on about three occasions in July and August 1961. In her accounts Keeler claimed more meetings over a longer period. On one occasion he borrowed the Bentley of his parliamentary colleague John Hare (Minister of Labour) for an outing with her. He took her for a drink with a former Cabinet minister, Geordie Ward, newly ennobled as Lord Ward of Witley, who later denied all memory of the occasion. On 3 August, while his family were holidaying on the Isle of Wight, Profumo had an evening with Keeler: she cooked sausages before they had sex in front of the television.

'I simply thought that she was a very beautiful little girl who seemed to like sexual intercourse,' Profumo explained two years later. 'She told me that she had done a certain amount of model-ling, and that she was now between jobs.' He gave her £20 for her mother, a cigarette lighter and some scent. It was the same perfume as his wife used: a trick of the practised adulterer who knows that a wife will be less suspicious if she smells her own scent on her husband, but alert if she detects the different scent of another woman. Valerie Profumo told her son David, 'He thought he could get away with it: after all, most of his friends did.'[8]

On 8 August, Profumo met Keeler again, and made another assignation with her for the next evening. Over the preceding three weeks they had probably met half a dozen times. Meanwhile, MI5 (whose men were monitoring Ivanov) apprised the Cabinet Secretary, Sir Norman Brook, of the attaché's contacts with Ward, and of Profumo's visits to Ward's home. Brook called Profumo to see him on 9 August. One version of this meeting suggests that Brook warned Profumo that MI5 was watching Ward's flat, because of the Ivanov connection, but that Profumo misinter-preted Brook's comments as a hint that MI5 knew of his affair with Keeler (MI5 did not hear of the affair until later). A more dubious notion is that Brook asked Profumo to help MI5 in compromising Ivanov, but that Profumo declined. There was no suggestion then that Ivanov was conducting an affair with Keeler.

After meeting Brook, Profumo sent Keeler a hasty, imprudent note on War Office paper – headed 'Darling' and signed 'Love J' – cancelling their meeting. Shortly afterwards he left for a holiday with his wife in Portofino. This was, according to Ward, one of five letters that Profumo sent to Keeler, which she left lying around. He claimed that he destroyed two, and that her quondam boyfriend Michael Lambton destroyed another.

Although Profumo claimed that he dropped Keeler after meeting Sir Norman Brook, his son suspects that there were sporadic assignations during the autumn – conceivably in a spirit of defiance of the Cabinet Secretary's condescending, head-masterly guidance. The hasty, imprudent note certainly mooted a further meeting with Keeler in September. One hypothesis is that their assignations continued until the autumn, and ended after Keeler refused Profumo's suggestion that she leave Ward's flat so that he could set her up in a flat of her own. According to this guesswork, Profumo thought Ward was a blabbermouth, who might gossip about his dalliance with Keeler (after Brook's warning, he certainly severed contact with Ward, whom he barely knew: the two men met only once again, by chance, in the Dorchester hotel in March 1963). The affair may have ended for a commonplace reason. The sexual fire between Keeler and Noel Howard-Jones had soon been banked: maybe the Minister tired of her as swiftly as the law student.

'The basic difference between a liaison and a marriage,' Sir Richard Glyn MP said in 1963, 'is that both parties in a liaison are likely to be unfaithful to each other.' By the early 1960s, according to Lord Annan, 'the Establishment accepted that men in public life slept with each other's wives or had a steady mistress, and might as a result land in the divorce courts. It did not accept that they might pick up girls casually at parties or through the network that passes on names and phone numbers. Jack Profumo when Secretary of State for War had the bad luck to have an affair with a girl who also knew a Soviet naval attaché. She claimed (although in his report Denning, the Master of the Rolls, disbe-lieved her) that he too was her lover. Worse still she was a girl who would say anything to hit the headlines.'[9]

In October 1961, when Profumo's affair with Keeler was either over or petering out, she accompanied Ward to the Rio Café in Notting Hill, perhaps with the intention of scoring cannabis. There she met Aloysius 'Lucky' Gordon, who had reached England from Jamaica in 1948, enlisted as a soldier but left in disgrace after two years following an attack on an NCO. Gordon, who sometimes sang in jazz clubs, had a runtish physique, dazzling smile, weedy moustache and receding hairline. He liked to act cool, but was easily spurred to violence. The Danish authorities had deported him after a furious incident with a girlfriend, and he had an English police record for assault and shop-breaking. Keeler alleged that Gordon introduced her and Ward to cannabis, that he later raped her while wielding a knife (which he denied) and much else. It is likely that she had smoked the drug before, uncertain that Ward had more than a few experimental inhalations, and certain that he disliked her use of the drug. Indeed, he later took her to a police station for a 'talking-to' on its ill-effects.

Previously, during August (a month after the Cliveden weekend), Khrushchev made a bellicose broadcast threatening to amass armaments on the Soviet bloc's western frontiers. Workmen began erecting the concrete wall, with guard towers, that encircled West Berlin and severed it from the rest of Germany. The Russians exploded a hydrogen bomb.

Doubtless at Ivanov's prompting, Ward persuaded Astor to send a busybody letter to the Foreign Office introducing Ward as an intimate of Ivanov's. Ward, Astor explained, could ensure that any information about Western intentions that the Foreign Office wished to reach the Soviets directly could be given to Ward for transmission to Ivanov. Any desired meeting with Ivanov could be arranged through Ward. The idea that an unstable meddler like Ward could surpass the Foreign Office in diplomatic liaison was a reversion to the worst days of Cliveden Set interference in Anglo-German relations in the 1930s. Nevertheless, Ward was invited to the Foreign Office, where he offered to act as an intermediary with Ivanov. His offer was rejected.

Ward arranged for Ivanov to dine at the House of Commons with one of his patients, a Tory backbencher called Sir Godfrey Nicholson. As a result of this meeting, Nicholson approached the Foreign Secretary, Lord Home, who advised him against private initiatives involving Ivanov. Despite this, Ward asked Nicholson to introduce him to Sir Harold Caccia, Permanent Under Secretary at the Foreign Office. On 5 April 1962, Nicholson held a luncheon for Ward and Caccia. Ward said that he felt anxious about Anglo-Soviet relations, and offered to open direct contacts between Caccia and Ivanov. Ward prized informality, intimacy, confidences and indiscretions, so it is easy to see why haphazard contacts between the Russian embassy and the Foreign Office appealed to him. Caccia, though, must have seen such contacts as time-consuming complications with a potential for muddle or mischief. He declined Ward's offer. The lunch, indeed, must have been frustrating to a busy man.

On 20 June, *The Times* printed a letter that the Colonial Secretary, Reginald Maudling, had addressed to his constituents scrutinising the reasons for his party's recent startling defeat in the Orpington by-election and offering cryptic criticism of Macmillan. It shows the uneasy, frugal sentiments in the national mood even before the publicity of the Profumo-Keeler imbroglio. 'The 1950s have passed and taken their problems with them; unless we turn to the problems of the 1960s we may find that we have worked ourselves out as the last Labour Government did,' Maudling warned. There was a 'new national mood' expressed in 'the growing sense that material affluence is not enough'. The Macmillan ethos, with its catchphrase 'You've never had it so good', seemed cynical, mercenary and complacent. Initiatives were needed 'to buttress prosperity with moral responsibility' and to inculcate 'self-discipline' so as to restore the 'moral purpose that is missing from the search for rising personal wellbeing'.[10]

Jasper More, Tory MP for Ludlow, called publicly in June 1962 for Macmillan to take an earldom and go to the Lords, while remaining Prime Minister, on the grounds that he looked 'periodically a man under an excessive physical and mental strain'. The Liberal-owned *Time & Tide* added on 5 July: 'Mr Macmillan would be surprised if he knew how many Tories are saying privately that he should take his coronet – without remaining

Prime Minister.' Further bad by-election results followed in mid-July, but Macmillan did not retire with an earldom. The earldom went instead to Kilmuir, his long-serving Lord Chancellor, who, when Macmillan sacked a third of his Cabinet, was pushed off the Woolsack to make room for Reginald Manningham-Buller in his new guise as Lord Dilhorne. After hearing that Kilmuir had complained that his cook would have been given more notice of dismissal than he had, Macmillan quipped that Lord Chancellors were easier to find than cooks. Maudling became Chancellor of the Exchequer.[11]

Macmillan was vexed when, in a *Panorama* television discussion of the Cabinet reshuffle, the insubordinate backbench MP Lord Lambton likened him to Macbeth. Antony Lambton was responsible for the glossy magazine *Queen* publishing a fortnight later, on 31 July, a theatrical spoof entitled 'Supermacbeth, a tragedy in three shuffles', in which the cast included John Wyndham as Lady Macbeth; Lord Beaverbrook as Hecate; Nigel Birch and Lords Hinchingbrooke and Lambton as the three witches; Profumo, Dilhorne, Hugh Fraser, Julian Amery, Keith Joseph and Enoch Powell as Supermacbeth's servants; and Macleod, Redmayne and Christopher Soames as murderers. It was preceded by Lambton's remonstrance addressed to the Prime Minister, in which he hectored Macmillan with the sentiments of his party's irreconcilable right-wing: 'You have been clever once too often, for in the last six years you have stripped the Conservative Party of all its tradition, and its beliefs, and given a continental twist to our politics . . . now you find yourself naked and friendless'. He urged Supermac to retire so as to give his party a chance of winning the next election: 'Don't you think that now is the time to go, as we can't afford to have a Prime Minister at this time whose genius and spark have gone, and who is now the tired and discredited symbol of Conservative decline?'[12]

This same issue of *Queen* contained a feature by its associate editor, Robin Douglas-Home, entitled 'Sentences I'd Like To Hear The End Of'. It contained a series of incomplete sentences by which Douglas-Home hinted at choice London gossip involving people like Clore, Lady Pamela Berry (wife of the chairman of the *Daily* and *Sunday Telegraphs*) and David Frost: '. . . she said next on Charlie's takeover list is . . .'; '. . . so completely innocently I said, "Lady Pamela, I'd like you to meet a friend of mine who writes the Medicine column in the Q . . ."'; '. . . overheard David saying that *he* still thought Michael Frayn funny because . . .'. One of the cryptic hints read: 'called in MI5 because every time the chauffeur-driven Zis drew up at her *front* door, out of the *back* door into a chauffeur-driven Humber slipped . . .'. Fleet Street realised that the Humber indicated a government minister, and the Zis a Soviet bloc diplomat.[13]

After a successful Conservative Party conference in October, Macmillan, in consultation with other ministers, began framing a new policy initiative which he called 'The Modernisation of Britain'. Then, on 22 October, the Cuban missile crisis erupted. The imminence of nuclear war provided Ward with the excuse for a new phase of otiose meddling. Ivanov used him to instigate Astor and Nicholson to urge the Foreign Office to advise that Macmillan's government should call an international peace conference. Ward was infatuated enough to believe that his interventions might prove momentous: they were, however, futile, and proved his naïveté. He was a tool of the Soviet tactics to make mischief in the Atlantic Alliance and create diversionary confusion by appealing to Macmillan's hankering for British leadership of world summitry. The Soviets wished, Home wrote in June 1963, 'to drive a wedge between ourselves and our American allies', and 'to test our resolve and lay a bait for our vanity'.[14]

On 25 October, during the Cuban crisis, Ward interrupted a conversation on the subject at an adjacent table in the Kenya Coffee House in Marylebone High Street with pro-Soviet apologetics. One of the men at the other table was called William Shepherd. When Shepherd left the café, Ward was waiting on the pavement, and asked if he wished to meet a Russian attaché to hear the Soviet side of the crisis. It is unlikely that Ward would have done this if he had not known that Shepherd was a Tory backbencher, though he gave no sign of recognising his target as a politician. Both men were regulars not only at the coffee house but at Murray's cabaret club: a waiter at either place might have identified Shepherd as an MP to Ward. It is less sure that Ward knew that Shepherd, like Henry Kerby, was an MI5 informant who regaled his handler with tales gleaned during his parliamentary duties and relayed information that MI5 wanted to be circulated in Parliament. Shepherd was also a conduit of information to and fro between the Commons and the upper echelons of the Metropolitan Police at Scotland Yard.

Shepherd, who, like Kerby, often railed against homosexuality, mistrusted Ward's predilections. 'I found his voice rather irritating,' Shepherd recalled a year after he had been accosted by Ward on the Marylebone pavement. 'It had a phoney, almost homosexual intonation. His whole manner was one to arouse suspicion.' Shepherd subsequently met Ivanov for drinks at Ward's flat on 31 October. The meeting degenerated into a slanging match about Soviet intentions. By Shepherd's self-dramatising account, Ivanov trumpeted the opinions of 'a big-fisted Stalinist', and was furious when Shepherd said, 'We didn't enter into a squalid pact in 1939 to share the milk with Hitler.' At the Wimpole Mews flat, said Shepherd, were both Rice-Davies and Keeler, whom he recognised from Murray's. He had already heard tales linking Keeler with Profumo. Seeing her with Ivanov, in the flat of this mysterious Dr Ward, alarmed him.[15]

So, too, did an incident that occurred as he was leaving. 'We must go, too,' said Ward, indicating Ivanov. 'We're going to have dinner with Iain Macleod.' This dropping of the Leader of the House of Commons' name was typical of Ward's distortions: he had no dinner invitation from Macleod, whom he never met, but had inveigled a youngster to bring him along with Ivanov for drinks with Macleod's teenage children. Shepherd reported the meeting to his MI5 handler: Ivanov knew both Ward and Keeler, he said, and Keeler was involved with Profumo. He also warned

Macleod that his name was being invoked by dubious characters. Finally, during the time of the Vassall homosexuality panic, possibly at the instigation of his MI5 handler, he sent Macmillan a letter threatening further exposures of ministers, and denounced several parliamentary colleagues to the Chief Whip, Redmayne. At the end of this meeting in November 1962, Shepherd claimed he told Redmayne: 'And there's a problem with Jack Profumo: you'd better be very careful.'[16]

Keeler had meanwhile met a former merchant seaman from Antigua, Johnny Edgecombe, who had served prison sentences for larceny, pimping and possession of drugs, and ran a shebeen in a Notting Hill flat leased from Rachman. She lived briefly with him in Brentford. After 'Lucky' Gordon then ambushed Keeler and knocked her to the pavement, she and Edgecombe confronted him outside the Flamingo jazz club in Wardour Street on Saturday 27 October. A fight erupted: Edgecombe knifed Gordon, who needed seventeen stitches in his face. Keeler went into hiding with Edgecombe, but left him in December because she found him domineering and sexually inconsiderate.

Although in October 1962, Rachman supposedly gave Rice-Davies £1,000 in cash, wrapped in brown paper, as an eighteenth birthday present, he was so morose that soon afterwards she left the Bryanston Mews premises where he kept her, and moved into Ward's spare bedroom at Wimpole Mews. A few weeks later, on Saturday night of the last weekend of November 1962, Rachman went gambling at the 150 Club in Earls Court. He left early because he felt queasy and, driving north to Hampstead Garden Suburb, had to stop the car because he felt so bad. For some time he sat hunched over the steering wheel in a St John's Wood street. At home, on Sunday morning, he suffered a heart attack, and was taken by ambulance to Edgware Hospital, where a second massive coronary thrombosis killed him.

On Friday 14 December, Keeler went to visit Rice-Davies at Ward's flat. Around one o'clock Edgecombe arrived there in a minicab, raging that she was consorting with Gordon, and furiously ringing the bell. Rice-Davies called to him from a first-floor window that Keeler was at the hairdressers. Edgecombe was not fooled and produced a gun, which he fired at the lock of the front door, then at the window from which Rice-Davies was gazing down. Having failed to climb a drainpipe he dropped his gun and fled. When the police arrived, Keeler, who often fibbed under pressure, said the gun was hers. Edgecombe was soon detained, and remanded for trial on a charge of attempted murder.[17]

In this period Keeler smoked cannabis often. Her hold on reality was slack; her days were a smudge of shapeless improvisation; her chatter was sometimes spry and amusing, occasionally indignant, but never discreet. On 23 December she accompanied Paul Mann to a Christmas party in Rossmore Court, a block of flats between Marylebone Station and the Regent's Park. There, with huffs of anger, she recounted her recent experiences to several unreliable confidants. Mann, who had been born in 1936, was a nimble-witted man without impractical ideals: although described in the press as a racing driver, at this time he ran a shirt business in Manchester. Another guest at the party – he lived a minute's walk from Rossmore Court – was John Lewis, the obnoxious former MP who had an inveterate hatred of Ward. To both of them Keeler talked of Ward, Profumo and Edgecombe's gunshots. Neither was a safe repository of secrets.

Mann approached journalists about selling the story; Lewis sneaked to a Labour MP called George Wigg on 2 January 1963. Keeler made further rash confidences to Michael Eddowes, a deceptively fatherly-looking man with patrician airs whom Rebecca West likened to a Peter Sellers imitation of an English gentleman. Eddowes ran a South Kensington restaurant called Bistro Vino. He was a plausible, self-aggrandising obsessive who cajoled the Texans into exhuming the body of Lee Harvey Oswald in 1981 to test his hare-brained theory that the man who shot President Kennedy was a Soviet imposter. Lewis saw the 'Darling' note which Profumo had written, and so probably did Eddowes. The letter was also seen (perhaps through Lewis) by a puffy-faced youngster called Lawrence Bell, who lived in the dingy London suburb of Wanstead and was a newspaper stringer. 'This started a train of malice and filth which went through a Mr Lawrence Bell to Colonel Wigg, and other Socialist members,' Ward later alleged to his MP, Sir Wavell Wakefield. It was almost amusing to see Ward, whom many people found unsavoury, complaining about Bell, who had (he believed) been involved with Lord Longford's prisoner aid charity and (less probably) was a friend of Wigg. 'Mr Bell has been arrested recently for persistent importuning,' he told Wakefield. 'It was he who set off the Fletcher-Cooke scandal with the papers.' Charles Fletcher-Cooke was a whimsical barrister-MP who had served as Parliamentary Under Secretary at the Home Office under Henry Brooke. He had been introduced by a tipsy Hove bachelor, Lord Maugham, to a nineteen-year-old ex-borstal lad (and policeman's son), Anthony Turner, who went to live in Fletcher-Cooke's house as a novel way of getting straightened out. The youth was stopped by the police for exceeding the speed limit in Commercial Road, Stepney, while driving Fletcher-Cooke's Austin Princess car. After Turner's appearance on 4 March at Bow Street magistrates' court (on charges of speeding and driving while disqualified and uninsured) Fletcher-Cooke resigned his Home Office post. When Bell later appeared in court on nine charges of indecency with guardsmen, his counsel described him as having been responsible for Fletcher-Cooke's resignation.[18]

Colonel George Wigg, for whom Lewis and Bell served as informers, was a suspicious, slippery, vindictive man with the mentality of a police grass. Wigg had joined the Tank Corps in 1919 when he was eighteen, rose from the ranks to be a non-commissioned officer, and had made a stealthy study of military organisation with the help of socialist writings. He resented the fact that the army of a twentieth-century industrial power was organised like a peasant levy led by the gentry and nobility: its outlook, hierarchy and discipline all reflected a social order based on the ancestral rights of the landed interest. Garrison life taught him, he said, to punch hard and below the belt. As a result of wartime service in the Education Corps he achieved the rank of colonel, which he persisted in using in peacetime. He was elected as a Labour MP in 1945.

When Wigg's elephantine ears caught a Tory ex-minister muttering a criticism of the Speaker during a Commons debate, 'the unspeakable Wigg broke every rule of behaviour by reporting this'. As the best-informed Labour MP on the Select Committee for Reform of the Army and Air Force Acts in the early 1950s, Wigg saw himself as the soldiers' protector from political incompetence or hanky-panky. Winston Churchill, as Prime Minister, and Antony Head, the then Secretary of State of War, 'adopted a foolish attitude towards Wigg, who was one of the few members of his party who really had the interests of the services at heart', recalled their parliamentary colleague Ian Harvey. 'They mocked him for being an Education Corps colonel, whereas he had previously had a long career in the Tanks Corps.' Wigg was a man who nursed his grievances. Profumo's handling of complaints about living conditions in the British Army on the Rhine and the ill-equipment of troops in Kuwait infuriated him. Already hell-bent on damaging Profumo before Lewis approached him, Wigg immediately opened a dossier in which he filed every tit-bit that he heard.[19]

On 15 January 1963, a fortnight after Lewis denounced Profumo to Wigg, Lord Radcliffe's Vassall tribunal began its public hearings. The following day, at Marlborough Street Court, the preliminary hearing of Edgecombe's case was held. Denning later reported that Ivanov last met Ward on 18 January, but like much that Denning printed, this may be untrue: the men perhaps never met after Christmas 1962. Ivanov returned to Moscow permanently on 29 January – perhaps to protect his embassy from being incriminated in the attempted shooting of a 'model' by a black hoodlum. Given all that followed, it is worth reiterating the opinion of the First Lord of the Admiralty, Carrington, that the security stunt raised over the tenuous Ivanov-Profumo connection was 'humbug from first to last'.[20]

Paul Mann had by then convinced Keeler that she could profit by selling her story to the press. On 22 January 1963, accompanied by Rice-Davies, she visited the Mirror Group's headquarters with Profumo's 'Darling' letter in her handbag. Cudlipp assessed her story together with Reg Payne, editor of the *Sunday Pictorial*, which some months later was renamed the *Sunday Mirror* following the restructuring that created the International Publishing Corporation. Having photographed the note, the *Sunday Pictorial* offered her £1,000 for the right to publish it. Keeler then tried to sell her story for a higher price to Peter Earle, crime reporter of the *News of the World*, but botched the negotiation. She therefore accepted the *Sunday Pictorial* offer, was paid £200 up front (with the second payment of £800 payable if the story was published), and was allotted two reporters to extract her story.

Keeler started chattering spicily about rich men in high places and Caribbean low-lifers. The questioning prompts from the two journalists soon showed her what they wanted: Profumo, Ivanov and sex. At one point she said that Ward had told her to ask Profumo when West Germany would get American secrets about atomic weapons. Ward did ask her this, as a joke; she knew it was a joke, and repeated it as a joke to the *Sunday Pictorial* men. No one who met her for half a minute would have mistaken her for a Mata Hari who could extract state secrets with pillow talk. No one could think that Profumo, in rapture or post-coital gratitude, would have supplied her with classified information, even if he knew it. Yet this was what journalists wanted excuses for pretending. In the *Pictorial*'s pompous re-writing of the joke, the following phrases were attributed to Keeler: 'I did find it worrying when someone asked me to try to get from Profumo the answer to a certain question. That question was: "When, if ever, are the Americans going to give nuclear weapons to Germany?" I am not prepared to say in public who asked me to find out the answer to that question. I am prepared to give it to the security officials. In fact, I believe now that I have a duty to do so.'[21]

Earle, after severing *News of the World* negotiations with Keeler, approached Ward for a story. Ward was aghast, telephoned Astor, and on 28 January the men consulted William Rees-Davies, a barrister who was a Tory MP. Billy Rees-Davies had lost an arm in the war, and usually wore a cloak, which made him look raffish. He was a gossip, a drinker and director of a public relations firm and of John Bloom's washing machine company. Ward explained that the *Sunday Pictorial* had bought Keeler's memoirs, which might compromise Astor, Profumo and himself. He feared that she might give a publicity boost to the memoirs when she testified in Edgecombe's imminent trial.

On hearing of these developments from Astor, Profumo requested a visit from MI5. Denning's report, relying on a brief supplied by MI5 which seems misleading, stated that Profumo was visited by the Director General of the Security Service, Sir Roger Hollis. Profumo's recollection, which is more credible, is that he was visited by a senior MI5 man: he asked his visitor if MI5 could suppress the *Sunday Pictorial* story on the basis that it compromised the 'honey-trap' operation against Ivanov, about which he knew. The MI5 officer doubted if anything of the sort could be done. Rees-Davies and Profumo's solicitor, Derek Clogg, began to negotiate with Keeler's solicitor, who demanded compensation of £5,000 for the annulment of her *Sunday Pictorial* contract.

Independently of this, Ward telephoned an assistant editor on *Sunday Pictorial* warning that there were factual errors in Keeler's story, and that he, Astor, Profumo and perhaps others would sue if the article was published. The *Sunday Pictorial* capitulated and withdrew the story. Ward had succeeded where the lawyers had failed. Keeler kept her £200, but was aggrieved that he had prevented her from collecting the extra £800.

On 26 January, Detective Sergeant John Burrows called on Keeler and Rice-Davies with a routine reminder that they would be required to testify as prosecution witnesses at Edgecombe's trial.

They poured out recriminations to him. Rice-Davies resented being usurped by Ward from the Bryanston Mews flat in which she had been installed by Rachman: he had moved there after being asked to vacate the Wimpole Mews flat in the aftermath of the shooting; she regarded it as her home, and had partly furnished it herself. Keeler blamed Ward for being £800 short of the *Sunday Pictorial* payout. She was by then well-coached by journalists in saying what would have impact.

Afterwards Burrows wrote a report: 'She said that Doctor Ward was a procurer of young women for gentlemen in high places and was sexually perverted; that he had a country house at Cliveden to which some of these women were taken to meet important men – the cottage was on the estate of Lord Astor; that he had introduced her to Mr John Profumo and that she had an association with him; that Mr Profumo had written a number of letters to her on War Office notepaper and that she was still in possession of one of these letters which were being considered for publication in the *Sunday Pictorial* to whom she had sold her life story for £1,000. She also said that on one occasion when she was going to meet Mr Profumo, Ward had asked her to discover from him the date on which certain atomic secrets were to be handed over to West Germany by the Americans, and that this was at the time of the Cuban crisis. She also said that she had been introduced by Ward to the Naval Attaché of the Soviet Embassy.'[22] Marylebone CID considered the accusation of procuring to be absurd, and decided not to investigate further.

Rees-Davies went to Peter Rawlinson, the Solicitor-General, with a summary of what he knew on 28 January (the Attorney-General, Sir John Hobson, being occupied all day at the Vassall tribunal). There followed an intricate sequence of consultations and interviews with Profumo. Hobson began by believing the rumours linking Profumo to Keeler, and thought him capable of puerile lies about his sex life. When, however, Profumo undertook that he would issue a libel writ against any newspaper that suggested that Keeler had been his mistress, Hobson accepted his vehement denials, because he did not think the minister was a hardened perjurer who would enter the witness box and break his oath. Rawlinson doubted Profumo's story, but loyally supported the official backing of the minister's credibility. He felt that the private lives of ministers should remain their own business: certainly he respected Profumo's resolve that he would not be hounded from his ministry by sleazy gossip of the sort that had assailed Galbraith.

Profumo's solicitor, Clogg, believed his client completely. Profumo's barrister Mark Littman was an exceptional man who had become a Queen's Counsel at the age of forty. Born in Hackney in 1920, his life was transformed when, still an Islington schoolboy, he read Proust's *A la recherche du temps perdu*. His wife was a Southern Belle who had been the confidante of Tennessee Williams and Christopher Isherwood. As all this suggests, Littman was humane and wise. He advised that Keeler's soliciting of £5,000 as a solace for not selling her story to Sunday newspapers provided grounds for a criminal prosecution for blackmail. With Clogg, he put this case to Mathew, the Director of Public Prosecutions, who declined to act. Littman was too inscrutable to show whether he, too, had been gulled by Profumo. It may be doubted.

On Friday 1 February 1963, Mark Chapman-Walker, former chief publicity officer at Conservative Central Office and now managing director of the *News of the World*, went to the Prime Minister's private office to see John Wyndham, whom he had first met in the Italian theatre of war. Chapman-Walker repeated what he had been told by Peter Earle: that the story was hurtling round Fleet Street that Profumo 'had compromised himself with a girl who was also involved with a negro in a case about attempted murder'. The 'girl' had sold her story, mentioning both Profumo and the Russian naval attaché, to the Mirror Group. Wyndham wrote a 'top-secret' minute giving a garbled summary of Chapman-Walker's story for Macmillan to read:

According to Mr Chapman-Walker, Mr Profumo is alleged to have met this girl 'Kolania' through Lord Astor at Cliveden, where they chased her naked round the bathing pool . . . it is also alleged that:

(i) 'Kolania' got into this company through the agency of a Mr Ward, who Mr Chapman-Walker described as a 'psychopathic specialist' of Wimpole Street;

(ii) Mr Profumo, visiting 'Kolania' in Mr Ward's house, passed in the passage the Russian Naval Attaché on his way out from 'Kolania';

(iii) 'Kolania' has two letters on War Office paper signed 'J' – although it is not suggested that these letters are anything more than ones of assignation.[23]

This triggered another bout of consultations. Wyndham's Downing Street colleague, Timothy Bligh, telephoned MI5 asking Hollis, the organisation's Director General, to come for a talk. As Hollis had left for a country weekend, his deputy, Graham Mitchell, who was being kept under twenty-four-hour surveillance as a suspected KGB agent, substituted for him: he was shadowed to the meeting by two MI5 watchers. Mitchell told Bligh and Wyndham that Profumo had been 'in and out of Miss Keeler's place', and had been warned against the association. MI5 were sure that there had been no security risk. Why, the private office asked, had they had not been told this earlier? 'This is a free country,' Mitchell replied, 'not a police state.' Wyndham and his colleagues continued to hear tales about the affair. Macmillan used to refer to 10 Downing Street as Vatican City – a citadel in which he was hopelessly insulated from gossip and changes of temper. Wyndham retrospectively felt that he had been slack in regaling back-talk as a good private secretary should: perhaps his knowledge of the Boothby-Dorothy Macmillan affair made him shy of discussing adultery with a Prime Minister whom he revered. The government's handling of the early phase of the Profumo Affair was not, Wyndham recognised, as tight as the circumstances merited.[24]

Bligh consulted Profumo, who asked him (in vain) not to tell the Prime Minister of the rumours. On 4 February (the day that Foster and Mulholland went to prison) Bligh and Profumo met again in the presence of Redmayne. Profumo repeated his denials, but asked Redmayne if he should resign. It is unlikely that the Chief Whip full-heartedly accepted Profumo's denials. However, the Radcliffe tribunal had not yet exonerated Galbraith: Redmayne, who feared the damage of another ministerial resignation on a security issue, advised that he should not resign. This judgement was understandable, but had fatal consequences.

Another showy, self-mystifying, soft-living figure now intruded into the story. Thomas Corbally was an American whose grandfather had founded a private detective agency. He too had been a private investigator, and in 1963 was based in London, ostensibly as an advertising executive, although he also worked for an American firm of corporate investigators and security consultants. On 29 January, Corbally visited the US embassy to report to Alfred Wells, assistant to the US ambassador David Bruce. Ward, he said, had treated him for a knee injury, and during a subsequent lunch had confided the Keeler-Profumo affair to him. Wells made a summary of Corbally's information, which he passed to Bruce. Probably Bruce gave the gist of this to Macmillan shortly after the Prime Minister read Wyndham's minute. Redmayne apprised Macmillan of the Profumo rumours on 4 or 5 February.

This palaver was not what the Prime Minister wished to give his energy and thought to. 'Harold's a very good Prime Minister as far as taking Cabinet goes: he takes it slowly, let's everyone have his say, and if they don't agree he doesn't mind calling an extra meeting,' one of his ministers had said in 1962. 'But as he grows older he thinks about fewer things – he's now mainly occupied with the Common Market, the Cold War and the Atlantic Alliance.'

Sexual gossip seemed a demeaning distraction from the old man's great priority of international settlement. In any case, Macmillan preferred cheerful rascals to solemn hypocrites.[25]

Ward was his own incubus. 'If only Stephen had kept his mouth shut, Profumo would never have been disgraced,' Corbally told Philip Knightley and Caroline Kennedy when they were researching their valuable book *Affair of State*. 'But Stephen talked about it, and talked about it. At every dinner party he went to, and everywhere else. There was no way to shut Stephen up. And he was greatly amused by it all . . . He loved being the centre of attention, loved being the one to come out with all the latest gossip.' Profumo's embarrassments had become a topic of smart cocktail-party gossip, as Lord Lambton warned Redmayne. Keeler and her friend Paula Hamilton-Marshall freely chattered about the situation to people they knew in Marylebone and north Kensington.[26]

On 8 March, an American named Andrew Roth, who had left the United States during the witch-hunt of communists and had a Commons lobby pass on the basis that he was correspondent of the left-wing French *L'Observateur*, published some explicit paragraphs in his thin, mimeographed weekly newsletter *Westminster Confidential*, which had under 200 subscribers (at six guineas a year). A story had 'run like wildfire through Parliament', Roth revealed.

> The best authenticated version is this: that two call-girls came into the limelight as a result of the effort of a Negro to kill them for having given him a venereal disease. This notoriety having made their calling difficult, the two girls started selling their stories to the Sunday newspapers, the *Sunday Pictorial* and *The People* . . .
>
> One of the choicest bits in their stories was a letter, apparently signed 'Jock' on the stationery of the Secretary for W+r. The allegation by this girl was not only that this Minister, who has a famous actress as his wife, was her client, but also the Soviet military attaché, apparently a Colonel Ivanov. The famous-actress wife would, of course, sue for divorce, the scandal ran. Who was

using the call-girl to 'milk' whom of information – the W+r Secretary or the Soviet military attaché? . . . It was probably knowledge about this story as well as the scandal concerning Charles Fletcher-Cooke and his young good-looking car-borrowing friend which led the Chief Whip, Brigadier Redmayne, to tell a correspondent with resignation: 'We have all the luck!'[27]

Roth's informant, significantly, had been the corrupt backbencher Henry Kerby, MI5's snooper. Kerby's fellow right-wingers in Parliament distributed copies of the newsletter. Profumo was disinclined to sue. His judgement was endorsed by both Clogg and Hobson, who felt that Roth's newsletter had too small a circulation to be worth suing, but forgot that its readership of journalists and MPs was influential. Profumo's friend Selwyn Lloyd was the only MP who was not a minister to confront him by seeking reassurances that the gossip was untrue. 'Selwyn had convinced himself,' wrote Ferdinand Mount who was Lloyd's bagman in the Conservative Research Department, 'that the whole thing would blow over. In any case, he always said, in his unworldly way, "I don't see how Jack could have had the time".' Lloyd reported Profumo's denials to Macmillan.[28]

In February 1963, a few weeks after opening his dossier on Profumo, George Wigg masterminded Harold Wilson's election as Labour Party leader by a combination of cajolery and threats to MPs about their future under Wilson. He remained Wilson's parliamentary enforcer. On 10 March he discussed tactics in exploiting the Profumo rumours with Wilson, who began planting the Profumo story in off-the-record briefings to journalists.

Harold Wilson had been the subject of an MI5 file since the late 1940s. He paid three visits to the Soviet Union while President of the Board of Trade, and revisited the country often while employed during the 1950s as economic consultant to a company importing timber from Russia. It was to preserve the quality of his business access that he refused to sign a condemnation by other left Labour MPs of the Soviet invasion of Hungary in 1956. The KGB prized his political gossip, gave him the codename 'Olding' and hoped to recruit him. In England, Wilson was as sly and self-conscious as Macmillan in the false image that he projected: sanctimonious frugality rather than patrician nonchalance. He would never have said, as Macmillan did, 'it's very important not to have a rigid distinction between what's flippant and what is serious'.[29]

A journalist who interviewed Wilson during his first year as Labour leader was handed a copy of that morning's *Daily Express* gossip column. 'The London season is over,' William Hickey had written. 'The last champagne glass has been smashed, the last gate-crasher has been repelled, the last escort has roared away in his sports car from the dying party down the empty dawn streets.' Wilson – in 1963 – professed to loathe such luxury. 'This sort of conspicuous consumption by a small but highly regarded class,' Wilson told his interviewer, 'is not merely repugnant to the vast majority but it makes it harder for us to do our job. There are more important things to do. What is wrong with our society is that those who make the money are more regarded than those who earn the money.' Wilson was adept at synthetic moral wrath. The parliamentary reporter Bernard Levin thought the jeering, hooting and barracking by Tory bullies in the Commons of their opponents was obnoxious. The Labour Party's equivalent parliamentary vice was 'elaborate displays of mock indignation; whenever any Minister announces a cut in a subsidy or an increase in the charge of some welfare service the Opposition explode in an imitation of fury loud enough to put an attacking band of Cherokees to shame. He who has not heard Mr Harold Wilson, with tears on his cheek and his tongue in it, accusing the Government of "taking it out of the kids" has not yet explored the lower depths of which the House of Commons is capable.'[30]

Barbara Castle gave a supper party for Wilson on 10 March. The other guests included Wigg, Crossman and Foot. 'George outlined the story to us,' Crossman reported, 'and we emphatically and unanimously repudiated it. We all felt that even if it was true that Profumo was having an affair with a call-girl, and some Russian diplomat had been mixed up in it, the Labour Party simply shouldn't touch it.' They took this attitude, he believed, because they were ashamed of George Brown's recent slurs about Galbraith. Their strong advice to Wilson 'squashed' Wigg.[31]

Journalists were eager for Edgecombe's trial to open at the Old Bailey on 14 March, for they expected Keeler to make admissions or commit indiscretions during her testimony which they could print as a report of court proceedings without risk of libel actions – and without the expense of paying her. Perhaps she might blurt that Edgecombe was jealous of her affair with Profumo? Might she mention that she had been visited in Wimpole Mews by Profumo and Ivanov? In the event, Keeler never testified, for on 8 March Paul Mann took her by car to Spain. Probably Mann realised that if she testified in court, much of her story would become available to all of Fleet Street *gratis*. By spiriting her away, and 'minding' her in seclusion from journalists, he raised her value in a future newspaper bidding war. In default of her testimony, Edgecombe was acquitted of wounding Gordon and of shooting with intent to do grievous bodily harm; but sentenced to seven years for possessing a firearm with intent to endanger life.

It was insinuated that Profumo, or his political allies, had spirited Keeler away: Ward later alleged to his MP, Sir Wavell Wakefield, that Lawrence Bell had been paid by the *Daily Express*, *News of the World* and *People* for the tale that she had been sent abroad by Profumo. This rumour gained such credence that Hobson asked Profumo point-blank if he had engineered her disappearance. Profumo's denial remains entirely credible. Photographs of Keeler soon appeared in the *Daily Express*, which was a more likely instigator of her vanishing beyond the reach of its rivals. It certainly maximised her story pugnaciously.

The front page of the *Daily Express* on Friday 15 March was headlined: 'WAR MINISTER SHOCK – Profumo: He asks to resign for personal reasons and Macmillan asks him to stay on.' (This story was not an invention, for Profumo had indeed suggested to Redmayne that he should resign, albeit likening his offer to the resignation of Galbraith, whom everyone agreed had been unfairly victimised.) Next to it there was a photograph of Keeler headlined 'VANISHED – Old Bailey Witness', with another photograph showing her kneeling on a rug, apparently naked, with a skimpy towel strategically clenched to her front, and giving a sexy sideward glance. The *Express* was adamant in its later evidence to Lord Denning's inquiry that this juxtaposition of stories was utter chance; it was a measure of Denning's selective gullibility that he swallowed this twaddle.[32]

Of the millions of *Daily Express* readers nationally, only a few hundred London insiders recognised the warning shot that Lord Beaverbrook was firing at the government and the Astors. Beaverbrook, who had been pursuing a vendetta against the Astor family since 1951, wanted to use his newspapers to stress the Cliveden connection. Beaverbrook, an incorrigible adulterer who for years had kept Jean Norton (the mother of Astor's first wife) as his mistress, instructed his editors to harry Astor as 'a callous libertine'. One of Beaverbrook's adjuncts was Marcus Lipton, an MP who, like Wigg, preferred to be known by a military prefix, in his case 'Lieutenant Colonel'. Lipton was a self-publicist who was always ready to provide Beaverbrook's London *Evening Standard* with a juicy quote or to help promote press stunts. On one occasion he complained to the Speaker that parliamentary privilege had been breached when it was suggested that among over 600 MPs there must be a few male homosexuals. His intervention justified the press in launching a short-lived burst of muckraking.[33]

Now, once again, he obliged the *Daily Express*, which reported the 'Vanishing Model Case' on its front page of 20 March: 'Christine was last seen in the West End. Mr Marcus Lipton, Labour MP for Brixton, is to ask Home Secretary Mr Henry

The Flamingo club in Wardour Street, Soho where black jazz lovers and hip white Mods congregated. It was outside the Flamingo that Johnny Edgecombe knifed 'Lucky' Gordon during a row over Christine Keeler.
(Getty Images)

Christine Keeler dressed for work at Murray's Club in Beak Street, Soho in 1960.
(AGIP/Epic/Mary Evans)

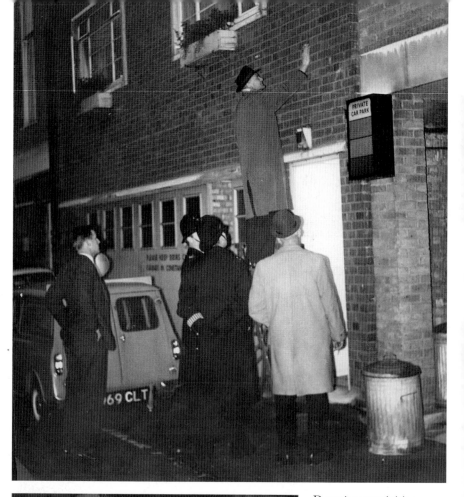

Detectives scrutinising the bullet holes after Johnny Edgecombe had shot at Christine Keeler at 17 Wimpole Mews in December 1962. (Rex Features)

The police coerced Christine Keeler into giving perjured evidence against 'Lucky' Gordon. He looked spruce when months later she was tried for conspiracy to pervert the course of justice during his trial. (Getty Images)

A gaunt but plucky Stephen Ward in his Bryanston Mews West home in June 1963 after his release from remand in prison. Mandy Rice-Davies had been detained on a trumped-up charge of stealing a similar television from the flat. (Mirrorpix)

Christine Keeler returning to Paula Hamilton-Marshall's flat in Devonshire Street after a police interview in June 1963. The flat was above the premises of the Genito-Urinary Manufacturing Company. (Mirrorpix)

Stephen Ward in a Bryanston Square flat preparing for the first day of his trial in July 1963. (Mirrorpix)

Mandy Rice-Davies leaving the Old Bailey in July 1963, after testifying at Ward's trial, seems serene amid the jostling, leering, taunting mob. (Getty Images)

Stephen Ward is carried from Noel Howard-Jones's flat in Chelsea after taking an overdose. Callous press photographers tried to force their way into the flat. (Getty Images)

Photographers harried Jack
Profumo when two months after his
resignation he flew to Scotland with
his son David for a holiday in August
1963 – between Ward's suicide and
publication of the Denning Report.
(Mirrorpix)

Lord Denning at Waterloo Station,
in high fettle at the publication of his
infamous Report in September 1963.
(Getty Images)

An envious crowd gawps as Christine Keeler followed by Paula Hamilton-Marshall leave their home to be tried for perjury in October 1963. (Getty Images)

Mandy Rice-Davies – jubilant, dauntless and ogled. She, more than Keeler, prospered in the decades that followed. (Mirrorpix)

The deposed leader in proud isolation: Harold Macmillan queuing for a taxi at Victoria Station in 1965. (Getty Images)

Brooke about the case.' Lipton also, as the *Daily Express* reported next day, interrupted a parliamentary question about tracing the missing ex-diplomat Philby (who had fled Beirut by sea two months earlier): 'Would it not be more in the public interest if the machinery of state were to concentrate on tracing the whereabouts in England of missing witnesses?'[34] Osbert Lancaster's front-page cartoon in the *Express* on 21 March contrasted Keeler's flight with the incarceration of Mulholland and Foster: a pompous man resembling Dilhorne asking of Maudie Littlehampton at dinner, 'Really, dear lady, how could we pursue this poor, defenceless girl and force her to give evidence – she's not a journalist!'

On the same day as the 'Vanishing Model' front page, a fearless champion of the People's Right to Know burgled Astor's house in Upper Grosvenor Street, and abstracted a file of letters. An accomplice broke into lockers at the school of Astor's eleven-year-old son, looking for heaven-knows-what. The boys thought the intruder was working on behalf of the *Daily Mirror*, but it might as easily have been the *Daily Express*. On 21 March, Spring Cottage was ransacked. A *News of the World* reporter admitted entering the cottage with a photographer, once the door or window had been broken open, but no one took responsibility for the break-ins.

Shortly before the Commons debate on the imprisonment of the Vassall reporters, Foster and Mulholland, scheduled for 21 March, Wigg tabled a parliamentary motion calling for 'severe financial penalties on the principal proprietors of newspapers which constantly indulge in adventurous sensationalism with little regard to truth'. In this he chimed with the view of many voters that journalists over-relied on 'that old enemy, the anonymous informer', and that the press, with its confusion of fact and inference, was 'one of the most corruptive influences in society today'.[35]

During the night of 21/22 March, Profumo became the victim, in Lord Hailsham's words, partly of his own poor judgement, but mostly 'of a really foul conspiracy between the late Dick Crossman (utterly unscrupulous) and the late George Wigg (positively evil), and some shockingly bad advice from friends'. After the Labour leadership had quashed Wigg at Barbara Castle's supper, and agreed not to exploit the rumours, Castle was briefed by the Labour-supporting *Daily Herald* to break the story during the Foster-Mulholland debate. Wigg and Crossman, disbelieving that a mere woman could be trusted to do an effective job, pre-empted her speech with interventions of their own. Wigg issued a challenge to Brooke, the Home Secretary, to deny the rumours implicating a government minister with 'Miss Christine Keeler and Miss Davies and a shooting by a West Indian', or else appoint a parliamentary investigation 'so that these things can be dissipated, and the honour of the Minister concerned freed from the imputations and innuendoes that are being spread'. Crossman followed Wigg in pursuit of a select committee to ferret out the truth of the rumours. The barrister-MP Reginald Paget interrupted Crossman, trying to nullify the impact of the allegation, but only made the story clearer to newspaper readers: 'What do the rumours amount to? They amount to the fact that a Minister is said to be acquainted with an extremely pretty girl. As far as I am concerned, I should have thought that was a matter for congratulation rather than enquiry.'[36]

Further into the debate Barbara Castle – primed by the *Daily Herald* as Lipton had been by the *Daily Express* – referred to 'the missing call-girl, the vanished witness', and went further in trying to implicate (unnamed) Profumo in a cover-up: 'What if it is a question of the perversion of justice?' she asked. 'If accusations are made that there are people in high places who *do* know [Keeler's whereabouts], and who are not informing the police, is it not a matter of public interest?'[37]

The Profumo Affair burst through the sound barrier of gossip. Valerie Profumo returned from the theatre that evening to find the Chester Terrace house surrounded by a loud, jostling rabble armed with notepads and cameras. The debate finished at 1.22 a.m. on Friday 22 March; afterwards Redmayne, Hobson and Rawlinson conferred with Iain Macleod, the Leader of the House of Commons and Chairman of the Conservative Party, and William Deedes, the ex-*Daily Telegraph* journalist who sat in the Cabinet as its public relations adviser. They decided to summon Profumo. Woozy from a sleeping-draught taken to obliterate the din of journalists besieging his house and banging on its door, Profumo hastened back to the Commons just before three that morning. In the Chief Whip's room, flanked by his solicitor, Clogg, he found the law officers with Redmayne, Deedes and Macleod. They confronted him with the choice of resignation or an immediate statement in the Commons denying the allegations. 'Look, Jack,' Macleod asked bluntly. 'The basic question is: did you fuck her?'[38]

It was as mismanaged a meeting as the one that forced Galbraith to resign because of his innocuous notes to Vassall. Ministers, from Macmillan downwards, were guiltily aware that they had overreacted to the Vassall press furore, and made a cowardly sacrifice of Galbraith. They were determined not to repeat the mistake, but they were exhausted men, whose talk was muddled. They neither tested Profumo's denials nor scrutinised the text of his 'Darling' note to Keeler. Clogg, Hobson and Rawlinson – the three lawyers – drafted the statement that Profumo was to make in the Commons at the start of parliamentary business later that day. Rawlinson never thought that Profumo was too drowsy from the effects of his sleeping-draught to understand the statement to which he was committing himself. His scepticism of Profumo's denials was finally quashed when Profumo made his personal statement at eleven that morning. Enoch Powell complained at a Cabinet meeting after the crisis broke in June that the ministers had been 'very credulous', but even Dilhorne said that he 'would not then have been prepared to disbelieve Profumo on account of the information then available'.[39]

The chief purpose of the statement was to refute the allegations that national security had been jeopardised and that Profumo had instigated Keeler's disappearance. His denial of adultery – with the uncharacteristically bloodless phrase, planted on him by

the lawyers, 'there was no impropriety whatsoever in my acquaint-
anceship with Miss Keeler' – seemed (to him) a side issue. The
statement *sounded* definite and conclusive. Under parliamentary
rules it could not be challenged or debated because the integrity
of MPs making a personal statement is accepted unreservedly. In
fact, the statement was artful, evasive and far from iron-clad, as
became evident once it was studied in print. 'There was hardly
anybody on the Tory side who didn't . . . assume that the stories
were true,' Crossman judged; but the fact that he, Castle and Wigg
had 'blown the gaff' rallied the Tories into stalwart loyalty. 'I left
with black rage in my heart because I knew what the facts were,'
Wigg later said, 'and I knew that . . . I had been trussed up and
done again.' Later that day, Stephen Ward gave an interview to
Independent Television News in support of Profumo's statement.[40]
Outside the Commons, and beyond Fleet Street, most people felt
that grubby, unfair rumours had been spread about Profumo, as
they had about Galbraith.

That Friday afternoon Jack and Valerie Profumo attended
Sandown races with the Queen Mother, a fact which Labour MPs
including Crossman saw as an objectionable gesture of support
by the Royal Family towards a miscreant. In the evening the
Profumos went to Quaglino's for a fundraising dinner in aid of
Hatch End Conservatives. Even the Beaverbrook press relented
the next day with a front-page photograph of the Profumos
'dancing cheek-to-cheek' at Quaglino's, and a lobby correspondent's assurance: 'Last night Whitehall made clear that Ministers
regard Mr Profumo's statement as closing the matter, and . . . a
similar attitude prevailed among Labour front-benchers.'[41]

Yet the mischief-making did not abate. On Saturday 23 March
the disreputable crank Michael Eddowes, in whom Keeler had
confided in December, visited her mother at Wraysbury claiming
to have been a friend of Ward's for twenty-five years and protesting
that he was worried Christine might be endangered. Sitting in
the converted railway carriages, he insisted that there was big
money to be made from the concoction that Keeler had been the

lover of Ivanov as well as Profumo, and had trafficked in state secrets. Keeler should, he urged, issue a statement acknowledging Ivanov as her 'boyfriend', and admitting that she extracted information from Profumo which she gave to Ivanov for 'a joke'. Eddowes added that Keeler would have to hold fast to this story once she had launched it, but that it was worth £5,000 to £10,000 for the press. 'She would be set up nicely with nothing to worry about because they could do nothing to her because she was a child of eighteen.' Eddowes predicted 'that the Government would be forced to open a Select Committee, and she would state these things and turn out a little heroine'. Keeler's mother was alarmed by the elaborate lies that Eddowes was inciting, for next day she went to report his mendacious conspiracy at her local police station.[42]

On 25 March, Keeler surfaced in Madrid. Mann arranged a £2,000 exclusive deal with the *Daily Express*, which next day carried a photograph of her in calf-length black boots, short skirt and tight sweater. She was wearing the same boots, as well as false eyelashes (and sipping whisky), when Roger Hall of the *News of the World* interviewed her. 'I am still utterly bemused and bewildered and astonished at the hue and cry which started when I left the country,' she supposedly told Hall. 'I have many friends who hold important positions in Britain, but I see nothing to be ashamed of in that. I was astonished that Mr Profumo should have been mentioned. Certainly both he and his wife were friends of mine. But it was a friendship no one can criticise.' She was, she suggested, the target of envious killjoys. 'The trouble is I am twenty-one, and many people consider me photogenic. I have lived in the West End of London and frequently been to parties with well-known people present. Presumably if I had been fifty-two and a housewife in Surbiton there would have been none of this trouble.'[43]

Apart from Profumo and Clore, Keeler knew no one of significance, but journalists eagerly spread their fib that Keeler had important friends. 'Leggy, red-headed Christine Keeler managed to move in Mayfair's smartest circles and numbered among her wide range of gentlemen acquaintances top names in London's political, social, diplomatic and show business worlds,' reported *Time* magazine on 29 March. 'A social gad-about named Stephen Ward' was the sponsor, *Time* continued, of the 'one-time waitress and full-time play-girl'.[44]

The *Daily Express* promised £500 to Rice-Davies for an interview. Their questions duly elicited her claim that she had gone to bed with Bill Astor. When challenged three months later, while testifying in Marylebone Magistrates Court, with the fact that Astor had denied her claim, she retorted: 'Well, he would, wouldn't he?' One of the cruellest details of the Profumo Affair is that this slick evasion has become Bill Astor's popular epitaph. It is still recycled by the lazy, unscrupulous and prim.

On the evening of 25 March, hours after Keeler was found in Spain, George Wigg was interviewed on BBC television's *Panorama* programme. His Commons intervention, like those of Castle and Crossman, had been ill-received in the parliamentary party, which, unlike certain newspapers, disliked mudslinging. On *Panorama* he therefore concentrated on security issues. He peppered his remarks with disparagement of Ivanov whom, he said, drove a sports car, was tailored in Savile Row, and haunted nightclubs – all of which seemed objectionably decadent to his brand of MP.

Ward, who for three months had been stimulated and talkative at being at the centre of commotion, made the capital error of telephoning Wigg to correct these mistakes about Ivanov: the Russian drove an Austin A40 or Humber Snipe, he protested, not a sports car; Ivanov bought his suits from John Barker's department store in Kensington High Street, not Savile Row; he was not a nightclub habitué. Wigg, who had a journalist named Wilfred Sendall eavesdropping on their conversation, agreed to meet Ward. Their long meeting on Tuesday 26 March began in the Harcourt Room of the House of Commons, which Ward insisted on leaving abruptly when an ex-minister whom he knew, Sir Robin Turton, entered the room. They retreated to an interview room to resume their discussion. It was typical of Ward that he exaggerated by calling Turton 'an ex-Cabinet Minister', which Turton, as an unsuccessful Minister of Health whom Macmillan had sacked, was not.

The object of Ward's lengthy explanations was to exculpate Ivanov, but he could scarcely have volunteered more stupidly damaging admissions, which Wigg could use as pretexts for a claim that security issues were involved. Ward said that he had been Ivanov's intermediary in communicating Soviet messages during the Cuban crisis; that Ivanov was under surveillance; that MI5 knew about Profumo's relations with Keeler because he, Ward, had told them; that when he had seen Profumo at the Dorchester hotel three weeks earlier, and had asked about Keeler, Profumo had given an inscrutable answer, 'Christine Keeler? Who's she?' He was bitter against Paul Mann, whom he alleged was 'a spiv' who 'would do anything for money and . . . thought that in the Keeler story he had a gold mine'. He also complained about Lawrence Bell (whom he believed to be a contact of Wigg's) selling stories to the *Daily Express* and *The People*.[45]

Wigg consulted Harold Wilson and Sir Frank Soskice, the Shadow Home Secretary. Soskice expressed 'moral disgust at the revelations', but Wigg was implacable that Labour spokesmen must not indulge in prissy sermonising, and ensured that Wilson confined himself to the security angle – bogus though both men knew it to be. On the last Sunday in March, Crossman had a reminder that the press were itching to damage the government while Foster and Mulholland remained in prison. He dined with Michael Berry, editor-in-chief of the *Daily Telegraph* and its Sunday sister paper launched in 1961, and his wife. Lady Pamela Berry was an able, ambitious woman who slaked her frustration at being denied formal responsibilities or power by outrushes of political malice. She praised Wigg's muckraking, but was indignant when Crossman explained that after Profumo's personal statement the matter was dead. 'That's intolerable!' she exclaimed. 'How can you hold back now that the whole press is waiting for you to go ahead?' Crossman incited her by describing Ward's meeting with Wigg, adding the untrue detail that Wigg had tape-recorded Ward. He subsequently repeated these indiscretions to the *Sunday Telegraph*'s Peregrine Worsthorne. As he calculated, his stories appeared in both Berry newspapers.[46]

Yet the fatal unintended consequence of Ward's interview with Wigg involved neither Labour nor the press. Ward did not visit the Commons with his head stifled under a blanket to hide his identity. He was not a man to slink down corridors quietly. His face was recognisable to MPs like Sir Robin Turton, who were his patients, and to journalists, who read their own papers. It is likely that Tory Party managers knew of the meeting before it was over.

A conference met at the Home Office on 27 March. It was attended by Henry Brooke (the Home Secretary), Sir Charles Cunningham (Permanent Under Secretary at the Home Office), Hollis of MI5 and Sir Joseph Simpson (Commissioner of Metropolitan Police). Ostensibly Brooke called the meeting to check the rumour that MI5 had in 1961 sent poison-pen letters to Valerie Profumo about her husband's adultery with Keeler. Hollis disavowed this absurdity. Brooke reportedly then enquired about prosecuting Ward under the Official Secrets Act. Hollis, who found the meeting 'difficult' and the Home Secretary 'excitable', mentioned Keeler's statement that Ward had asked her to quiz Profumo about nuclear warheads for Germany, but dismissed the idea of taking action. Brooke turned to Simpson, who said that there was a chance of prosecuting Ward for living off immoral earnings. Perhaps the old pimping allegations inspired by John Lewis had resurfaced from police files, although they had no more substance than the tales that Clore had been convicted of obscenity in the 1930s. Once Hollis had confirmed after this conference that there was no chance of a successful prosecution under the Official Secrets Act, Simpson authorised a Metropolitan Police investigation into Ward's sexual influence.[47]

The launching of this investigation immediately after Ward's conspicuous Commons colloquy with Wigg raises suspicions that

Brooke wanted a criminal investigation that would either scare Ward into silence, or discredit him. It is more probable that Brooke was casting for ways to get Ward because he felt, like his Labour counterpart Soskice, 'moral disgust at the revelations'. He was 'a very virtuous and conscientious man', according to an official who worked with him for years. 'Brooke was as straight as a die, the most honest politician I have ever known,' agreed a Cabinet colleague. 'To him politics is not the art of the possible: it is simply doing what he considers right.' After his appointment as Home Secretary in 1962, Brooke had declared his distaste for moral laxity. 'At this time,' he said in a revealing phrase, 'when a growing number of people feel free to do anything not specifically condemned by Act, we should be slow to loosen up.' Part of his duty at the Home Office, he told Alec Douglas-Home, was 'helping the young of our country to grow up straight'. His wife, with whom he shared deep Christian beliefs, described Profumo as 'a man who has sinned against our standards'.[48]

Brooke, who was the least politically adept or imaginative Home Secretary since Joynson-Hicks in the 1920s, blundered forward at his conference with Hollis and Simpson intent on keeping the young straight and punishing those who loosened national standards. He was too sure of his moral course to reflect that after Profumo's personal statement had quelled the Commons, it was ruinous to the government's interests to instigate police dredging of sludgy depths that might lead to sensational arrests, a flamboyant trial and months of torrid publicity. In fairness to Brooke, the notion that he instigated the police investigation of Ward, or that Ward's prosecution was motivated by political malice, was always denied by Peter Rawlinson, who believed that the police faced a situation in which they would be suspected of shielding influential men unless they acted. Girls whom Ward knew seemed conveniently available for his male acquaintances; and it was unthinkable to the official mind that they might be sexually independent young women capable of making their own choices.

*

Whatever the reasoning, Brooke's conference and the ensuing police investigation proved calamitous for Macmillan's government. The inquiry was headed by Chief Inspector Samuel Herbert, who had joined the police seventeen years earlier after being demobbed from the army, in which he held the rank of sergeant. Herbert was abetted by Detective Sergeant John Burrows, and assisted by two police sergeants.

From the outset this was an exceptional investigation which deviated from usual police procedure. Usually officers are despatched when a crime has been committed. They are charged to find evidence which will secure the criminal's conviction. Their instructions in Ward's case were to investigate a specific individual in order to see if he could be charged with a crime. This reversal of usual detective methods suggests special instructions. Herbert set out to find, or create, evidence which he might fix on Ward to secure the conviction which his political masters sought. From 2 April to 8 June he interviewed between 125 and 140 prospective witnesses. The sergeants filed daily progress reports. Within a short time, ten copies were being circulated of each daily report. Some went to Whitehall and Westminster.

On 4 April, Herbert and Burrows first visited Keeler at the Marylebone flat where she was staying. Herbert's interrogations were terse and overbearing, while Burrows was gently probing. They told her that she might face charges under the Official Secrets Act if she did not cooperate, for they were investigating espionage and protecting national security. On Friday 5 and Saturday 6 April, they interviewed her again – that is, on three consecutive days – at Marylebone police station. During the second interview she confirmed her affair with Profumo. Having got her to admit this, they asked if she had gone to bed with Astor. They asked the same questions about every man whom they thought she had met through Ward.

Keeler was slow to realise that Herbert aimed to charge Ward under the Sexual Offences Act. It was only when he demanded to know about abortions that she suspected something was amiss.

She was asked to name each of the men with whom she had sex, or had given her money, since her first meeting with Ward. She mentioned a man called Charles, from whom she accepted a present of money (this episode with Clore was to prove fatal to Ward). She was questioned a total of twenty-four times by Herbert and Burrows before Ward's appearance in a magistrates' court on 28 June. Under their pressure, she was spasmodic, turbid and fitful in her stories. Keeler, who had a history of dependence on men who abused her, developed a semi-masochistic reliance on her contacts with Herbert and Burrows, with whom she spoke by telephone almost daily.[49]

Police investigators used the hoary technique of attrition. Witnesses were kept waiting for hours in police stations until they were too weary to resist signing inaccurate statements. On 10 April, John Hamilton-Marshall, an epicene, larcenous twenty-two-year-old who dabbled in antiques and was devoted to Ward, who had always treated him kindly, signed a police statement which implicated the osteopath in obtaining an illegal abortion for a girl of his acquaintance. He retracted this part of the statement at the Marylebone Magistrates Court hearing in June. 'I was there,' he explained, 'for six hours: I skimmed through it, because I was glad to get out.' At Ward's Old Bailey trial, the prostitute Ronna Ricardo testified that a police statement which she had signed on 6 April contained several notions that had been implanted by the police: 'At the police station I was kept so long I was ready to sign anything.' She had been confined in the interview room at Harrow Road police station for four hours before the statement was read aloud to her at two in the morning, when she was tired and vulnerable. 'I didn't want to sign that statement. I didn't want to have anything to do with it . . . I wanted the police to leave me alone.'[50]

The Astors were in America for six weeks until 12 April. Lord Astor was stunned when, on the thirteenth, he was asked to give a police interview. Herbert and Burrows asked for the names of women he had taken to bed; whether he had met them through

Ward; and whether he had paid for sex. They elicited from Astor that he had once given Keeler and Rice-Davies a cheque to cover the rent of their flat in Barons Court. As Herbert and Burrows believed both women to have had sex in that flat with men, they decided Astor was guilty of keeping a brothel, and sought to develop a case against him. Although this line was dropped, with all fire concentrated on Ward, Astor was shattered by this minatory inter-rogation. He asked Ward to leave Spring Cottage forthwith.

The police amassed their rickety evidence by exploiting antipathies, flustering witnesses, treating loyalty as a sign of guilty affections, and threatening, framing and arresting both leading and bit-part players in the drama. On 17 April, at a flat at 33 Devonshire Street occupied by her friend Paula Hamilton-Marshall (above premises supplying catheters), Keeler had 'a battle-royal' with the latter's brother John. (The siblings had an Italian father who had devised an anglicised surname for himself; their mother Ruby Milton was a sometime next-door neighbour of Lucien Freud, who painted some of the family.) Keeler accused the youth of reading or rifling her papers, and, according to his account, she challenged him to hit her – which he did. 'We really fought: she went for me, and I went for her,' he testified six months later. 'I punched her in the eye, and her face split above the eyebrow.' He also kicked her repeatedly in the backside. In one of her habitual telephone calls to Herbert's team, Keeler told them that she was bruised with a black eye. They suggested that she should lure 'Lucky' Gordon to the flat, call Marylebone police station, and then accuse him of assaulting her.[51]

Keeler telephoned Gordon's friends telling them where she was. Gordon duly came banging on the front door. There was a scuffle in the hallway, and Keeler, who was unsteady after smoking dope, fell over and crawled away. There is no evidence that Gordon did more than shove her. Two West Indian men, her current boyfriend Rudolph 'Truello' Fenton and a friend of Paula Hamilton-Marshall's called Clarence 'Pete' Camacchio, were in the flat. They restrained Gordon. Keeler, having set the trap, telephoned the police. Gordon, at the suggestion of Fenton and Camacchio, scarpered. Two police cars arrived quickly under the control of Inspector Basil Mitackis, whose reputation for political deftness was such that a year later he was seconded from the Metropolitan Police to serve under United Nations auspices as an adviser to the police force in Burundi. Fenton and Camacchio, who as black men had learnt to be wary of the Metropolitan Police, hid in a bedroom at Keeler's suggestion; but the sole interest of the officers under Inspector Mitackis's command was in nailing Gordon. 'Miss Keeler,' Detective Sergeant Sidney Whitten reported, 'had recently been assaulted on the premises by a coloured man known as Lucky Gordon.' The story, as later adapted by the police, was that Gordon had ambushed her on the pavement, knocked her down, punched and kicked her.[52]

On 18 April, Gordon was arrested and charged with inflicting grievous bodily harm on Keeler. Herbert led questioning of him about Ward procuring 'girls' for well-known Society men: if Gordon made a statement that would help secure Ward's conviction, the assault charge might be dropped. Gordon however refused to cooperate and the police proceeded to prosecute him for assaulting Keeler, although they knew John Hamilton-Marshall was responsible. Keeler was the chief prosecution witness, acting under police direction, in Gordon's trial, which was to prove a calamity for her.

Another arrest to coerce a witness against Ward soon followed. On 23 April, Rice-Davies went to Heathrow airport for a Madrid flight. Hitherto, she had – like Gordon – refused to make a police statement about Ward. After cavorting for the flash-photographers, she was detained as she went to board her aircraft. The pretext for her arrest was that when Rachman had given her a Jaguar car as a seventeenth birthday present, he had also provided her with a false driving licence, which she had subsequently shown when renting a car. Now she was charged with possessing a forged licence, making false statements to obtain insurance, and driving without insurance. Exceptionally on such minor charges, Rice-Davies was sent overnight to Holloway prison by magistrates who next day set bail at the exorbitant figure of £2,000. In Holloway she was told by the police that if she raised the bail, they would re-arrest her on another charge as soon as she was released – requiring yet more bail. She was subjected to body searches, her pubic hair was shaved and she was locked in her cell for twenty hours a day. After two days she was desperate to be free. Chief Inspector Herbert returned with Burrows. 'Mandy,' he said, 'you don't like it in here very much, do you? So you help us, and we'll help you.' She told them what they wanted to hear about Ward and his parties.[53]

On 1 May, when her motoring offence came to court, she was fined £42. She left immediately for Spain, but when she returned, Burrows arrested her again at Heathrow. On 16 June she was charged with stealing a television worth £82. This was a set that she had rented for the Bryanston Mews flat; but she had been excluded from the flat after Rachman's death, and knew nothing of the set's whereabouts. At Marylebone police station she was told she would be released if she entered into a bond of £1,000 due on 28 June, the date on which the case against Ward was to be presented at Marylebone Magistrates Court. On 28 June, she duly testified against Ward, with the threat of a second police prosecution levelled at her. The trumpery criminal charge was then dropped, ostensibly because she paid £82 to the television rental company.

Ronna Ricardo, meanwhile, was interviewed nine times by the police. Herbert pressed her to say that when she visited Bryanston Mews, Ward asked her to go to bed with men. She said that a police car stayed outside her flat to intimidate her. Threats were made that her younger sister, who was living with her, would be taken into care. When another prostitute, called Vickie Barrett, was arrested for soliciting, police found Ward's telephone number in her handbag. Herbert went to interrogate her. She said that she had whipped Ward at his flat. 'Wouldn't it be better if you said you whipped other men at the flat?' Herbert suggested. 'Why should I say that?' she asked. According to Barrett, Herbert replied: 'If you don't say that you'll never be able to show your face in

Notting Hill again.' In mid-May, Lawrence Bell, who had been a stringer with the early Keeler and Fletcher-Cooke stories in Fleet Street, was arrested, and held in prison for sixteen days 'almost incommunicado' before being charged in June with nine charges of homosexuality with guardsmen. He was brutalised in prison. All this gave the appearance, said his barrister in open court, of 'political chicanery and frame-up'.[54]

The police put Ward under surveillance, including telephone-tapping. They found no criminal activity. Herbert and Burrows positioned themselves outside Ward's consulting rooms, questioning patients as they arrived and left. Male patients were asked if Ward had ever introduced them to a woman. Female patients were asked if Ward had made 'an improper suggestion' to them. Clients naturally cancelled appointments. Ward's friends were visited, and asked for the names of women to whom he had introduced them.[55]

On 7 May, Ward telephoned Timothy Bligh asking for an appointment. Bligh reported this to Macmillan and Redmayne. He also consulted Simpson, who told him that the police investigation of Ward was proceeding: 'an arrest possible in a week or so but the case against him not at present very strong'. Bligh saw Ward later that day in the presence of an MI5 officer, Lieutenant Colonel Malcolm Cumming, who secretly tape-recorded the discussion while Bligh made a show of taking notes. Ward, in a cascade of words and speaking under stress, made clear that Profumo's personal statement in the Commons was untrue. 'I'm being completely destroyed, enormous pressure is being brought to bear on me . . . I have been battered steadily into the ground.' The 'horrid and ghastly' police harassment of him was politically motivated: 'I don't know whether you have any feelings about this, whether there is anything you can do,' he told Bligh (according to Cumming's tape). 'There is a great deal of potentially extremely explosive material in what I have told you.'[56] Bligh, Macmillan and later Denning interpreted this as an attempt to blackmail Downing Street into ordering Henry Brooke to halt the police investigation.

It is equally possible that Ward was reminding Bligh and Cumming that MI5 had used him as an intermediary to Ivanov.

When it became clear that his overtures to Bligh and Cumming had failed, Ward made explicit in a letter of 19 May to the Home Secretary, Henry Brooke, that Profumo had lied in his personal statement. Ward gave a summary of this letter to the Press Association and other news agencies, which all refused to circulate the statement to newspapers. Next day he wrote to his MP, Sir Wavell Wakefield, and to Harold Wilson. 'It is obvious,' Ward complained to Wakefield in large, flowing handwriting, that the Marylebone police have been 'acting on Home Office instructions' in harassing his visitors and other contacts. His osteopathic practice was 'being utterly ruined because of constant police enquiries amongst my patients and friends', he told Wilson. 'The line of the enquiries clearly indicates that I am under suspicion among other things of living on immoral earnings. This, of course, is complete nonsense . . . Obviously my efforts to conceal the fact that Mr Profumo had not told the truth in Parliament have made it look as if I myself had something to hide. It is quite clear now that they must wish the facts to be known, and I shall see that they are.'[57]

Wilson sent a copy of Ward's letter to Macmillan, whom he met on 27 May, with their Chief Whips, Redmayne and Herbert Bowden, in attendance. Wilson was deft in dressing-up mean insinuations with earnest concern about non-existent security risks. 'Mr Wilson went on to say that Ward was a self-confessed intermediary,' records the official minute of the meeting. 'It was beyond dispute that Ward hobnobbed with Ivanov. He must be regarded as a tool of Russian communism. Ministers had frequently met Ward: indeed Mr Profumo said in his statement to the House of Commons that he had been to his flat on half a dozen occasions. Did Ministers know that Ward was a Security risk? It would seem from the amount of mingling that had gone on that Ministers had not been told.' Macmillan replied that 'he doubted whether Stephen Ward bore quite the character or role which Mr Wilson had suggested'. Certainly, it was 'possible to exaggerate the role that Stephen Ward had played during the Cuban crisis'.[58]

Macmillan confided his own account of this meeting to his diary: 'The case of Mr Ward (who got Profumo into trouble) is being actively pursued by Harold Wilson, Wigg and one or two of that ilk. Wilson has sent me some so-called evidence that Ward was a spy or agent of the Russians. (The security people do not believe this, but believe that he was a pimp, not a spy.) Wilson came to see me on a fishing expedition on Monday. He is clearly not going to leave this alone. He hopes, under pretence of security, to rake up a "sex" scandal, and to involve ministers, and members of "the upper classes" in a tremendous row, wh. will injure the "Establishment". Wilson, himself a blackmailing type, is *absolutely* untrustworthy. No one has ever trusted him without being betrayed.'[59]

The official minute of Wilson's discussion with Macmillan was copied to Sir Roger Hollis who, on 29 May, informed Macmillan for the first time that Keeler had in January told Detective Sergeant Burrows that Ward had suggested she ask Profumo about atomic secrets involving West Germany. Ward's feeble joke, which the *Sunday Pictorial* had induced Keeler to take seriously as a way of grabbing attention and making money, was now incorporated into her repertoire. Hollis's news unnerved Macmillan and his Downing Street staff. The magazine *Time & Tide* on 30 May reported the existence although not the contents of Ward's letter to Henry Brooke, and added: 'There is pressure for an investigation into a subject which could bring down the Government.' Two Labour MPs tried to table questions to Brooke about the letter. Macmillan decided that he must appoint an inquiry into security breaches under the Lord Chancellor, Dilhorne. 'I am sure in my own mind,' he wrote to Wilson on 30 May, 'that the security aspect of the Ward case has been fully and efficiently watched, but I think it important that you should be in no doubt about it.'[60]

Lord Dilhorne was flabby, myopic, gruff and irritable with the obdurate, put-upon expression of a man who was beset by urgent pressure. He crashed through life with formidable, armour-plated confidence. 'What the ordinary careerist achieves by making himself agreeable, falsely or otherwise, Reggie achieved by making himself disagreeable,' wrote a fellow jurist, Lord Devlin. 'He was a bully without a bullying manner. His bludgeoning was quiet. He could be downright rude but he did not shout or bluster. Yet his disagreeableness was so pervasive, his persistence so interminable, the obstructions he manned so far flung, his objectives apparently so insignificant, that sooner or later you would be tempted to ask yourself whether the game was worth the candle: if you asked yourself that, you were finished.' When Anthony Wedgwood Benn appeared before the Commons Privileges Committee, Dilhorne had 'hacked at me as if I was a man who had been caught red-handed in the act of rape and was then pleading mistaken identity. He really behaved in a most unpleasant and hostile way.'[61]

On 31 May, the Profumos flew to Venice, and stayed at the Cipriani hotel. It had been settled that Jack Profumo would see Dilhorne on Thursday 6 June (a day after his scheduled return), but at the Cipriani he received a message that Dilhorne wished him to return for an interview on the Tuesday. Knowing Dilhorne's character, this demand for his early return suggested that his bluff was being called. His nerve broke. The ex-premier Lord Avon heard that it was Redmayne who telephoned Profumo in Venice, warning that 'the truth had been discovered and that he must return'. Perhaps the Chief Whip did intervene, for the news that Keeler had started a new round of taped interviews was contained in the daily police reports that were received by the Home Secretary, Brooke, and probably available to Redmayne.[62]

Profumo told his wife the truth over a Bellini cocktail before dinner. They determined to return to London, which they reached on Whit Monday. Profumo then telephoned Bligh asking for an urgent appointment with the Prime Minister. Macmillan was in Argyllshire, staying with the Duke of Atholl's mother, so Bligh settled to meet him on Tuesday morning. Redmayne attended their meeting, either at Bligh's request, or possibly because he had instigated Profumo's return from Italy. Profumo confirmed to both men (of which they can have had little doubt) that his personal statement had been untrue, and that he intended to resign from Parliament and the government.

On 5 June – the Wednesday that Lucky Gordon appeared in court charged with causing actual bodily harm to Keeler – Profumo's resignation was announced. That morning his son David had returned to Hill House preparatory school in Knightsbridge after half-term. He knew something was amiss when the headmaster's wife, Beatrice Townend, fetched him from the classroom to their private flat, where she gave him a cup of warm milk. 'I sat on the edge of the sofa, but simply could not look her in the eye. The thickly applied make-up appeared a clown's face, the kindly attention a skewed version of what appeared maternal.' He was then taken to the house off Kensington High Street belonging to his uncle Harold, Lord Balfour of Inchrye.

There in the sunlit conservatory overlooking the garden his parents, and some other relations, were perched on cane chairs. A butler dispensed sherry from a decanter. On a table there stood a thermos jug of hot consommé, with plates of chicken sandwiches – the white bread quartered into triangles, with the crusts cut off. As David Profumo sucked orangeade up a straw, his mother told him: 'Daddy's decided to stop being a politician. He told a lie in the House of Commons, so now we're going to have a little holiday in the country – all together. Now, doesn't that sound fun?' His aunt, Lady Balfour, lit a Du Maurier cigarette, and squinted at him through the smoke.[63]

TEN

Show Trials

In the summer of 1963 there was a Profumo spree. Rumour-mongers were like hungry lions prowling the London streets in search of fleshy prey on which to pounce. The stuffier members of the Establishment were apoplectic; newspapers incited daily fits of hysterics; and lawyers planned vindictive ways to reassert authority. Some boisterous people enjoyed the cheerful smut flying about, but others flinched at the filth. There was little agreement on how to treat the scandal. MI5 considered that the affair between Profumo and Keeler was a private matter; Wilson's Labour Party claimed that it was a security issue; *The Times* sermonised that it was a moral issue; lascivious newspapers dribbled over pretty girls at orgies; Hailsham bellowed that it was a question of Profumo's integrity; Nigel Birch sniped that it was a product of Macmillan's ineptitude; the running dogs of Mirror Newspapers barked that it was the sordid, humiliating death-throe of the Establishment.

That was the state of affairs until the end of June. Then, with the sex stories sub judice before Ward's trial, and with a clamp on spy stories while the Law Lord, Denning, investigated espionage rumours, editors plumped for Rachman's antics as a slum landlord as the new source of devilment. Finally, from mid-July onwards, as Ward's show trial was staged at the Old Bailey, with solemn judicial handling of perjurers and tainted police evidence, and the Court of Criminal Appeal performed deplorable tricks, and

Denning titillated himself, lawyers took the leading parts for the last act of the drama.

On the mornings of 5, 6 and 7 June, Christine Keeler arrived for Gordon's trial at the Old Bailey in a Rolls-Royce (hired by Robin Drury, her temporary business manager). She was dressed in mauve, like a film-star ready for priceless photo opportunities. She testified – as Marylebone police officers had instructed – that Gordon had assaulted her in Paula Hamilton-Marshall's flat on 17 April. Despite being asked by Keeler and his sister to keep away from the trial, John Hamilton-Marshall felt that Gordon should not be prosecuted for something that he had done. He appeared at the court on the first morning, and spoke to a policeman, who sent him away. Hamilton-Marshall was a voluble, gesticulating youth with criminal convictions: he was deterred from speaking out. As he had previously told the truth of what happened to Ward, Ronna Ricardo and *Sunday Pictorial* reporters, several people knew that Gordon's was a show trial.

Gordon insisted upon defending himself. He was not allowed to cross-examine Keeler directly, but put questions to her designed to show the extent of her lies. To the gratification of reporters he repeatedly introduced Ward's name, and demanded to know whether 'she asked me to find a coloured girl for her brother Stephen so we could make up a foursome'. Keeler agreed that this was true. Later she was ejected from the court for raising a screaming brouhaha when Gordon claimed that she had infected him with venereal disease. Gordon wanted to call Profumo and Ward as defence witnesses, as well as Camacchio and Fenton, the men who had been at the Devonshire Street flat when Keeler's telephone calls had lured him there. He added that the policeman who arrested him had said that he was investigating Ward for procuring girls for Society men.

Ward appeared on ITV's *This Week* programme to deny that he was a procurer, and reiterated that he had told MI5 of the Profumo-Keeler entanglement early on. Burrows, the policeman handling Gordon's prosecution, told the court on 7 June that Camacchio and Fenton could not be produced as defence witnesses because they were untraceable – an odd claim, because it transpired (too late for Gordon) that Camacchio was remanded on bail, and his whereabouts were ascertainable. The jury took ten minutes to find Gordon guilty of assault, but acquitted him of wounding with intent to cause grievous bodily harm. He was sentenced to three years.

In the hectic days following Profumo's resignation, Wigg was ruthless in ensuring that the Labour Party emphasis was exclusively on the security issue, bogus though he knew this to be. The rhetoric of class conflict was just beneath the surface: 'The trial of Keeler and her Negro friends must have been the biggest shock to public morality which has been known in this century,' Crossman wrote after Gordon's conviction. 'I can't think of a more humiliating and discrediting story than the Secretary of State for War's being involved with people of this kind. It has social seediness and some fairly scabrous security background concerning Ivanov, the lying, the collusion, and the fact that Royalty and the Establishment back Profumo.' Crossman predicted that if the Queen saw Profumo when, as was the custom for retiring ministers, he returned his seals of office, 'this would do the Establishment enormous harm . . . in fact enormously undermine the Government, and so assist in creating the conditions for a Labour Party victory'.[1]

On Saturday 8 June, in an act of political revenge, Ward, wearing carpet slippers, was arrested in Hempstead Road, Watford, outside the house of his friend Pelham Pound, the features editor of *Woman's Mirror*. He was charged with living wholly or partly on the earnings of prostitution, although there was some juggling with the indictment as the police tried to agree with prosecutors what charges had a hope of sticking. David Astor's protégé Patrick O'Donovan wrote: 'You only had to say, "I see they've arrested him," and everyone knew whom and what you meant.'[2] Few people could be other-worldly about the Profumo Affair, although a Wykehamist who met Christine Keeler at this time, and felt he recognised the surname, asked her if she was related to the Keiller marmalade family.

The next day the *News of the World* published its scoop 'Confessions of Christine', for which it had paid her £24,000. It contained such squalid idiocies as the claim that Ward led her through the Marylebone streets on a lead with a dog collar encircling her neck. Peter Earle also publicised real or imaginary goings-on which had nothing to do with Ward, but were prejudicial to his case. Although the offences with which Ward was charged were misdemeanours, not felonies, he was refused bail. Accordingly he spent three weeks isolated in Brixton prison.

'The established order went into battle against this man, whose sole offence was a nonconformity in sexual matters that met with the same kind of relentless reaction from the prosecuting authorities that characterised the persecution of *Lady Chatterley's Lover*,' wrote the jurist Louis Blom-Cooper. 'Dr Ward's arrest and removal to police custody, the refusal to grant him bail until the start of the committal proceedings, the refusal to allow him to organise from prison the sale of his paintings, his committal to the Old Bailey for trial rather than to Quarter Sessions, his trial before a High Court Judge rather than before the Recorder of London or the Common Sergeant – all these things betokened a sense of persecution, even if each event was by itself, but not cumulatively, explicable to those versed in legal procedure.'[3]

Most Tory MPs felt that Redmayne as Chief Whip, and Macleod as Leader of the House of Commons, who had both interrogated Profumo, had been inexcusably gullible about his replies and slack in informing Macmillan of backbench disquiet on the subject. A few blamed the Prime Minister for not easing Profumo from office: they felt his judgement had been clouded by his wish not to repeat the injustice dealt to Galbraith during the Vassall crisis. The *Sunday Telegraph* was the most hostile newspaper: Lady Pamela Berry was gunning for Macmillan; and its right-wing followers fomented trouble in the parliamentary party. The

Observer editorialised that Profumo had blundered by denying 'so explicitly that he had had an affair with Miss Keeler – a lie which was all the more foolish since it was widely regarded as such even before his confession'. The paper hoped (in vain) that as Labour had 'already gained a large electoral advantage by the revelation of these scandals', it would not 'dress up the desire to exploit a political advantage as a concern for national security'. To drum up a panic about state secrets would add a new dimension of hypocrisy to an affair already brimming with it.[4]

Redmayne offered his resignation to Macmillan. 'If you resign, I shall resign,' Macmillan replied on 9 June. 'No man was ever better served in all these difficulties than I have been by you. All this will come right if we have courage and determination. We have nothing with which to reproach ourselves, except perhaps too great a loyalty.' To compound his woes, Macmillan learnt that Kim Philby, who had vanished from Beirut in January, was in Moscow, and thus knew that another spy scandal was looming. He hoped that he could carry off the Profumo incident with nonchalant bluff. He announced what had been kept secret hitherto: the existence of Lord Dilhorne's inquiry into the security aspects of the affair.[5]

On 11 June, *The Times* published Haley's notorious editorial, 'It *Is* a Moral Issue', which quoted a phrase from the *Washington Post* about 'widespread decadence beneath the glitter of a large segment of stiff-lipped society'. The next day a Tory peer, Lord Caldecote, complained to Rab Butler that Macmillan's mishandling of the scandal proved the need for a change of leadership. 'I have been tremendously struck by the opinion of so many of my friends, all staunch Conservatives, who are utterly sick of the standard of integrity, of the lack of moral courage and of the politics of expediency. We would suffer both personally and nationally from a Socialist government,' Caldecote continued, 'but if this is the only way of clearing up the mess . . . so be it.'[6]

Lord Poole, joint chairman with Macleod of the Conservative Party, Redmayne and officials at the party's headquarters expected that provincial voters would prove to be more puritanical than metropolitan: 'the main trouble is going to be in the sticks'.[7] This conventional wisdom was gainsaid by a survey of hundreds of people conducted by the *Banbury Guardian*, a newspaper owned by a Labour MP, Woodrow Wyatt, in the week after Profumo's resignation. The newspaper's catchment area included the southern edge of Profumo's constituency. Wyatt's survey deserves detailed consideration.

There were three issues, the *Banbury Guardian* judged: national security; the 'private morals of a public figure'; and lying in the House of Commons (for which ninety-five per cent of *Banbury Guardian* respondents condemned Profumo). One outstanding fact emerged from the survey: that the minority who condemned his morality were mostly middle-aged or elderly. Younger people were neither offended nor condemnatory. 'Despite assertions from the national Press and MPs that the public has been shocked and disgusted by the morality aspect, the survey showed conclusively that this was not so,' the newspaper reported:

> What may have shocked our grandfathers fifty years ago is now accepted – even if it is not condoned. Few of the people questioned were shocked by Mr Profumo's affair with Christine Keeler. They agreed that 'this sort of thing goes on' . . . As one man put it, 'Those who are shocked by the affair are obviously out of touch with life in the twentieth century.' . . .
>
> Despite the disgrace that is obviously felt in some of the villages, there is still a tremendous feeling of loyalty to the Profumo family, especially in Kineton and Shotteswell, where members of his family still live. National newspaper reporters in Kineton last week offered up to £100 for information leading to the present whereabouts of the former War Minister. They were met with a stony silence.

Jack and Valerie Profumo spent thirteen days secreted in a stone house in the Warwickshire village of Radway with his constituent, Air Commodore Victor Willis DSO, commandant of the RAF Staff College at Andover, and pioneer of blind-approach landing, signals intelligence and electronic warfare. If a few Radway villagers knew Profumo was there, none of them blabbed. 'To them he is still "a gentleman" who had been unlucky to be dragged into the Christine Keeler affair. And some – particularly the women – wouldn't hear a word spoken against him. They have already forgiven him – and would vote for him again in an election.'[8]

Two pages of the *Banbury Guardian* were devoted to *vox populi*. 'What he does in his spare time is his own affair,' said F. A. H. Townsend of 3 Dene Close, Kineton. Ethel Bowden, aged sixty-six, and mother to fourteen children, said: 'This business has got nothing on *Lady Chatterley's Lover* – you could not put this affair in a book, and his wife has my sympathy.' Mrs S. Parker, of Market Hill, Southam, thought the MP was a good man and felt grieved by his humiliation. She blamed Christine Keeler: 'I think she ought to keep her thoughts to herself and not sell her story to the papers.' Mrs J. Morgan of Bishops Itchington said: 'I am a Labour Party supporter, so from my point of view this is a good thing. The best thing he could do now would be to leave the country rapidly.'

Several neighbours from Station Road in Fenny Compton gave their views. Mrs B. Spencer 'did not think the affair should be "public property" and did not like to discuss it. But she commented: "I would love to know just what Ministers get up to, but I suppose I shall read about it in the papers".' Sidney Hughes felt Ministers must conduct their lives in a manner befitting their position. 'They should keep their noses clean in the same way a policeman has to. I feel sorry for Mr Profumo now, but he must take his punishment.' Mrs Emily Robbins sympathised with Profumo. 'If he stood for election again, I would not hold this against him. He has always been a good Member, and I think this was just a bit of bad luck.'

Many of his Ratley constituents in South Warwickshire were polled. Gordon Leys, aged sixty-eight, had believed his MP when he made his statement in the Commons and felt let down: 'I am surprised that after doing such a thing he could go to the races and back a winner.' Mrs W. Halliday of 3 Town Hill Cottages was shocked by the disclosures because she had thought her MP was a good man. 'You look up to people in the Commons and they have your respect. This was a shock and makes you wonder whether there are any more like him.' Her son-in-law, a Ratley soldier, 'who would not give his name because he was afraid the War Office would take action against him under the Official Secrets Act', added: 'I am not concerned with the War Minister's private life but . . . a few people in high places will have red faces before this is finished.' Mrs D. M. England of 1 Council Houses, Town Hill, said: 'I expect my MP to lead a blameless life, and this is dreadful. I cannot forgive him . . . there is still more to come out, and I think there will be other important people involved.'[9]

In contrast to this compassionate tolerance, there was a much-publicised speech by the Bournemouth MP, John Cordle, while opening a church fête at Drayton, near Banbury (which raised £40). Cordle was a handsome, vaunting puritan with smug illusions about himself. Parliamentary colleagues treated him as a sickening humbug. Henry Kerby told Andrew Roth after Cordle's adoption in Bournemouth (secured partly because he was a rip-roaring supporter of the death penalty for murderers) that local Tory women were aghast at his success claiming that he was 'a man they dared not leave alone with their early-teen daughters'. After becoming proprietor of the *Church of England Newspaper* in 1959, Cordle vowed that it would campaign for 'high standards of public life, discipline in the home and a decisive approach to hooliganism'. He opposed 'easy divorce', but his own conduct failed the standards that he set for others. When his first wife, from whom he was divorced in 1956, sought his imprisonment in 1964 for breaching a custody order, Cordle only escaped by pleading parliamentary privilege: the judge condemned his conduct as 'utterly disgraceful'. During the collapse of his second marriage in 1971, he imposed a 7 p.m. curfew on visitors to his wife. His third and final wife, who was thirty-five years his junior, had been his children's nanny. Cordle, who was a disciple of the American evangelical Billy Graham, felt driven to visit strip clubs in order to be able to denounce them with authority, anathematised Sir Roger Casement's sodomitical diaries, demanded that copies of *Lady Chatterley's Lover* be dumped in the sea, and blamed venereal diseases among teenagers on 'filthy books'. Fourteen years after denouncing Profumo, he resigned his parliamentary seat after entangling himself in venalities that also disgraced the former Home Secretary, Maudling.[10]

Cordle was an example of the soapy scum that flowed after the sluices of self-righteous scurrility were opened. 'We have all been shocked recently by the belated disclosure of a Minister's deceit and misconduct,' he pronounced at the church fête. The nation required strong leadership, both moral and political, in these difficult days. 'It is our duty as citizens to maintain the highest standards of rectitude in public life . . . For the sake of national wellbeing and strength, we cannot afford to have bad security risks in high office. For this reason, men who choose to live in adultery, men who are homosexuals, or men whose highest interest is against the highest interests of the nation ought not to be invited to serve our Queen and Country. Nor should they be tolerated in office if they adopt these destructive practices.' Cordle added that he was 'appalled to hear that our beloved Queen should be so wrongly advised to give an audience' to the disgraced minister: 'It seems to me surely an affront to the Christian conscience of the nation.' As a result of Cordle's intervention, Profumo did not return his seals of office personally to the monarch, as was customary.[11]

On 13 June, Lord Hailsham, venting hot air like an explosive volcano, and in such a tantrum that his head seemed to change shape on screen, gave a notorious BBC television interview denouncing Profumo for having 'lied and lied; lied to his family, lied to his friends, lied to his solicitor, lied to the House of Commons'. In the *Daily Mirror* the columnist Cassandra commented that Hailsham's rant seemed 'a rather unattractive mixture of genuine rage and seemingly simulated indignation that only served to heighten the skill and patient questioning of the interviewer'. The irate Hailsham, according to another television viewer, resembled Evelyn Waugh berating a trespasser: 'It had to be seen to be believed.'[12]

Hailsham accused Robert McKenzie of trying to exploit 'a security problem' as party politics. 'A Secretary of State cannot have a woman shared with a spy,' he fulminated, 'without giving rise to a security risk.' The security services, of course, had long before discounted the fantasy that the minister had shared a woman with a spy – a story that first surfaced six months earlier when the woman in question was trying to make £1,000 by selling her story to Peter Earle, Reg Payne and Hugh Cudlipp. When McKenzie countered by asking why, if it was not a party issue, the Tory whips had issued a three-line whip, Hailsham was cornered: like Profumo in a fix, he lied. Hailsham insisted that a three-line whip was a summons to attend Parliament, rather than a document of party discipline to ensure a strong vote.

This fib outraged MPs. In the Commons Reginald Paget decried Hailsham as a 'lying humbug' and 'hysterical demagogue, with a brutal tinge'. He mocked, too, the Leader of the House of Lords as a bully and glutton: 'From Lord Hailsham we have had a virtuoso performance in the art of kicking a fallen friend in the guts. It is easy to compound for sins we are inclined to by damning those we have no mind to. When self-indulgence has reduced a man to the shape of Lord Hailsham, sexual continence involves no more than a sense of the ridiculous.' This was striking hard, because Hailsham liked to discuss sexual acts and bedroom etiquette with metaphors drawn from the table: 'If you gobble your food, it's not quite so nice. If you eat HP sauce like [Harold Wilson], it's not so good as oysters and Quenelles de Sole Newburg.' In distinguishing good sex from bad, he would say, 'the whole difference is between crêpes suzettes and pigs' trotters'.[13]

In the opinion of most voters, Profumo's resignation was

mandatory because (to quote the *Economist*) it was 'essential to insist – quite remorselessly – that no minister should ever be allowed with impunity to tell lies in the House of Commons'. They did not add that he would have been equally forced to resign if he had told the truth. Politicians, too, were indignant that he had lied to colleagues, despite themselves lying robustly on occasions. Lying is a means for politicians to prove their power: they make a resounding declaration, which their listeners know is untrue but do not dare to challenge; and by doing so they affirm their invulnerability and raise their status. Selwyn Lloyd, as Foreign Secretary, gave a flat denial to the Commons on 31 October 1956 of collusion as the Israelis invaded Egypt. Kilmuir, Lord Chancellor at the time of Suez, had the effrontery to declare in his memoirs published in 1964 that 'the wild accusations of collusion between the British, French and Israeli governments which were hurled by the Labour Party had absolutely no foundation in fact'. The deliberate inaccuracies similarly tumbled like acrobats in Kilmuir's parliamentary speech opposing Lord Mancroft's Privacy Bill of 1961.[14]

In 1964, Nyasaland became the independent state of Malawi under the presidency of Dr Hastings Banda. Dilhorne, the Lord Chancellor, who five years earlier as Attorney-General had told the Commons that Banda had planned to massacre every European in the country, from the governor down to infants, and moreover had convinced the Tory majority to pretend to believe him and give him an ovation, represented the British government at the independence celebrations and congratulated Banda on his assumption of power. On the Labour side, Harold Wilson's smears of Lord Poole in the Bank Rate Leak stunt of 1957 were calculated mendacity. Crossman perjured himself in a notorious libel action against the *Spectator*. George Brown, 'half-seas-over', lied when he appeared on television on the night of the Kennedy assassination, declaring 'Jack Kennedy was one of my best friends', when they had met only twice in formal interviews.[15]

It seemed to sober, rational minds that the Macmillan government was 'about to be overthrown by a twenty-one-year-old trollop'. The greatest threat to him came from the restive right-wing of his party. During the previous year his most trenchant backbench critics had been Nigel Birch, Lord Lambton and Sir Harry Legge-Bourke. Birch's parliamentary colleagues believed that he was one of the few attackers whom Supermac feared. 'There is something about his fierce wit, his supercilious grouse-moors manner, his superior snobbery, which seems to demoralise the Prime Minister – who goes to some lengths to pacify him. Birch is the kind of man that Macmillan admires – General's son, Etonian, brilliant businessman, first-class intellect. But Birch regards Macmillan as a sham, a played-out actor and a trickster.' Macmillan doubtless felt dread when he heard that Birch intended to speak in the Profumo debate immediately after the Commons reconvened on Monday 17 June.[16]

Wilson returned from a visit to Khrushchev two days earlier, and spent the weekend mastering Wigg's dossier and honing his indict-ment of the Prime Minister. 'We've got him on toast,' Wilson said when the speech was written.[17]

Wilson's intervention proved formidable. 'This is a debate,' he declared, 'without precedent in the annals of this House. It arises from disclosures which have shocked the moral conscience of the nation.' He asked whether ministers – soiled by their contact with 'a sordid underworld network' – connived in Profumo's lies, or were negligent in accepting them. He told MPs about Ward's calamitous meeting with Wigg, and Wigg's written summary of it: 'a nauseating document taking the lid off a corner of the London underworld of vice, dope, marijuana, blackmail, counter-black-mail, violence and petty crime'. He accused Macmillan of 'indolent nonchalance' and reckless bluff. 'After the Vassall case he felt that he could not stand another serious security case involving a Ministerial resignation, and he gambled desperately and hoped that nothing would ever come out. For political reasons he was gambling with national security . . . this is why he was at such pains to demonstrate to me his unflappability.' Although Ward had been working with MI5, he was vilified by Wilson as 'a tool' of the Soviets, who exemplified a 'sleazy sector of society'. Wilson denounced hereditary privilege and skewed pay differentials: 'there is something utterly nauseating about a system which pays a harlot 25 times as much as it pays a Prime Minister, 250 times as much as it pays its Members of Parliament, and 500 times as much as it pays some of its ministers of religion'. Egalitarianism, he suggested, would prove the necessary moral purgative of 'a diseased excrescence, a corrupted and poisoned appendix of a small and unrepresentative section of society that makes no contribution to what Britain is, still less can be'.[18]

Macmillan's response was moving to his friends, but sounded querulous to less sympathetic listeners and gave the impression of a spavined old warhorse. 'On me, as head of the Administration, what has happened has inflicted a deep, bitter, and lasting wound,' he said. 'I could not believe that a man would be so foolish, even if so wicked, not only to lie to colleagues in the House, but be prepared to issue a writ in respect of a libel which he must know to be true.' Macmillan stated that he had not been told of the security aspect to the business, but did not give the reason: that Ward's remark to Keeler that she should ask about atomic warheads for Germany had been a joke, which was never taken in earnest by MI5. Only low journalists pretended to take it seriously.[19]

Birch's speech scorned the government for being so easily duped by Profumo: 'He never struck me as a man at all like a cloistered monk, and Miss Keeler was a professional prostitute,' Birch declared (although Keeler was never a professional prostitute). 'There seems to me to be a certain basic improbability that their conduct was purely platonic.' Humphry Berkeley was in Iraq when he was summoned by Redmayne to vote in the debate. He was incredulous to learn that Macmillan had never confronted Profumo about the rumours, and disappointed by the quavering tone of the old man's speech. He was one of twenty-seven Tory abstentions in the vote. Several MPs only supported the government on Redmayne's assurance that Macmillan would resign by autumn.[20]

Sir Peter Smithers, the wise and gentle Tory MP for Winchester, said that panic overwhelmed the Commons at this time. 'I use the word panic, for panic it was. Every MP remembered his own transgressions, great or small, past or present.' The panic centred on the Smoking Room, where everyone worried who was going to be denounced next, and the Press Bar, which swirled in rumours.[21]

Anthony Sampson watched MPs work themselves into frenzy after the Commons reassembled on 17 June. 'Absurd rumours, involving half the Cabinet, were believed, repeated and elaborated. Plots and conspiracies to overthrow the Prime Minister were hatched around every corner. Wild stories and schemes were leaked to the Press who, in turn, built up the crisis and generated still further alarm. Members of Parliament who returned to England in the midst of the furore were astonished to find that Parliament had apparently lost its head.' Mark Bonham Carter, after his spell as a Liberal MP, likened the Commons to a boarding school in a memorable interview for Sampson's *Anatomy of Britain*. The parliamentary hysterics of June 1963 reminded Sampson of one of those sudden moral panics that overwhelmed boarding schools. 'The shock vibrates through the school and so terrible is it to the splendid traditions of the place that wave upon wave of rumours emerge, each one more preposterous than the last, suggesting that the entire school has, for years past, been corrupt and obscene. The processions, Latin mottoes and founders prayers seem to have been no more than a front. Every prefect and every master has some secret vice ascribed to him, and the headmaster himself is accused of the most sinister complicity.'[22]

Bill Astor, with his peaceable nature, was thrown into vertiginous uncertainty as the Pharisees hounded him. Malise Hore-Ruthven, who had joined the Moral Rearmament movement to save the world from sin and communism, tried to bully his sister-in-law, Lady Gowrie, into forsaking Parr's Cottage at Cliveden to protect her grandsons from Astor depravity. At Royal Ascot, during the second week of June, Astor's supposed friends cut him dead, and boasted of it afterwards. A newspaper refused to publish a letter by him on coordinating relief to victims of natural disasters. On 19 June, just as his Ascot guests were dispersing, Chief Inspector Herbert appeared at the house with Burrows. When they told Astor that they were collecting evidence to charge him with allowing a brothel at Spring Cottage, he nearly collapsed. The Astors were ineluctably stigmatised as leaders of 'the spiv aristocracy', of which Nicholas Mosley had recently written: 'foursomes in the brothels of Marseille, voyeurs and exhibitionists, the modern ways of making love'.[23]

Those who did not live through this period cannot imagine how the words 'intercourse' and 'prostitute' suddenly entered daily parlance. I recall, as a ten-year-old-boy, asking a racy great-aunt, who lived in a flat above the King's Road, Chelsea, how to pronounce the word which I found on front pages of the cook's *Daily Express*. 'Pros-ti-tutty' was my original shot. Lip-smacking revulsion provided an adult awakening for an observant child. My coeval Tom Utley was boarding at a preparatory school in Suffolk in June 1963. He was puzzled that the broadsheet newspapers arrayed in the school library for boys to read after breakfast were cut to tatters every morning. Only the Court and business pages seemed to evade extensive scissoring. His father, in answer to a letter asking the reason for these holes, sent a detailed account of the Profumo Affair, which the school matron confiscated.[24]

On 22 June, Macmillan attended a fundraising garden party in his constituency. He had a dazed air amidst the coconut shies and lucky dips. As he posed for a photograph with the daughter of a constituent, someone hissed: 'Take your hands off that little girl. Don't you wish it was Christine Keeler?' It was in this fetid atmosphere that Macmillan submitted to Labour's demand to appoint an inquiry into the rumours besmirching the integrity of public figures. He decided to have a one-man inquiry, by the Master of the Rolls, Lord Denning, who had been a wartime divorce judge and was President of the Lawyers' Christian Fellowship. Macleod, as Leader of the Commons, argued with Macmillan about this. 'I was against it from the beginning, and believed we ought not to give an inch to all the filthmongers.' When he went to dissuade Macmillan, he found the Prime Minister 'in a terrible state, going on about a rumour of there having been eight High Court judges involved in some orgy. "One," he said, "perhaps, two, conceivably; but eight – I just can't believe it." I said, if you don't believe it, why bother with an inquiry? But he replied, "No, terrible things are being said. It must be cleared up."'[25]

Osbert Lancaster's front-page cartoon in the *Daily Express* of 22 June showed his heroine Maudie Littlehampton flourishing a newspaper headlined: '"WHIPS! WHIPS! MASKS!" SAYS MANDY.' 'Honestly, darling,' she tells her husband, 'I do really think that National Kinky Week has gone on quite long enough!' The *Economist* that day, as *Time & Tide* had a year earlier, urged Macmillan 'to retire to an Earldom as soon as the Party can definitely determine his successor'.[26]

The most devastating bombardment was directed not at Macmillan individually but at the governing class of which he was a luminary. Hugh Cudlipp engineered a devastating special issue of the *Sunday Mirror* on 23 June. Under the front-page headline, 'Who Runs This Country, Anyhow?' the *Sunday Mirror* declared: 'The man who torpedoed Macmillan's hopes of leading the Tories into the next election is not John Profumo, but a civil servant . . . Name: Lord Normanbrook of Chelsea.' The Cabinet Secretary, so Cudlipp's scribes reported, had confronted the Secretary for War about his visits to Ward's flat in 1961, but had not informed the Prime Minister. 'Is it safe for the Mandarins of Whitehall, who know so little of life outside their own narrow world, to wield such influence?' Officials were, after all, 'in no way accountable to Parliament or to the People'. The *Sunday Mirror* mercifully did not know the story of the Warden of an Oxford college recalling Normanbrook's arrival there as an undergraduate from Wolverhampton Grammar School. 'Very quick, Brook,' said the Warden, 'learned the tricks. Came up with a front pocket stuffed full of pens. Soon disappeared inside.' The Cudlipp-King school of journalism scorned such class assimilation. Normanbrook remained a bugbear to the Labour left: 'a real old Establishment figure', Anthony Wedgwood Benn reckoned in 1964.[27]

Elsewhere in the *Sunday Mirror*, Malcolm Muggeridge was master of revels at 'The Slow, Sure Death of the Upper Classes'. The upper class had passed away, he gloated, in the week since the Profumo parliamentary debate: 'We who have watched their demise with enthralled interest, amusement and satisfaction certainly do not want to see them rise again.' In forty years of journalism he had never heard such a tidal wave of slander. Yet, he warned, 'there have been scandals in plenty before, and the Upper Classes have managed to survive them'. Muggeridge, who had a reiterated repugnance of homosexuality, recalled that during Oscar Wilde's trials 'the Channel Steamers were full of Top People who felt that a trip abroad would be expedient'. They were soon back practising their filthy tricks with impunity. 'The dirty linen of Debrett is frequently given a public washing in the divorce courts. Promiscuity is more evident in stately homes than in semi-detached villas, if only because there are more bedrooms and longer corridors.' The Profumo scandal was 'the culmination of a series of episodes all calculated to undermine the repute, not just of Upper Class individuals and circles, but of the class system.' Abuse was well-deserved: 'the Upper Classes have always been given to lying, fornication, corrupt practices and, doubtless as a result of the public school system, sodomy'.[28]

Richard Crossman was deployed to attack Whitehall officialdom. Macmillan's explanation to the Commons had confirmed that the 'British government and British administration – which used to be recognised as the best in the world – are fast becoming a standing example of amateurism and incompetence'. Macmillan, with his 'indecision and personal empire-building at the top', was culpable for the 'incompetence and corruption' festering beneath. The people were stuck with 'an establishment still dominated by the mandarin mind which despises the expert and the technician and relies on a genteel amateurism out-of-date even in Edwardian Britain', Crossman explained. This class-bound dilettantism was the cause of the successive 'security scandals which have disgraced Macmillan's regime'.[29]

The foreign correspondent James Cameron explained to *Sunday Mirror* readers 'Why the World is Mocking Britain'. Macmillan, he wrote, was 'scarcely a real person himself, but a kind of self-induced illusion'. Diplomats were anti-democratic conspirators in the Century of the Common Man. 'Every man jack of our Foreign Service abroad is a creature not of the Government of the day, but of the permanent staff of the Foreign Office, owing allegiance not to any popular administration but to the Machine.' Their disinterested, non-partisan ethos was deplorable because the diplomatic service was manned by 'gentlemen of impeccable tastes and great civility; they are always excellently educated, and usually well-born'. (One wonders if Cameron wished to have populist diplomats who were bad-mannered and ill-educated.) He recalled that when Ernie Bevin became Foreign Secretary in 1945, 'it was claimed that the Diplomatic Service was going to be revolutionised, democratised, disinfected of its almost total adherence to the upper-class myth, purged of its insistence on the Public School and Oxbridge'. Instead Britain would be represented abroad by 'technicians, businessmen, trade unionists'. However, 'the great crushing irresistible weight of the Establishment overlaid the plan ... and left the FO exactly as it was: the pasture of the public school, the grazing-ground of the upper-class intellectual, above all the haven of the play-safe'. Cameron then swung his diatribe towards the Profumo scandal. 'If the Old Etonian Counsellors advise the Old Harrovian Ambassadors who advise the Old Etonian Foreign Secretary to advise or not advise the Old Etonian Premier, WHO decides what goes on in the mind of the Old Ukrainian City Scholar who runs the Soviet Union? Maybe the same people who knew all about Christine Keeler, and didn't let on ... the faceless gentlemen of unchallengeable upbringing who protect statesmen from the business of statesmanship and insulate Government from the troubles of governing, and care not that Premiers come and Premiers go, for they go on forever.' [30]

Throughout the summer weeks that followed, the *Sunday Mirror* had other eloquent articles instilling this post-Profumo message about ruling-class corruption, traitors and modernisation. Significantly when, in early July, Macmillan, Wilson, Redmayne and Bowden met to discuss the Denning inquiry, Wilson mooted a connection between Ward and the licentious Duchess of Argyll, who was being noisily divorced by her duke. Fourteen months later, Britain had a general election in which Labour squeaked past the Tories with a majority of four seats: a victory swung by Mirror Group newspapers deploying special features like this.[31]

Macmillan, when he announced the Denning inquiry in the Commons on 21 June, referred to 'rumours . . . which affect the honour and integrity of public life in this country'. Tom Denning in turn used this phrase when calling witnesses to appear before him. He was a judge with a corrective spirit who did not believe that he often overreached himself. It was impossible, he felt, to demarcate crime from sin: libertines should be harried, disgraced and scourged. In 1957, during a parliamentary debate on the Wolfenden recommendations, he urged that it should be a criminal offence for a man to undergo a vasectomy which enabled him to have 'the gratification of sexual intercourse without any of the responsibilities'. Whether heinous sexual acts were criminalised should depend on whether they were reckoned 'morally reprehensible . . . in the minds of right-thinking people', or struck 'at the safety or wellbeing of society', as did 'unnatural vice' which threatened 'the integrity of the human race'. He continued his speech by warning that if homosexuality was no longer a criminal offence, the unthinkable might happen: a man might be charged with assault for punching another man who flirted with him. 'In all these cases the law must either condemn or condone,' he told his fellow peers. 'Is it not the case that for so many people now it is the law alone which sets the standard? If you reprove such a one for his conduct, he will say "Why should I not do it? There is no law against it" . . . I am afraid that Hell Fire and eternal damnation hold no terrors nowadays. The law should condemn this evil, for evil it is, but the judges should be discreet in their punishment of it.'[32]

The People on 7 July, under the headline 'THREE MINISTERS NAMED IN JUDGE'S PURGE', noted of Denning: 'His probe may lead to a purge of public life generally, with a view to excluding the risk that politicians who "sin" in private will be blackmailed by enemy agents.' Scotland Yard and Special Branch officers, under Commander Arthur Townsend, were enquiring 'into the private morals of public men' in parallel with Denning. 'They are compiling a dossier covering homosexual practices as well as sexual laxity alleged against civil servants, Service officers and MPs.' A Special Branch man supposedly told *The People*: 'the Russians jump at the chance of exploiting any moral weakness'. Startling information, he added, was pouring in.[33]

In the second week of June 1963, some days after Ward's arrest, there was a meeting at the Athenæum club in Pall Mall. All of the men who attended held responsible jobs; most had been Ward's patients; some knew him socially too. Each of them had been asked by Ward's solicitors if they would appear at the Old Bailey to testify to his good character. Each wanted to know what the others had decided. One of those present was a high-ranking Foreign Office man, who twenty years later spoke non-attributably about the Athenæum discussion. 'On the one hand we liked and respected Ward and we wanted to help him. On the other, if we were seen to be involved in such a sordid case in no matter what role, then we would be ruined. We decided that if Bill Astor, Ward's oldest friend and patient, was not going to give evidence on Ward's behalf, then we could also decline.' They felt that Ward's legal team would not subpoena them lest, 'in order to save our own skins, we turned hostile. We've all had to live with our decision. For my part I can't tell you of the moral awfulness of abandoning a friend when he needs you most, and a friend, moreover, who was completely innocent of the charges against him.'[34]

The risks to Ward's acquaintances in coming forward in his defence were real. Vasco Lazzolo, the portrait painter, who had known Ward since 1946, agreed to give evidence on his friend's behalf. He was threatened by Chief Inspector Herbert that if he did so, the police might visit his studio, plant some pornography and arrest him.

On Friday 28 June, Ward's committal proceedings opened at Marylebone Magistrates Court. He was charged with eight violations of the Sexual Offences Act of 1956, including brothel-keeping, procuring, living off the earnings of prostitutes, and abortion offences. This was a preliminary hearing before a magistrate to determine whether the prosecution had enough evidence to justify sending the accused for trial in a higher court. The defence case was not heard at all. Whereas in France examining magistrates hear the prosecution's case *in camera*, in England the hearings can be fully publicised – with prejudicial publicity in lewd cases like Ward's. The charges involving abortion and brothel-keeping, together with the initial procuring charges, were dropped before Ward's trial three weeks later; but the prejudicial damage had been done. Reports of the magistrate's hearings created two opposed impressions. 'The first was of ineradicable grubbiness,' wrote Sybille Bedford, 'a feeling that Ward might well be a procurer, a ponce, a pimp, and that . . . the fellow was untouchable with a barge pole. The other impression was that the actual evidence against him was inconclusive and of tainted origin; in fact that the prosecution case was thin.'[35]

The prosecution was led by Mervyn Griffith-Jones, a tall, imposing man who, as prosecuting counsel in the *Lady Chatterley's Lover* obscenity trial three years earlier, had asked the jury whether it was a novel that they would wish to be read by their 'young sons, young daughters, because girls can read as well as boys'. Was it, he continued, a book that they would leave lying around the house: 'a book that you would even wish your wife or your servants to read?'[36] He had no thought that the jury might not have servants, or that if they did, the servants had minds of their own to decide what to read. At Ward's committal proceedings Griffith-Jones showed that he felt sullied by the case by refusing to speak directly, except in court questioning, to any of the prosecution witnesses, including the police. Nor did he let them speak to him. All contact was delegated to junior counsel, Michael Corkery. He addressed the court in the tones of a public school bully, using his privileges as counsel to humiliate anyone who thwarted his case, interrupting witnesses in mid-sentences, scorning their testimony. His voice was cold, rasping and stiff. His testy arrogance and sardonic morality at the committal proceedings deterred witnesses from volunteering to speak in Ward's defence at the criminal trial. The police opposed bail by claiming that Ward might vanish or interfere with witnesses. It was widely reported that the magistrate set bail at the high figure of £2,000, which intensified the notion that Ward was an arch-villain from whom society needed protection.

Under the Sexual Offences Act of 1956, a man who was 'habitually in the company of a known prostitute' had the onus of proving that he was not living off her earnings. Ward faced three counts of living on earnings of prostitution: from Keeler, when she had lived at Wimpole Mews from June 1961 to July 1962; from Rice-Davies, when she had been his lodger at Wimpole Mews during September to December 1962; and from two prostitutes, Vickie Barrett and Ronna Ricardo, who had visited Bryanston Mews between January and June 1963. Another section of the Sexual Offences Act criminalised those who introduced a man to a woman aged between sixteen and twenty-one if sexual intercourse ensued.

During cross-examination by Griffith-Jones at Marylebone Magistrates Court, Keeler testified that during a meal at the Brush & Palette restaurant with Ward, they had seen a nineteen-year-old called Sally Norie with a youth. The two couples started talking and flirting: Keeler paired with Norie's boyfriend, while Ward later went to bed with Norie. Ward's counsel interrupted this evidence, as it was extracted by Griffith-Jones, with a jibe and a protest: 'Even a honeymoon would sound obscene in the hands of my learned friend,' he said of Griffith-Jones. 'Here is a case where a man, looked at in its worst context, asked a girl he was with to give him an introduction to another girl. Then it is suggested that they made love. It is said that this is a criminal offence. We must not take leave of our senses.' He then asked the magistrate, 'How can it be a criminal offence for two persons, if they choose, to enter into an intimate relationship?' The magistrate replied, 'If one introduced someone knowing it was for the purpose of intercourse, it becomes procuring.'[37]

'Everyone is lying to grind his own axe,' a battered but impenitent Ward told Dominic Elwes, who stood bail for him. 'Every witness who does not give the answer the police want is tampered with . . . Every motive I had is twisted. All I have left between me and destruction is a handful of firm friends, the integrity of the judge and the twelve men on the jury. God alone knows what will happen. I know that one day the truth will eventually come out. And the truth is very simple: I loved people – of all types – and I don't think there are very many people the worse for having known me.'[38]

Bill Astor's Cliveden friend Maurice Collis visited Feliks Topolski's studio under an arch on the South Bank after the committal proceedings. 'When we were seated over a vodka,' Collis recorded, 'we got talking, as was inevitable, on the Ward case which literally has set the whole word buzzing, as it has all the elements of a popular shocker, as presented by the press, with spying and leakage of vital secrets to Russia, orgies, a broken Minister, prostitution, organised vice, flagellation, voyeurism, the threatened fall of the Conservative government, all with the sauce that a noble lord, very rich, owner of racehorses, a great mansion, a wife famous formerly as a model, and a name which for a generation or more has been news on account of his mother's wit and eccentricities, had been mixed up in the imbroglio.' Topolski recognised the Ward prosecution as a stunt: 'His was not a real case of living on immoral earnings, arranging abortions, maintaining a brothel. When the laws were framed they had not in view men like Ward, but underworld racketeers.' Topolski felt sure that if the police succeeded in securing Ward's conviction on any charge, it would be a miscarriage of justice.[39]

Bill Astor, too, believed that the prosecution evidence was so weak that Ward would be acquitted. He wanted to speak, but his lawyers advised against volunteering evidence. Neither prosecuting nor defending counsel called him during Ward's trial. When Collis commiserated on his ordeal, Astor replied with a sigh: 'The only thing to do is to keep up one's dignity, go on as before and not engage in a public slanging match with those women. After all, I don't live like that, Maurice. Hundreds of people know exactly how I live, what my interests are, how I occupy my time, what I do in the public service, what my private life consists of. We are being pestered by the press, spied on; the press helicopters are the worst, hovering over the house.'[40]

On 1 July, Edward Heath, the Lord Privy Seal, confirmed that Kim Philby had been the Third Man. After David Astor's *Observer* then revealed that Philby had been appointed as its Beirut correspondent at the Foreign Office's request, the *Daily Mirror* launched a new fusillade:

Hardly a day goes by without some fresh revelation of how the Old Boys work in high places to keep the Old Boys in high places. Don't worry, Old Boy, if you're found out – there are buckets and buckets of surplus whitewash in Whitehall, and your friends will see you through . . .

Look at what happened to Maclean. Working for the Foreign Office in Cairo he was as soused as a herring, involved in wild and disgraceful episodes which no business concern would tolerate for a second in its messenger boys.

Fired? Not on your life, Old Boy. Dear old Donald was given

a rest until his hangovers cleared up, and then he was given another Foreign Office top job.

Look at jolly Jack Profumo – Harrow, Brasenose College, Oxford, fifth Baron of the late United Kingdom of Italy, and all that taradiddle. If Jack says he calls all his lady friends 'Darling' (including Miss Keeler) then why shouldn't we believe him?

Once you're in the gang they let you down gently. You're given the benefit of the doubt. If you're a cat that walks at night, even into the wrong bedroom, you're given nine lives – like all the other Top Cats.

It is no use Mr Macmillan telling Mr Wilson, as he did in the Commons yesterday, that he must learn to distinguish between invective and insolence . . . This sort of wigging for people who aren't in the Club is merely whimsical. But is it any good blaming Mr Macmillan any more? It is beginning to look as if the whole of the Tory Party approves of the cover-up, hush-up, keep-it-dark, Old Boys technique of getting in power and staying in power – and to hell with what the country thinks.

Such ebullitions were dispiriting for Whitehall mandarins, and indeed weakening for national governance. 'It is a bore that the facts have not got across to the public; but I am afraid that the Press are determined to misunderstand or misrepresent whatever they can,' Normanbrook wrote to Macmillan on 6 July. 'I hope that all this will blow over when Denning has reported and the Ward trial is finished.'[41]

With the Ward prosecution sub judice between the committal proceedings and trial, attention switched to Rachman, who could not sue: 'an easy target', said a Polish photographer who was pursued by journalists for pictures of the dead landlord 'with his girls, his Rolls-Royce, and his big fat cigars'. On 8 July, Ben Parkin, Labour MP for Paddington, intervened in a debate on housing. Parkin, a sincere campaigner about slum conditions with a prurient interest in the street-walkers who were conspicuous in his constituency, now plunged into unscrupulous sensation. 'All Fleet Street is full of the idea that he is not dead,' he announced of Rachman. 'It would be an easy thing to switch bodies – dead on arrival at Edgware General Hospital . . . a very good idea for a substitution and very useful, too – just ten days before all hell broke loose.' Rachman, of course, had been alive and talking when he reached hospital, and could not have foreseen that ten days later Edgecombe would shoot up the Bryanston Mews flat: still less could he have substituted a dead body – even if, as gossip suggested at Daquise, the Polish restaurant where he played chess, he had a twin brother, who had conveniently died. 'I *know* he's dead,' Parkin told a member of a Notting Hill tenants' association, 'but don't tell anyone, and keep the rumours going, because if Rachman is dead, our case is dead too.'[42]

Much might be written on the frenetic press investigations of Rachman, bribes to unreliable informers, and racial prejudice intended to sustain tension before Ward's trial. Police obtained signed statements from David Waxman, the Mill Hill physician who was treating him for heart disease, as well as Fortis Green ambulancemen, confirming that it was Rachman who died. The matron at Edgware Hospital said scornfully, 'I do not permit body-switching in my hospital.' On 16 July, Sir Charles Cunningham wrote to Sir Joseph Simpson stating that Brooke, the Home Secretary, had commented, after reading the file on Rachman: 'He is now believed to be dead, but what about his business associates and his sponsors, particularly Colonel Sinclair of Farnham Common? Do the police keep themselves informed about that man's other activities?' These questions are a pointer to how the Home Office may have directed the Metropolitan Police's attention to Ward after the latter's colloquy in the Commons with Wigg became known.[43]

Ward's trial opened at the Old Bailey on 22 July and closed on 31 July. The judge, Sir Archie Marshall, was a plump little man with a vain bustle and long experience of criminal cases in the

Midlands. He rejected an application for an adjournment until September so that the defence might be better prepared, because he said it was in the public interest to have an early trial. 'We at the Bar are men of the world,' he declared while intervening in the cross-examination of Ronna Ricardo – upon which Ludovic Kennedy commented that this was a common delusion of judges: 'theirs is one of the most cloistered of all the professions.' Lawyers of Marshall's generation, and Denning's, stubbornly adhered to creeds that were sundered from real human experience.[44]

There were five charges: three of living off the immoral earnings of Keeler, Rice-Davies and the two other women; and two of procuring. Griffith-Jones's opening address (delivered with harsh, cold fervour) made assertions that exceeded the evidence that he later brought. He also made assertions involving matters about which Ward was not being prosecuted. He proceeded by innuendo, posturing, and distortion. He dealt in unfounded inferences and reckless characterisations. He liked a righteous wallow in indignation. He seemed to threaten witnesses that they would be branded as sexually corrupt, and deserving of social ostracism and professional ruin, if they did not reply in the terms that he wished. Yet repeatedly they gave responses that seemed the opposite of what he expected. The trouble appeared to be that the witnesses had been chivvied into falsehoods in their police statements so many months earlier that they could not remember what they were supposed to say. The overall impression of the prosecution case was of startling inconsistencies which Griffith-Jones knocked aside.

Ludovic Kennedy, who attended the trial, wrote that Griffith-Jones assumed the role not merely of state prosecutor of criminals, 'but as the state guardian of private morals . . . acting as a sort of Establishment front-man for an ethos which few people besides himself any longer believed in'. This, perhaps, accorded with Henry Brooke's hopes when he initiated the police investigation of Ward four months earlier. Griffith-Jones's cross-examinations gave Kennedy the impression 'not that Ward had committed a single obvious crime which cried out for justice, but rather that the prosecution were trying very hard to elicit facts which would bring Ward's activities into the compass of a recognised crime'. The prosecution case depended upon 'uncorroborated statements by proven liars: it was a hotchpotch of innuendoes and smears covered by a thin pastry of substance. It was a tale of immoralities, rather than crimes.'[45]

The two-way mirror in Rachman's flat had been smashed by Rice-Davies, and there was no such mirror in any of Ward's flats. Yet one was repeatedly mentioned by Griffith-Jones in order to emphasise Ward's association with vice. The jury was given the impression that Ward's claim to have helped MI5 was a fantasy. Griffith-Jones exploited the fact that Rachman was now a national hate-figure to state categorically but falsely that Ward had introduced Keeler to the slum landlord (in truth, they had met by chance while flat-hunting), and to suggest that Ward was responsible for Keeler becoming Rachman's kept woman.

Amidst the welter of extraneous material, contradictory allegations and inconsistent accusations from palpable liars, Griffith-Jones scored two hits. Keeler testified that she had been introduced by Ward to a man called Charles, who lived in a house off Park Lane. She claimed to have forgotten Charles's surname (which was Clore) despite pressure from counsel and judge to remember it. He had given her £50 after 'intercourse'. Some of this money she had used to repay a loan from Ward.

The more damaging episode involved a story which Rice-Davis produced under police pressure after her arrest on the concocted television-set charge when she was desperate not to return to Holloway prison. She said that while visiting the Marylebone High Street coffee bar with Ward they met a man who became her short-term boyfriend. In court he was referred to as 'the Indian doctor'. In fact the man was a Ceylonese confidence trickster known as Emil Savundra, who had once been extradited from England to serve a prison sentence in Belgium, and by 1963 was masterminding a grandiose insurance swindle which resulted in a long prison sentence in 1967. Rice-Davies said that Savundra left between £15 and £25 after each visit to Wimpole Mews – a total over £100. Griffith-Jones alleged that Ward got £2 or £3 from each visit. It is striking that neither Clore nor Savundra were called to corroborate, amend or deny these stories.

The Old Bailey was besieged by mobs. There were police constables, crime reporters, foreign correspondents, press photographers, taxi men, law clerks with heavy files; but supremely, an ugly, screeching mob. 'Going out of the main entrance of the Old Bailey,' wrote Rebecca West, who covered the trial for the *Sunday Telegraph*, 'was to walk into one vast leer, a concupiscent exposure of dentures, the significance of which was quite clear to anyone who had been caught in one of the crowds who mobbed Christine Keeler in her car. She was a pitiful spectacle, sitting in terrified dignity, her face covered with a pancake make-up which levels out the natural toning of the skin, and her determination to make a good show levelling her features to the flatness of a mask. First, the photographers surrounded her, then they fell away, and their place was taken by women, mostly old or in late middle-age, and they were without exception ill-favoured and unkempt, and elderly men of the unprosperous sort. Their cries and boos expressed the purest envy.' West was shocked that this old rabble was jealous of Keeler's rackety vulnerability.[46]

The trial was slow-motion horror. As the injustices proceeded, the philosopher A. J. Ayer came as near to publishing a protest as anyone could without risking Marshall summoning them for contempt of court. His article, headed 'Morality 1963', was published in *Punch* on 31 July. It began: 'We do right to be concerned with public morality. It is our chief, indeed almost our only protection, against tyranny and exploitation.' Then, in carefully oblique terms, he addressed the Ward trial. 'Among all the forms of official wickedness, the perversion of justice outrages us the most. Not that the egoism or even the stupidity of a politician, or the corruption of a civil servant, may not do more harm.' Yet the palpable injustice when scapegoats like Dreyfus, Sacco and Vanzetti were prosecuted should arouse 'more resentment than a naked exercise of tyranny, just because it makes a mockery of the law. One of the most appalling features of totalitarian purges is that they are made to masquerade as trials.' The parallel was clear if implicit.[47]

A travesty of justice was about to occur in the Court of Criminal Appeal. During Ward's trial, Keeler said repeatedly that her April injuries had been caused by Lucky Gordon. When Gordon's denial that he had caused her injuries was put to her, she replied: 'The man is mad. Of course they were.'[48] She repeated her denials that Camacchio and Fenton had been present in the flat. This was the second time she had lied on oath about these matters. Once she had been set on this course by the police, she could not retreat. However, Robin Drury, a sidekick of Ward's who briefly convinced Keeler that he should become her business manager because he had held the same job for the lyricist Lionel Bart, had in May tape-recorded ten hours of her (sometimes stoned) reminiscences with a view to ghosting a book. When their agreement fell into acrimonious disarray, he offered these tapes, in which she revealed that Fenton and Camacchio had been in the Hamilton-Marshall flat when Gordon arrived, to Peter Earle of the *News of the World*, who baulked at his price of £20,000. The tapes reached a young man named Alex Wharton and a freelance hack twenty years his senior called Alastair Revie.

Wharton was an energetic youth (born in Scunthorpe in 1939), who as a teenager had sung in the earliest production of the musical *Fings Ain't Wot They Used To Be*, and had been part of a hit duo called The Most Brothers, performing in a basement coffee bar in Old Compton Street that was run by an Australian wrestler. At the age of twenty he became a boy-prodigy producer with Decca Records, for whom he created a string of hits; later he managed the band The Moody Blues. In the summer of 1963 it was thought that this lively youngster was so attuned to the spirit of the age that he might help to present a saleable Keeler memoir. Revie was a ghost-writer (responsible for the melodramatic junkie memoirs of Barry Ellis, *I Came Back from Hell*) whose trashy novel *That Kind of Girl* was published in 1963 with the strapline: 'Her Sin Was Ignorance – Her Reward Was Shame'.

Wharton and Revie, from worlds that were fearsome and incomprehensible to Griffith-Jones and Marshall, came near to wrecking the ruthless pomposities at the Old Bailey. Revie not only heard Drury's tapes, but met John Hamilton-Marshall, who told him, as he also told solicitors representing both Ward and Gordon, that he rather than Gordon had been Keeler's assailant in the Devonshire Place flat. Revie informed Wigg that Keeler had committed perjury during Gordon's trial. Wigg passed Revie's letter to the Attorney-General, Sir John Hobson. At Hobson's instigation, Scotland Yard obtained Drury's tapes a week before Ward's trial opened, and began transcribing them. The police, who during Gordon's trial had protested that Camacchio and Fenton were untraceable, now found them easily. Camacchio made a statement exonerating Gordon from the attack on Keeler; Hamilton-Marshall reiterated that he was the man who hit her; and other evidence pulled the frame apart. Gordon was granted leave to appeal by Lord Parker of Waddington, the Lord Chief Justice.

When Parker was chosen by Macmillan in 1958 it had been expected that he would prove to be a lenient influence. As a barrister, though, he had been a Treasury counsel, and was therefore predisposed towards the government. When criminal appeals came before him he so often increased rather than reduced prison sentences that barristers advised clients not to risk the Court of Criminal Appeal. In 1961 he sentenced the spy George Blake to forty-two years' imprisonment. When the Profumo Affair came under his influence, he evinced a ruthless, prim malice which he believed served the public good.

On Tuesday 30 July, the day that Griffith-Jones made his closing address at Ward's trial, three judges at the Court of Criminal Appeal, sitting an hour earlier than usual so that few onlookers were in attendance, took just nine minutes to set aside Gordon's conviction. Gordon had been sent to prison for seven years only six weeks earlier. The reasons for his swift release were suppressed by the judges who made the decision. Keeler had, of course, perjured herself, under police pressure, at Gordon's trial. Yet Lord Parker emphasised when delivering the court's judgement that this was based on the new evidence from Camacchio, Fenton, Hamilton-Marshall, Revie and others and that the court did not hold that Keeler's evidence was untruthful: indeed that she may have been speaking the truth. As her evidence was contradicted by everyone else, this was unlikely.

Parker and his fellow judges read the witness statements, but not aloud. They neither asked the witnesses to testify nor said in court what the new witnesses had revealed. They thus concealed Keeler's extensive perjury from the public. If the court had revealed the new evidence, and Parker had then maintained that Keeler might be telling the truth, he would have been scorned. The Lord Chief Justice's decision was taken by shorthand writers, checked and revised by him, then sent by special messenger from the Court of Criminal Appeal to the Old Bailey.

This exceptional proceeding – this corrupt, contemptible sequence of events – was undertaken by Parker in order to undermine Ward's defence. It enabled Griffith-Jones to say during his final address: 'Gordon's appeal has been upheld. That does not of course mean to say that the Court of Criminal Appeal have found that Miss Keeler is lying. As I understand it from the note I have, the Lord Chief Justice said it might be that Miss Keeler's evidence was completely truthful, but in view of the fact that there were witnesses now available who were not available at the trial, it was felt that the court could not necessarily say that the jury in that case would have returned the same verdict as they did if those two witnesses had been called. That is all it amounts to.' Nevertheless, once Ward was convicted, Keeler was tried for perjury in the Gordon case, and sentenced to nine months' imprisonment. As she had been told to perjure herself by Marylebone police officers, this was hard justice; but what does it say of the justice of Parker of Waddington?

323

In his closing address, Griffith-Jones indicted Ward for moral turpitude rather than immoral earnings. 'The evil,' he insisted, 'goes very deep.' He spoke of 'this doctor, so-called'; harked on Rachman's two-way mirror; and referred to the defendant as a man who plunged 'the very depths of lechery and depravity'. In words that struck hard, he suggested that there was a patriotic duty to convict: 'Members of the jury, you may think that it is in the highest public interest to do your duty and return a verdict of guilty.' Griffith-Jones had an overpowering effect, as a juror told Knightley and Kennedy over twenty years later. 'He called Stephen Ward a thoroughly filthy fellow, and we all knew he must be a thoroughly filthy fellow. Then a string of girls was paraded through the court, and we really didn't know what was going to come next.'[49]

The judge's summing-up was hostile to Ward, as his interruptions had been during the trial. He instructed the jury that the Appeal Court's decision in the Gordon case was extraneous, and must not influence the Ward case, and again quoted Parker's crafty wording which seemed to uphold Keeler's reliability as a witness. He pitched phrases like 'sink of iniquity' and 'filth and vice', applying them to newspaper coverage, but in a way that reflected on Ward. The evidence showed that Ward had subsidised Keeler and Rice-Davies from his earnings as an osteopath rather than taking their earnings from prostitution. Neither woman, indeed, was a common prostitute, street-walker or call-girl. Marshall's summing-up nevertheless directed the jury that Keeler and Rice-Davies came within the legal definition of prostitution: he used a loose interpretation which criminalised tens of thousands of unmarried women who did not share his notions of shame.

Ward heard all this with a quailing heart. For fifteen years he had struggled against the shackles of convention, and now revenge was being taken by conventional people. On this Tuesday evening, after hearing Marshall's summing-up, he telephoned a Home Office assistant with a message for Denning. A few hours later, before the last day of the trial on which Marshall was to conclude his summing-up, he took thirty-five grains of barbiturate at the Chelsea flat of his stalwart ally, Noel Howard-Jones, where he had taken refuge during the trial. He was found in a deep coma by Howard-Jones on the morning of Wednesday 31 July. After the ambulance took away his friend, Howard-Jones wrestled his way upstairs to slam his front door before a scrum of photographers could tumble into the flat.

Marshall refused to halt the trial, finished his address to the jury, which he rushed into reaching verdicts while Ward remained alive. Later that Wednesday, after four and a half hours in the jury room, the jury acquitted Ward of the two pimping charges, and of the accusations involving Vickie Barrett, but found him guilty on the charges relating to Keeler and Clore, and to Rice-Davies and Savundra. Marshall suspended proceedings, stating that he hoped that Ward would be fit enough to attend court to receive his sentence on Tuesday 6 August (after a Bank Holiday weekend). Instead, Ward died three days after his conviction on Saturday 3 August. If justice had been permissible under Parker's regime in the Court of Criminal Appeal, his conviction would have been quashed.[50]

'The case to end all cases,' as Cassandra of the *Daily Mirror* called it, 'snowballed with scandal and shock and squalor and depravity into a situation that for human interest (admittedly often of a gloating and morbid kind) has never been equalled in my time.' Those who sent flowers to the hospital as Ward lay dying were proffering garlands to depravity, Cassandra said. Magnanimity was not a Mirror Group virtue.[51]

Peter Earle's *News of the World* profile of Ward on the day after he died was frank about the dubious evidence on which the conviction rested. 'Look at the muck the Crown had to rely on at the Old Bailey. Lying whores; frightened little scrubbers; irresponsible little tarts.' He admitted, approvingly, that what was on trial was not so much Ward personally as 'moral laxity and sexual decadence. Mr Justice Marshall knew it. Upon his red-cloaked shoulders fell an additional mantle of responsibility. This was a straight fight between good and evil.' Ward was 'a diabolical, malevolent mischief-maker' who lived in a 'cess-pit' and was responsible for 'the stealthy corruption of the innocent, the worsening of the already bad', according to Earle: 'quite literally my flesh crawled sometimes in his presence'. No holds were barred in belabouring a man who could not fight back. 'If he ever did good, I swear it was but a means of doing something else far worse.' The epithets flew from Earle: 'that fiendish laughter of his – those strange protruding blue eyes flashing an inner fire of wicked triumph'; 'demon'; 'devil'; 'depraved'; 'disgusting perversions'. Earle even suggested that Ward's 'snake-like cunning' had been behind the marriage of 'top fashion model' Bronwen Pugh to Lord Astor. This outpouring ended on a vile note: 'The last and biggest crime of all of Ward in the eyes of decent men was that at the pinch – he just couldn't take it.'[52]

The front-page story of the Mirror Group's *People* was fairer than Earle's. 'Ward was no backstreet ponce. Nor was he at the centre of a call-girl ring serving London Society, as rumours had it. His offences in respect to Christine Keeler and Mandy Rice-Davies were minor, almost technical.' In truth he was 'the victim' of misrepresentation of his relations with women: 'He did not exploit them. He did not ravish them . . . Ward was a "kickster", a connoisseur of sensual experience. He would do almost anything for "kicks".'[53]

The Times refused to publish a letter from Hugh Leggatt, Ward's art dealer, stating that he knew dozens of men who had asked him to arrange for Ward to sketch their wives or girlfriends, that Ward had never pounced on these women, and that he could not understand why these men had not volunteered to speak in Ward's defence. Many who had known Ward were appalled by his posthumous vilification. 'Poor Stephen,' said Pamela Cooper, 'became the universal scapegoat: security risk, promoter of orgies for the rich and powerful; consorter with racketeers; pimp who lived off the immoral earnings of the prostitutes he introduced to his clients.

Like the medieval church, which outlawed then hunted lepers, witches, Jews and prostitutes, the press promptly set itself up as the protector of the Ordinary Decent Folk of England against the licentious aristocracy and governing classes.'[54]

As Ward lay dying, a Beaverbrook reporter was sent to Cliveden to pester and humiliate Bill Astor, who was depicted as a man skulking in disgrace. 'Lord Astor cannot entirely retire behind the walls of Cliveden,' the *Daily Express* threatened. The family that had dispensed lavish hospitality in the past was now boycotted: 'Today, Cliveden has plenty of sightseers, but very few visitors.' John Gordon, editor of the *Sunday Express*, brandished a quote which he attributed to Ward: 'Bill could have spoken up for me. His silence crucified me.' Gordon then noted that Cliveden had been given to the National Trust 'to evade death duties in the normal way some of the abnormally rich evade them'. This gave him the pretext for nonsensical spite with which to flurry the Astors: 'The Trust must be disturbed about the disrepute brought upon the estate it owns. What if it decided to cancel the arrangement and return the estate to Lord Astor bringing the shadow of future death duties back upon his family? That would certainly be a popular retribution.'[55]

'In the Profumo Affair,' wrote Wayland Kennet in 1963, 'the political frivolity, the moral myopia and the herd credulity of latter-day Toryism led to convulsion and the sacrifice of one life, of one career and several reputations. What happened was horrible.' A few days after Ward's death, with the press storm abating, Macmillan (revived in optimism) wrote jauntily, 'There is, perhaps, quite a hand to be played yet.'[56]

ELEVEN

Safety Curtain

'The Profumo Affair did Mr Macmillan more harm than anything else in the whole of his administration,' thought his secretary John Wyndham, 'and it did a lasting damage to the Conservative Party.' The Astors's staunch friend Pamela Cooper agreed: 'Not only was Macmillan destroyed, but the Tory Party too, as it then was. It wouldn't be too much to say that the Profumo scandal was the necessary prelude to the new Toryism, based on meritocracy, which would eventually emerge under Margaret Thatcher.' Certainly the scandal sounded a death-knell to the confidence of traditional hierarchical authority. 'The whole Establishment did everything possible to rally round the Profumos, and to try to save them from their fate,' Richard Crossman claimed. The fact that they failed was welcome proof to Anthony Wedgwood Benn that June 1963 marked 'the decay of the old British Establishment'.[1]

Hailsham considered Denning's appointment to enquire into the circumstances of Profumo's resignation 'a panic measure' and 'ghastly error' which 'should never be repeated'. For once he was right. A fortnight into the inquiry, Macmillan contemplated resignation over its repercussions: 'If things go badly with the Denning Report, there will be no choice. I shall have been destroyed by the vices of some of my colleagues.' By 2 August, Denning had forewarned Macmillan he had established that Ernest Marples, the Minister of Transport, had resorted to prostitutes. Denning also found that Denzil Freeth, a young MP who cut a dash as a Commons speaker and was Hailsham's deputy at the Ministry of

Science, had three years earlier enjoyed some hours of intimacy with a man whom he had met at 'a party of a homosexual character'. Denning omitted references to Marples and Freeth on the basis that their conduct, though 'discreditable', did not jeopardise national security. Marples survived in government, but Freeth – who hit the bottle briefly under the strain of his solitary, precarious and secretive existence – left the government, and did not seek re-election in 1964. He became a City stockbroker and Kensington *bon viveur*, dying nearly half a century later as a respected High Churchman.[2]

Radcliffe's tribunal had found a scapegoat in Herbert Pennells, civil assistant to the Director of Naval Intelligence, who had died at the age of sixty-three shortly before Vassall's arrest. Pennells was presented as an industrious but unimaginative official who proved 'remiss' in selecting men to serve in Russia. Denning took Radcliffe's strictures on a man who was safely dead as a model for his report; but his investigatory methods were disgraceful, his deductions slipshod and his report-writing nastier than Radcliffe's. He penned his report, with a copy of the Bible close to hand, in tabloid-newspaper prose with chapter titles such as 'The Slashing and the Shooting' and 'The Man in the Mask'. Published on 26 September, it sold over 100,000 copies in a few days.

Although Denning hardly mentioned Ward's trial, he drew on the prosecution speeches. The report is awash with the spite of a lascivious, conceited old man. He cited allegations from Keeler and other 'girls', but either did not read the trial transcript or suppressed the rebuttals of their allegations by defence counsel. He took the verdict of the trial as unchallengeable, although it would probably have been overturned on appeal if Ward had lived. Several reputable friends of Ward volunteered to testify to Denning, but none were called. Instead, the dead man was treated as a repugnant, irredeemable wretch. The report's third chapter is entitled 'Stephen Ward Helping the Russians', and gives only half the story of his work as Ivanov's messenger. The Foreign Office asked that references to schemes to subvert foreign diplomats be underplayed. In consequence, Denning omitted MI5's plan to use Ward in a honey-trap to decoy Ivanov into defection. This omission was desirable on security grounds, but Denning thus suppressed the facts of Ward's cooperation with MI5 instructions and his reports to Wagstaffe ('Woods'). In other respects, Denning regurgitated his Security Service briefings in a trusting if not gullible spirit. He also reported that MI5 knew Ward as 'the provider of popsies for rich people', managing 'a call-girl racket', although Ward did neither of these things.[3]

Denning's prurient thrill is almost audible as one reads his calumnies of Ward. Civil servants working in nearby offices when Keeler and Rice-Davies were questioned recall the *frisson* in the corridors. He sent his shorthand writers out of the room while he questioned some of the young women about their business. A dominatrix who explained that she never had intercourse with the men she flogged was asked by Denning why her clients had these tastes: he may have squirmed inwardly with tut-tutting excitement as she replied that 'it went back to their nannies. Bus drivers and people like that who don't have nannies don't ask you to whip them.' Denning was avid for salacious rumours, and sinners to pillory. When he interviewed George Wigg, he asked if he knew anything about the Duke of Argyll's divorce, which had nothing to do with security.[4]

Referring to a photograph published in the *News of the World* on 3 February 1963 of Keeler in a bikini ('the slightest of swimming garbs,' Denning called it), her languorous arms stretched behind her head, the Law Lord commented: 'most people seeing it would readily infer the avocation of Christine Keeler'. Did he mean that all models who posed in bikinis were whores, or that all women who allowed themselves to be photographed in swimwear were sluts? It is moreover untrue that Keeler was a prostitute in 1961, when Profumo met her, or indeed in 1963 when she was photographed, or thereafter. Denning prided himself on what he called his 'sophisticated mind', but as Lord Annan observed, 'the sanctimonious tone of Denning's report suggested that, like many a judge, he was not all that aware of how men and women behave'.[5]

Denning wrote that Ward 'seduced girls', as if the osteopath was a bold bad baronet with twirling moustaches called Sir Jasper, ruining simple, trusting, innocent milkmaids. 'He used to pick up pretty girls of the age of sixteen or seventeen, often from nightclubs,' Denning wrote, and 'procured them to be mistresses for his influential friends.' This assertion masked the fact that despite interviewing over a hundred witnesses, the police only brought two charges of procuring, on both of which the jury had acquitted Ward. 'He catered also for those of his friends who had perverted tastes. There is evidence that he was ready to arrange for whipping and other sadistic performances.' The 'evidence', to use Denning's word, came from the least reliable witness at Ward's trial, Vickie Barrett; and again the jury acquitted him on this count. Denning indicted Ward as Keeler's exploiter in a prim, snobbish phrase: 'He introduced her to many men, sometimes men of rank and position, with whom she had sexual intercourse.' Denning depicted Ward almost as a white slaver who corrupted Keeler with 'the drug Indian hemp and she became addicted to it'. The truth is that Ward deplored her use of the drug.[6]

Twenty years after writing his report, Denning continued his vituperative falsification. On television in 1984 he maintained that Ward was the most evil man whom he had ever met. A few years later he repeated that Ward was 'really wicked', 'filthy' and steeped in 'vice'. Ward's flat was a 'corrupt, immoral set-up' with 'all these two-way mirrors and all that sort of thing' (Ward's flat had no two-way mirrors, as Marshall had conceded in his summing-up). During the 1980s, Denning still hankered after the idea that lawyers could inhibit fornication: while Master of the Rolls he rejected the appeal of a young woman who had been expelled from a teaching training course after taking her boyfriend to her bedroom, declaring that it was inconceivable that decent parents would wish their children to be taught by such a woman. He was so keen to suppress criticism of the Ward trial that he advocated changes in libel laws to enable the families of the dead lawyers to sue authors who brought them into ridicule or contempt. In retirement in 1987 he insisted in a tetchy letter to *The Times* 'that Stephen Ward was fairly and properly prosecuted, tried and convicted. He was not "framed" by the police. The charges against him were not "bogus". The conduct of the trial was beyond reproach.' This querulous bluster was published with perhaps intentional irony under the caption: 'Ward case and libelling the dead'.[7]

Denning inflicted lasting harm on his country. His report criticised the law officers Hobson and Rawlinson, as well as Redmayne, Deedes and Macleod, for concentrating on whether Profumo had committed adultery when they confronted him. Denning maintained that their test should have been whether his conduct would lead ordinary people to believe that he had committed adultery. In doing so, he drew an analogy from divorce law, whereby a wife had just cause for leaving her husband not only if he had committed adultery, but also if she had reasonable cause to believe that he was adulterous. Lord Dilhorne advised Macmillan, apropos Denning's conclusions: 'It would be opening the door to McCarthyism if Ministers could be hounded from public life because an influential section of the people held a reasonable belief – based on rumour and gossip – that a Minister had misconducted himself.' Hobson similarly wrote that *pace* Denning, 'people, including wives, partners and colleagues, ought to be condemned, or at least disposed of, if there are reasonable grounds for believing that they have done wrong, even if you accept from them that they have not in fact erred.' Five years later Harold Wilson's solicitor Lord Goodman called Denning's inquiry, with its focus on rumour, 'the most startling invasion of privacy in recent years'. Denning's upholding of the primacy of cheap suspicions inaugurated a period when newspapers could publicise moronic gossip, hound and humiliate their victims by innuendo and accusation, treat paid informers as heroes, solemnify hoaxes and turn ill-fame into a lucrative commodity.[8]

In despoiling Ward's memory, Denning set the tone for succeeding generations. When Keeler was tried for perjury and conspiracy to obstruct the course of justice, her counsel's rhetoric might have been taken from Denning: 'Dr Ward was a man of charm, he had great artistic flair, and he won his way into a snob world of power, taking with him this young girl. He groomed Keeler.' He did not dwell on the conditions that had victimised her: reared in a railway carriage without mains water or electricity; ill-educated, malnourished; scared by her stepfather; exploited by the fathers of the children she babysat; only employed in London because of her looks. Ward had been considerate and unselfish to the feckless girl who had been exploited by the US airman who impregnated her, the ruffians who hit and screwed her, the police who manipulated and broke her, the false friends who battened on her notoriety.[9]

Tendentious references to the events of 1963 persist in books: journalists spread their casual inaccuracies. In 2010, the *Daily Telegraph* described Keeler as 'procured for Lord Astor's "Cliveden Set" by Stephen Ward, an osteopath with a sideline in high-class prostitution'. The truth, however, is that Keeler was never procured for Lord Astor or his guests, and Ward did not have an auxiliary income as a pimp. Another national newspaper, in 1999, listed 'Christine Keeler, Call Girl' as one of the 'Accidental Heroes of the Twentieth Century', though a less fortunate or inspiring heroine cannot be imagined.[10]

On 8 October 1963, a fortnight after publication of Denning's report, Macmillan was admitted to hospital with inflammation of the prostate gland. The stress of recent months had shaken his health. Always prone to anxieties about those ailments that Turgenev named the calling-cards of death, he reacted badly when told that he had a benign or malignant tumour. Next day, drugged, suffering physical pain and mental distress, convinced that he had cancer, he wrote a resignation letter to the Queen, and drafted a letter to be read by Home to the imminent party conference at Blackpool explaining that he was too weak to lead the Tories into the next general election. This impulsive haste was unnecessary. Within a day, Macmillan's physicians had confirmed that he neither had cancer nor must retire through poor health. Minimal reflection showed that such an announcement was bound to throw the conference into disarray. When Home visited the hospital, Macmillan told him of the intended resignation and urged him to become a prime ministerial candidate. Home made no kindly effort to dissuade the sick, muddled man from quick resignation: there were no calming or temporising suggestions from the Foreign Secretary. Instead, Home made a ruthless killing of the Macmillan premiership. He started the train of events whereby he reached Downing Street by hastening to Blackpool, where he wrecked the conference by reading out the resignation message before the Prime Minister could be dissuaded by wiser heads.

Home's was the act neither of a disinterested friend nor of a man indifferent to the succession. He later claimed that he was surprised when Macmillan urged him to disclaim his earldom and contest the leadership; but Macmillan had mooted Home's succession to him a few days earlier. Other insiders had foreseen it as a possibility. In 1961, Normanbrook, the Cabinet Secretary whom the *Daily Mirror* decried, had been asked who should succeed as Prime Minister if some ill befell Macmillan. 'Alec Home,' replied Normanbrook: 'he is the only one who would do it well.' A year later, after the Cuban crisis, Macmillan had warned Rab Butler, who saw himself as the likeliest next Prime Minister: 'There is only one Minister now who could displace me, and that is Alec Home . . . Alec had some special genius, probably from his Lambton mother.' Home's succession seemed impossible in November 1962, for a peer had not held the premiership for sixty years. However, legislation which came into force on 31 July 1963 enabled members of the House of Lords to disclaim their peerages and stand for the Commons. This enabled Hailsham, after Home's announcement at Blackpool, to declare his candidature for the premiership and renunciation of his viscountcy. Macleod, the Tory minister whom Wilson most feared, was too tarnished by his part in the late-night ministerial conclave that weakly quizzed Profumo to be *papabile*. Hailsham, like Maudling, spoiled his hopes by an ill-judged speech: Hailsham brayed and Maudling baulked like two mismatched mules hitched together on their way to market. Butler's interventions, too, were stumbling. When Boyd-Carpenter dined with Colonel 'Juby' Lancaster MP, his host interrupted a discussion of leadership prospects. Didn't they know, he asked, that Home would be chosen: 'It's all arranged,' he said. Nigel Birch, asked about the succession, replied: 'I'm an Alec Home man. There aren't any other possibilities. He's going to get it.'[11]

Dilhorne, his haunches perched uncomfortably on a creaking chair besides an unmade bed in his small, stuffy room in the Imperial hotel, interviewed Cabinet members, and noted their preference as Macmillan's successor. His manner was correct, but it was evident that he did not share John Boyd-Carpenter's choice, Maudling. Elsewhere, Redmayne polled other ministers. Reginald Bevins, the self-styled Tory democrat who was Postmaster General, recalled giving his preferences: 'Maudling and Butler in that order. Long pause. We looked at each other. "What about the peers – Alec and the other one?" No pause. I said: "Not at any bloody price." That was an unfortunate answer, all carefully recorded on Martin Redmayne's foolscap.' After Home had won, and the other candidates were bested, a young backbencher, Paul Channon, tried to console Butler. 'This last cruel blow brought about by Nigel Birch and Macmillan relations when you were ahead in every poll will merely show how decadent the Tory Government and Party had become in 1963 and how extraordinary Mr Macmillan's decisions had become in his last few months of office.'[12]

Home's elderly mother, who was a Labour voter, told a television interviewer that he had been a very ordinary child, and that Butler should have bested him. His aunt, Lady Ellesmere, said he was an *extraordinary* choice; his uncle Lord Durham said it was a disaster. Sir Alec Douglas-Home (as he became after disclaiming his earldom) was Prime Minister for a year: he proved to have more resolve and resilience than Butler, Hailsham and Maudling could have mustered, and lost the general election of October 1964 by only four seats. David Butler's masterful study of the election concluded: 'It was the *Daily Mirror* rather than Mr Wilson which sustained the Labour campaign to a polling day climax.' The Cudlipp-King newspapers ran stories about Rachmanism, stop-go economics, underspending in schools and hospitals, defence muddles, impoverished pensioners, and Tory tiredness. Supremely, they capitalised on the message that they had instilled during the Profumo scandal: that Britain faced a modernisation crisis which was class-bound; that the Establishment, headed by a disclaimed fourteenth earl with expansive grouse-moors, was a travesty of power; that the old order must be hurried away in tumbrils.[13]

Once the general election was launched in 1964, Cudlipp sent his star interviewer Donald Zec to meet Wilson. The resulting profile, published over two days, was the market-branding of Wilson by the *Mirror* that swung the election for Labour. The message had been easier to implant since June 1963. 'I did not get a pheasant's eye view of him behind a twelve-bore gun nor did I face him in the Edwardian gloom of some Top People's Club,' Zec wrote. Wilson took him into the kitchen of his Hampstead Garden Suburb home ('the sort of home you'd find anywhere . . . in Britain'), and gave him a cup of tea from a tea-pot embossed with a print of the Forth Bridge. 'If a home reflects the man – as, say, a grouse moor might show up the marksman from the boys – then Mr Wilson's untidy but comfortable habitat is a real give-away . . . Up-ended plank on wheels in overgrown garden, former property of younger son,

Giles. Rain-faded note on defunct doorbell says "Please knock". There was homely virtue, the Labour message seemed to say, in doorbells that did not work and an improvised go-cart hammered out of cast-off wood: none of the effete knick-knacks with which the Profumos, say, had arrayed their primrose and eau-de-nil drawing room. To emphasise Labour's pretence of anti-materialism, Wilson told Zec: 'We in the Labour Party absolutely reject the insulting doctrine that the British People are only interested in gambling, making money, new washing machines and the latest refrigerator. Look at the magnificent work being done by Oxfam, the "Freedom From Hunger" campaign, War on Want, and the societies for helping spastics.' He turned on his patriotic indignation, too. 'We are a great country,' he said angrily. 'Let nobody sell us short. But we could be a hell of a lot greater.'[14]

In the *Daily Mirror*'s next issue, Zec continued his profile interview of Wilson, 'this former council schoolboy, born at No 4, Warneford Road, Milnsbridge, Huddersfield (twelve shillings a week, plus rates)'. Wilson believed that future battles 'must be fought less on the playing fields of Eton – more in the science laboratory', according to Zec. 'He does say there is no place in politics for the gentlemanly amateur, now as obsolete as that snob game, Gentlemen versus Players.' Wilson was earnest about re-drawing Britain's social landscape. 'Land racketeers, their wings severely clipped, will not be so happy in it. Those Etonians who still believe in the survival of the smuggest will want no part of it. Boardroom "Blimps" who slid into power through money and influence may gnash their gold teeth at it. *But the young, the dynamic, the brainy, the well-intentioned and the just will flourish in it. So promises Mr Harold Wilson.'* Wilson believed that the election would be won by the votes of 'young people, the courting and the newlyweds' who sought affordable homes: 'House prices have doubled in six years and land racketeering has run riot.' A Labour priority, said Wilson, would be 'curbing the racketeer'. A few years later he was mired in the notorious slag-heap land deal, and recommending dicey wideboys for public honours. In 1964, though, he promised the 'young citizens' who were *Daily Mirror* readers, "*The squalid property deals which merely produce vast profits and ultimately send up the prices of people's home have no place in a new Britain*".[15]

The *Daily Mirror* campaign message was reinforced daily. 'Sir Alec, with his comic knickerbockers and clicking teeth peering over half a pair of glasses, is absolutely convinced that the women of Britain are going to carry him forward to victory,' wrote Marjorie Proops in the issue of 7 October. 'I am sick to the bone of . . . Alec and all the rest of the Tories who have sat on their smug rears in Westminster for thirteen endless, weary years.' Next day there was an array of quotes from modish reformers. 'I will vote Labour,' declared Alan Sillitoe, 'because I believe in equality. Equality is a cliché, except to those who haven't got it.' A. J. Ayer was voting Labour because the party 'will put science to a more intelligent use, and are more likely to bring about social reform – better than voting Conservative because I'm-all-right-Jack'. The jazz singer and club owner Annie Ross told the *Mirror*: 'I will vote Labour because I hate class distinction.'[16]

On election night in October 1964, Paul Raymond's Revuebar had a gimmick. After voting closed, five naked showgirls appeared on stage, each with a ribbon in their hair. The one with the blue ribbon represented the Conservatives, the pink ribbon Labour, yellow for Liberal, red for Communists and white for independents. As the result in each constituency was declared, the girl representing the victorious party took a chiffon scarf of the right colour and tied it round herself. None of the girls wanted to be the Communist, not from political scruples, but because they did not want to be shivering without a single scarf for the whole night. The pink chiffon scarves won.

Only the most partisan spirit could say that the new administration, with its mix of sincere idealists, quarrelsome intellectuals, crafty trade union time-servers, bullies and small-minded envy-ridden puritans, was more effective, or less prone to cronyism and trickery, than the preceding government, with its practitioners of noblesse oblige, Old Etonians, retired officers, glossy playboys, bullies and expense-account company directors. One network of egotists, with an intricate history of mutual obligations, murky pacts and tacit promises, was replaced by an opposing alliance, no more qualified or efficient, held together by similar bargains, ambition and vanity. The notion that the change of government in 1964 brought purity or progress was naïve.

George Wigg was rewarded by Wilson with the appointment of Postmaster General, with direct access to him on security matters. By dint of Westminster intrigues, melodramatic antics in Downing Street and hectoring late-night telephone calls, he pummelled Wilson for several years, until his harassed punchbag exiled him to the House of Lords. Subsequently he developed a senescent taste for kerb-crawling in Park Lane. In 1976 he was in the dock denying charges of insulting behaviour and endangering the peace after repeatedly accosting women from his car. Wigg protested that he had been looking for a street news vendor selling late editions. *Private Eye* photographed him getting out of a car in a dirty raincoat, with an urgent look on his face, and a bubble caption saying, 'I'm desperate for a good *Evening Standard*'.

Cecil King's Rolls-Royce had a flagstaff inserted behind the Silver Lady emblem so that he could fly a Red Flag, inscribed 'Vote Labour', during the 1964 general election. The mistrustful alliance between him and Wilson fissured after the election, when Wilson, who had previously announced that he would not recommend the Queen to create further hereditary titles, offered King a life peerage. King retorted that he wanted an earldom, so as to out-rank his uncles Northcliffe and Rothermere, to say nothing of other newspaper proprietors, Camrose, Kemsley and Southwood. Wilson reiterated that no hereditary peerages would be created at his recommendation. King then produced precedents for life earldoms (Darlington, Walsingham and Yarmouth were all granted as life earldoms in the eighteenth century), but

339

to no avail. His applications however ended with his termagant wife being made a dame. King was the man of whom Anthony Sampson said admiringly in 1962: 'he dislikes Eton, titles, pomposity and humbug in high places, and he loves attacking the Establishment'. His megalomania led to his expulsion from the Mirror Group in 1968. 'I do not feel I have ever been fully stretched – and I have never been allowed to serve my country as I could have wished,' he told me in 1972 at a time when, he complained, 'newspapers are full of trivial news and irrelevant comment'.[17]

One person to prosper from the scandals of 1963 was Samuel Herbert, whose strenuous, pitiless fixing of evidence was rewarded with promotion from chief inspector to superintendent. He died of a heart attack at the age of forty-eight in 1966. His character as a shameless rascal was fortified by the posthumous discovery that he had £30,000 squirrelled away – a small fortune for a policeman at that time. This was the sum that Keeler said she had been offered by John Lewis to secure Ward's conviction and reduce Macmillan's government to a rubble heap.

Keeler was treated viciously after Ward's death. On 4 August, the Mirror Group's second Sunday family paper, *The People*, carried the front-page headline: 'KEELER, THE SHAMELESS SLUT', and called her 'an empty-headed trollop, skilled only at using her body to bewitch and betray'. 'She smoked marijuana and loved orgies', seldom washed (although it also claimed 'she sat in a bath drinking champagne with a boyfriend'), had soiled underwear, and 'boasted of picking up down-and-outs in the street and taking one of the scruffiest of them to sleep with her'. They found a man who claimed, as a butler, to have served coffee to Profumo and Keeler in bed together. The article claimed John Hamilton-Marshall was her lover – which would have been against his nature – and that they lived together in Sheffield Terrace, Campden Hill. A friend had written a reference to their landlady there, *The People* pretended: 'If you want your house turned into a brothel, with coloured layabouts all over the place, drug orgies and all that jazz, accept Miss Keeler as a tenant.' Even Louis Blom-Cooper, a jurist who epitomised compassionate urbanity, in his damning commentary on Denning's report, dismissed Keeler and Rice-Davies as 'adolescent drabs, for whom little public sympathy should be wasted'.[18]

On 5 September (three weeks after Ward was cremated with only six mourners daring to show their faces), Keeler and Paula Hamilton-Marshall were arrested and charged with perjury and conspiracy to obstruct the course of justice by not revealing the presence of Camacchio and Fenton in their flat at the time when Gordon was put in a police frame for attacking Keeler. There were preliminary hearings at Marylebone Magistrates Court in October, a sensational trial opened in November, and on 6 December, Keeler was sentenced to nine months in Holloway prison. 'Tales of kicks, thumps, and slaps, bribes, and sex orgies, lies and blackmail threats, kept alive the spirit of the "Ward *galère*",' reported the *Glasgow Herald* gleefully.[19]

In order to confuse matters further, Robin Drury (who was months away from bankruptcy) was induced to testify that Keeler had told him that her bruises and black eye were inflicted by an unknown woman with whom she participated in an afterdinner orgy in the Hamilton-Marshall flat. Although John Hamilton-Marshall – bedecked in a pink candy-striped shirt, black satin waistcoat and blue collarless felt jacket – testified that he, not Gordon, had brawled with Keeler (testimony that the police had discouraged him from volunteering at Gordon's trial), the police and prosecution case focussed on the hiding of Fenton and Camacchio. They did not disavow the false story that Gordon was her assailant, but implied that there was truth in it, for there could be no suggestion after the Ward trial that police officers coerced its prime witnesses into giving false evidence in that or

341

related cases. Nor did Keeler's counsel complicate or prejudice her defence by mentioning police entrapment or police-incited perjury in her original evidence about Gordon.*

What is striking about October 1963 is that while Cabinet Ministers donned homburgs, fobs and morning suits, disclaimed peerages, delivered dud perorations at Blackpool, and promised with lifeless, orotund phrases to restore normative stability, a kid pop impresario like Alex Wharton, and rootless young risk-takers such as Drury, Hamilton-Marshall and Mann – the foot-scouts of that inchoate, unruly, destabilising, protean phenomenon that was to be called 'Swinging London' – traipsed into the witness box. These two social spheres, distant though they seemed, had converged during the modernisation crisis of 1963.

The *Daily Sketch* marked Keeler's release in 1964 from Holloway prison, where she suffered cruelly, by publishing her telephone number: thereafter she was deluged with abusive telephone calls. When in 1965 she married, she was ruthlessly doorstepped by photographers, who scrabbled round like crabs in a bucket snapping at her. Keeler's life has been unpleasantly chequered since then. She has collaborated in several unreliable memoirs. In one she depicted the early 1960s a time when 'Dukes and Ministers fought side by side by sadists, masochists, homosexuals and lesbians against the barriers of a frustrated society'. In another, she indicted Ward as 'a spymaster' involved in placing Moscow's double agent, Sir Roger Hollis, as Director General of MI5. 'My Svengali,' she called Ward: 'a spider with a malevolent web,' who

---

*John Hamilton-Marshall was arrested in Paddington for a breaking-in offence in December 1967, rearrested while on remand in Stoke Newington in March 1968 in possession of stolen silver and charged with burglary, and then committed to a mental hospital because of drug addiction. He was part of a gang involved in stealing paintings from the dramatist Christopher Fry, silverware from the architectural historian Alec Clifton-Taylor, ceramics worth over £10,000 from Lady Mountbatten's nephew Noel Cunningham-Reid, and other burglaries. The investigation led to the prosecution of a police officer for corruption and conspiracy to pervert the course of justice. Hamilton-Marshall committed suicide by carbon monoxide poisoning in an open-backed truck in a wood near Winding Hill at Selling in Kent, in 1984, aged forty-three.

'would have killed me as easily as light my cigarette. He stitched me up, stitch after very neat stitch. He was bad.'[20]

Shortly before the general election of 1964, the Astors went to stay at the Cipriani in Venice, where Profumo eighteen months earlier had forfeited his bluff. Bill Astor spent some days sketching at Freya Stark's nearby home. 'He is such a poor little waif of a man,' she wrote. 'I sometimes feel it is just some rather expensive clothes walking around and no one in particular inside them. But she is rare and beautiful, and *good*, with lovely honest eyes which she never plays with. They are rather a touching couple, he always with a well-intentioned but silly value and she quietly putting it right.' A few days later Bill Astor had a heart attack. He became a wretched invalid, and died two years later. His daughter, who was aged four at the time, later worked for Winston's Wish, the charity that helps bereaved children.[21]

Clore was not publicly identified as the 'Charles' who featured in the Ward trial until after his death in 1979. He embarked on a course of outstanding philanthropy by establishing the Clore Foundation in the general election year of 1964. Amongst its benefactions to cultural institutions and Jewish causes, the most famous is the Clore Gallery housing the Turner collection at Tate Britain.[22]

During the summer of 1963, the Territorial Army headquarters in Shropshire, where Profumo had unveiled the foundation stone during the previous winter, applied for the inscription to be re-cut with Profumo's name erased. 'This stone was meant to be something of an inspiration to the young fellows,' explained Colonel Guy Thornycroft, vice-chairman of Shropshire TA. 'Now we think it better to strike out Mr Profumo's name. It would be a permanent reminder of Mr Profumo.' Yet the Profumo legacy was not easily erased. For forty years, whenever he and his wife entered a room, all conversation stopped for a moment. He was chastened for a time, but never tamed. In his desk he stored ballpoint pens adorned with pictures of naked women. The conventional view is that he expiated his misdoings during decades of voluntary work in the East End of London. Certainly, and deservedly, he was rehabilitated. The Queen Mother remained his champion. At a dinner in her honour, sitting between her and a seventeen-year-old Guinness heiress, the old satyr whispered to the latter during the first course: 'Ever been fucked by a seventy-year-old? No? You should try it.'[23]

The Profumo Affair was not only a body-blow to Macmillan's government. It was the death-blow of an England that was deferential and discreet. Home said in June 1963 that he was 'disgusted and angry' at the way that one man's lapse had impugned the belief that British public life was conducted 'by men who have the highest sense of integrity and public duty'.[24] That summer inaugurated the raucous period when authority figures were denied respect even when they deserved it. Denning's recommendation that ministers should become suspicious snoopers on one another, and that rash, random rumours ought to be solemnly investigated, performed euthanasia on notions of privacy. Until 1963, newspapers protected politicians who were detected in adultery, or caught in the bushes with guardsmen. After 1963, Fleet Street's emetic brew of guilty joys, false tears, nasty surprises and dirty surmises seemed limitless. From the moment of Profumo's resignation, newspapers started deploying outrageous headlines for non-existent stories: 'PRINCE PHILIP AND THE PROFUMO SCANDAL – RUMOUR UTTERLY UNFOUNDED', boomed a *Daily Mirror* headline of June 1963, above paragraphs that failed to specify the imaginary rumour.

There were strenuous efforts after the summer of 1963 to pretend that nothing had changed. Ward had been hounded to death; Profumo was shunned; Keeler went to prison; Astor became a crumpled ruin; Rachman's name coined an unpleasant new epithet. Villainy had been punished; transgression had been anathematised; the national morality based on newspaper pillorying had been raised to the level of auto-da-fé. Although Labour strategists kept alive the sense that the scandal had been proof of Establishment corruption, the general mood was to shrug off what had happened, as if awakening from a lurid, turbulent nightmare.

In fact the trauma had been too horrendous for the status quo to be restored. Traditional notions of deference had been weakening for years, but after June 1963 they became mortally sick. Authority – however disinterested, well-qualified and experienced – was increasingly greeted with suspicion rather than trust. Respect and deference, even when merited, were increasingly seen as a species of snobbery. Notoriety became a money-spinner: it became profitable to behave destructively. If Keeler had been born thirty-five years later, she would have starred on *Celebrity Big Brother* and consulted her publicist every time her footballer boyfriend knocked her about.

People's visions were distorted forever by the outlandish novelties of the summer of 1963. Afterwards everything still looked reassuringly familiar, but was weirdly twisted. It was as if a stolid householder – one of Profumo's Stratford constituents, say – had left his house at a summer dusk to post a letter in the red pillarbox on the corner of his neat privet-lined street; had murmured 'Good Evening' to the vicar out with his spaniel and sidestepped the whistling schoolboy on his Raleigh bike; and returning a few minutes later with the assurance of a woman going to *The Sound of Music* for the twentieth time and knowing every song, did not at first notice that his cosy living-room had swapped places with the living-room in the Windolene-burnished mirror hanging above the hearth; and that the air was hazy with unnameable secrets and squalid grudges.

ACKNOWLEDGEMENTS

Sieska Cowdrey, Patric Dickinson (Clarenceux King of Arms), David Kynaston, Gina Thomas and Richard Thorpe have provided me with written materials that helped in the writing of this book. Mark Amory, Horatia Harrod and Anna Vaux, as review editors of the *Spectator*, *Sunday Telegraph* and *Times Literary Supplement*, have sent me books that have informed my own. So, too, have the memoirs that I received as a judge of the J. R. Ackerley Memorial Prize: I thank my fellow judges, Georgie Hammick, Peter Parker and Colin Spencer, for recruiting me to their counsels. The late Colin Matthew and Sir Brian Harrison, as successive editors of the *Oxford Dictionary of National Biography*, revived my boyhood interest in the Profumo Affair by commissioning me to write entries on Henry Brooke, Charles Clore, Jack Cotton, Perec Rachman, Emil Savundra, Stephen Ward and Edward Sugden (the abortionist who provided the pills that killed Ward).

Kind friends – Miranda Carter, Edward Davenport and Alexander Games – read draft chapters of this book with lynx-like attention. Each of them made shrewd, vigilant and imaginative suggestions which I have gratefully adopted. As they have more arduous and demanding lives than mine, the time they allotted to me was especially generous. My editor at Harper Press, Martin Redfern, let me run on a long leash, but brought me sharply to heel when I went too far. His combination of easy tolerance and sharp curbs make him a delightful employer.

I thank the Hon. Rupert Carington, on behalf of the Carington family, for permission to quote from the diaries of the Marquess of Lincolnshire; the executors of the Literary Estate of Lord Dacre of Glanton for permission to quote from the writings of Hugh Trevor-Roper; Lord Gage for a letter sent to him; and the Harry Ransom Center of the University of Texas at Austin, for extracts from Sybille Bedford's unpublished account of Stephen Ward's trial, 'The Worst We Can Do'. Other extracts are reproduced from the archive of the late Harold Macmillan, Earl of Stockton, by kind permission of the Trustees of the Harold Macmillan Book Trust. Lord Astor has agreed to my quotations from his father's letters, and was generous in correcting a few nuances and details after reading the manuscript draft of chapter three.

Parts of this book were researched or drafted in the London Library, where the amenities remain, as ever, indispensable. I am grateful to Jeremy Lewis, the biographer of David Astor, who was proprietor of *Twentieth Century*, the quarterly seminar magazine which I found on the open shelves of the London Library, and which proved so informative. Richard Astor has kindly acceded to my use of his father's unpublished correspondence.

When the possibility of writing a book about the events of 1963 was only dimly imaginable, I had conversations with several bystanders of the Profumo Affair, who had witnessed events at Cliveden, Notting Hill or elsewhere. As these talks were social or informal, it is better not to name my informants or to provide the sources for certain details. However, it is right to thank Nicolas Barker, the late John Grigg, Dominic Harrod and my kindest boyhood mentor, Alan Walter Pearce (1925–95), who all described to me incidents that are recounted in this book.

I am grateful to the Bodleian Library, Oxford (papers of the Marquess of Lincolnshire, the Earl of Stockton, Earl Winterton, the Earl of Woolton, Viscount Crookshank); British Library (papers of Sir Edward Hamilton and the Earl of Cromer as Lord Chamberlain); Christ Church, Oxford (papers of Lord Dacre of Glanton); Harry Ransom Center at the University of Texas at Austin (Sybille Bedford typescript); House of Lords Record Office (papers of Lord Beaverbrook); King's College, Cambridge (papers of Lord Annan); the National Archives (Assizes records, and Directorate of Public Prosecutions, Home Office, Metropolitan Police, Premier's and Security Service files); Reading University Library (papers of Viscountess Astor); and Trinity College, Cambridge (papers of Lord Butler of Saffron Walden).

The working papers of the Wolfenden Committee on Homosexual Offences and Prostitution, which are an important source for this book, were first released by the Home Office to the National Archives as the result of my representations in the late 1980s. My book *Sex, Death and Punishment* (1990) was the first to quote them. I mention this as other writers have since claimed to have been the first to use this material, or even to have obtained its release. The police file on Charles Clore quoted in these pages was opened (with timid redactions) following my application under the Freedom of Information Act. The redactions in the dossiers on Rachman held in the National Archives are equally silly: one chunk of blackened text, for example, tries to protect the reputation of Rachman's 'winkler' Norbert Rondel (1927–2009), an ex-rabbinical student who once bit off a pimp's ear in a fight and gouged one of his eyes. It was at his gambling den, the Apartment in Rupert Street, that Rondel organised the Spaghetti House robbery in Knightsbridge in 1975 during which restaurant staff were held hostage for 122 hours. Rondel, who was acquitted at trial as the result of jury-nobbling, became a secondhand car dealer, grew the beard of a shaman, and liked to stand on his head.

Hundreds of words would be needed if I was sufficiently to thank Jenny Davenport and Christopher Phipps, who together incited and honed my writing of this book. Nothing would be possible without them: Phipps, additionally, has compiled an index for which every discriminating reader will be grateful.

Kensington & Le Meygris, May 2012

NOTES

Overture

1. Peter Forster, 'Peeling the Politicians', *Spectator*, 9 October 1959, p. 469; David Butler and Richard Rose, *The British General Election of 1959* (1960), p. 89.
2. Richard Crossman, *Diaries of a Cabinet Minister*, III (1977), pp. 206–07.

PART ONE: CAST

One: Prime Minister

1. Crossbencher, 'Macmillan prepares to go', *Sunday Express*, 2 December 1956, p. 6; Lord Rawlinson of Ewell, *A Price Too High* (1989), pp. 71–2; Richard Cockett (ed.), *My Dear Max: The Letters of Brendan Bracken to Lord Beaverbrook 1925–58* (1990), p. 199.
2. Philip Williams (ed.), *The Diary of Hugh Gaitskell 1945–56* (1983), p. 450.
3. D. R. Thorpe, *Supermac* (2010), pp. 53–8; Alistair Horne, *But What Do You Actually Do?* (2011), p. 262.
4. Diary of Harold Macmillan, 1 and 10 November 1959, dep d 37, ff 60 and 66, Bodleian Library.
5. Mark DeWolfe Howe (ed.), *Holmes-Laski Letters*, I (1953), p. 676; Grover Smith (ed.), *Letters of Aldous Huxley* (1969), p. 379.
6. Stuart Ball (ed.), *Parliament and Politics in the Age of Baldwin and MacDonald: The Headlam Diaries 1923–35* (1992), p. 296; 'Harold Macmillan', *National Review*, 150 (March 1958), p. 105; Earl of Swinton,

Sixty Years of Power (1966), p. 175; Lord Egremont, *Wyndham and Children First* (1968), p. 193.

7. Stuart Ball (ed.), *Parliament and Politics in the Age of Churchill and Attlee: the Headlam Diaries 1935–51* (1999), p. 209; Egremont, *Wyndham and Children*, p. 193.

8. John Barnes and David Nicholson (eds), *The Empire at Bay: the Leo Amery Diaries 1929–45* (1988), p. 846; Egremont, *Wyndham and Children*, p. 194.

9. Sir Robert Rhodes James, *Bob Boothby* (1991), pp. 41, 126.

10. Anthony Powell, *The Acceptance World* (1955), p. 171.

11. Rhodes James, *Boothby*, pp. 118, 120.

12. Charlotte Mosley (ed.), *In Tearing Haste: Letters Between Deborah Devonshire and Patrick Leigh Fermor* (2008), p. 52; Peter Catterall (ed.), *Macmillan Diaries*, II (2011), pp. 99, 182, 228.

13. Harold Wilson, House of Commons debates, 17 June 1963, Vol. 679, col. 44.

14. Robert Boothby to Lady Cynthia Mosley, 14 September 1932, Boothby papers M/689, quoted in Thorpe, *Supermac*, p. 97; Dorothy Macmillan to Nancy Astor, nd [January 1933] and Duchess of Devonshire to Nancy Astor, 24 January 1933, Astor 3748. On the Duchess, see Mark Girouard, *Enthusiasms* (2011), pp. 172–92.

15. Harold Macmillan to Nancy Astor, nd [?31 January 1933], Astor 3748.

16. Harold Macmillan to Nancy Astor, two letters dated 1 February 1933, and Duchess of Devonshire to Nancy Astor, 9 February 1933, Astor 3748.

17. Horne, *But What Do You Actually Do?*, p. 256.

18. Thorpe, *Supermac*, p. 363; information from Nicolas Barker, 21 December 2011; Sir Edward Heath, *The Course of My Life* (1998), p. 181; Alistair Horne, *Macmillan 1957–1986* (1989), p. 5.

19. Thorpe, *Supermac*, p. 372; Catterall, *Macmillan Diaries*, I, p. 615.

20. R. A. Butler, aide-memoire of 22 October 1957, Butler papers G31.

21. Diary of Earl Winterton, 17 February 1919 and 15 May 1920, Winterton papers 22 and 25, Bodleian.

22. R. A. Butler, aide-memoire of 24 January 1962, Butler papers G38; Swinton, *Sixty Years*, p. 187.

23. Ian Harvey, *To Fall Like Lucifer* (1971), p. 82.

24. Diary of Harold Macmillan, 14 December 1959, Macmillan dep d 37, f 91; Macmillan diary, 17 March 1957, Macmillan dep d 28, f 74, Bodleian; Catterall, *Macmillan Diaries*, II, p. 427; Roy Jenkins, 'A

Resounding Finale', *Spectator*, 8 July 1960, p. 52.

25. Diary of Harold Macmillan, 27 November 1959, Macmillan dep d 37, f 80, Bodleian; Tom Hopkinson, 'Waiting for Lumumba', *Twentieth Century*, 169 (January 1961), p. 8.

26. Lord Boyd-Carpenter, *Way of Life* (1980), pp. 151–52.

27. Catterall, *Macmillan Diaries*, II, p. 559; George Thomson, 'Parties in Parliament 1959–63', *Political Quarterly*, 34 (1963), p. 250.

28. 'The New Chancellor', *National Review*, 150 (February 1958), pp. 51–2.

29. 'Lord Elliott of Morpeth', *Daily Telegraph*, 23 May 2011; Charles Curran, 'The Politics of Envy', *Spectator*, 6 December 1957, p. 781.

30. Lord Egremont, *Wyndham and Children* (1968), p. 161.

31. Egremont, *Wyndham and Children*, p. 165; Patrick Gordon Walker, 'On Being a Cabinet Minister', *Encounter*, 6 (April 1956), p. 21.

32. Kenneth Rose, 'Official Residences', *National Review*, 154 (April 1960), p. 125; Sir Brian Harrison, *Seeking a Role* (2009), p. 111; Lord Hennessy of Nympsfield, *Having It So Good* (2008), p. 542.

33. Lord Altrincham, 'Organised Hypocrisy', *National Review*, 148 (February 1957), pp. 63–4; 'Harold Macmillan', *National Review*, 150 (March 1958), p. 104; 'The Boothby Letter', *Time & Tide*, 43 (15–22 November 1962), p. 35.

34. Lord Kilmuir, *Political Adventure* (1964), pp. 158–59.

35. William Rees-Mogg, 'The Selection of Parliamentary Candidates', *Political Quarterly*, 30 (1959), p. 218 (Gerald Nabarro did not, at this time, describe himself as Jewish); Sir Julian Critchley, *A Bag of Boiled Sweets* (1994), p. 69.

36. Christopher Hollis, 'Government by Etonians', *Spectator*, 4 January 1957, p. 10; Critchley, *Boiled Sweets*, p. 71.

37. Henry Kerby, 'Government by Etonians', *Spectator*, 18 January 1957, p. 83.

38. Angus Maude, 'Tory Democracy at Westminster', *Spectator*, 26 April 1957, p. 540.

39. C. H. P. Mayo, *Reminiscences of a Harrow Master* (1928), pp. 150–51; Anthony Sampson, *Anatomy of Britain* (1962), p. 52; Earl Ferrers, *Whatever Next?* (2011), p. 146.

40. Diary of Earl Winterton, 1 August 1951, Winterton papers 54.

41. Critchley, *Boiled Sweets*, p. 74; Anthony Wedgwood Benn, 'The Tory Party from the Outside', *National Review*, 149 (December 1957), p. 267.

42. Diary of Earl Winterton, 24 June 1959, Winterton papers 56.

43. Critchley, *Boiled Sweets*, p. 69; Humphry Berkeley, *Crossing the Floor* (1972), p. 83.
44. Harold Macmillan to Michael Fraser, 17 February 1957, NA PREM 11/1816.
45. 'A Shade Too Optimistic?', *Bedfordshire Times and Standard*, 26 July 1957, p. 8.
46. Thorpe, *Supermac*, p. 392; Quentin Skinner, 'The Queen, the Workers, the Jews', *London Review of Books*, 22 September 2011, p. 4.
47. Peter Kennerley, 'They Call it "Britain's Sin City"', *Sunday Pictorial*, 10 May 1959, p. 22.
48. Louis Blom-Cooper, 'Prostitution: a Socio-Legal Comment on the Case of Dr Ward', *British Journal of Sociology*, 15 (March 1964), p. 70; Viscount Hailsham QC, 'Homosexuality and Society', in Tudor Rees and Harley Usill (eds), *They Stand Apart* (1955), pp. 21–2, 24–6, 28–9.
49. Geoffrey Lewis, *Lord Hailsham* (1997), pp. 181–82.
50. 'Candidates State Their Cases as the Election Enters its Final Stage', *Stratford-upon-Avon Herald*, 2 October 1959, p. 1.
51. Hugh Trevor-Roper to Nicolas Gage, 24 March 1959, Gage papers, Firle; Albert Finney, 'Making Them Feel', *Twentieth Century*, 169 (February 1961), p. 141; Anthony Fell, 'The British in Danger of Slavery', *Time & Tide*, 30 August 1962, p. 9.
52. Michael Wharton, 'Beyond a Joke', *Twentieth Century*, 169 (July 1961), pp. 13–14; Bernard Levin, 'Violence at Blackpool', *Spectator*, 17 October 1958, pp. 506–07; compare the pompous bluster of Lord Hailsham, 'Incidents at Blackpool', *The Times*, 18 October 1958, p. 7e.
53. Bernard Williams, 'Fairlie, the Establishment, and the BBC', *Encounter*, 13 (November 1959), pp. 64–5; Henry Fairlie, 'The BBC – Voice of the Establishment', *Encounter*, 13 (August 1959), p. 13.
54. Sir David Cannadine, 'John Harold Plumb', *Biographical Memoirs of Fellows of the British Academy*, III (2004), p. 286 and seriatim; J. H. Plumb, 'Hall of Fame', *Spectator*, 16 March 1962, p. 339.
55. R. H. S. Crossman, 'Power and Personalia', *New Statesman*, 13 July 1962, p. 49.
56. Simon Raven, 'The Listener's Book Chronicle', *Listener*, 12 July 1962, p. 69.
57. Malcolm Bradbury, 'The New Language of Morals', *Twentieth Century*, 172 (summer 1963), pp. 81–2.

Two: War Minister

1. Dame Rebecca West, *The Meaning of Treason* (1965), p. 295; John Galsworthy, *Another Sheaf* (1919), pp. 91–3; Giles Playfair, *My Father's Son* (1937), pp. 71–2.
2. Christopher Tyerman, *A History of Harrow School 1324–1991* (2000), p. 442.
3. Playfair, *My Father's Son*, p. 113.
4. Sir Cyril Norwood, *The English Tradition of Education* (1929), pp. 71, 73, 75, 76, 228; Brian Glanville, 'Laggards in the Sex War', *Truth*, 19 April 1957, 157, pp. 435–36.
5. Geoffrey Gorer, 'This is the English – A Race Torn by Inner Conflicts', *The People*, 30 September 1951, p. 4.
6. Hugh Trevor-Roper, *Wartime Journals* (2011), p. 47; Hugh Trevor-Roper to David Stephens, 10 February 1960, quoted Alex Danchev, *Oliver Franks* (1993), p. 152; John Mortimer, *Clinging to the Wreckage* (1982), p. 57; J. Mordaunt Crook, *Brasenose* (2008), p. 370; David Profumo, *Bringing the House Down* (2006), p. 66.
7. Profumo, *House Down*, p. 77.
8. Cyril Ray, 'The Cinema', *Spectator*, 182 (24 June 1949), p. 853; Virginia Graham, 'Cinema', *Spectator*, 188 (29 February 1952), pp. 260–61.
9. Profumo, *House Down*, p. 53.
10. Boyd-Carpenter, *Way of Life*, p. 108.
11. '15 Guests at Wedding of MP and Actress', *Stratford-upon-Avon Herald*, 7 January 1955, p. 1.
12. John Whiting, 'From My Diary', *Twentieth Century*, 169 (February 1961), p. 198.
13. 'Bunny, Flockie and Co.', *New Statesman*, 51 (26 May 1956), p. 588.
14. James Morris, 'Patriotism', *Encounter*, 18 (January 1962), p. 17.
15. Macmillan diary, 7 January 1959, Macmillan dep d 34, f 33, Bodleian; Profumo, *House Down*, p. 139; Sir Colin Coote, *Editorial* (1965), p. 284.
16. Murphy, *Lennox-Boyd*, p. 110; Profumo, *House Down*, pp. 151–2.
17. John Charnley, *Churchill* (1993), p. 203; Murphy, *Lennox-Boyd*, p. 164.
18. Catterall, *Macmillan Diaries*, I, p. 580; Macmillan diary, 8 April 1957, Macmillan dep d 28, f 124, Bodleian.
19. Profumo, *House Down*, p. 154.
20. 'Only Five Nights to Go', *Stratford-upon-Avon Herald*, 2 October 1959, p. 1.

NOTES TO PP. 62-75

21. Margaret Stacey, *Tradition and Change: a Study of Banbury* (1960), pp. 8–9.
22. Stacey, *Tradition and Change*, p. 9.
23. Shirley Green, *Rachman* (1979), p. 23.
24. Maurice Richardson, 'Television Clowns', *Twentieth Century*, 169 (July 1961), p. 88.
25. Harold Macmillan, *Winds of Change* (1966), p. 100; Berkeley, *Crossing the Floor*, pp. 81–2; Catterall, *Macmillan Diaries*, II, p. 651.
26. Maurice Collis, *The Journey Up* (1970), p. 193; Robert Hardman, *Our Queen* (2011), p. 241.
27. Wilfred Fienburgh, *No Love for Johnnie* (1959), p. 114.
28. Brian Sewell, *Outsider* (2011), p. 72; 'Fall Out! 11 Forces men can't be MPs', *Daily Express*, 4 March 1963, p. 7; 'Carry On Sergeant!', *Daily Express*, 5 March 1963, p. 1.
29. Pat Jalland, *Death in War and Peace: A History of Loss and Grief in England, 1914–1970* (2010), pp. 172–73.
30. Ray Gosling, *Sum Total* (1962), pp. 22, 34.
31. John Braine, 'The Month', *Twentieth Century*, 163 (February 1958), pp. 169–70.
32. Frederic Raphael, *Personal Terms* (2001), pp. 97–8.

Three: Lord

1. Diary of Sir Edward Walter Hamilton, 25 January 1893 and 15 October 1893, BL Add ms 48659, 48661; Diary of Marquess of Lincolnshire, 11 July 1895 and 30 May 1896, Bodleian.
2. Diary of Marquess of Lincolnshire, 4 November 1897 and 13 January 1899, Bodleian.
3. Diary of Marquess of Lincolnshire, 7 July 1900, Bodleian; Derek Wilson, *The Astors 1763–1992* (1993), pp. 133, 177.
4. Diary of Earl Winterton, 10 November 1919, Winterton papers 23, Bodleian.
5. Diary of Earl Winterton, 24 June 1950, Winterton papers 53, Bodleian.
6. Wilson, *Astors*, p. 342.
7. Bill Astor to Nancy Astor, [1926], Astor papers 1416/1/3/24; David Astor to Nancy Astor [c. 1926], Astor papers 1416/1/3/28; Richard Cockett, *David Astor and the Observer* (1991), p. 11.
8. Bill Astor to Nancy Astor, [1926], and to Waldorf and Nancy Astor, [1928], Astor 1416/1/3/28.

9. Bill Astor to Waldorf and Nancy Astor, [1928], 19 February 1929, and [Vienna, 1929], Astor 1416/1/3/28.

10. Norman Rose, *The Cliveden Set* (2000), pp. 180, 183; Anthony Julius, *Trials of the Diaspora* (2010), p. 317; Sir Harold Nicolson, *Diaries and Letters 1930–39* (1966), pp. 326–27, 396–97.

11. Lord Astor, House of Lords debates, 22 November 1955, 194, col 711, and 10 July 1956, 198, cols 699–704.

12. Bill Astor to Nancy Astor, [September 1952?], Astor papers 1416/1/3/28.

13. Peter Stanford, *Bronwen Astor* (2000), pp. 162–63.

14. Gorer, 'This is the English', p. 4; Lord Carrington, *Reflect on Things Past* (1988), p. 74.

15. 'Why French Horses Win Classic Races', *Listener*, 12 July 1956, p. 45; Pamela Cooper, *A Cloud of Forgetting* (1993), p. 306; Stanford, *Bronwen Astor*, p. 157; Maurice Collis, *Diaries 1949–69* (1977), p. 74.

16. Collis, *Diaries*, p. 70.

17. Isaiah Berlin, *Enlightening: Letters 1946–60* (2009), p. 449; Stanford, *Bronwen Astor*, p. 284.

18. Lord Astor, House of Lords debates, 1 November 1956, 199, cols 1321–132, and 31 October 1957, Vol. 205, col 750; Collis, *Diaries*, p. 85.

19. Hugh Thomas, *The Suez Affair* (1967), p. 142; Frederick Bishop to Anthony Eden, 16 November 1956, NA PREM 11/1127.

20. Sir Sherard Cowper-Coles, *Cables from Kabul* (2011), p. 273; Cooper, *Cloud of Forgetting*, p. 306.

21. S. J. D. Green, *The Passing of Protestant England* (2011), p. 185.

22. Wilson, *Astors*, p. 361.

23. John Paterson-Morgan, 'Behaviour of the Press', *The Times*, 21 January 1958, p. 9.

24. Lord Astor, House of Lords debate, 2 February 1960, Vol. 220, cols 838–43.

25. Catterall, *Macmillan Diaries*, II, p. 304; 30 May 1960, Macmillan dep d 39, ff 46–7.

26. Viscount Astor, 'Shah Aly Khan', *The Times*, 14 May 1960, p. 10a.

27. Bishop Gordon Savage, quoted Wilson, *Astors*, p. 345; Stanford, *Bronwen Astor*, p. 151.

28. Anne Chisholm and Michael Davie, *Beaverbrook* (1992), pp. 492–93; Nancy Astor to Lord Beaverbrook, Friday [17 July 1931], and 'HOLD GORDON', 22 July 1958, both HLRO BBK C/15.

29. Katharine Whitehorn, 'Elegance comes out of chaos', *Picture Post*, 1 April 1957, pp. 28–30.
30. David Litchfield, *Thyssen Art Macabre* (2006), pp. 254–55.
31. Stanford, *Bronwen Astor*, pp. 146–47.
32. Stanford, *Bronwen Astor*, pp. 147, 157.
33. Stanford, *Bronwen Astor*, pp. 5, 191.
34. Nicky Haslam, *Redeeming Features* (2009), pp. 117–18.

Four: Doctor

1. 'Randolph Churchill's Column', *News of the World*, 7 and 14 August 1960, p. 9.
2. *Oxford Dictionary of National Biography*.
3. Evelyn Waugh, *A Handful of Dust* (1934), chapter 2 (pp. 35, 39 of 2002 edn); Geoffrey Murray, 'Bone and Sinew', *Spectator*, 28 October 1960, p. 644.
4. Lord Gladwyn, *The Diaries of Cynthia Gladwyn* (1995), p. 288; Sir Colin Coote to Philip de Zulueta, 6 June 1963, NA PREM 11/4369; Coote, *Editorial*, pp. 285–86.
5. 'Rebel MPs Defiant', *The Times*, 14 November 1946, p. 4d; Diary of Earl Winterton, 1 August 1951, Winterton papers 54, Bodleian; Philip Knightley and Caroline Kennedy, *An Affair of State* (1987), pp. 42–5.
6. Coote, *Editorial*, p. 288; Kennedy, *Trial of Stephen Ward*, p. 21; 'The Enigma of Stephen Ward', *Observer*, 4 August 1963, p. 5.
7. Trevor-Roper, *Wartime Journals*, p. 258; Gladwyn, *Cynthia Gladwyn*, p. 288; Collis, *Diaries*, p. 131.
8. Profumo, *House Down*, pp. 156–57; Cooper, *Cloud of Forgetting*, pp. 305–06; Stanford, *Bronwen Astor*, p. 226.
9. Christine Keeler, *Scandal!* (1989), p. 46; Christine Keeler, *The Truth at Last* (2001), p. 32; Christine Keeler, *Secrets and Lies* (2012), pp. 35–6.
10. 'The Enigma of Stephen Ward', *Observer*, 4 August 1963, p. 5.
11. Sir Colin Coote to Philip de Zulueta, 6 June 1963, NA PREM 11/4369.
12. Stanford, *Bronwen Astor*, pp. 8, 223.
13. Keeler, *Truth at Last*, p. 33; Coote, *Editorial*, p. 288.
14. Margery Allingham, *The Patient at Peacocks Hall* (1954), pp. 12, 20–21; Richard Davenport-Hines, *The Pursuit of Oblivion* (2001), pp. 237–38.
15. Harold Macmillan to Sir Anthony Eden, 29 September 1957, Macmillan

dep c 310; Sir Arthur Porritt, 'Views from the Top', *Twentieth Century*, 171 (autumn 1962), pp. 82, 85.

16. Kenneth Barrett, 'These Doctors Make Me Angry', *News of the World*, 17 January 1960, p. 7.

17. Memorandum of British Medical Association, December 1955, CHP/95, NA HO 345/9. Dr Ernest Claxton was secretary to the sub-committee which prepared the report, and wrote much of it.

Five: Good-Time Girls

1. Elizabeth Taylor, *A Game of Hide-and-Seek* (1951), p. 56; 'Anne Crossman', *The Times*, 13 October 2008; Janice Galloway, *All Made Up* (2011), p. 85.

2. C. C. Cabot, 'You've hooked him but he wants you to go too far', *Sunday Pictorial*, 18 November 1962, p. 22; see also Jessica Mann, *The Fifties Mystique* (2012), pp. 130–32.

3. Simon Szreter and Kate Fisher, *Sex Before the Sexual Revolution: Intimate Life in England, 1918–63* (2011), p. 127; Victor Durand QC, Lewes Assizes, 26 March 1963, NA ASSI 36/387; John Bloom, *It's No Sin to Make a Profit* (1971), p. 154.

4. Personal recollection; Colin MacInnes, *Out of the Way* (1979), p. 248.

5. Siriol Hugh-Jones, 'We Witless Women', *Twentieth Century*, 169 (July 1961), pp. 16–17.

6. BBC Panorama interview with Nancy Astor 1959, accessed youtube. com 11 May 2011; Lord Llewellin, House of Lords debates, 4 February 1953, 180, col 220.

7. Lord Rea, House of Lords debates, 3 December 1957, 206, col 629; Earl Ferrers, ibid, cols 709–11; Ivy Compton-Burnett, *Pastors and Masters* (1925), p. 111.

8. Jessica Mann, *The Fifties Mystique* (2012), is a cool, sane account of Englishwomen's experiences in the 1950s.

9. Fienburgh, *No Love for Johnnie*, p. 128; Michael Rubenstein, 'When a Marriage Starts to Split', *Twentieth Century*, 172 (summer 1963), p. 77.

10. 'Marriage and Happiness', *New Statesman*, 31 March 1956, p. 296; Oliver McGregor, 'Why Our Sexual Ethics are in a Mess', *Twentieth Century*, 171 (spring 1963), p. 112.

11. Dorothy Macmillan to Nancy Astor, Chatsworth, nd [January 1933], Astor papers 3748.

12. Wayland Young, 'Sitting on a Fortune', *Encounter*, 12 (May 1959), pp. 20–1.

13. Lena Jeger, 'The Politics of Family Planning', *Political Quarterly*, 33 (1962), pp. 48–9; Hera Cook, *The Long Sexual Revolution* (2004), pp. 131–35.

14. Joyce Robinson, 'Speaking from Experience', *Twentieth Century*, 172 (summer 1963), pp. 85, 86, 88.

15. Celia Imrie, *The Happy Hoofer* (2011), p. 13; Peter Scott, 'A Clinical Contribution', in Sir Norwood East (ed.), *The Roots of Crime* (1954), pp. 56, 66.

16. Conversations with Dr Ann Dally; Mann, *Fifties Mystique*, pp. 162–64; Paul Addison, *No Turning Back* (2010), p. 96; W. H. Allchin, 'Looking for Trouble', *Twentieth Century*, 169 (winter 1962), p. 53.

17. Lord Ailwyn, House of Lords debates, 1 May 1961, Vol. 230, col 1091.

18. Cecil King, 'The Dangers when Sex is Mistaken for Love', *The Times*, 12 April 1969, p. 9e; Lord Jenkin of Roding, 1979, quoted Addison, *No Turning Back*, p. 356.

19. Mann, *Fifties Mystique*, p. 99; Marjorie Proops, 'Well, Who Cares What the Men Think?', *Daily Mirror*, 23 September 1964, p. 9.

20. Isabel Quigly, 'Filthy Pictures', *Spectator*, 15 April 1960, pp. 544, 546.

21. 'Pamela Green', *Daily Telegraph*, 17 May 2010.

22. Denis Thomas, 'The Daily Dynamic', *Truth*, 1 March 1957, 157, p. 226; Damon Wise, *Come by Sunday: the Fabulous, Ruined Life of Diana Dors* (1998), p. 63.

23. Wise, *Come by Sunday*, p. 68; Green, *Rachman*, p. 71; Bloom, *No Sin*, pp. 61–2.

24. Diana Dors, 'Strip Poker', *News of the World*, 31 January 1960, p. 4.

25. Diana Dors, 'Wild and Wicked – Secret of the Mirror in the Guest Room', *News of the World*, 24 January 1960, p. 5.

26. Geoffrey Willans, *Down With Skool!* (1959), p. 29.

27. Robert Hancock, '41:19:36', *Spectator* (9 August 1957), pp. 184–85; '"Women of the Year" Contrasts', *The Times*, 28 September 1956, p. 6b; 'Our London Correspondence', *Manchester Guardian*, 28 September 1956, p. 8.

28. Peter Evans, 'Mink is My Security', *Daily Express*, 19 March 1963, p. 17.

29. Angela Thirkell, *Close Quarters* (1958), pp. 32–3; Elizabeth Taylor, *In a Summer Season* (1961), pp. 139–40; Ralph Harris, 'A Competitive Market', *The Times*, 22 July 1964, p. 11e.

30. Bloom, *No Sin*, pp. 104–05.
31. Testimony of Harvey Holford, 26 March 1963, NA ASSI 36/387; 'The Blue Gardenia Trial: Holford – Christine – Bloom', *Daily Express*, 22 March 1963, pp. 8–9.
32. Testimony of Harvey Holford, 26 March 1963, NA ASSI 36/387.
33. 'Judges Reject Holford Plea for a Jury', *Daily Express*, 5 March 1963, p. 9.
34. 'The Blue Gardenia Trial: At the Villa', *Daily Express*, 23 March 1963, p. 9.
35. 'The Blue Gardenia Trial: Holford – Christine – Bloom', *Daily Express*, 22 March 1963, pp. 8–9; 'The Blue Gardenia Trial: At the Villa'; 'The Blue Gardenia Trial: The Last Letter', *Daily Express*, 26 March 1963, p. 10.
36. 'Holford in the Box', *Daily Express*, 27 March 1963, p. 6.
37. Arnold Latcham and Tom Mangold, 'Three Years for Holford', *Daily Express*, 30 March 1963, p. 1; Arnold Latcham and Tom Mangold, 'Summing Up', *Daily Express*, 30 March 1963, p. 2; Arnold Latcham, 'No Full Acquittal', *Daily Express*, 29 March 1963, p. 6.
38. J. H. Walker to Sir Austin Strutt, 23 September 1953, NA HO 302/10.
39. Paul Johnson, 'Are Virgins Obsolete?', *New Statesman*, 4 January 1963, p. 9; 'This England', *New Statesman*, 7 December 1962, p. 821.
40. 'Oh, Marje! The Easter Brides have never had a word in their ears at the bedroom door like this!', *Sunday Mirror*, 14 April 1963, p. 13; Marjorie Proops, 'Giving the lie to "love makes the world go round"', *Sunday Mirror*, 7 July 1963, p. 13.
41. 'Night Life at the Grotto', *News of the World*, 18 November 1962, p. 4.
42. Keeler, *Scandal!*, pp. 27–8.
43. Jean Dawnay, *Model Girl* (1956), pp. 82, 174, 198.
44. Anthony Powell, *At Lady Molly's* (1957), p. 182.
45. Paul Willetts, *Members Only: The Life and Times of Paul Raymond* (2010), p. 69.
46. 'Deep Freeze', *Sunday Pictorial*, 24 February 1957, p. 7.
47. Clive Irving, Ron Hall and Jeremy Wallington, *Scandal '63* (1963), p. 8.
48. 'David Murray', *Daily Telegraph*, 20 October 2004.
49. Knightley and Kennedy, *Affair of State*, pp. 56–7.
50. Knightley and Kennedy, *Affair of State*, p. 62.
51. Profumo, *House Down*, p. 163; private information, 12 March 2012.
52. Sybille Bedford, 'The Worst We Can Do: A Concise Account of the Trial

of Dr Stephen Ward', Harry Ransom Center, University of Texas at Austin, folio 9.

53. Penelope Fitzgerald, *Human Voices* (1980), chapter 8, p. 224; Rice-Davies, *Mandy*, pp. 7, 18.
54. Knightley and Kennedy, *Affair of State*, p. 204.
55. Keeler, *Truth at Last*, p. 58; Keeler, *Secrets and Lies*, pp. 61–2.

Six: Landlords

1. Muriel Spark, *The Girls of Slender Means* (1963), chapter 1 (Everyman, 2004), p. 129.
2. Robert Irwin, *Memoirs of a Dervish* (2011), p. 6.
3. Isabel Quigly, 'Kindest Cuts', *Spectator*, 8 April 1957, p. 177; London's sexual ecology is explored in Frank Mort, *Capital Affairs: London and the Making of the Permissive Society* (2010), although this book's bias, especially apropos the Profumo Affair, is deplorable: see Richard Davenport-Hines, 'Class Action', *Times Literary Supplement*, 20–27 August 2010, pp. 11–12.
4. Richard Hornsey, *The Spiv and the Architect: Unruly Life in Postwar London* (2010), pp. 14–15, 46–7, 71–4; Judith Walkowitz, *Nights Out: Life in Cosmopolitan London* (2012), pp. 289–91.
5. Wilfred Fienburgh, 'The Politics of Welfare', *Twentieth Century*, 158 (July 1955), p. 29.
6. Charles Gordon, *The Two Tycoons* (1984), p. 17.
7. Sid Chaplin, 'My Money – and My Life', *Twentieth Century*, 172 (winter 1963), p. 41.
8. Oliver Marriott, *The Property Boom* (1967), pp. 28, 271.
9. Marriott, *Property Boom*, p. 155.
10. Marriott, *Property Boom*, pp. 156–57.
11. Anthony Sampson, *Anatomy of Britain* (1962), p. 499; William Hickey, 'Charles Forte is Now the Squire', *Daily Express*, 22 March 1963, p. 3.
12. Gordon, *Two Tycoons*, p. 5; Lord Weidenfeld, *Remembering My Good Friends* (1995), p. 166.
13. Gordon, *Two Tycoons*, p. 5; private information.
14. Raphael, *Personal Terms*, p. 93.
15. Stacey, *Tradition and Change*, pp. 27–8, 31.
16. Chief Inspector Harold Hawkyard, 'Strictly Confidential' report of 18 September 1943, NA MEPO 3/2657; George Titman, memoranda 'Sourire

de Paris', 15 January and 22 February 1934, Lord Chamberlain's corre-spondence, British Library; 'Theatre Officials Fined', *The Times*, 22 February 1934, p. 16e; 'West End Revue Censored', *Daily Telegraph*, 22 February 1934; 'Vulgarity in a Revue', *Courier-Mail* (Brisbane), 23 February 1934, p. 13h. On the Prince of Wales Theatre, see also Walkowitz, *Nights Out*, p. 273; Graham Greene, 'The Theatre', *Spectator*, 7 March, 6 June and 27 June 1941, pp. 251, 677, 771.

17. 'London Casino to Reopen', *The Times*, 21 February 1939, p. 12c; Sir William Morren, Chief Constable of Edinburgh, to Sir Norman Kendal, Assistant Commissioner of Metropolitan Police, 26 August 1943, and Kendal to Morren, 27 August 1943, NA MEPO 3/2657; Matthew Sweet, *West End Front* (2011), p. 79.

18. Anonymous letter [probably written by Charles Gale, former general manager of the Token Construction Company] to Director of Public Prosecutions, 11 December 1946; anonymous postcard to Chief Commissioner of Scotland Yard; report by Detective Inspector A. Bishop, 7 March 1947, MEPO 3/2657.

19. Niall Ferguson, *High Financier: the Lives and Times of Siegmund Warburg* (2010), p. 184; Bracken, *My Dear Max*, p. 152.

20. Anthony Crosland, 'The Case against Takeover Bids', *Listener*, 2 September 1954, p. 347; Goronwy Rees, *The Multi-Millionaires* (1961), p. 139; Michael Flanders and Donald Swann, 'Sounding Brass'.

21. Donald Coleman, *Courtaulds*, III (1980), p. 24; Martin Weiner, *English Culture and the Decline of the Industrial Spirit 1850–1980* (1981), p. 150; Sampson, *Anatomy of Britain*, p. 505.

22. Richard Sheppard, 'Seven Keys to Good Architecture', *Twentieth Century*, 171 (winter 1963), p. 148.

23. Weidenfeld, *Remembering My Good Friends*, pp. 165, 270–71; Jeremy Banks, 'Charles Clore: Country Squire', *Queen*, 8 May 1962, p. 70; Gordon, *Two Tycoons*, p. 43.

24. Gordon, *Two Tycoons*, pp. 44–5.

25. Henry Fairlie, 'Why so few lifemen in the Lords?', *Time & Tide*, 6 January 1961, p. 6; Simon Raven, 'The Listener's Book Chronicle', *The Listener*, 12 July 1962, p. 69.

26. Personal recollection; Gordon, *Two Tycoons*, p. 46.

27. Sir Cecil Beaton, *The Years Between* (1965), p. 53; Charles Ritchie, *The Siren Years* (1974), p. 68; Sweet, *West End Front*, pp. 82, 91, 95.

28. Gordon, *Two Tycoons*, pp. 35–6; John Gale, 'Jack Cotton Explains',

Twentieth Century, 171 (summer 1962), p. 82.

29. Gale, 'Cotton Explains', p. 78; Rayner Heppenstall, 'The Month', *Twentieth Century*, 166 (October 1959), p. 297.

30. Sampson, *Anatomy of Britain*, pp. 416–17; Gale, 'Cotton Explains', p. 77; Sir Osbert Lancaster, *Mixed Notices* (1963), p. 27 (reproducing cartoon of 10 April 1962).

31. Robert Head, 'Tycoon Cotton Quits', *Daily Mirror*, 4 July 1963, p. 1.

32. Gordon, *Two Tycoons*, p. 175.

33. Express City Editor, 'Sergt Flack the Property Magnate dies at 47, alone in his flat', *Daily Express*, 23 March 1963, p. 7.

34. Gordon, *Two Tycoons*, pp. 169–70. Flack's arms were blazoned: Or, a cross floretty azure, and two Flasques gules masoned argent; with, as a crest, a seahorse argent, scaled and finned azure, holding a silver Flask corded Or.

35. Gordon, *Two Tycoons*, p. 173. Prince von Loewenstein was the great-grandson of Lord Pirbright, a forgotten Victorian financier with Rothschild blood.

36. Amos Oz, *A Tale of Love and Darkness* (2004), pp. 183–84.

37. Green, *Rachman*, p. 11.

38. Green, *Rachman*, p. 14.

39. Green, *Rachman*, pp. 7, 64.

40. Green, *Rachman*, pp. 26, 28.

41. Anthony Powell, *The Acceptance World* (1955), p. 1.

42. 'Full House in Notting Hill', *Economist*, 9 December 1961, p. 1033.

43. Green, *Rachman*, p. 41.

44. Christopher Isherwood, *Diaries 1970–83*, III (2012), p. 314; Irwin, *Memoirs of a Dervish*, pp. 143–47.

45. Lynn Barber, *An Education* (2009), p. 42.

46. Blake Modisane, 'Sorry, No Coloureds', *Twentieth Century*, 170 (Spring 1962), pp. 96–7.

47. Green, *Rachman*, pp. 57–8, 60.

48. Green, *Rachman*, p. 106.

49. Detective Superintendent George Taylor to Chief Superintendent C. Macdougall, 27 July 1959, and Taylor to Chief Superintendent F. Pollard, 26 October 1963, NA MEPO 2/10077.

50. Barry of Directorate of Public Prosecutions to Sir Joseph Simpson, Commissioner of Metropolitan Police, 4 August 1959, NA MEPO 2/10077.

51. Green, *Rachman*, p. 154.
52. Keeler, *Scandal!*, p. 58.
53. Green, *Rachman*, pp. 198–99.
54. Patrick Hutber, 'Obsessions on the Left', *Twentieth Century*, 172 (spring 1964), pp. 57–8; Marjorie Proops, 'So Alec thinks I'm his SECRET WEAPON', *Daily Mirror*, 7 October 1964, p. 17.
55. 'Railway Land Sold Cheaply to "Spiv Tycoons"', *The Times*, 7 July 1964, p. 8f; Donald Zec, 'The Britain I Want to See', *Daily Mirror*, 25 September 1964, pp. 16–17.

Seven: Hacks

1. Stanley Cohen, *Folk Devils and Moral Panics* (1972), p. 45.
2. W. T. Stead, evidence to Royal Commission on Divorce, 21 December 1910, Q 43403.
3. Hugh Cudlipp, 'Sex, Crime and the Press', *Daily Mirror*, 12 November 1953, p. 2.
4. Cyril Connolly, 'This Gale-Swept Chip', *Encounter*, 21 (July 1963), p. 95.
5. Sir Michael Redgrave, 'Expendable Faces', *Twentieth Century*, 169 (February 1961), p. 146; Ruth Langdon Inglis, 'An American View of England', *Twentieth Century*, 173 (Spring 1965), pp. 90–1; Tom Mangold, 'Procter-Land Paradise', *British Journalism Review*, booksaboutjournalism.com/procter (accessed 7 August 2011).
6. Peter Wildeblood, *Against the Law* (1955), pp. 29–32; Arthur Christiansen to Lord Beaverbrook, 6 March 1952, HLRO BK H/155; Adrian Bingham, *Family Newspapers?: Sex, Private Life and the British Popular Press, 1918–78* (2009), p. 27.
7. Ronald Knox, *Double Cross Purposes* (1937), p. 21.
8. 'The New MAN!' and 'The Sins of Mayfair!', *Sunday Pictorial*, 6 March 1939, pp. 6, 10.
9. Mary Soames, *A Daughter's Tale* (2011), p. 342.
10. Stanley Evans, House of Commons debates, 28 July 1949, 467, col 2774. The so-called 'Little Kinsey' report was published in a five-part serial in the *Sunday Pictorial* from 3 to 31 July 1949. Several historians and sociologists, who refer to it in their writings, have plainly never looked at it. This Mass Observation work is most easily accessible, and intelligently analysed, in Liz Stanley, *Sex Surveyed 1949–94* (1995).

11. 'Press Council View on "Sex Exploitation"', *The Times*, 28 October 1953, p. 8e; 'Press Council Conclusions on Hanging Controversy', *The Times*, 2 May 1956, p. 6e (for the defiant insolence of the editor of the *Daily Sketch* when the War Office complained of the heartless harassment of the widow of a soldier killed in Cyprus).

12. 'Exploitation of Sex', *The Times*, 25 November 1953, p. 4c; Sir Victor Gollancz, *More for Timothy* (1953), pp. 211–12, 306; C.S. Lewis, 'After Priggery – What?', *Spectator*, 7 December 1945, p. 536.

13. Cudlipp, 'Sex, Crime and the Press', *Daily Mirror*, 13 November 1953, p. 2; Cecil King, 'The Morality of the Popular Press', *Twentieth Century*, 171 (Spring 1963), p. 99.

14. Lord Mancroft, House of Lords debates, 13 March 1961, 229, col 608.

15. Sir Richard Glyn, 'The Responsibilities and Defects of the Press', *The Times*, 22 March 1963, p. 13e. For the clamorous occupation by journalists and photographers of the garden of a Bromley house containing children whose three mothers had been killed together in a motoring accident, see Gillian Lynne, *A Dancer in Wartime* (2011), p. 8.

16. Harry Street, 'Privacy and the Law', *Twentieth Century*, 170 (Spring 1962), p. 39.

17. Catterall, *Macmillan Diaries*, II, p. 405.

18. William Gerhardi, 'Hard Sharp Point', *Spectator*, 16 March 1962, p. 331; Ephraim Hardcastle, 'When Sir John threw a chair at his sister', *Sunday Express*, 21 July 1963, p. 5; Sir Isaiah Berlin, *Personal Impressions* (1980), p. xxvi; Berlin, 'The Anglo-American Predicament', *Listener*, 42 (29 September 1949), pp. 518–19, 538; 'Mr Berlin', *Evening Standard*, 3 October 1949; Catterall, *Macmillan Diaries*, II, p. 58.

19. J. B. Priestley, 'Taking The Lid Off', *Twentieth Century*, 170 (Spring 1962), p. 32.

20. Hugh Cudlipp, *At Your Peril* (1962), pp. 25, 31, 47; Hugh Trevor-Roper, *Letters from Oxford* (2006), pp. 125–26.

21. Denis Thomas, 'The Paper with the Mostest', *Truth*, 8 February 1957, 157, pp. 148–49.

22. Catterall, *Macmillan Diaries*, I, pp. 396, 563, and II, p. 70.

23. Hugh Cudlipp, *Publish and Be Damned!* (1953), pp. 282–283; Cudlipp, *At Your Peril*, p. 25.

24. Ruth Dudley Edwards, *Newspapermen* (2003), p. 44; King, 'Morality of Popular Press', p. 100; Cecil King, 'The Dangers when Sex is Mistaken for Love', *The Times*, 12 April 1969, p. 9e.

25. Edwards, *Newspapermen*, pp. 138, 141.
26. Edwards, *Newspapermen*, pp. 107, 284, 285–6, 320–1.
27. Edwards, *Newspapermen*, p. 132.
28. Charles Wilberforce [Cudlipp's pseudonym], 'The NEW Woman!', *Sunday Pictorial*, 12 March 1939, p. 7.
29. 'Hugh Cudlipp – Journalist Tycoon', *Observer*, 18 June 1961, p. 9.
30. Edwards, *Newspapermen*, p. 312.
31. Pertinax, 'Fit for a King', *Time & Tide*, 20 January 1961, p. 92.
32. Cudlipp, *At Your Peril*, p. 314.
33. Wilfred Fienburgh, 'The Politics of Welfare', *Twentieth Century*, Vol. 158 (July 1955), pp. 20–21.
34. Janet Morgan, *The Backbench Diaries of Richard Crossman* (1981), p. 714; Cudlipp, *At Your Peril*, pp. 120–22; Cecil King, 'The Morality of the Popular Press', *Twentieth Century*, 171 (Spring 1963), pp. 98–9.
35. Cudlipp, *At Your Peril*, pp. 113, 116.
36. King, 'Morality of Popular Press', p. 102; Philip Purser, 'Viewers, Voyeurs and Victims', *Twentieth Century*, 170 (Spring 1962), p. 76.
37. Sir Brian Harrison, *Seeking a Role* (2009), p. 462.
38. Penelope Fitzgerald, *Human Voices* (1980), chapter 2 (p. 163 of Everyman edition, 2003); Henry Fairlie, 'The BBC', *Encounter*, 13 (August 1959), p. 8.
39. Wilfred Greatorex, 'Television', *Twentieth Century*, 173 (Spring 1965), pp. 85–6.
40. Malcolm Bradbury, 'The New Language of Morals', *Twentieth Century*, 172 (Summer 1963), p. 81; Pat Williams, 'Enemies of the Imagination', *Twentieth Century*, 171 (Spring 1963), pp. 81–2; Michael Frayn, 'More About Comedy', *Twentieth Century*, 169 (Autumn 1961), p. 182.
41. Connolly, 'Gale-Swept Chip', p. 95; Purser, 'Viewers, Voyeurs and Victims', p. 79.

Eight: Spies

1. Lord Dacre of Glanton to Sir Isaiah Berlin, 9 October 1981, Dacre papers 1/31/1; Adam Sisman, *Hugh Trevor-Roper* (2010), p. 464; Sir Michael Howard, 'Cowboys, Playboys and Other Spies', *New York Times*, 16 February 1986.

2. Information from Nicolas Barker, 21 December 2011.
3. Rebecca West, *The Meaning of Treason* (1982), p. 293; B2A minute, 13 May 1952, and Lambert Titchener to G.A. Carey-Foster, 9 May 1952, NA KV 2/1636.
4. Rebecca West, 'Annals of Treason', *New Yorker*, 14 February 1953, p. 37.
5. Marshall's statement to Special Branch, 13 June 1952, f 36, NA KV 2/1638; B2A report, 'The Case of William Martin Marshall', 19 June 1952, NA KV 2/1639.
6. Howard Johnson, 'Downfall of a Dupe', *Daily Mirror*, 11 July 1952; 'Our Son', *Reynolds News*, 13 July 1952.
7. W. J. Skardon, report: 'William Martin Marshall: Interview at Wormwood Scrubs on 19.2.53', 24 February 1953, NA KV 2/1641.
8. Harold Elvin, *A Cockney in Moscow* (1958); West, *Meaning of Treason*, pp. 293–302.
9. B2A, 'Note for file', 24 July 1952 [interview with Anthony Hibberson], NA KV 2/1639.
10. 'The Squalid Truth', *Sunday Pictorial*, 25 September 1955, p. 1; Cudlipp, *At Your Peril*, p. 317.
11. 'Who is Hiding the Man Who Tipped Off These Sex Perverts?', *Sunday Pictorial*, 25 September 1955, p. 1; Rawlinson, *Price Too High*, p. 37; Horne, *But What Do You Actually Do?*, p. 55.
12. George Brown, 'FO Flops: Spies are Not the Only Trouble', *Sunday Pictorial*, 25 September 1955, p. 11; Catterall, *Macmillan Diaries*, II, pp. 450–51; Macmillan diary, 16 February 1962, dep d 45, f 23.
13. Lord Astor, House of Lords debates, 22 November 1955, 194, cols 708–15.
14. Catterall, *Macmillan Diaries*, I, pp. 452, 456; Richard Aldous, *Macmillan, Eisenhower and the Cold War* (2005), p. 57; Malcolm Muggeridge, 'England, Whose England?', *Encounter*, 21 (July 1963), pp. 14–15.
15. Honor Balfour, 'Paris and After', *National Review*, 154 (June 1960), pp. 209, 211–12.
16. Sir Harold Evans, *Downing Street Diary* (1983), p. 113; Horne, *Macmillan*, II, p. 231; Aldous, *Macmillan, Eisenhower*, p. 163.
17. Geoffrey Stone, 'Conventions', *Twentieth Century*, 169 (January 1961), p. 13.
18. Rawlinson, *Price Too High*, p. 88; Sir Theobald Mathew, undated memorandum, CHP/7, NA HO 345/7.

19. Marcus Cunliffe, 'The Comforts of the Sick-Bay', *Encounter*, 21 (July 1963), p. 98.

20. John Vassall, *Vassall, the Autobiography of a Spy* (1975), p. 21; West, *Meaning of Treason*, pp. 361–62.

21. Vassall, *Vassall*, p. 39.

22. Vassall, *Vassall*, pp. 37–8, 53, 55–6, 62–3, 91.

23. West, *Meaning of Treason*, pp. 367–68.

24. Catterall, *Macmillan Diaries*, II, p. 501.

25. Brendan Mulholland, 'Courier', *Daily Mail*, 23 October 1962; Radcliffe report, para 222.

26. Arthur Christiansen to Lord Beaverbrook, 10 November 1955, HLRO BBk H/177.

27. John Vassall, '42 Faces of the Spy Who Bares His Soul', *Sunday Pictorial*, 28 October 1962, pp. 9–10.

28. John Deane Potter, 'Twilight Traitors', *News of the World*, 28 October 1962, p. 15.

29. William Shepherd, House of Commons debates, 26 November 1958, 596, cols 425–30; Knightley and Kennedy, *Affair of State*, pp. 114–16.

30. George Brown, House of Commons debates, 5 November 1962, 666, col 714; Morgan, *Crossman Backbench Diaries*, p. 991; Sir Maurice Bowra, *New Bats in Old Belfries* (2005), p. 150; Lord Montagu of Beaulieu, *Wheels within Wheels* (2000), p. 131.

31. Stephen Robinson, *The Remarkable Lives of Bill Deedes* (2008), pp. 218, 265.

32. 'A Whitehall Farce', *Guardian*, 8 November 1962, p. 8; Percy Hoskins, 'Don't forget they knew for 18 months there was a spy around', *Daily Express*, 8 November 1962, p. 5; Evans, *Downing Street Diary*, p. 55; Carrington, *Reflect on Things Past*, pp. 173–75.

33. House of Commons debates, 14 November 1962, 667: Harold Macmillan, col 401, Nigel Birch, cols 411–15, Michael Foot, col 480; Publius, 'Where Was Lord Carrington's Smile?', *Time & Tide*, 43 (22–29 November 1962), p. 4.

34. Evans, *Downing Street Diary*, p. 229; Catterall, *Macmillan Diaries*, II, pp. 518–19; Macmillan diary, 15 November 1962, dep d 47, ff 101–02.

35. Radcliffe report, paragraphs 63, 66; Lionel Crane, 'How To Spot a Potential Homo', *Sunday Mirror*, 28 April 1963, p. 7; Ken Livingstone, *You Can't Say That* (2011), pp. 104–05.

36. Paul Johnson, 'London Diary', *New Statesman*, 22 March 1963, p. 417.

PART TWO: DRAMA

Nine: Acting Up

1. Christopher Andrew, *The Defence of the Realm* (2009), pp. 495–96.
2. Henry Vane, 'From Evening Dress to Sloppy Joes', *Twentieth Century*, 163 (May 1958), pp. 454–56; Frederic Raphael, *The Earlsdon Way* (1958), p. 78.
3. Profumo, *House Down*, p. 157.
4. Information from Dominic Harrod, 27 October 2011.
5. Profumo, *House Down*, p. 157; Richard Lamb, *The Macmillan Years* (1995), pp. 455, 463.
6. 'More Confessions of Christine', *News of the World*, 16 June 1963, p. 4.
7. Stanford, *Bronwen Astor*, p. 222; Profumo, *House Down*, p. 159.
8. Profumo, *House Down*, pp. 163, 167.
9. Sir Richard Glyn, House of Commons debates, 17 June 1963, 679, col 119; Lord Annan, *Our Age* (1990), p. 137.
10. 'New Solutions Needed for Problems of 1960s', *The Times*, 20 June 1962, p. 5a.
11. 'Mr Macmillan resignation possibilities', *Time & Tide*, 5 July 1962, p. 5; R.F.V. Heuston, *Lives of the Lords Chancellors 1940–70* (1987), pp. 177–78.
12. Lord Lambton, 'Dear Prime Minister', *Queen*, 31 July 1962, p. 18.
13. Robin Douglas-Home, 'Sentences I'd Like To Hear The End Of', *Queen*, 31 July 1962, p. 18.
14. Catterall, *Macmillan Diaries*, II, p. 507; Knightley and Kennedy, *Affair of State*, p. 109; Andrew, *Defence of the Realm*, p. 497; Lord Home, despatch 315 of 10 June 1963, NA PREM 11/4369.
15. Irving, *Scandal 63*, p. 60. Italics added.
16. Knightley and Kennedy, *Affair of State*, pp. 113–16.
17. The official file of Edgecombe's shooting trial is NA CRIM 1/4086.
18. Stephen Ward to Sir Wavell Wakefield, 20 May 1963, NA PREM 11/4368; 'Boy Driver of MP's car is charged', *Daily Express*, 5 March 1963, p. 5.
19. Lord Wigg, *George Wigg* (1972), p. 67; Diary of Earl Winterton, 13 March 1951, Winterton 53; Harvey, *To Fall Like Lucifer*, p. 78.

20. Carrington, *Reflect on Things Past*, p. 178.
21. Denning report, paragraph 66. Keeler signed the proofs of this *Sunday Pictorial* story as true on 8 February 1963, but it was never published.
22. Keeler, *Truth at Last*, p. 165; Knightley and Kennedy, *Affair of State*, p. 139.
23. John Wyndham, 'Top Secret', 1 February 1963, NA PREM 11/4368.
24. Egremont, *Wyndham and Children*, pp. 187–88, 190.
25. Sampson, *Anatomy of Britain*, p. 134.
26. Knightley and Kennedy, *Affair of State*, p. 197; private informant, 13 January 2012.
27. 'That Was The Government That Was!', *Westminster Confidential*, 8 March 1963, p. 1, NA PREM 11/4368.
28. Ferdinand Mount, *Cold Cream* (2008), p. 258.
29. Horne, *But What Do You Actually Do?*, p. 256.
30. Patrick Hutber, 'Obsessions on the Left', *Twentieth Century*, 172 (Spring 1964), p. 57; Taper, 'Punch-Drunk Parliament', *National Review*, 149 (October 1957), pp. 164–65.
31. Morgan, *Crossman Backbench Diaries*, p. 991.
32. 'Photonews Dossier in the Case of the Vital Witness Who Vanished', *Daily Express*, 15 March 1963, p. 5.
33. Stanford, *Bronwen Astor*, p. 238.
34. 'Vanishing Model Case Raised Before Judge', *Daily Express*, 20 March 1963, p. 1; 'MP Wants "Lost Witness" Count', *Daily Express*, 21 March 1963, p. 1.
35. John Owen, 'Home of Model's Friend Despoiled', *Daily Telegraph*, 21 March 1963; 'Call for Fine on Sensationalism', *The Times*, 13 March 1963, p. 5a; M. E. C. Pumphrey, 'In the Public Interest', *The Times*, 11 March 1963, p. 11e; R. C. Carrington, 'A Proper Defiance', *The Times*, 12 March 1963, p. 11e.
36. Hailsham, *Sparrow's Flight*, p. 331; George Wigg, House of Commons debates, 21 March 1963, 674, col 725; Reginald Paget, col 727.
37. Barbara Castle, House of Commons debates, 21 March 1963, 674, cols 740–41.
38. Profumo, *House Down*, p. 180; Robinson, *Remarkable Lives of Bill Deedes*, p. 231.
39. Rawlinson, *Price too High*, p. 95; Lord Dilhorne to Harold Macmillan, 12 June 1963, NA PREM 11/4370.
40. John Profumo, House of Commons debates, 22 March 1963, 674, cols

809–10; George Wigg, House of Commons debates, 17 June 1963, 679, col 102.

41. 'Out Dancing Cheek to Cheek', and 'Mr Profumo Ends the Whispers', *Daily Express*, 23 March 1963, pp. 1, 2.

42. Statement of Julia Ellen Huish, Slough, 24 March 1963, NA PREM 11/4370; Macmillan, House of Commons debates, 17 June 1963, 679, cols 73–74; Evans, *Downing Street Diary*, p. 259.

43. Rodney Hallworth and Frank Howitt, 'After 17 days of silence', *Daily Express*, 26 March 1963, p. 1; Roger Hall, 'My friends – by Christine', *News of the World*, 31 March 1963, NA PREM 11/4368.

44. 'Case of the Sensitive Osteopath', *Time*, 29 March 1963, p. 25.

45. George Wigg, memorandum [April 1963], NA PREM 11/4368; Irving, *Scandal 63*, p. 115.

46. Morgan, *Crossman Backbench Diaries*, pp. 989, 995–96, 997.

47. Andrew, *Defence of the Realm*, p. 498.

48. Sir Alec Cairncross (ed.), *The Robert Hall Diaries 1954–61*, II (1991), p. 95; Bevins, *Greasy Pole*, p. 50; Timothy Raison, 'Crime is the Priority', *New Society*, 4 October 1962, p. 20; Henry Brooke to Sir Alec Douglas-Home, 19 February 1964, NA PREM 11/4848; 'Lady Brooke of Ystradfellte', *The Times*, 5 September 2000, p. 23a; Rawlinson, *Price Too High*, p. 96.

49. Knightley and Kennedy, *Affair of State*, p. 167.

50. Kennedy, *Trial of Stephen Ward*, pp. 86–7, 90–1.

51. 'Argument, then "I hit Miss Keeler"', *Guardian*, 3 October 1963, p. 5; 'Witness Describes a "Fight" with Keeler', *Glasgow Herald*, 3 October 1963; 'Charges Christine with Bribing Witnesses', *Daily News* (St John's, Newfoundland), 3 October 1963, p. 1f; 'Offer of £1,000 by Christine Keeler Alleged', *The Times*, 3 October 1963, p. 6d.

52. Knightley and Kennedy, *Affair of State*, p. 171; NA CRIM 1/4130 contains the official dossier on Gordon's trial for wounding Keeler.

53. Mandy Rice-Davies, *Mandy* (1980), pp. 131–33.

54. Kennedy, *Trial of Stephen Ward*, pp. 242–47; Tom Lambert, 'Profumo Probe Turns to Dr Ward Inquiry', *Montreal Gazette*, 20 June 1963, p. 1.

55. Knightley and Kennedy, *Affair of State*, p. 175.

56. Tim Bligh, Note for the Record, 7 May 1963, and [Malcolm Cumming eavesdrop] Record of a Conversation between Dr Stephen Ward and Mr Bligh at Admiralty House on Tuesday 7 May 1963, NA PREM 11/4368.

57. Stephen Ward to Sir Wavell Wakefield and to Harold Wilson, both 20 May 1963, NA PREM 11/4369.
58. Bligh, Top Secret Note for the Record [of 27 May meeting], NA PREM 11/4369.
59. Catterall, *Macmillan Diaries*, II, p. 569.
60. Knightley and Kennedy, *Affair of State*, p. 183; 'A Private Letter from Dr Ward', *Time & Tide*, 30 May 1963, p. 5.
61. Lord Devlin, *Easing the Passing* (1985), p. 39; Tony Benn, *Years of Hope* (1994), p. 368.
62. Gladwyn, *Cynthia Gladwyn*, p. 288.
63. Profumo, *House Down*, pp. 189–90.

Ten: Show Trials

1. Morgan, *Crossman Backbench Diaries*, pp. 999–1000.
2. Patrick O'Donovan, 'The price of being caught', *Observer*, 16 June 1963, p. 11.
3. Louis Blom-Cooper, 'Prostitution: a Socio-Legal Comment on the Case of Dr Ward', *British Journal of Sociology*, 15 (March 1964), p. 65.
4. 'Tory rank and file angry', and 'Sex and Politics', *Observer*, 9 June 1963, pp. 1, 10.
5. Harold Macmillan to Martin Redmayne, dictated 8 June and sent 9 June 1963, NA PREM 11/4369.
6. Lord Caldecote to R.A. Butler, 12 June 1963, Butler G46.
7. Irving, *Scandal 63*, p. 154.
8. 'Constituents stay loyal to "perfect MP"', *Banbury Guardian*, 13 June 1963, p. 4.
9. 'The Profumo Affair', *Banbury Guardian*, 13 June 1964, p. 5.
10. Andrew Roth, 'John Cordle, Tory MP who preached Christian morality', *Guardian*, 25 November 2004; John Barnes, 'John Cordle, Moralistic Conservative MP', *Independent*, 9 December 2004.
11. 'Tory MP Hits at Chief Whip', *Observer*, 9 June 1963, p. 1; 'Tory MP Hits Out at Chief Whip', *Banbury Guardian*, 14 June 1963, p. 4.
12. Cassandra, 'Bell and Bathing Costume', *Daily Mirror*, 2 July 1963, p. 6; Maurice Richardson, 'Lord Hailsham hits his wicket', *Observer*, 16 June 1963, p. 25.
13. Reginald Paget, House of Commons debates, 17 June 1963, 679, col

151; Donald Zec, *Some Enchanted Egos* (1972), pp. 190, 197.

14. 'After Mr Profumo', *Economist*, 8 June 1963, p. 994; Kilmuir, *Political Adventure*, p. 278.

15. Morgan, *Crossman Backbench Diaries*, pp. 1041–42.

16. 'The Prime Minister's Crisis', *Economist*, 15 June 1963, p. 1115; Pendennis, 'The enemies of Macmillan', *Observer*, 16 June 1963, p. 8.

17. Anthony Howard and Richard West, *The Making of the Prime Minister* (1965), p. 49.

18. Harold Wilson, House of Commons, 17 June 1963, 679, cols 34, 38, 39, 41, 42, 53–4.

19. Harold Macmillan, House of Commons debates, 17 June 1963, 679, cols 54, 65.

20. Nigel Birch, House of Commons debates, 17 June 1963, 679, col 97; Berkeley, *Crossing the Floor*, p. 85. Sir Julian Critchley, *Palace of Varieties* (1989), p. 87.

21. Cooper, *Clouds of Forgetting*, pp. 309–10.

22. Anthony Sampson, 'Morality in Government', *Punch*, 28 August 1963, p. 296.

23. Stanford, *Bronwen Astor*, p. 246; Nicholas Mosley, *Meeting Place* (1962), p. 179.

24. Ludovic Kennedy, *The Trial of Stephen Ward* (1964), p. 19; Tom Utley, 'If the Christine Keeler Scandal Happened Today, She Wouldn't Be in Disgrace – She'd Be on "I'm a Celebrity"', *Daily Mail*, 29 October 2010.

25. Howard and West, *Making of Prime Minister*, pp. 51–2.

26. Sir Osbert Lancaster, *Mixed Notices* (1963), p. 64; *Economist*, 'The Succession', 22 June 1963, p. 1236.

27. 'Who Runs This Country Anyhow?', *Sunday Mirror*, 23 June 1963, pp. 1–2; Harrison, *Seeking a Role*, p. 194; Tony Benn, *Out of the Wilderness* (1987), p. 183.

28. Malcolm Muggeridge, 'The Slow, Sure Death of the Upper Classes', *Sunday Mirror*, 23 June 1963, p. 7.

29. Richard Crossman, 'The Peril of the Whitehall Mandarins', *Sunday Mirror*, 23 June 1963, p. 8.

30. James Cameron, 'Why the World is Mocking Britain', *Sunday Mirror*, 23 June 1963, p. 9.

31. Tim Bligh, Note for the Record on meeting on 11 July 1963, NA PREM 11/4371.

32. 'Security Inquiry May Set Wider Powers', *The Times*, 22 June 1963, p. 8a; Lord Denning, House of Lords debates, 4 December 1957, 206, cols 806–11.
33. 'Three Ministers Named in Judge's Purge', *The People*, 7 July 1963, p. 1.
34. Knightley and Kennedy, *Affair of State*, p. 209.
35. Sybille Bedford, 'The Worst We Can Do: A Concise Account of the Trial of Dr Stephen Ward', Harry Ransom Center, University of Texas at Austin, folios 5–6.
36. Faramerz Dabhoiwala, *The Origins of Sex* (2012), pp. 356–57.
37. Iain Crawford, *The Profumo Affair* (1963), pp. 112–13.
38. Knightley and Kennedy, *Affair of State*, pp. xi–xii.
39. Collis, *Diaries*, p. 162.
40. Collis, *Journey Up*, p. 198.
41. 'Danger: The Old Pals' Act', *Daily Mirror* editorial, 3 July 1963, p. 2; Lord Normanbrook to Harold Macmillan, 6 July 1963, NA PREM 11/4371.
42. Green, *Rachman*, pp. 214–17; 'The Life and Times of Peter Rachman', *Sunday Times*, 7 July 1963, p. 5; 'The Technique of Rachmanism', *Sunday Times*, 21 July 1963, p. 5; 'How the Housing Racket Works', and 'The Lessons of Rachman', *Observer*, 21 July 1963, pp. 5, 8; 'A landlord unable to live at peace – with himself', *Guardian*, 10 August 1963, p. 2.
43. Green, *Rachman*, p. 215; Chief Inspector George Taylor, CID, report of 25 July 1963, and Sir Charles Cunningham to Sir Joseph Simpson, 16 July 1963, both NA MEPO 2/9999.
44. Kennedy, *Trial*, p. 87.
45. Kennedy, *Trial*, pp. 24, 68, 153.
46. Rebecca West, 'Who is to Blame for Dr Ward?', *Sunday Telegraph*, 4 August 1963, p. 10.
47. A. J. Ayer, 'Morality 1963', *Punch*, 31 July 1963, p. 147.
48. Kennedy, *Trial*, p. 51.
49. Knightley and Kennedy, *Affair of State*, p. 216.
50. Knightley and Kennedy, *Affair of State*, p. 245.
51. Cassandra, 'The Seal of Tragedy', *Daily Mirror*, 1 August 1963, p. 6.
52. *World*, 4 August 1963, pp. 6–7.
53. 'Ward Died As He Promised, "I Won't Let Them Get Me"', *The People*, 4 August 1963, p. 1.

54. Hugh Leggatt, 'Stephen Ward', *Daily Telegraph*, 16 October 1969; Cooper, *Cloud of Forgetting*, p. 308.
55. 'At the Silent House of Astor', *Daily Express*, 3 August 1963, p. 6; John Gordon, 'Current Events', *Sunday Express*, 4 August 1963, p. 12.
56. Wayland Kennet, *The Profumo Affair* (1963), p. 111; Harold Macmillan to Tim Bligh, 6 August 1963, NA PREM 11/4371.

Eleven: Safety Curtain

1. Egremont, *Wyndham and Children*, p. 187; Cooper, *Cloud of Forgetting*, p. 310; Morgan, *Crossman Backbench Diaries*, p. 997; Benn, *Out of the Wilderness*, p. 30.
2. Hailsham, *Sparrow's Flight*, p. 332; Catterall, *Macmillan Diaries*, II, pp. 575, 583; Timothy Bligh to Lord Poole, 2 August 1963, NA PREM 11/4371; Lamb, *Macmillan Years*, p. 480.
3. Radcliffe report, paragraph 84; Denning report, paragraph 231.
4. Howard and West, *Making of Prime Minister*, p. 59; Tim Bligh, Note for the Record, 4 July 1963, NA PREM 11/4371.
5. Denning report, paragraph 58; Annan, *Our Age*, p. 137; 'Model in shots case', *News of the World*, 3 February 1963, NA PREM 11/4368.
6. Denning report, paragraphs 11, 16; Andrews, *Defence of the Realm*, p. 499.
7. Knightley and Kennedy, *Affair of State*, p. 251; 'Denning Suggests Libel Law Changes', *The Times*, 4 June 1987, p. 3e; Lord Denning, 'Ward case and libelling the dead', *The Times*, 3 June 1987, p. 13d.
8. Lord Dilhorne to Macmillan, 18 September 1963, and Sir John Hobson, 'Memo on Denning Report from the Attorney General' [24 September 1963], NA PREM 11/4372; 'Liberty Steadily Eroded', *The Times*, 28 March 1968, p. 2e.
9. Jeremy Hutchinson QC, quoted in 'Keeler Gets Nine Months after Pleas of Guilty', *The Times*, 7 December 1963, p. 6a; Dominic Sandbrook, *Never Had It So Good* (2005), pp. 634–35.
10. Stephen Adams, 'Christine Keeler Found Prison "Like School"', *Daily Telegraph*, 22 July 2010; 'Accidental Heroes of the 20th Century', *Independent*, 10 April 1999.
11. Sir John Colville, *Those Lambtons* (1988), p. 155; R. A. Butler, aide-memoire of 18 November 1962, Butler papers G38; Boyd-Carpenter,

Way of Life, p. 174; Howard and West, *Making of Prime Minister*, p. 74.

12. Bevins, *Greasy Pole*, pp. 143, 147; Paul Channon to R. A. Butler, 18 October 1963, Butler papers G40.

13. David Butler and Anthony King, *The British General Election of 1964* (1965), p. 151.

14. Donald Zec, 'Wilson – the Challenge of a Lifetime', *Daily Mirror*, 24 September 1964, p. 17.

15. Donald Zec, 'The Britain I Want to See', *Daily Mirror*, 25 September 1964, pp. 16–17.

16. Marjorie Proops, 'So Alec thinks I'm his SECRET WEAPON', *Daily Mirror*, 7 October 1964, p. 17; 'Top People, Too, Are Voting Labour', *Daily Mirror*, 8 October 1964, p. 17.

17. Sampson, *Anatomy of Britain*, p. 117; Cecil King to author, 23 November 1972, Davenport-Hines papers.

18. Ken Gardner and Len Adams, 'Christine Keeler: the Shameless Slut', *The People*, 4 August 1963, pp. 10–11; Blom-Cooper, 'Prostitution', p. 66.

19. 'Witness Describes a Fight with Keeler', *Glasgow Herald*, 3 October 1963; NA CRIM 1/4187.

20. Keeler, *Scandal*, p. 76; Keeler, *Truth at Last*, p. xv; Keeler, *Secrets and Lies*, pp. xxv–xxvi.

21. Freya Stark, *Letters*, 8 (1982), p. 80.

22. Mark Girouard, *Big Jim: the Life and Work of James Stirling* (1998), pp. 217–23.

23. 'The Army rub Profumo's name off a stone', *Daily Mirror*, 1 August 1963, p. 4; Haslam, *Redeeming Features*, p. 272.

24. Sir Oliver Wright to Timothy Bligh, 26 June 1963, NA PREM 11/4371.

INDEX

reputation 333, 342; published memoirs 342–3
Character & characteristics: appearance 144, 145, 320; cannabis use 252, 253, 259, 284, 331; conversation 145, 259; homes xi, 140, 144, 150; impatience 141; independence 109; sexual attractiveness 144, 145; tomboy 140; vulnerability 144, 333
Relations with: Bill Astor 135, 284; Charles Clore xiii, 135, 160, 263, 319; Johnny Edgecombe 258–9; 'Lucky' Gordon 252–3; Paula Hamilton-Marshall 145, 268; Noel Howard-Jones 144–5, 246, 252; Yevgeny Ivanov 248–9, 251; men 111, 139–40, 141, 144–5, 146–7, 283, 333; Jack Profumo 65–6, 145, 250–52, 262; Peter Rachman 126, 160, 185–6, 319; Mandy Rice-Davies 146, 148, 262; Stephen Ward 99, 102–3, 105, 144–5, 248, 257, 262, 264, 324, 331, 333, 342–3

Keeler, Colin 140
Keeler, Peter 141
Kelly, Felix 246
Kemsley, Gomer Berry, 1st Viscount 172, 201, 339
Kendal, Sir Norman 161–2
Kendall, Kay 53
Kennedy, Caroline, *An Affair of State* 144, 268, 324
Kennedy, Jacqueline 56
Kennedy, John F. 15, 233, 259, 302
Kennedy, (Sir) Ludovic 100, 318–19
Kennerley, Peter 35
Kennet, Wayland Young, 2nd Baron 119, 327
Keppel, Alice 71
Kerby, Henry 29, 223–4, 257, 269, 299
Kettering 50
Keynes, John Maynard, 1st Baron 6
KGB 231, 270
Khrushchev, Nikita 104, 217, 223, 225–7, 253, 303

Kiev 22, 226
Kilmuir, David Maxwell Fyfe, 1st Earl of 16, 27–8, 198, 255, 302
Kind Hearts and Coronets (film) 53
Kineton, Warwickshire 62, 297, 298
King, Cecil: family background 193, 200; early life 200–201; death of brothers 200; control of *Daily Mirror* 194; editorial director of *Sunday Pictorial* 201; business empire 159–60, 192, 202, 203, 209; business trips to Africa 203–4; marriages and children 204–5, 210; political exploitation of Profumo Affair 187, 192–3, 308; and 1964 general election 336, 339; seeks earldom 339–40; later life 340
Character and characteristics: appearance 203; drinking 208; grouse-shooting 203; megalomania 340; moods 201; psoriasis 201; resentments and jealousies 210, 340; self-belief 200; sexual appetites 204–5; unpleasantness 202, 203
Views on: consumerism 212; the Establishment 187, 210–212; homosexuality 222–3; human weakness 203; role of the Press 196, 211; sex 194, 204–5; women 122, 204–5
King, Michael 210
King and I, The (musical) 55
King's Lynn 142
Kinsey reports 137–8, 194
Kipling, Rudyard 6
Kirksville, Missouri 97
Knave of Hearts (film) 118
Knightley, Philip, *An Affair of State* 144, 268, 324
Koestler, Arthur, *Darkness at Noon* 77
Korean War 66
Kramer, Abraham 178–9
Kramer, Dorothy 179
Kuznetsov, Pavel 218–20, 245